wet moon™

book 3:
further realms of fright

written & illustrated by
Ross Campbell

Cleo's diary pages by Jessica Calderwood

*design by Ross Campbell, Steven Birch @ Servo
& Keith Wood*

edited by Douglas Sherwood & James Lucas Jones

Published by

Oni Press, Inc.

Joe Nozemack, *publisher*

James Lucas Jones, *editor in chief* **Keith Wood,** *art director*

George Rohac, *director of business development*

Tom Shimmin, *director of sales and marketing* **Jill Beaton,** *editor*

Charlie Chu, *editor* **Troy Look,** *digital prepress lead*

Robin Herrera, *administrative assistant*

"The Chronicles of Riddick" property of Universal Studios/Vin Diesel/David Twohy/all those folks
Wikipedia tonsilitis image property of someone who needs a doctor right now

Oni Press, Inc.
1305 SE Martin Luther King Jr. Blvd.
Suite A
Portland, OR 97214

onipress.com • twitter.com/onipress
facebook.com/onipress • onipress.tumblr.com
mooncalfe.blogspot.com • twitter.com/rosscampbelll

First Edition: November 2007

ISBN 978-1-932664-84-3

3 5 7 9 10 8 6 4 2

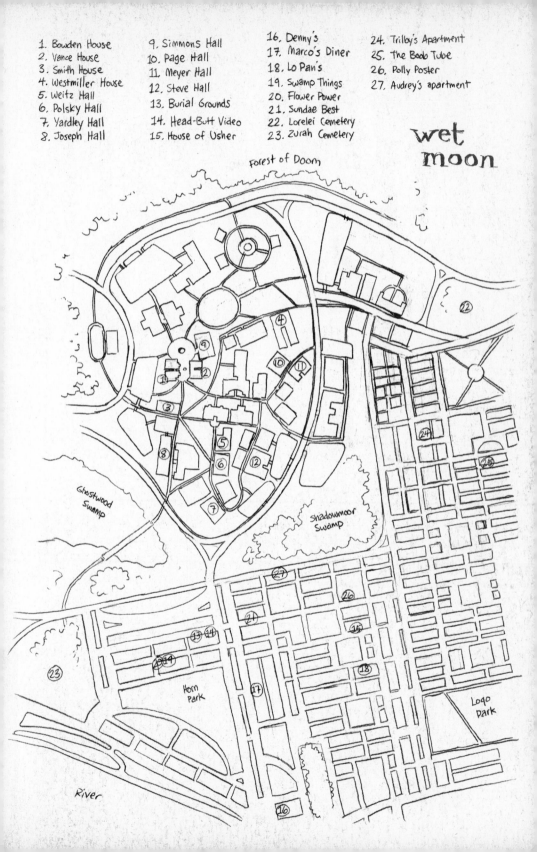

1. Bowden House
2. Vance House
3. Smith House
4. Westmiller House
5. Weitz Hall
6. Polsky Hall
7. Yardley Hall
8. Joseph Hall
9. Simmons Hall
10. Page Hall
11. Meyer Hall
12. Steve Hall
13. Burial Grounds
14. Head-Butt Video
15. House of Usher
16. Denny's
17. Marco's Diner
18. Lo Pan's
19. Swamp Things
20. Flower Power
21. Sundae Best
22. Lorelei Cemetery
23. Zurah Cemetery
24. Trilby's Apartment
25. The Boob Tube
26. Polly Poster
27. Audrey's apartment

wet moon

Forest of Doom

Ghostwood Swamp

Shadowmoor Swamp

Horn Park

Logo Park

River

28. The Lovedrop Residence
29. The Swanhilde Residence
30. Wet Moon High School
31. The Shoe Tree
32. The Bernarde Residence
33. The Zuzanny Residence

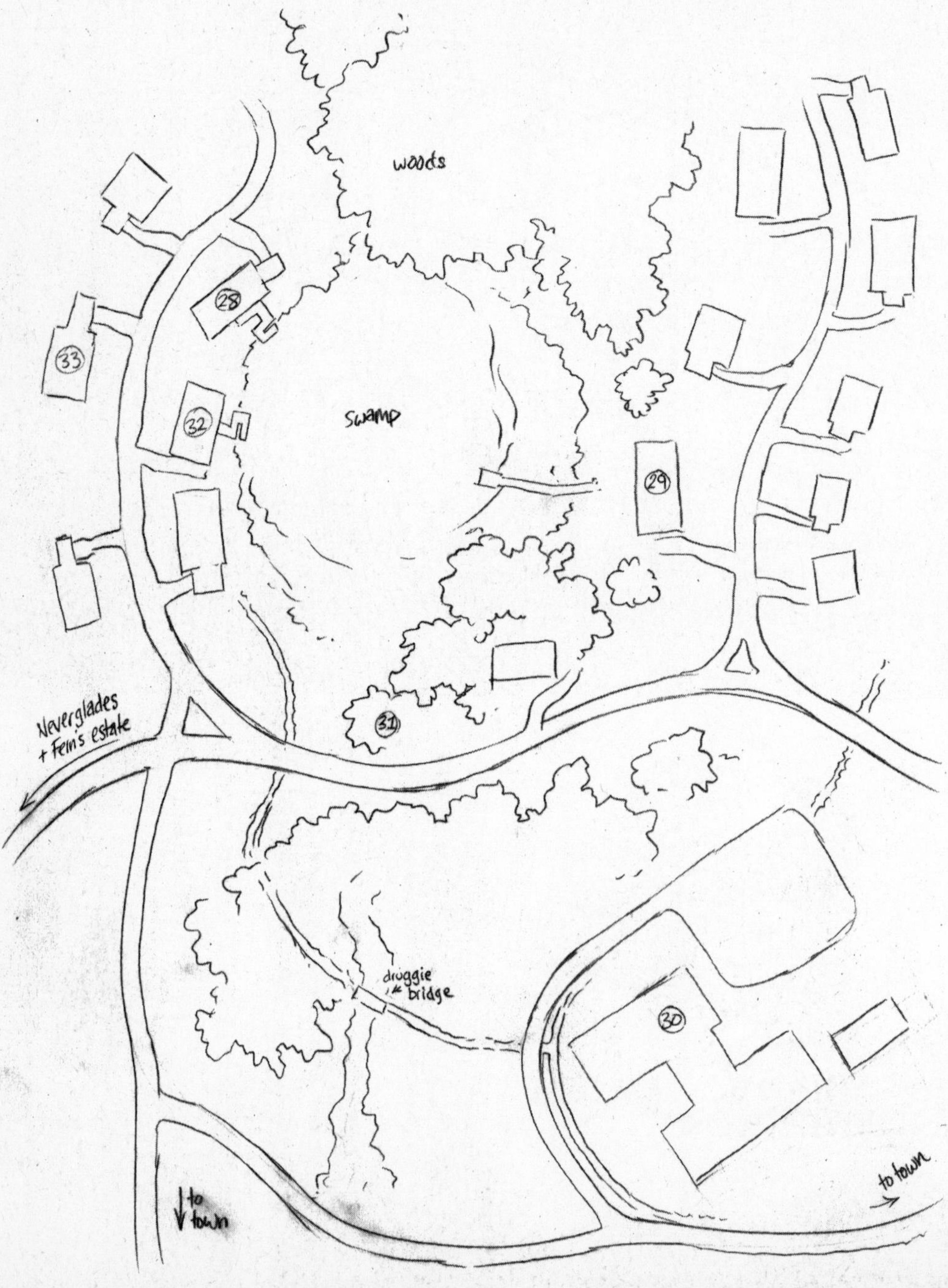

woods
swamp
28
29
30
31
32
33
Neverglades
+ Fern's estate
druggie
bridge
to
town
to town

wet moon
v.3

2007

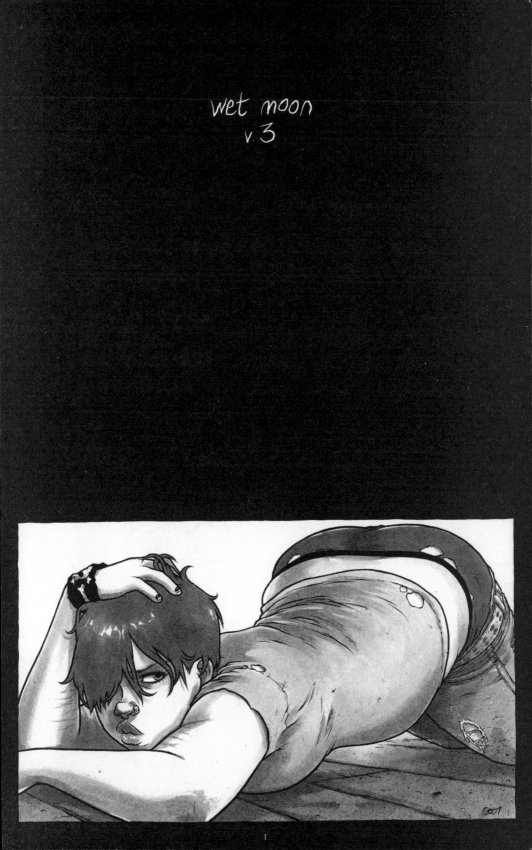

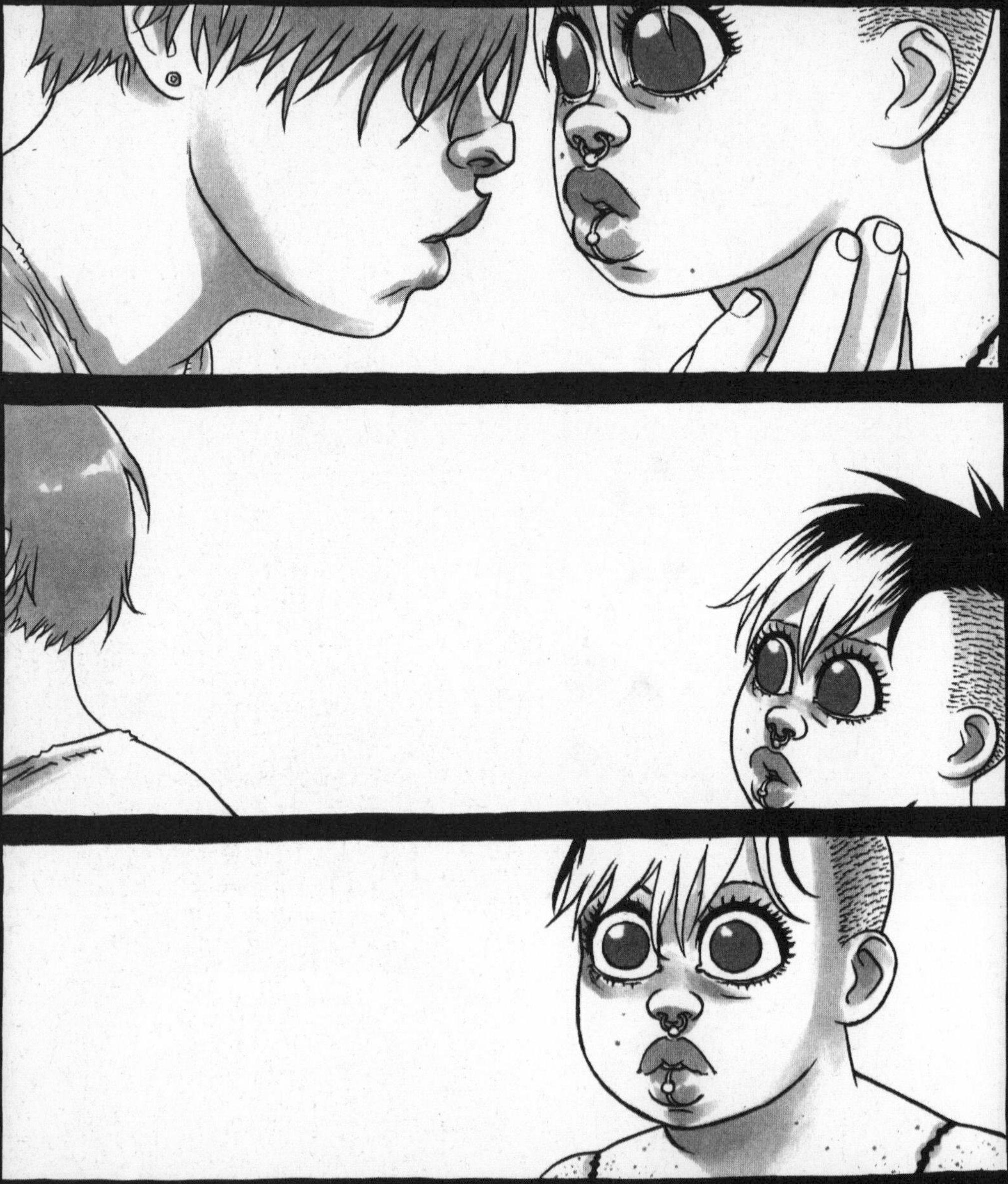

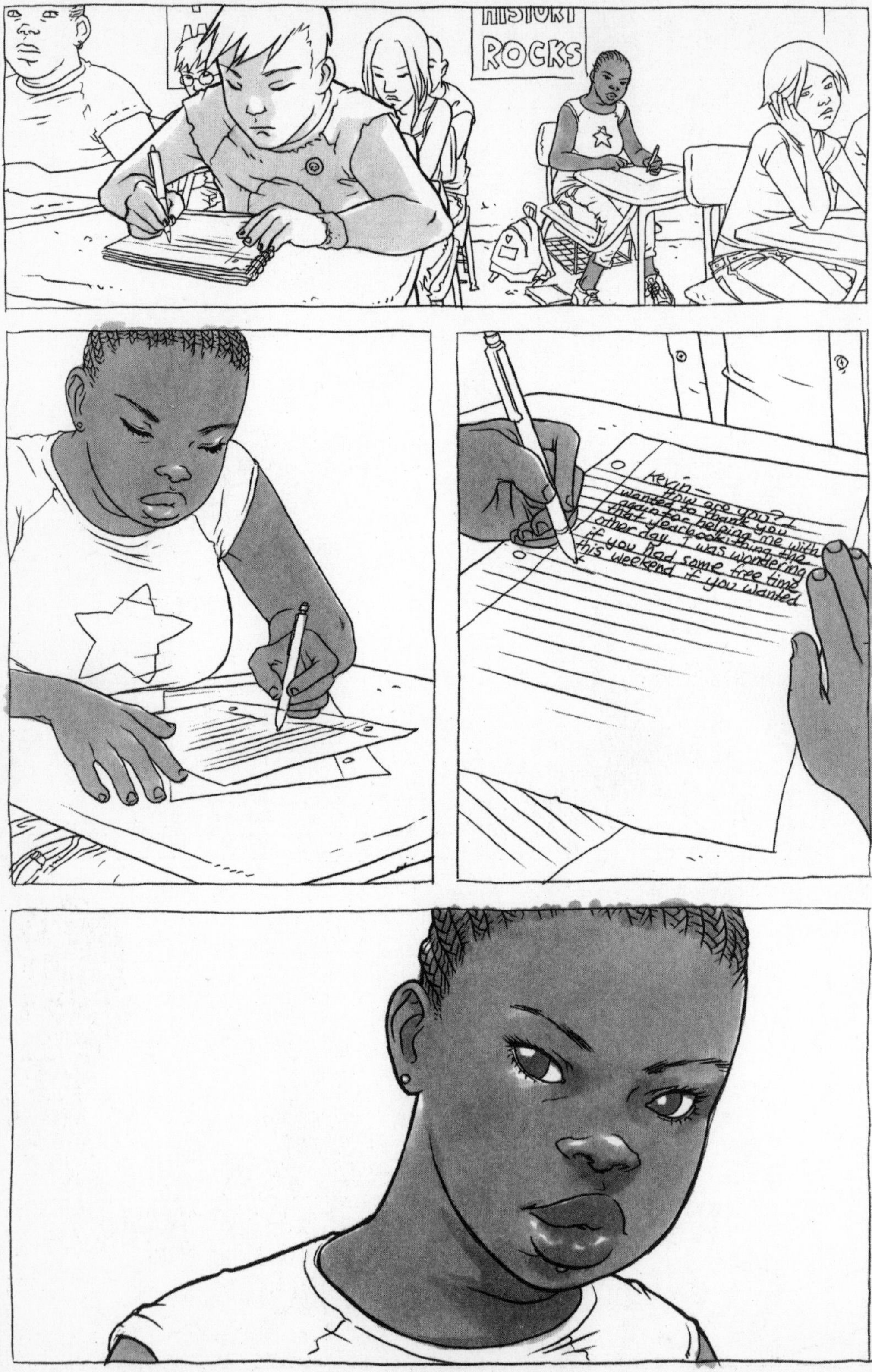
HISTORY ROCKS
Kevin—
How are you? I
wanted to thank you
again for helping me with
that yearbook thing the
other day. I was wondering
if you had some free time
this weekend if you wanted

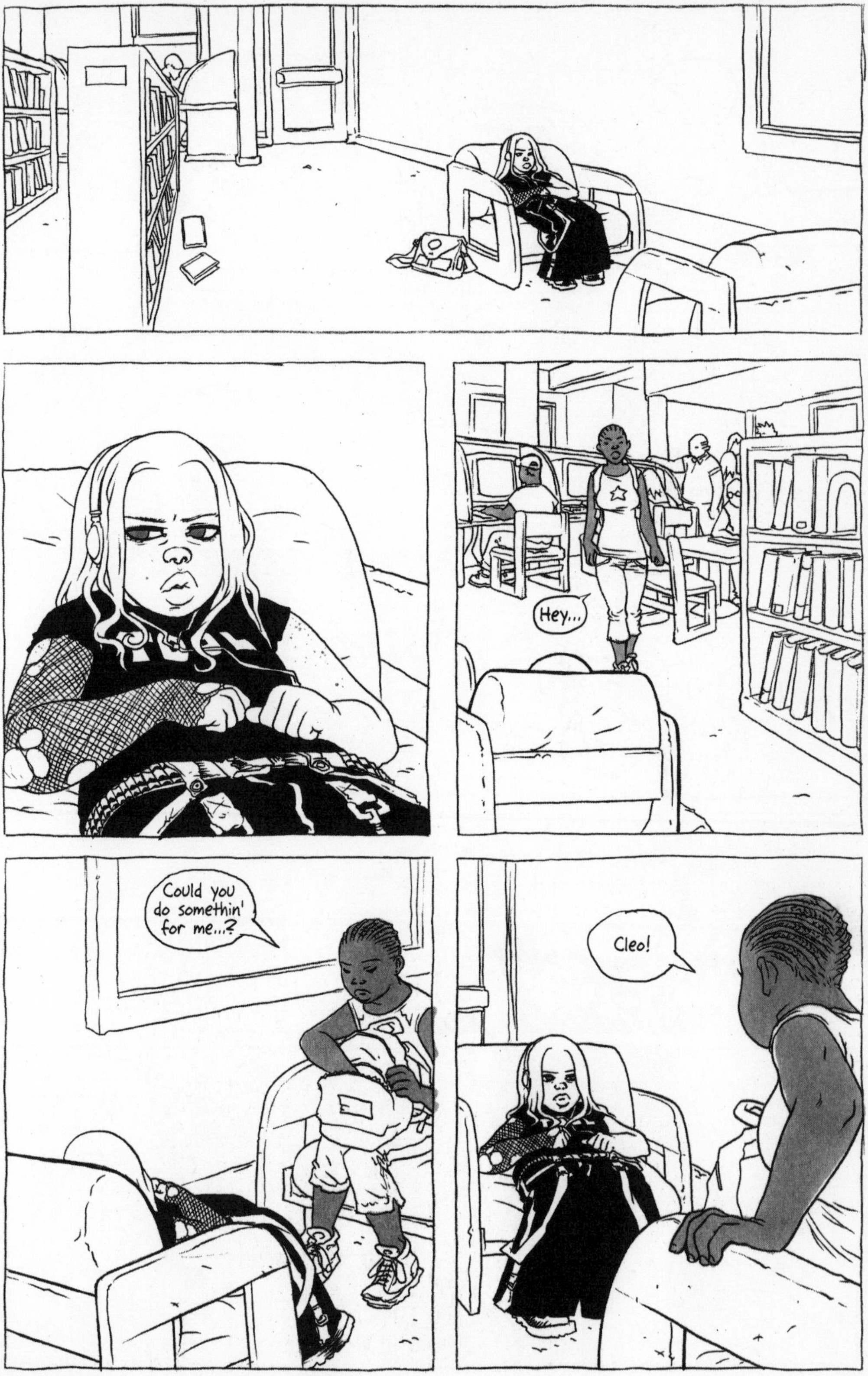
Hey...
Could you do somethin' for me...?
Cleo!

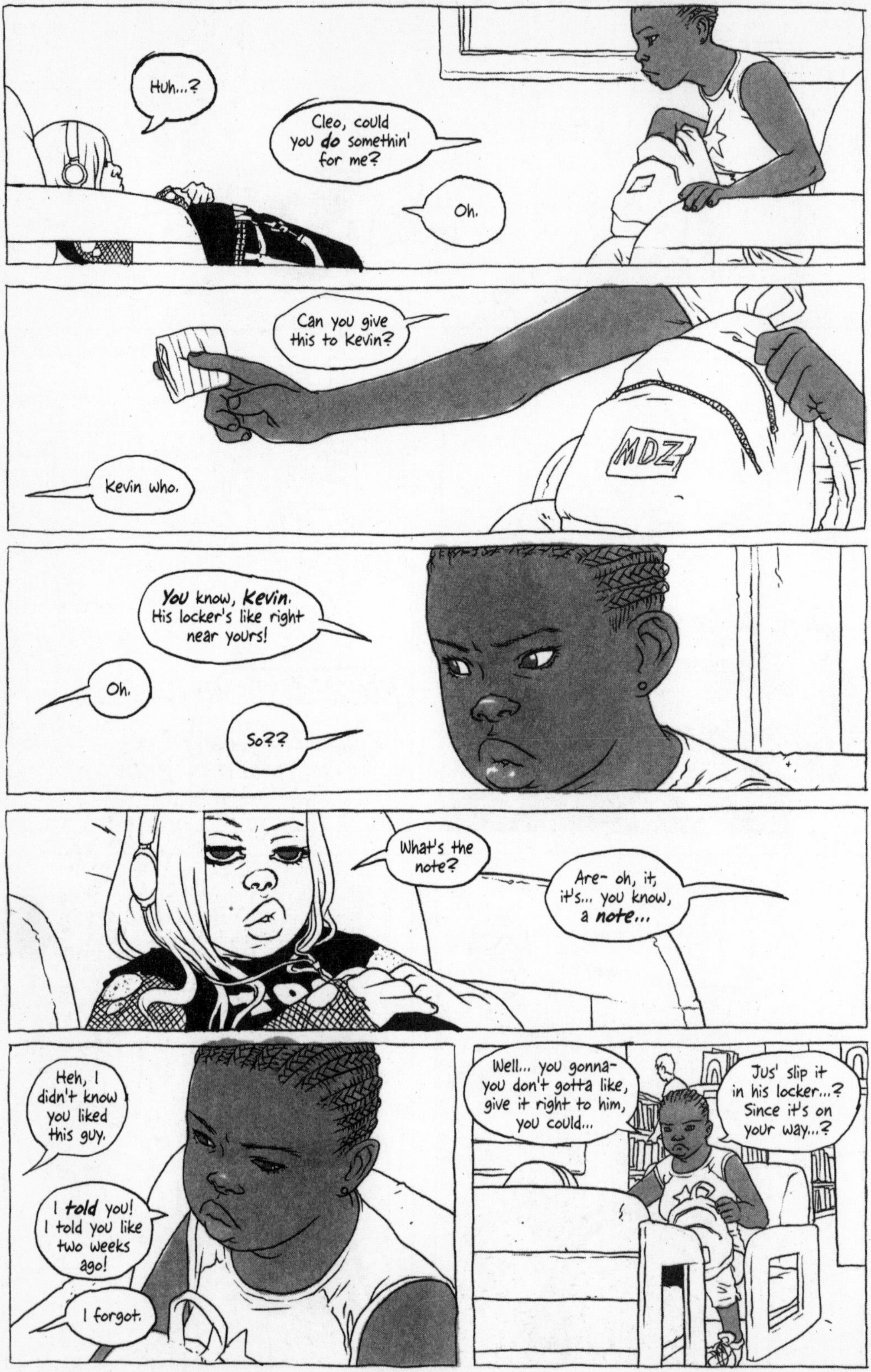
Huh...?
Cleo, could you **do** somethin' for me?
Oh.
Can you give this to Kevin?
MDZ
Kevin who.
You know, **Kevin**. His locker's like right near yours!
Oh.
So??
What's the note?
Are- oh, it, it's... you know, a **note...**
Heh, I didn't know you liked this guy.
I **told** you! I told you like two weeks ago!
I forgot.
Well... you gonna- you don't gotta like, give it right to him, you could...
Jus' slip it in his locker...? Since it's on your way...?

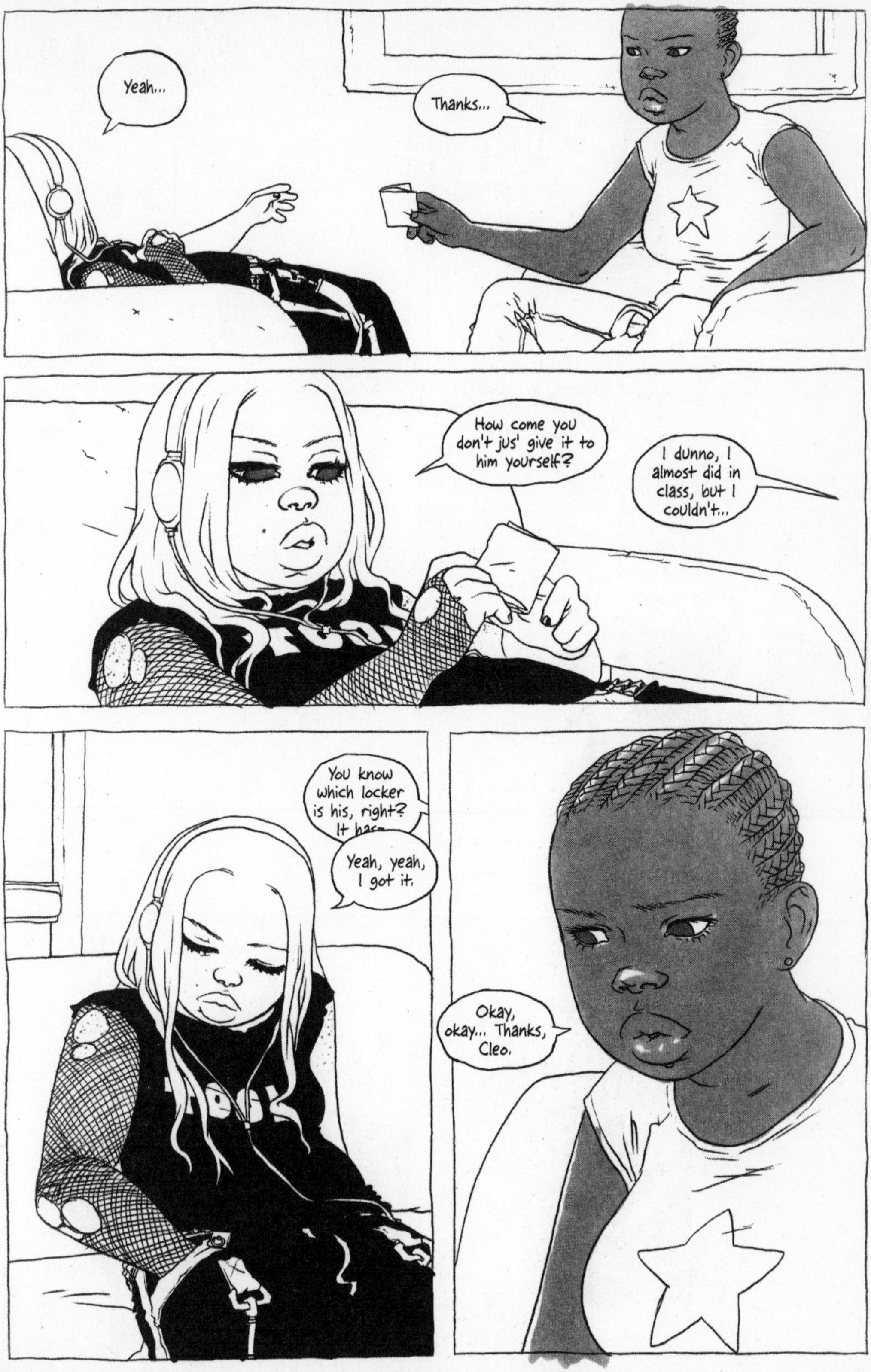
Yeah...
Thanks...
How come you don't jus' give it to him yourself?
I dunno, I almost did in class, but I couldn't...
You know which locker is his, right? It has-
Yeah, yeah, I got it.
Okay, okay... Thanks, Cleo.

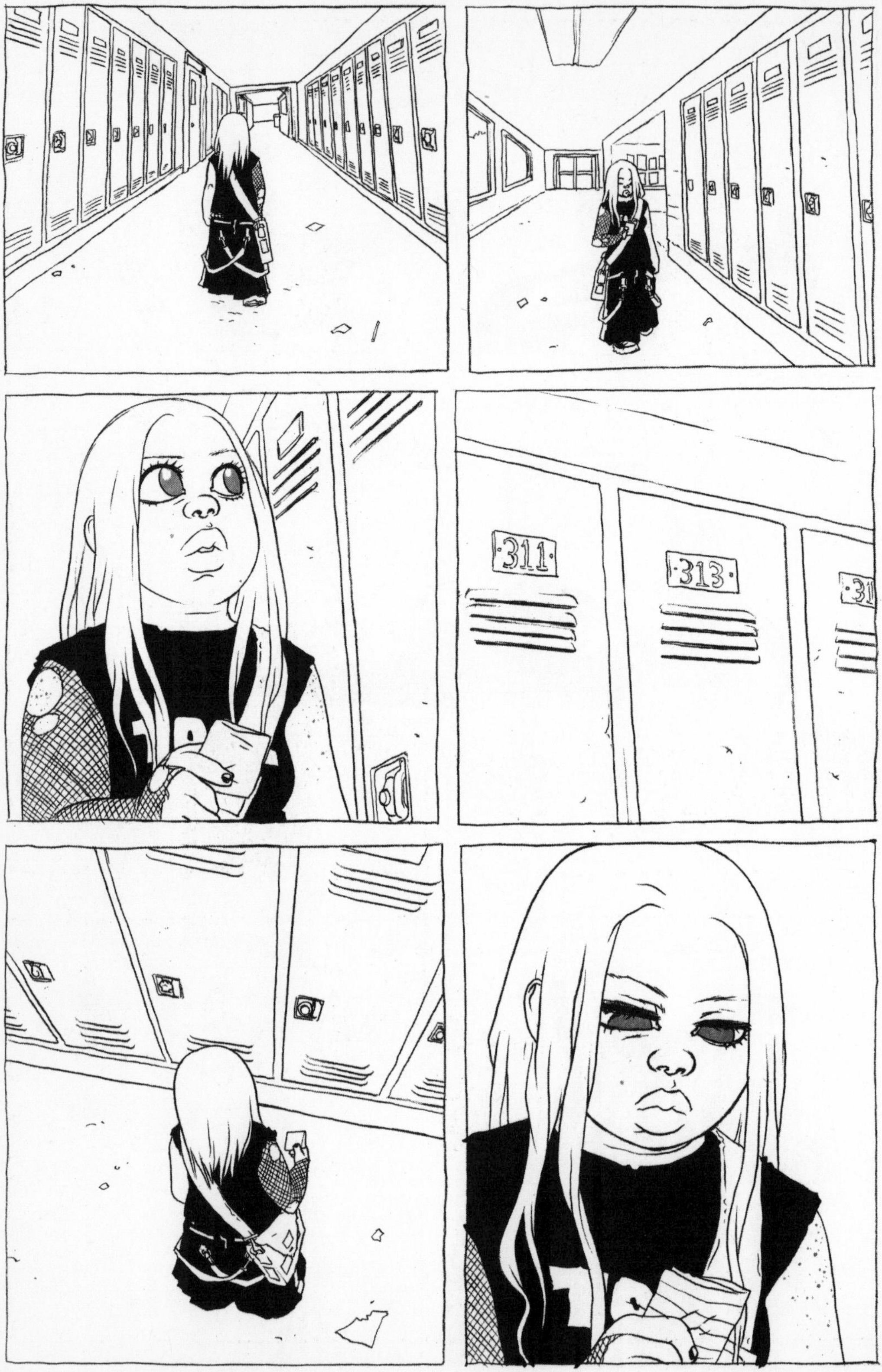
·311·
·313·

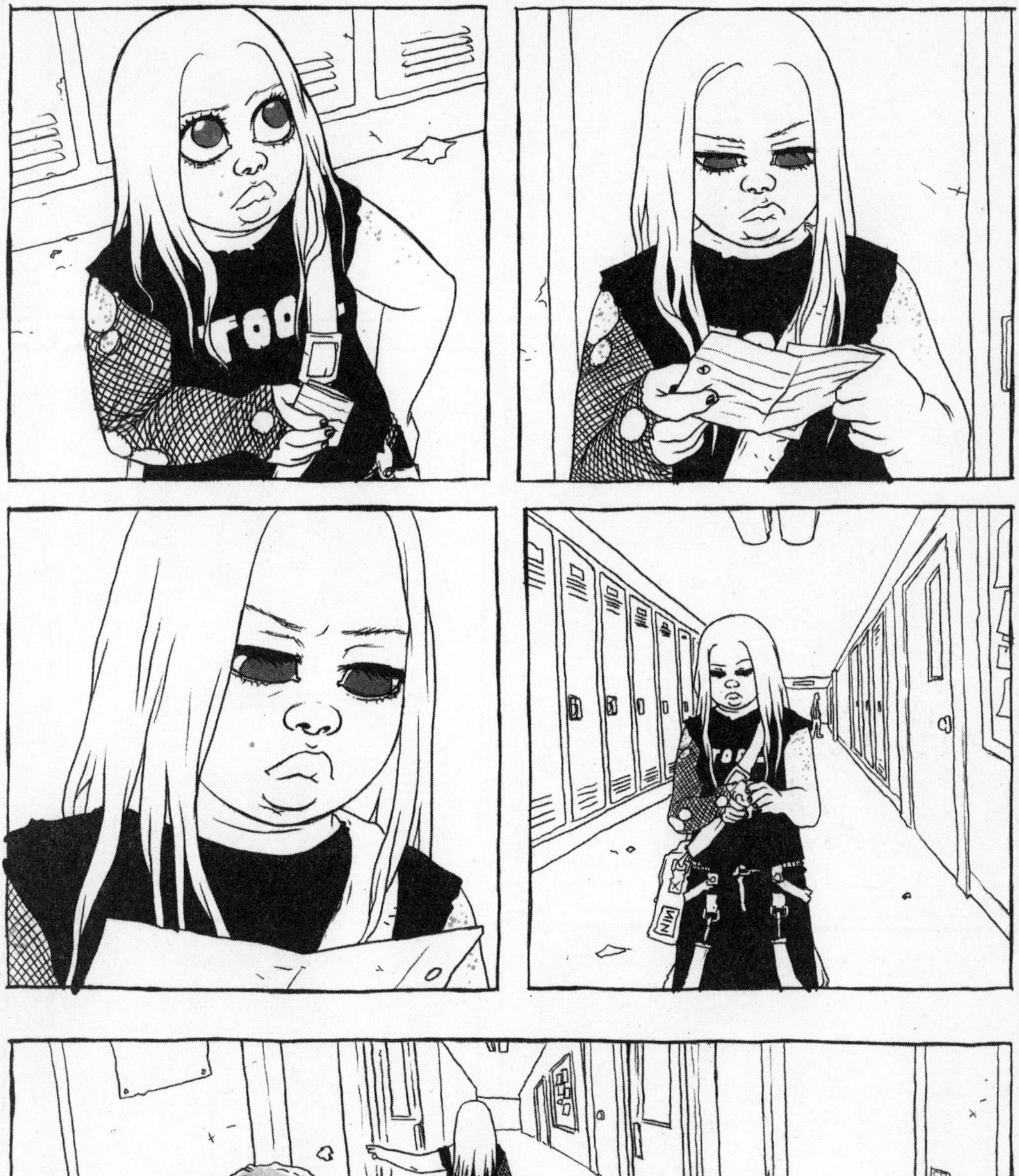

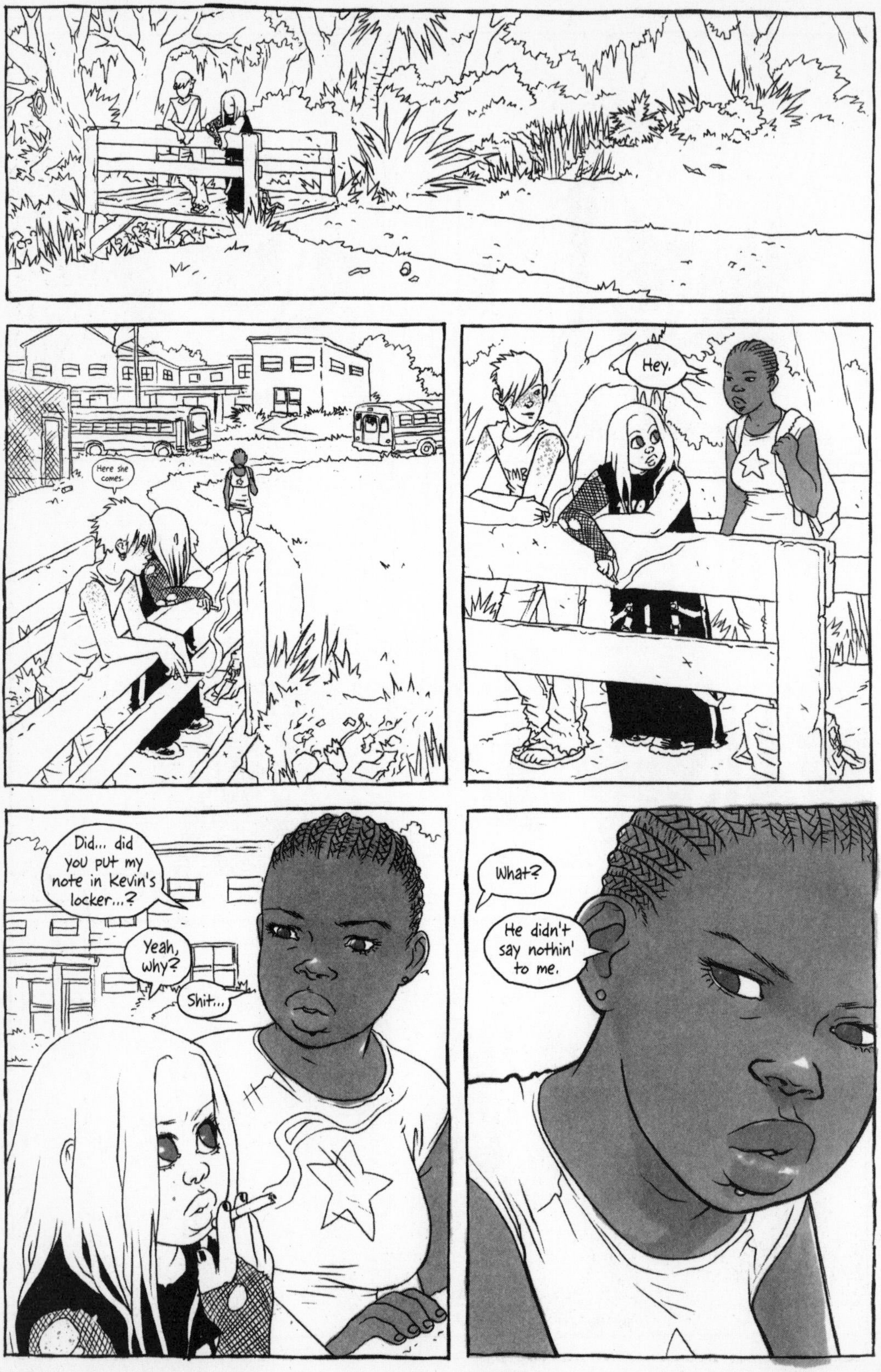
Here she comes.
Hey.
Did... did you put my note in Kevin's locker...?
Yeah, why?
Shit...
What?
He didn't say nothin' to me.

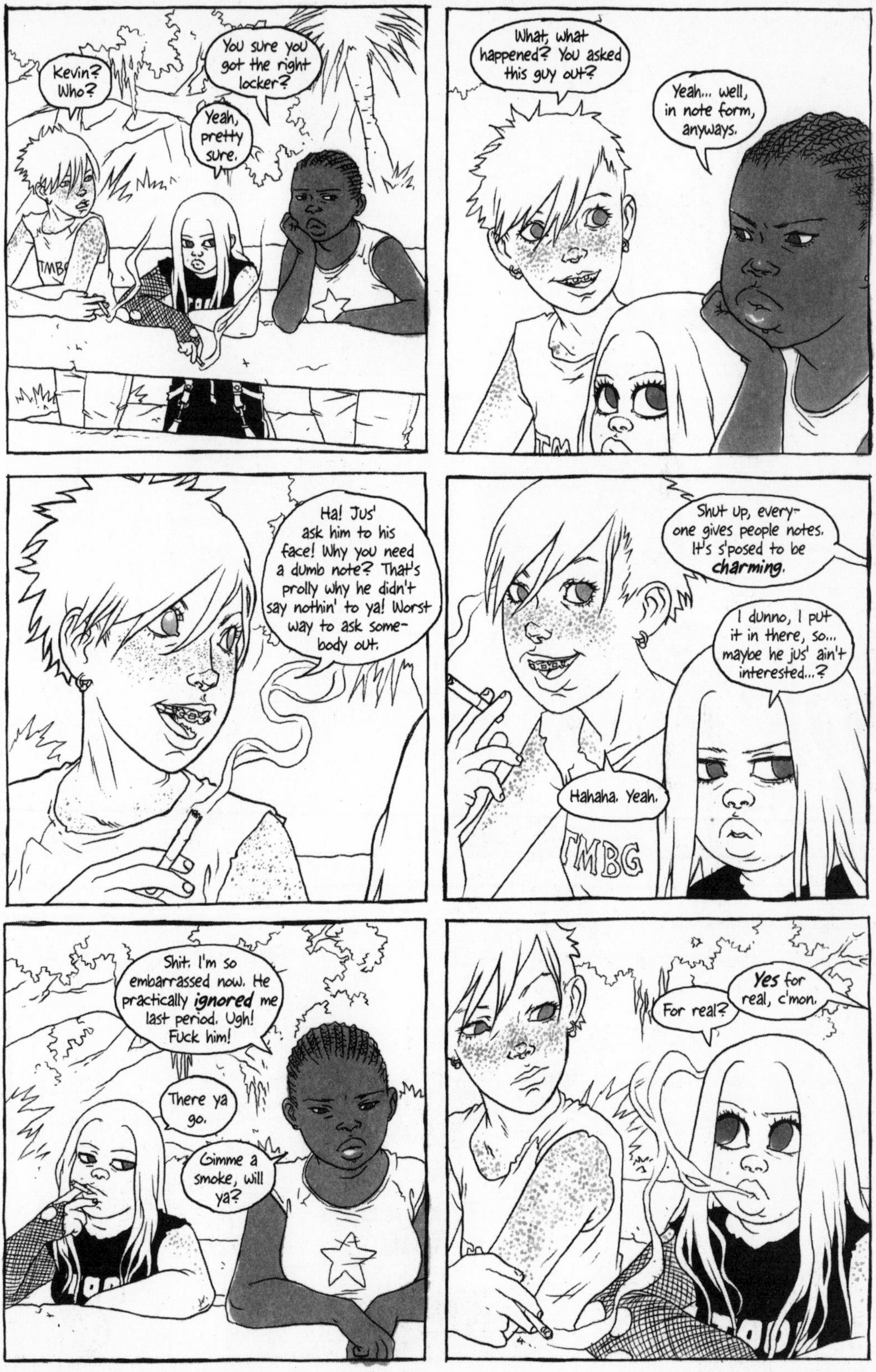
Kevin? Who?
You sure you got the right locker?
Yeah, pretty sure.
What, what happened? You asked this guy out?
Yeah... well, in note form, anyways.
Ha! Jus' ask him to his face! Why you need a dumb note? That's prolly why he didn't say nothin' to ya! Worst way to ask some-body out.
Shut up, every-one gives people notes. It's s'posed to be **charming**.
I dunno, I put it in there, so... maybe he jus' ain't interested...?
Hahaha. Yeah.
TMBG
Shit. I'm so embarrassed now. He practically **ignored** me last period. Ugh! Fuck him!
There ya go.
Gimme a smoke, will ya?
For real?
Yes for real, c'mon.

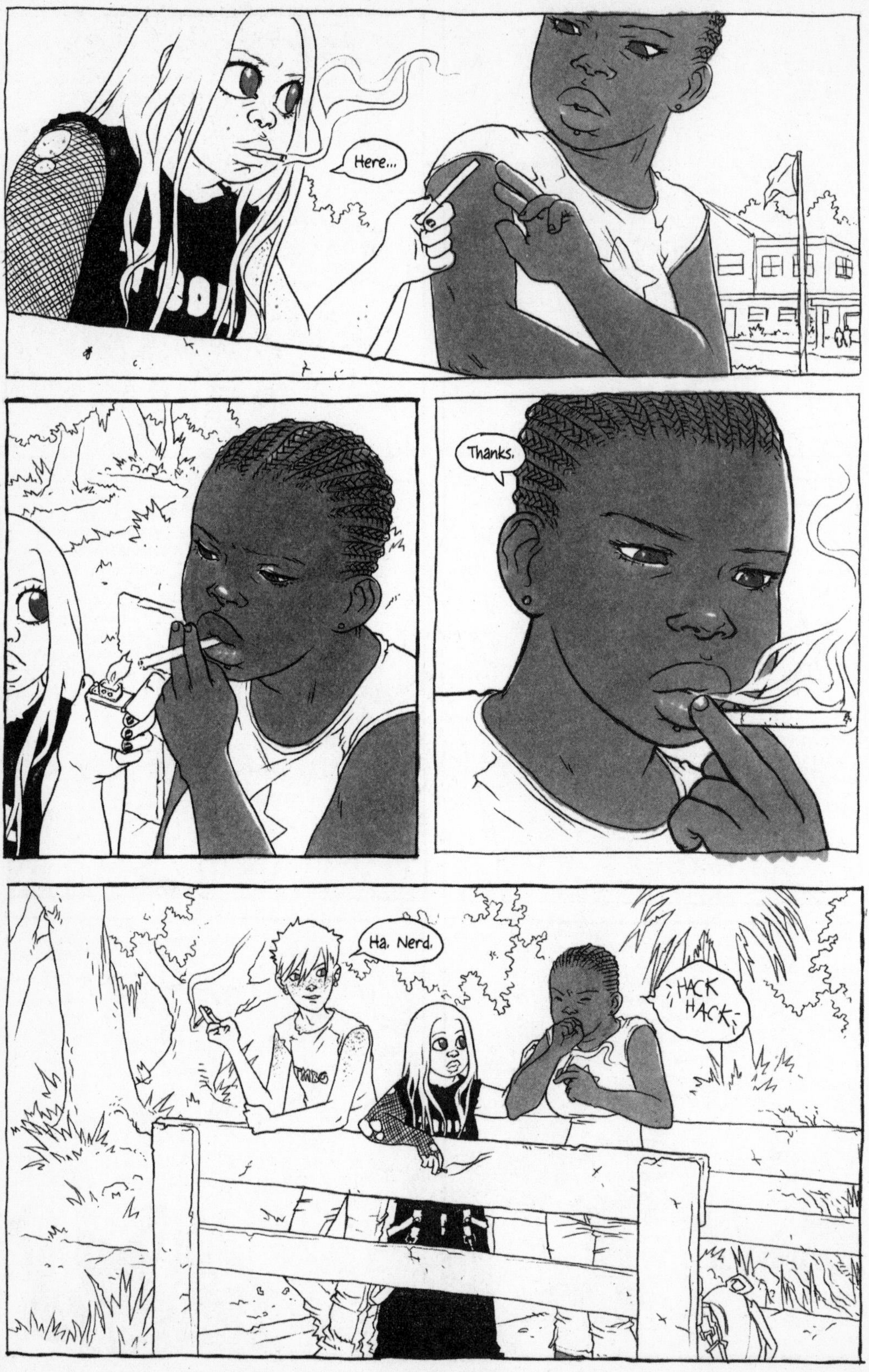
Here...
Thanks.
Ha. Nerd.
HACK HACK

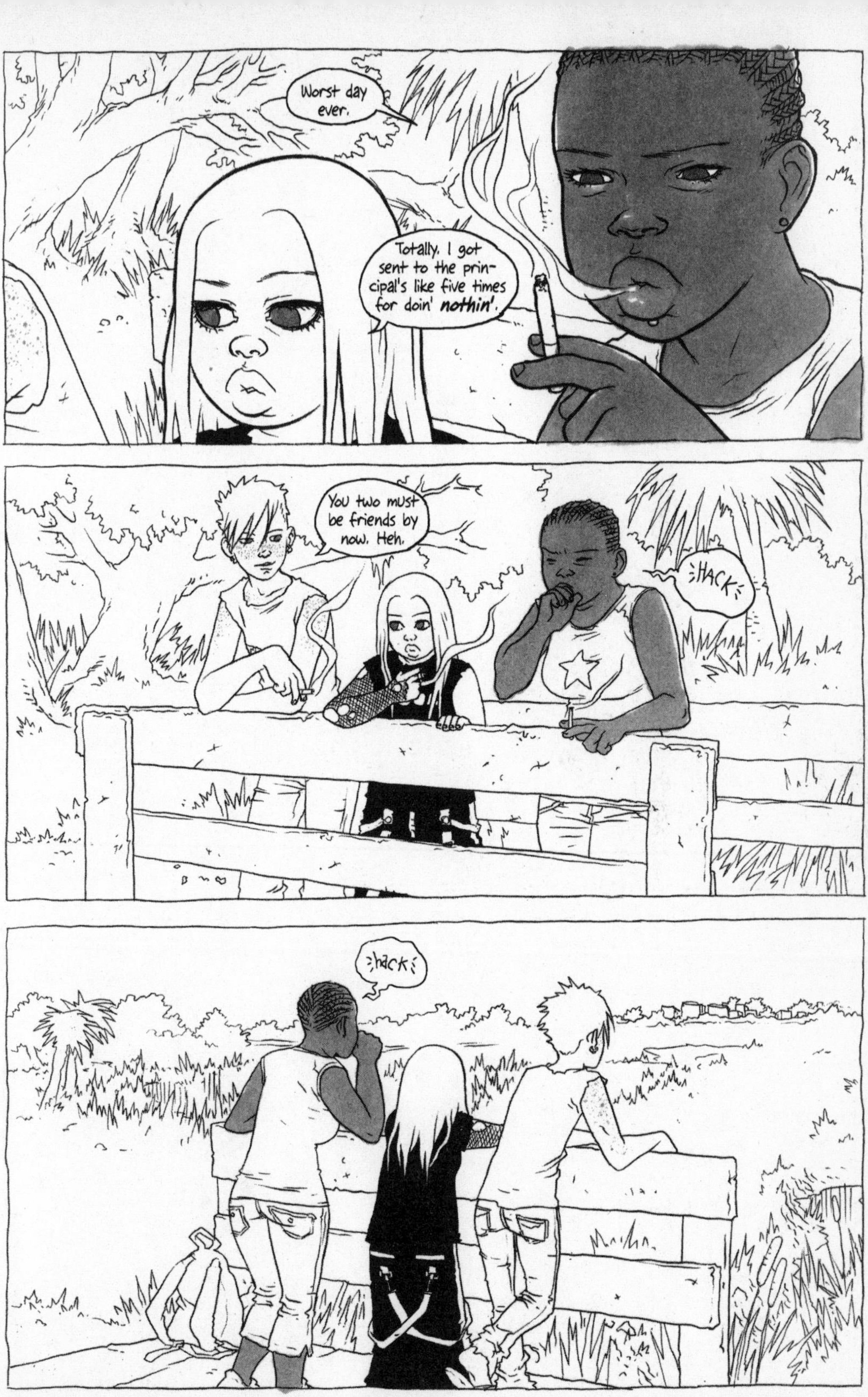
Worst day ever.
Totally. I got sent to the principal's like five times for doin' ***nothin'***.
You two must be friends by now. Heh.
HACK
hack

II

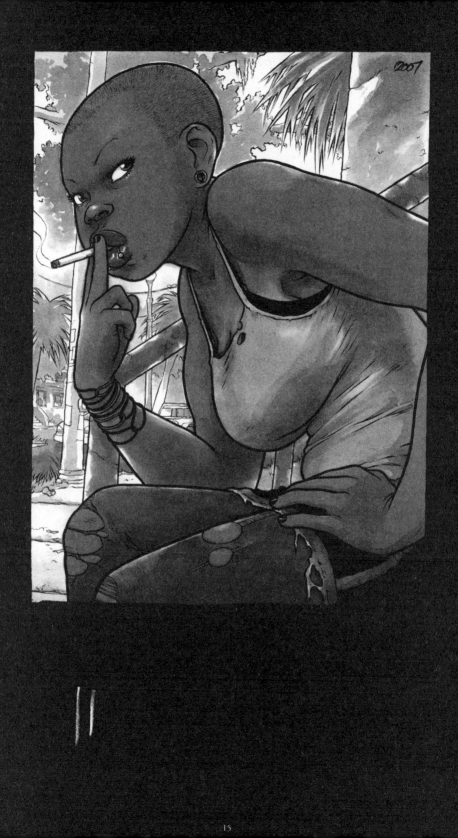

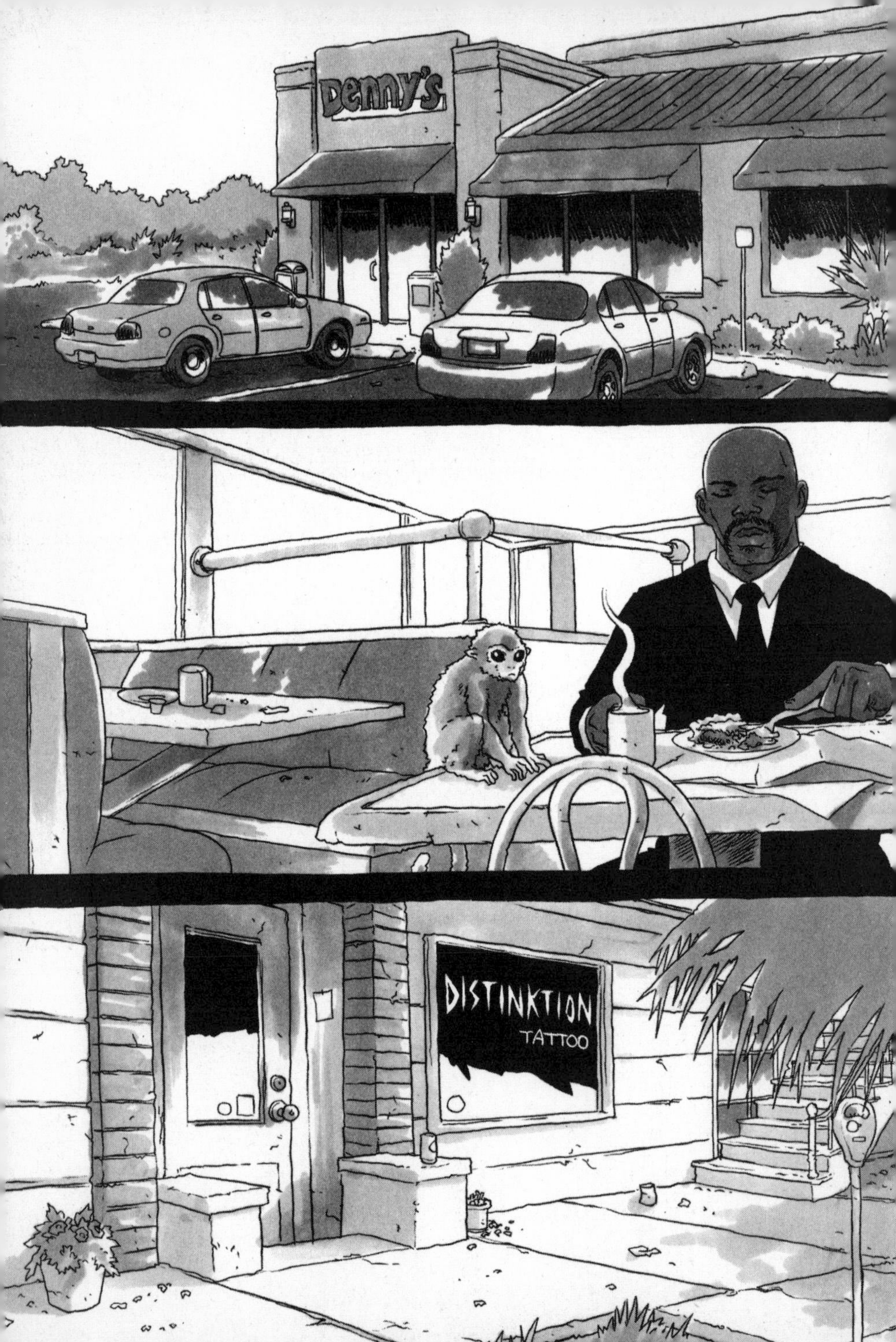
Denny's
DISTINKTION
TATTOO

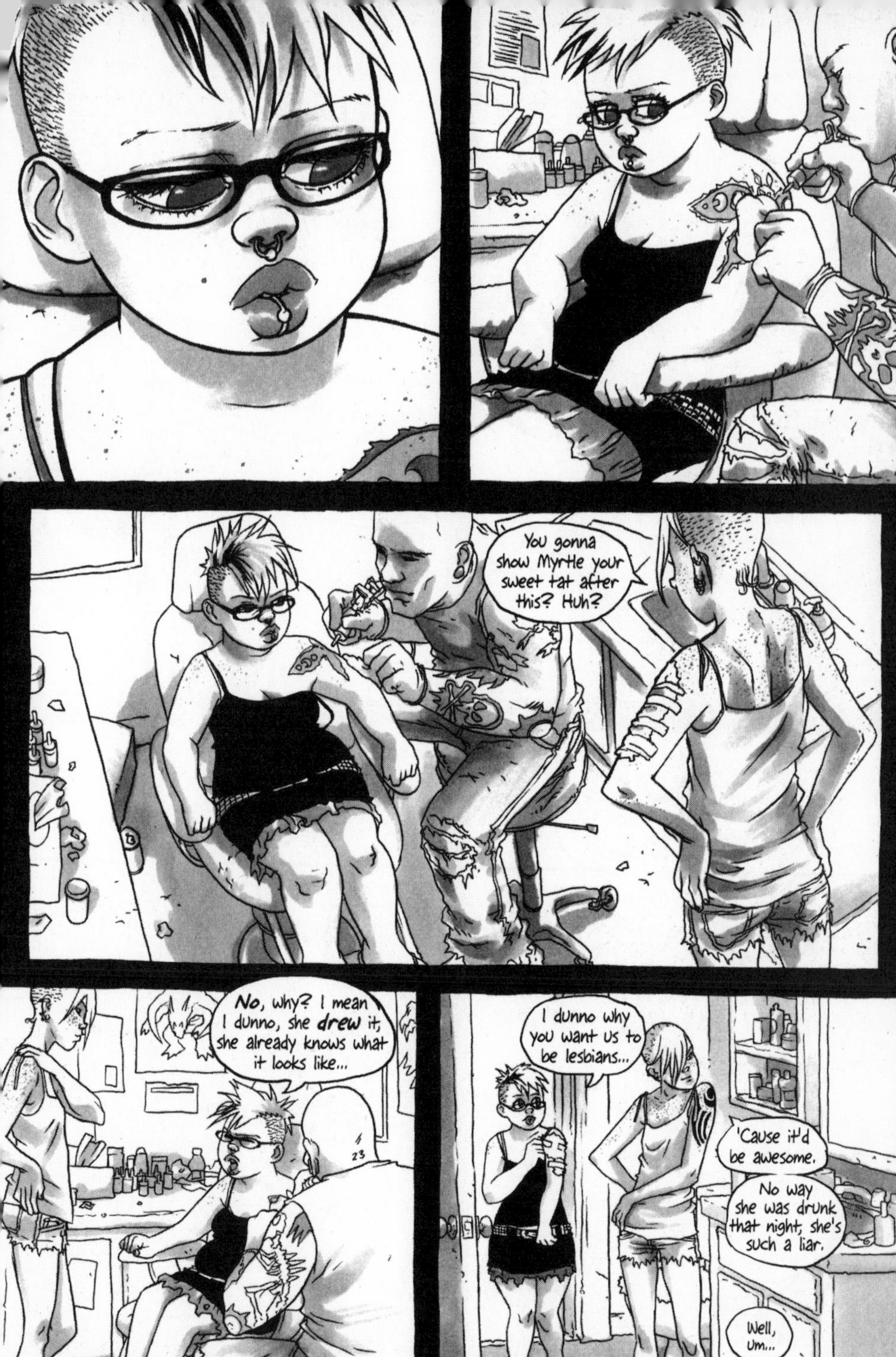
You gonna show Myrtle your sweet tat after this? Huh?
No, why? I mean I dunno, she drew it, she already knows what it looks like...
23
I dunno why you want us to be lesbians...
'Cause it'd be awesome.
No way she was drunk that night, she's such a liar.
Well, um...

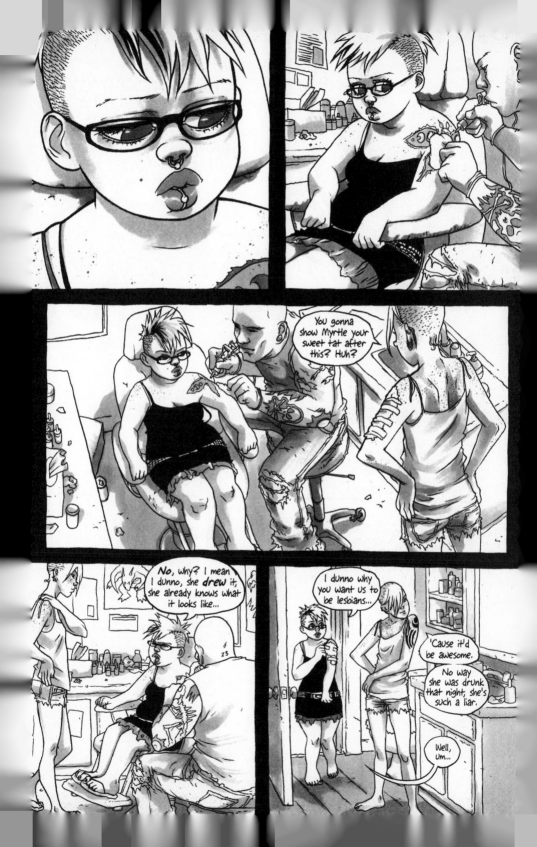

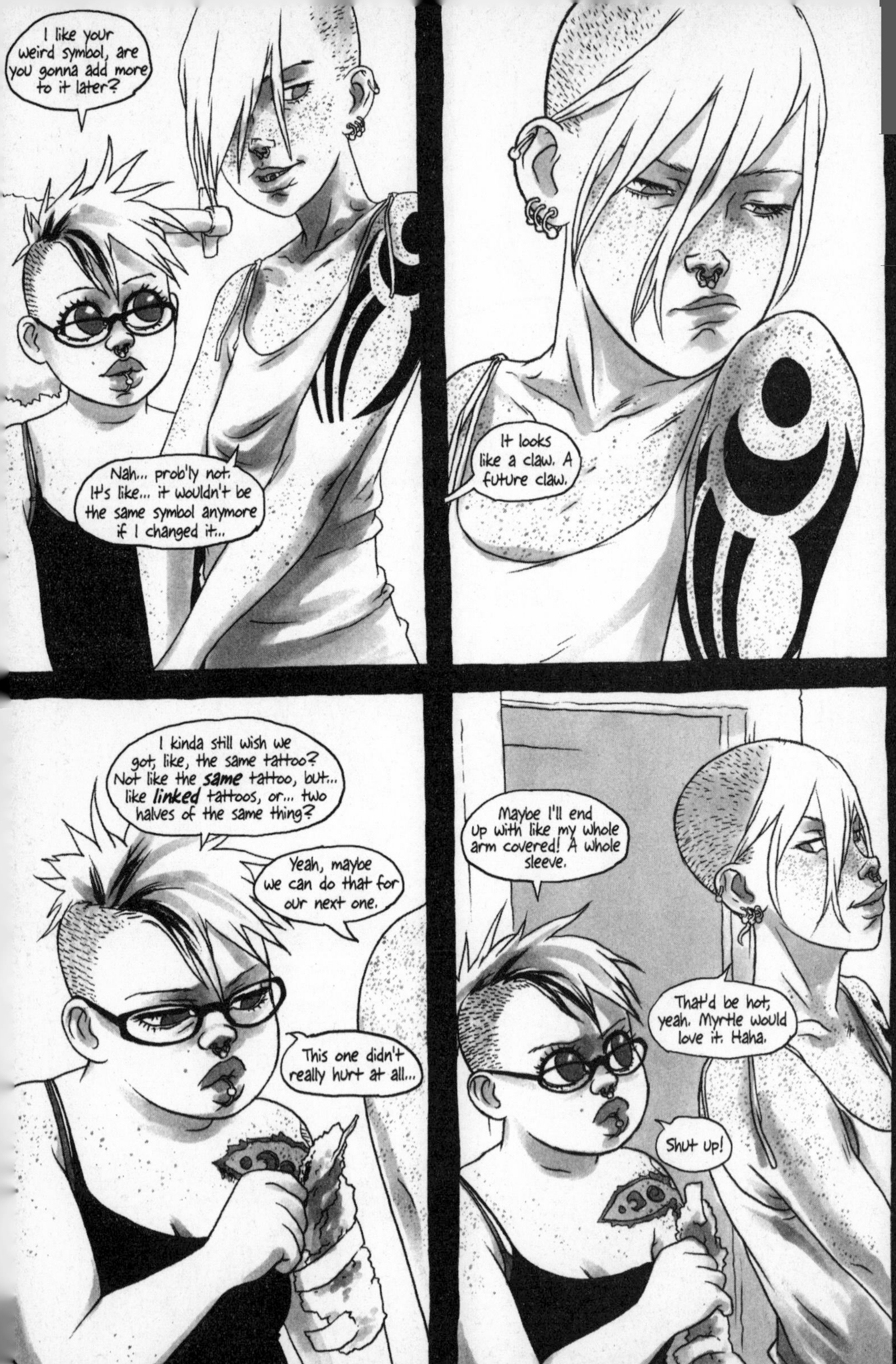
I like your weird symbol, are you gonna add more to it later?
Nah... prob'ly not. It's like... it wouldn't be the same symbol anymore if I changed it...
It looks like a claw. A future claw.
I kinda still wish we got, like, the same tattoo? Not like the **same** tattoo, but... like **linked** tattoos, or... two halves of the same thing?
Yeah, maybe we can do that for our next one.
This one didn't really hurt at all...
Maybe I'll end up with like my whole arm covered! A whole sleeve.
That'd be hot, yeah. Myrtle would love it. Haha.
Shut up!

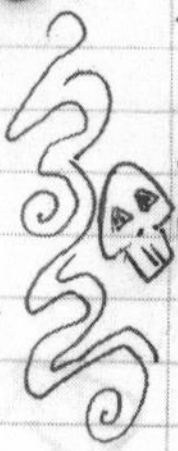

October 9th

Trilby and I got our tattoos done! We look so good. I decided to get that death's head luna moth design that Myrtle drew for me, and I got it done real big so it even goes onto my chest sort of. I thought it would be a better choice than the bone wings, because Beth just got some bone wing stuff and I didn't want to copy her. the manager guy at the parlor, Erwan, gave us some tattoo care things and a list of what to do. Some of it is kind of a hassle, like putting the lotions on all the time, and right after you get it you have to wipe off the ooze that keeps coming out of your skin, and you're not supposed to stay out in the sun for a long time or even go swimming (or get it wet! no showers! I'm prepared to be stinky). We were supposed to go to the beach sometime this week or next, but now I don't know. Maybe if we stay under a big umbrella and go on a cloudy day.

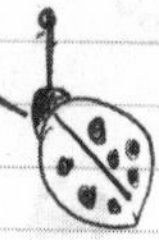

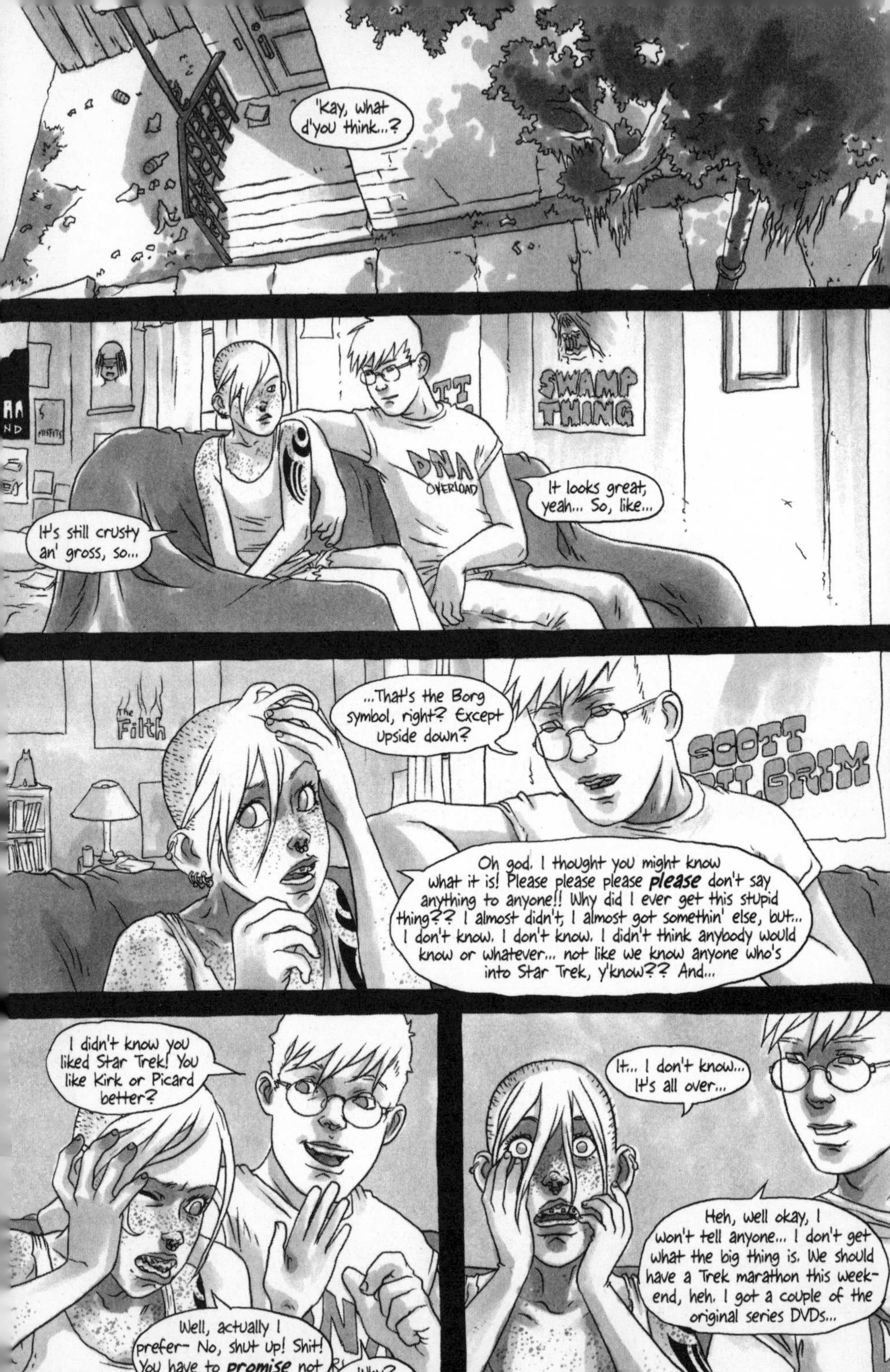
'Kay, what d'you think...?
It's still crusty an' gross, so...
It looks great, yeah... So, like...
SWAMP THING
DNA OVERLOAD
...That's the Borg symbol, right? Except upside down?
Oh god. I thought you might know what it is! Please please please **please** don't say anything to anyone!! Why did I ever get this stupid thing?? I almost didn't, I almost got somethin' else, but... I don't know. I don't know. I didn't think anybody would know or whatever... not like we know anyone who's into Star Trek, y'know?? And...
The Filth
I didn't know you liked Star Trek! You like Kirk or Picard better?
Well, actually I prefer- No, shut up! Shit! You have to **promise** not to say anything!!
Why? Who cares?
It... I don't know... It's all over...
Heh, well okay, I won't tell anyone... I don't get what the big thing is. We should have a Trek marathon this week-end, heh. I got a couple of the original series DVDs...

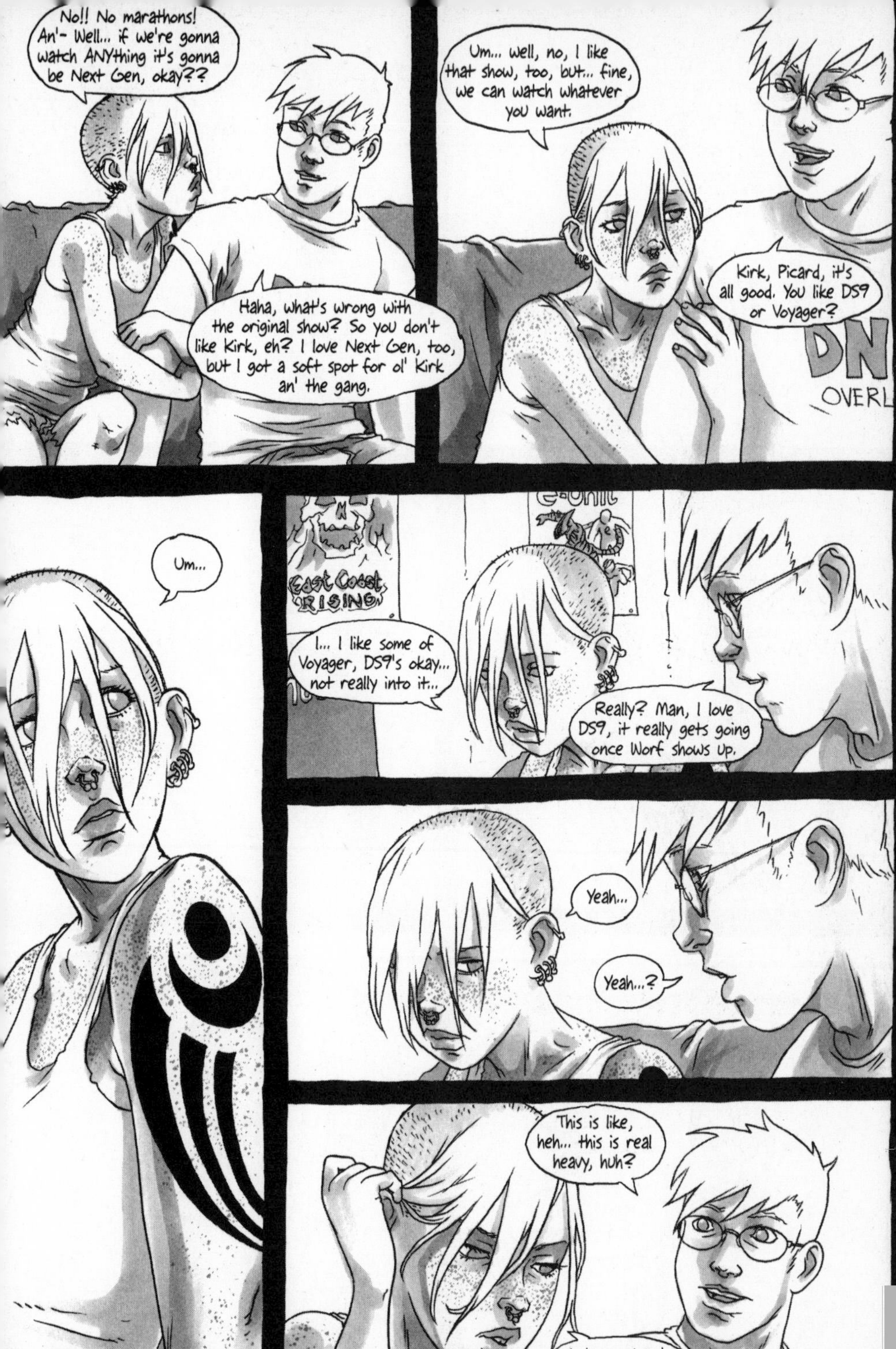
No!! No marathons! An'- Well... if we're gonna watch ANYthing it's gonna be Next Gen, okay??
Haha, what's wrong with the original show? So you don't like Kirk, eh? I love Next Gen, too, but I got a soft spot for ol' Kirk an' the gang.
Um... well, no, I like that show, too, but... fine, we can watch whatever you want.
Kirk, Picard, it's all good. You like DS9 or Voyager?
OVERL
Um...
East Coast RISING
I... I like some of Voyager, DS9's okay... not really into it...
Really? Man, I love DS9, it really gets going once Worf shows up.
Yeah...
Yeah...?
This is like, heh... this is real heavy, huh?
I dunno, I jus'... I don't want Cleo or Mara to know.

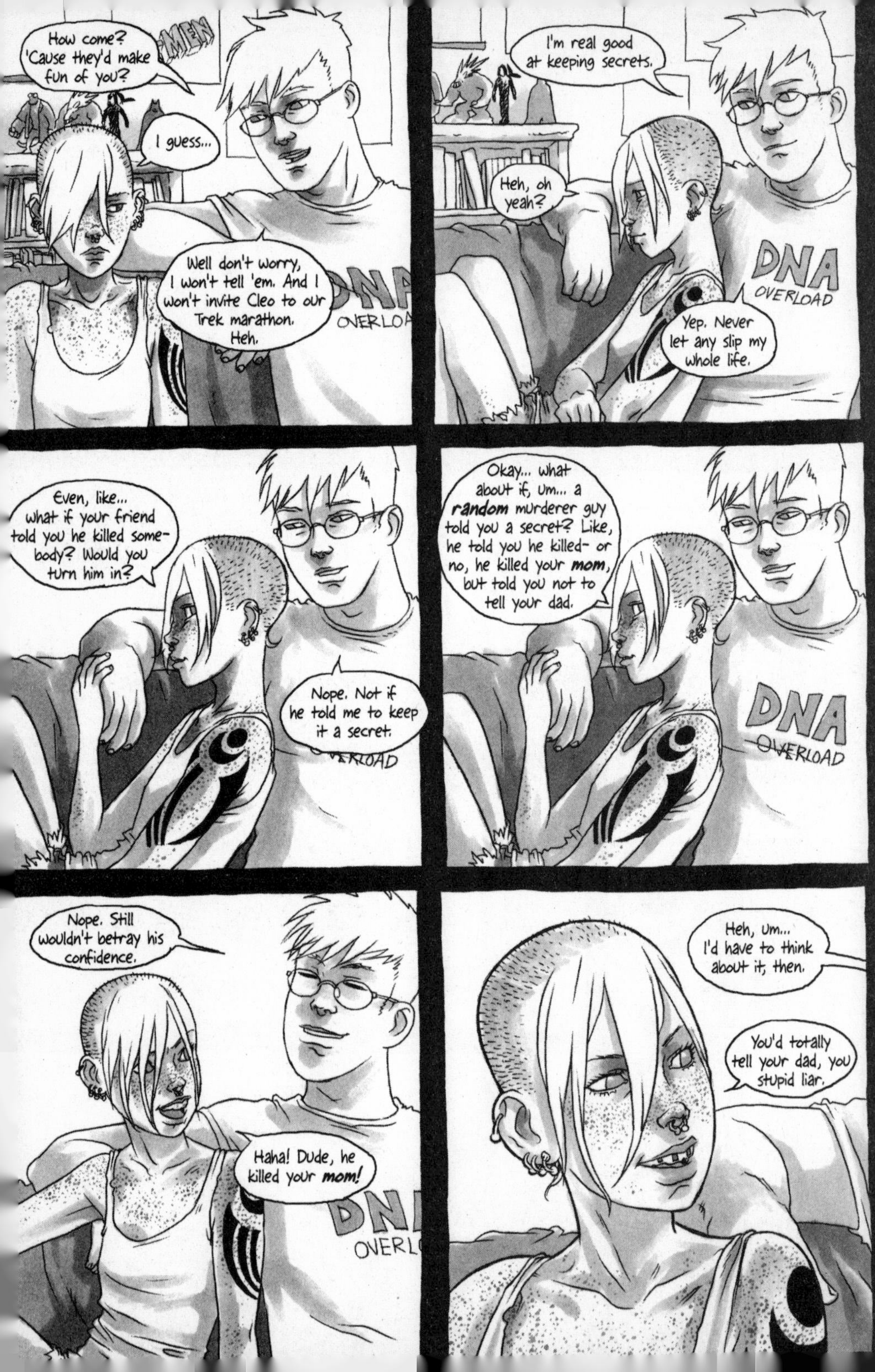

How come? 'Cause they'd make fun of you?
I guess...
Well don't worry, I won't tell 'em. And I won't invite Cleo to our Trek marathon. Heh.
I'm real good at keeping secrets.
Heh, oh yeah?
Yep. Never let any slip my whole life.
Even, like... what if your friend told you he killed somebody? Would you turn him in?
Nope. Not if he told me to keep it a secret.
Okay... what about if, um... a random murderer guy told you a secret? Like, he told you he killed- or no, he killed your mom, but told you not to tell your dad.
Nope. Still wouldn't betray his confidence.
Haha! Dude, he killed your mom!
Heh, um... I'd have to think about it, then.
You'd totally tell your dad, you stupid liar.

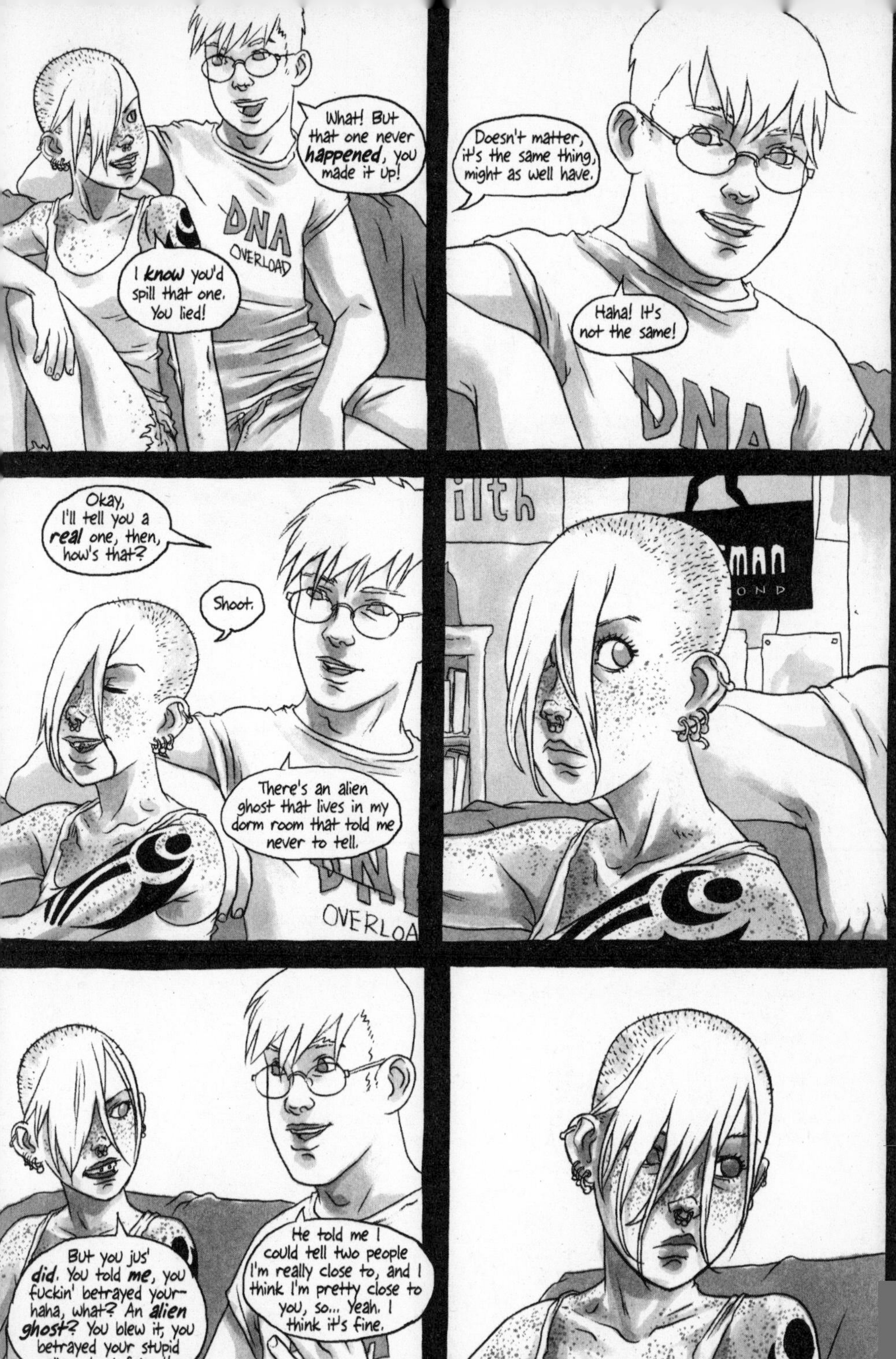
What! But that one never happened, you made it up!
DNA OVERLOAD
I know you'd spill that one. You lied!
Doesn't matter, it's the same thing, might as well have.
Haha! It's not the same!
Okay, I'll tell you a real one, then, how's that?
Shoot.
There's an alien ghost that lives in my dorm room that told me never to tell.
But you jus' did. You told me, you fuckin' betrayed your– haha, what? An alien ghost? You blew it, you betrayed your stupid alien ghost friend!
He told me I could tell two people I'm really close to, and I think I'm pretty close to you, so... Yeah. I think it's fine.

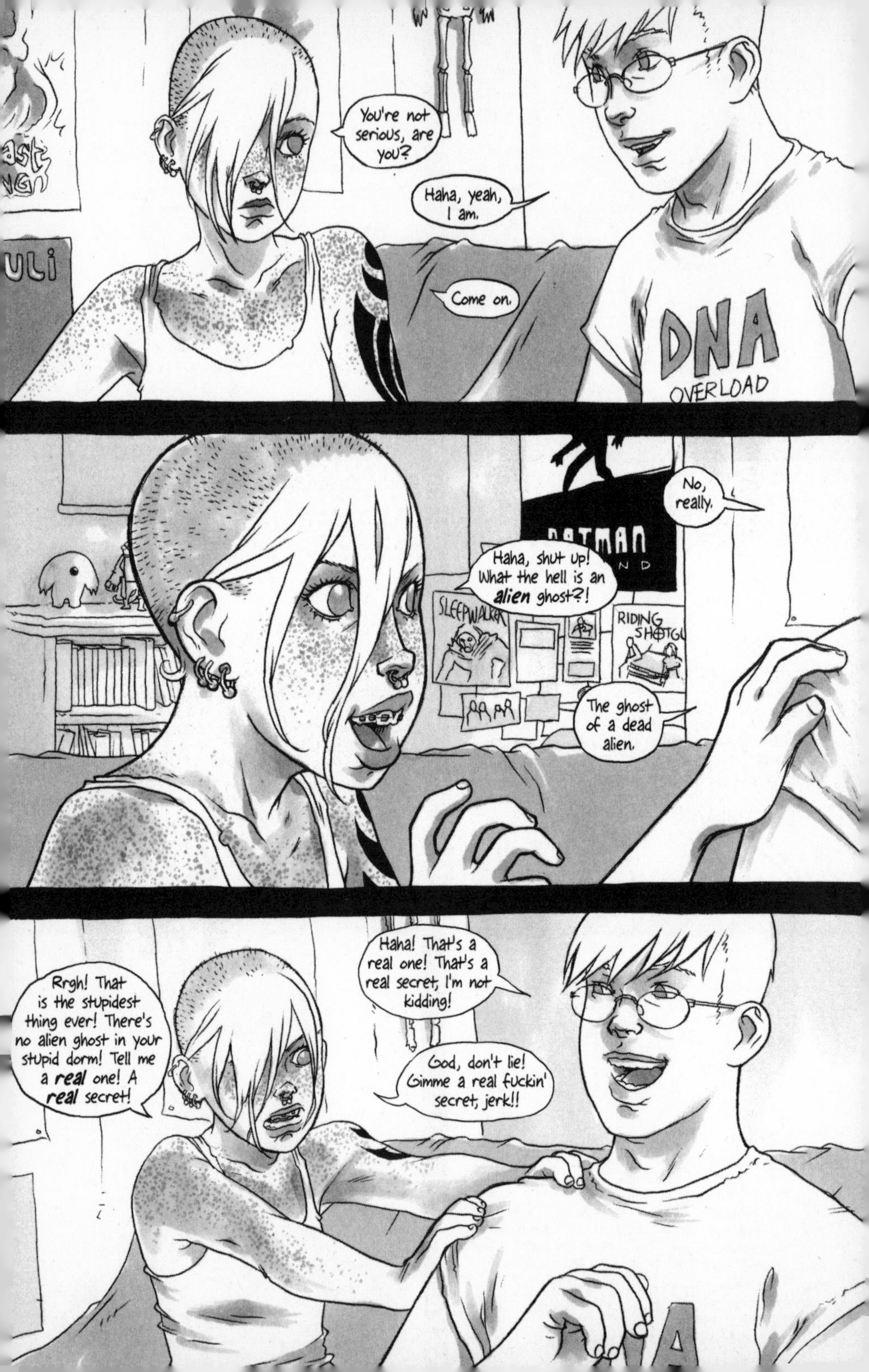

You're not serious, are you?
Haha, yeah, I am.
Come on.
DNA OVERLOAD
No, really.
Haha, shut up! What the hell is an **alien** ghost?!
The ghost of a dead alien.
SLEEPWALKER
RIDING SHOTGU
Rrgh! That is the stupidest thing ever! There's no alien ghost in your stupid dorm! Tell me a **real** one! A **real** secret!
Haha! That's a real one! That's a real secret, I'm not kidding!
God, don't lie! Gimme a real fuckin' secret, jerk!!

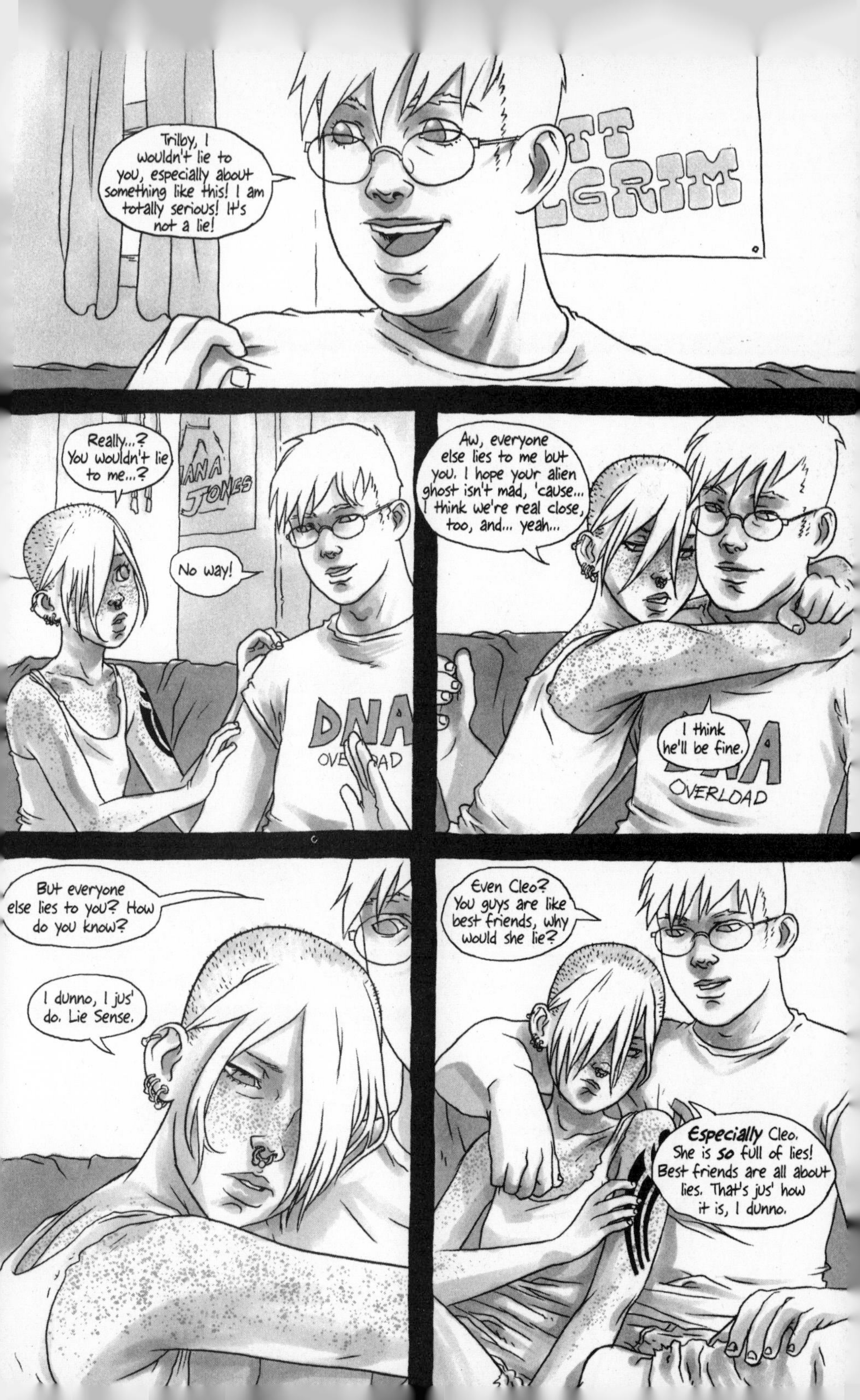

Trilby, I wouldn't lie to you, especially about something like this! I am totally serious! It's not a lie!
TT LGRIM
Really...? You wouldn't lie to me...?
No way!
ANA JONES
DNA OVERLOAD
Aw, everyone else lies to me but you. I hope your alien ghost isn't mad, 'cause... I think we're real close, too, and... yeah...
I think he'll be fine.
OVERLOAD
But everyone else lies to you? How do you know?
I dunno, I jus' do. Lie Sense.
Even Cleo? You guys are like best friends, why would she lie?
Especially Cleo. She is **so** full of lies! Best friends are all about lies. That's jus' how it is, I dunno.

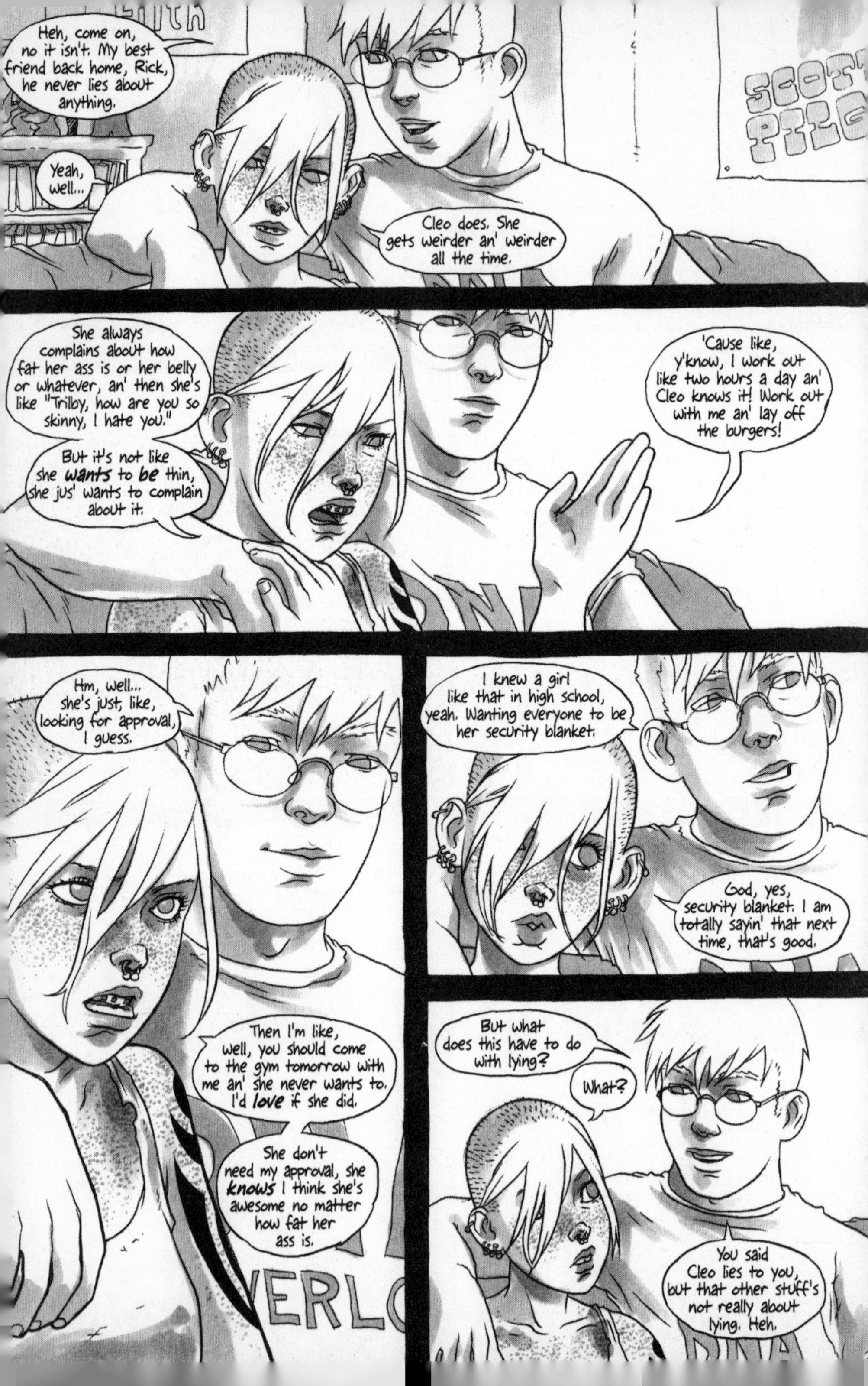

Heh, come on, no it isn't. My best friend back home, Rick, he never lies about anything.
Yeah, well...
Cleo does. She gets weirder an' weirder all the time.
She always complains about how fat her ass is or her belly or whatever, an' then she's like "Trilby, how are you so skinny, I hate you."
But it's not like she **wants** to **be** thin, she jus' wants to complain about it.
'Cause like, y'know, I work out like two hours a day an' Cleo knows it! Work out with me an' lay off the burgers!
Hm, well... she's just, like, looking for approval, I guess.
Then I'm like, well, you should come to the gym tomorrow with me an' she never wants to. I'd **love** if she did.
She don't need my approval, she **knows** I think she's awesome no matter how fat her ass is.
I knew a girl like that in high school, yeah. Wanting everyone to be her security blanket.
God, yes, security blanket. I am totally sayin' that next time, that's good.
But what does this have to do with lying?
What?
You said Cleo lies to you, but that other stuff's not really about lying. Heh.

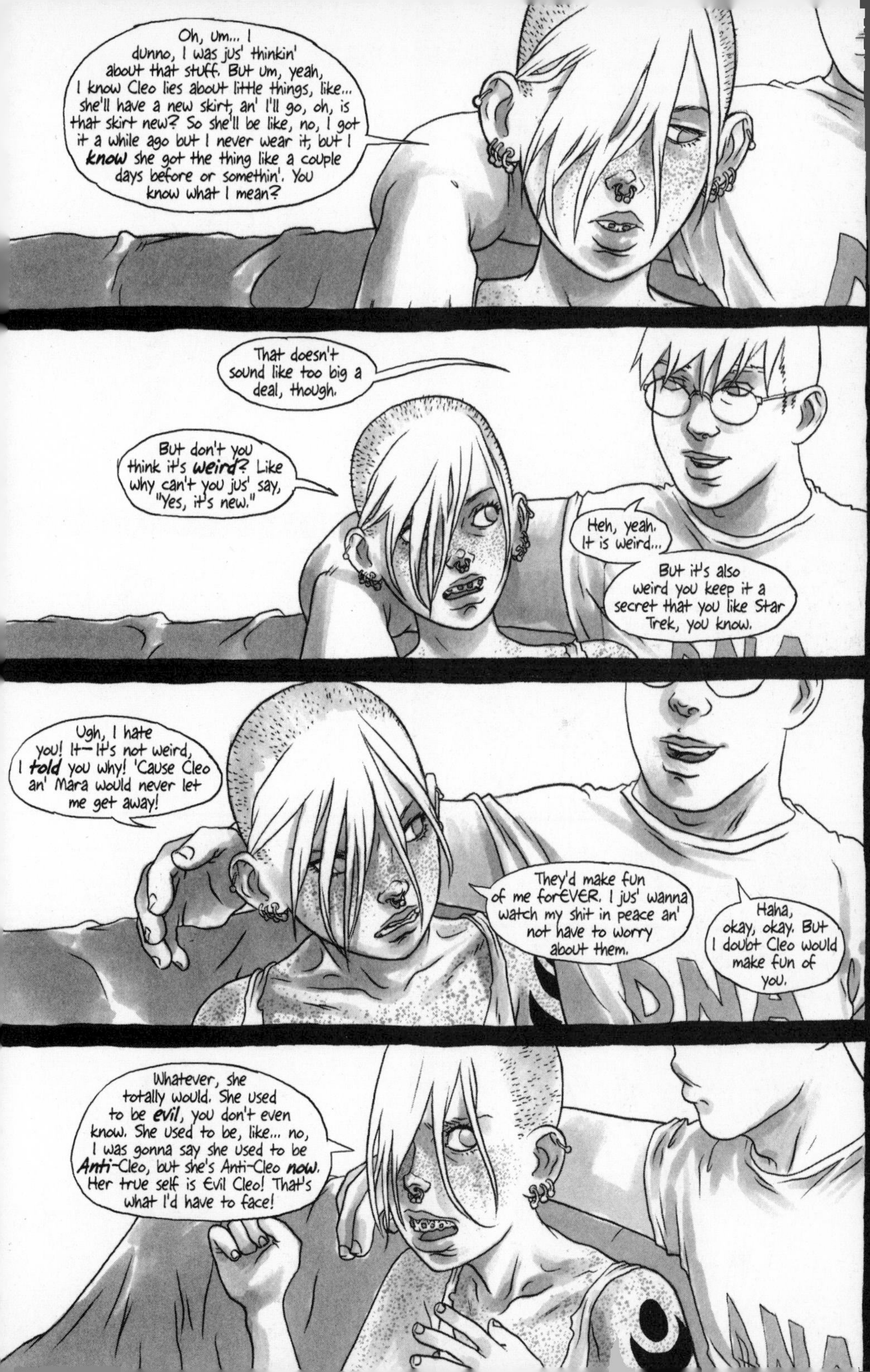
Oh, um... I dunno, I was jus' thinkin' about that stuff. But um, yeah, I know Cleo lies about little things, like... she'll have a new skirt, an' I'll go, oh, is that skirt new? So she'll be like, no, I got it a while ago but I never wear it, but I **know** she got the thing like a couple days before or somethin'. You know what I mean?
That doesn't sound like too big a deal, though.
But don't you think it's **weird**? Like why can't you jus' say, "Yes, it's new."
Heh, yeah. It is weird...
But it's also weird you keep it a secret that you like Star Trek, you know.
Ugh, I hate you! It— It's not weird, I **told** you why! 'Cause Cleo an' Mara would never let me get away!
They'd make fun of me forEVER. I jus' wanna watch my shit in peace an' not have to worry about them.
Haha, okay, okay. But I doubt Cleo would make fun of you.
Whatever, she totally would. She used to be **evil**, you don't even know. She used to be, like... no, I was gonna say she used to be **Anti**-Cleo, but she's Anti-Cleo **now**. Her true self is Evil Cleo! That's what I'd have to face!

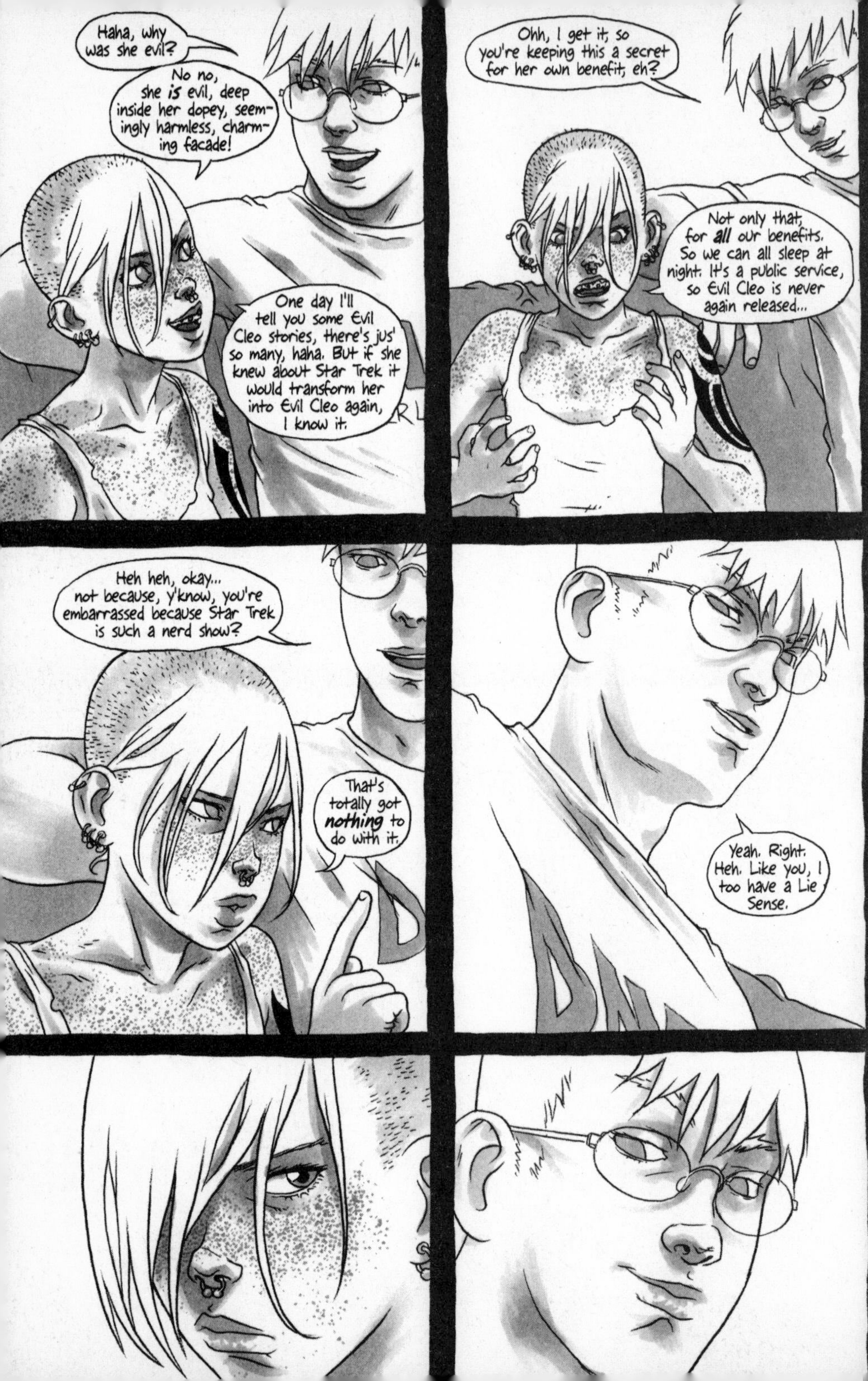
Haha, why was she evil?
No no, she *is* evil, deep inside her dopey, seemingly harmless, charming facade!
One day I'll tell you some Evil Cleo stories, there's jus' so many, haha. But if she knew about Star Trek it would transform her into Evil Cleo again, I know it.
Ohh, I get it, so you're keeping this a secret for her own benefit, eh?
Not only that, for **all** our benefits. So we can all sleep at night. It's a public service, so Evil Cleo is never again released...
Heh heh, okay... not because, y'know, you're embarrassed because Star Trek is such a nerd show?
That's totally got ***nothing*** to do with it.
Yeah. Right. Heh. Like you, I too have a Lie Sense.

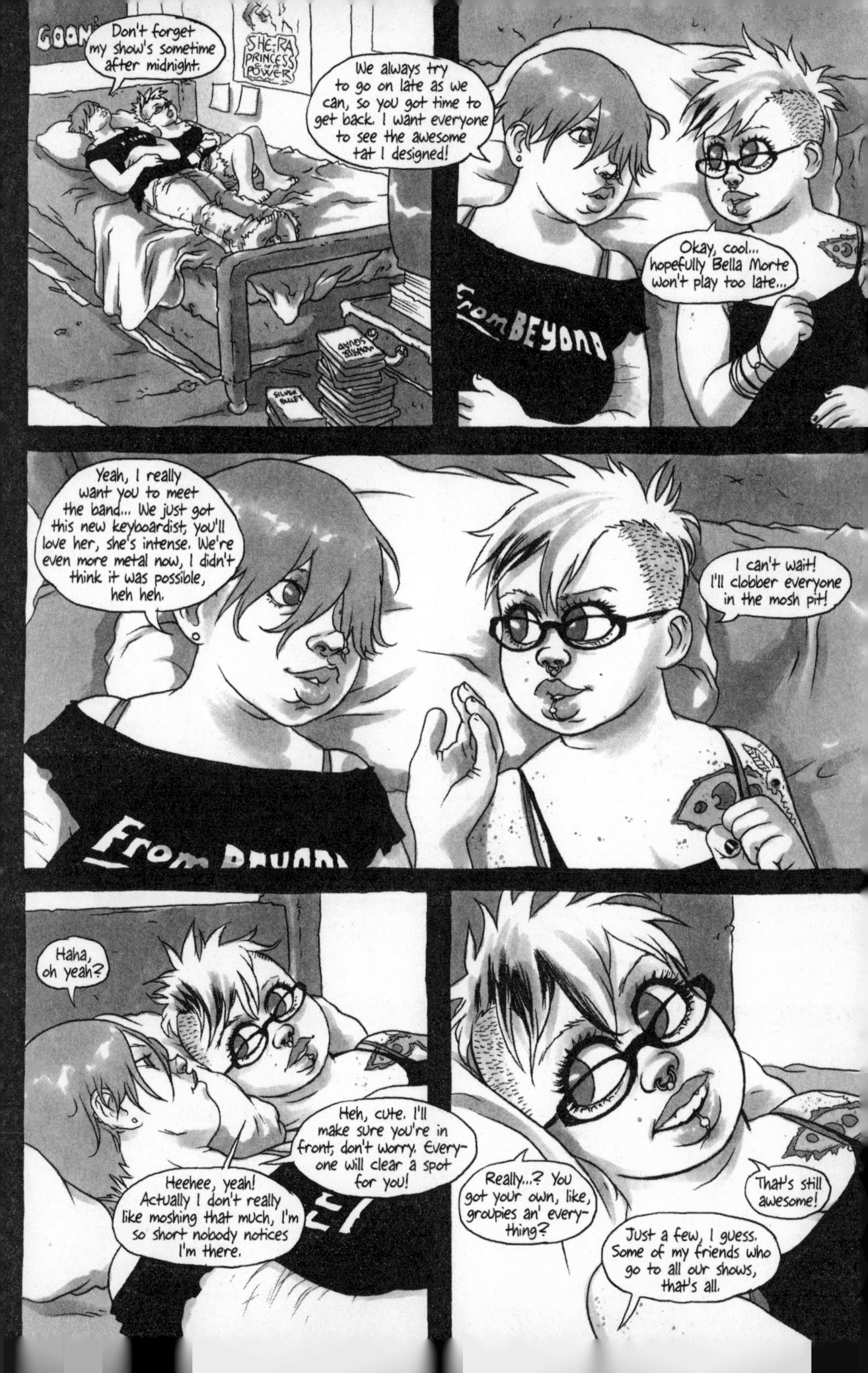
SHE-RA PRINCESS of POWER
Don't forget my show's sometime after midnight.
We always try to go on late as we can, so you got time to get back. I want everyone to see the awesome tat I designed!
From BEYOND
Okay, cool... hopefully Bella Morte won't play too late...
Yeah, I really want you to meet the band... We just got this new keyboardist, you'll love her, she's intense. We're even more metal now, I didn't think it was possible, heh heh.
I can't wait! I'll clobber everyone in the mosh pit!
Haha, oh yeah?
Heehee, yeah! Actually I don't really like moshing that much, I'm so short nobody notices I'm there.
Heh, cute. I'll make sure you're in front, don't worry. Everyone will clear a spot for you!
Really...? You got your own, like, groupies an' everything?
Just a few, I guess. Some of my friends who go to all our shows, that's all.
That's still awesome!

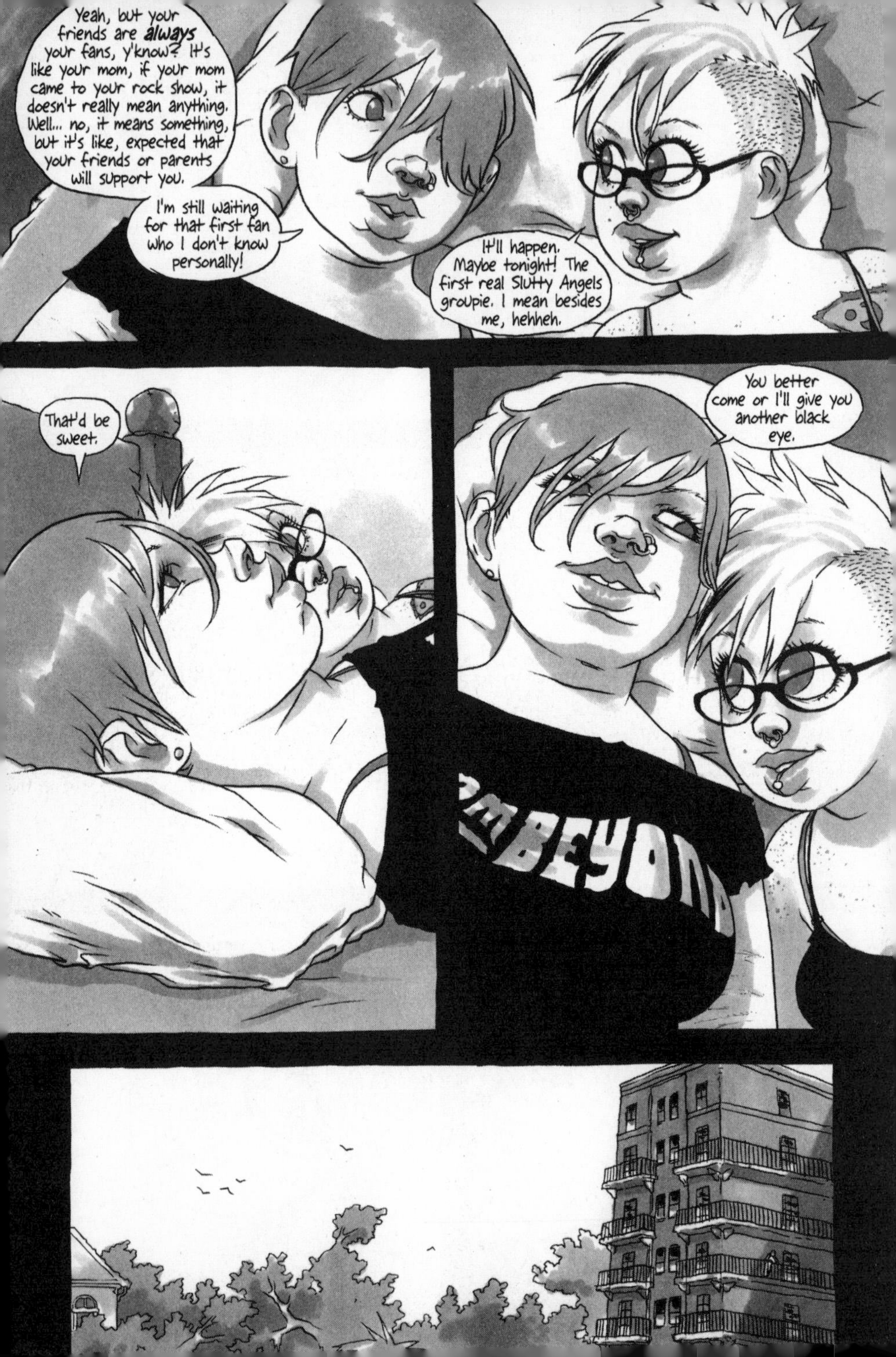

Yeah, but your friends are **always** your fans, y'know? It's like your mom, if your mom came to your rock show, it doesn't really mean anything. Well... no, it means something, but it's like, expected that your friends or parents will support you.
I'm still waiting for that first fan who I don't know personally!
It'll happen. Maybe tonight! The first real Slutty Angels groupie. I mean besides me, hehheh.
That'd be sweet.
You better come or I'll give you another black eye.

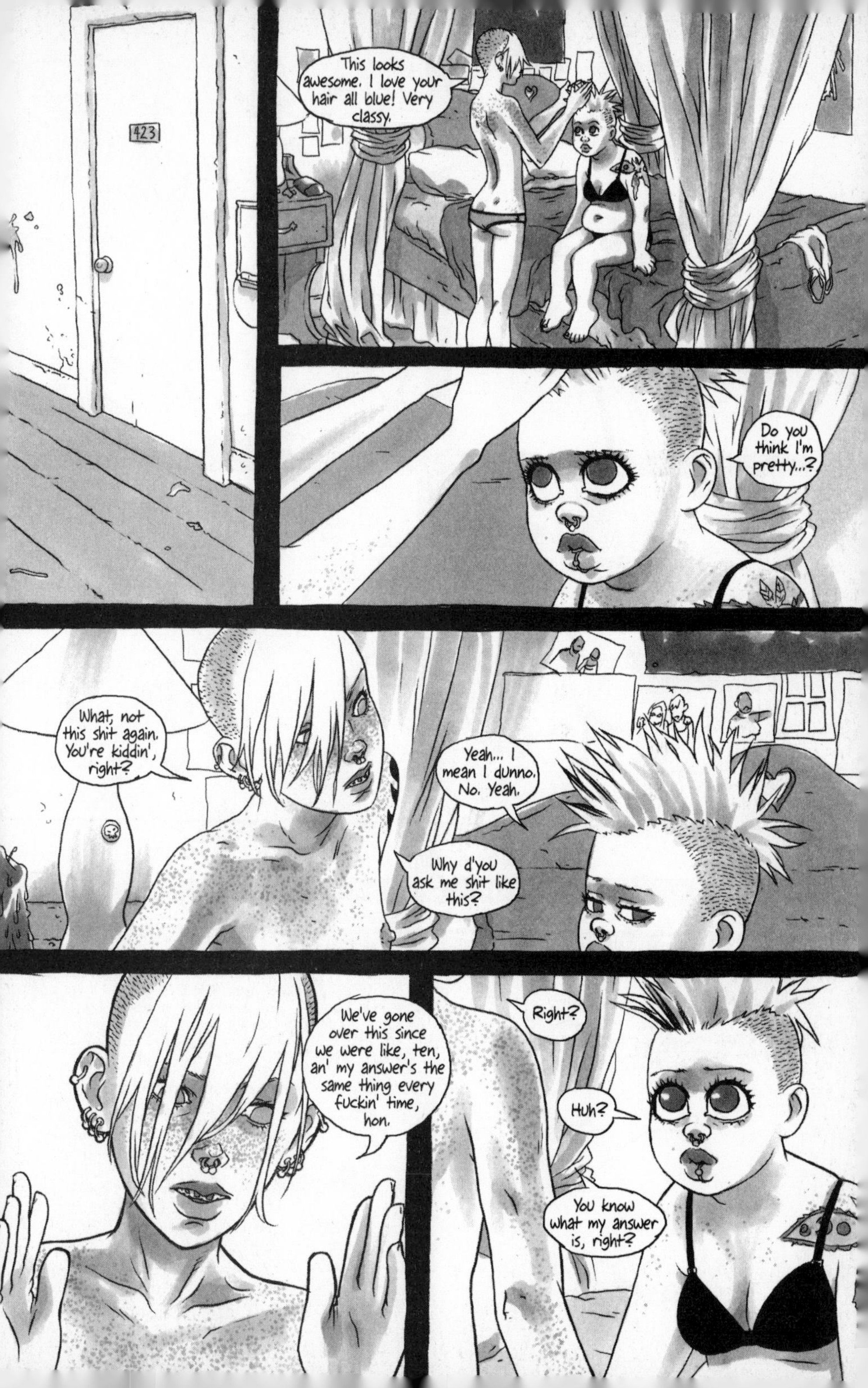
This looks awesome. I love your hair all blue! Very classy.
Do you think I'm pretty...?
What, not this shit again. You're kiddin', right?
Yeah... I mean I dunno. No. Yeah.
Why d'you ask me shit like this?
We've gone over this since we were like, ten, an' my answer's the same thing every fuckin' time, hon.
Right?
Huh?
You know what my answer is, right?

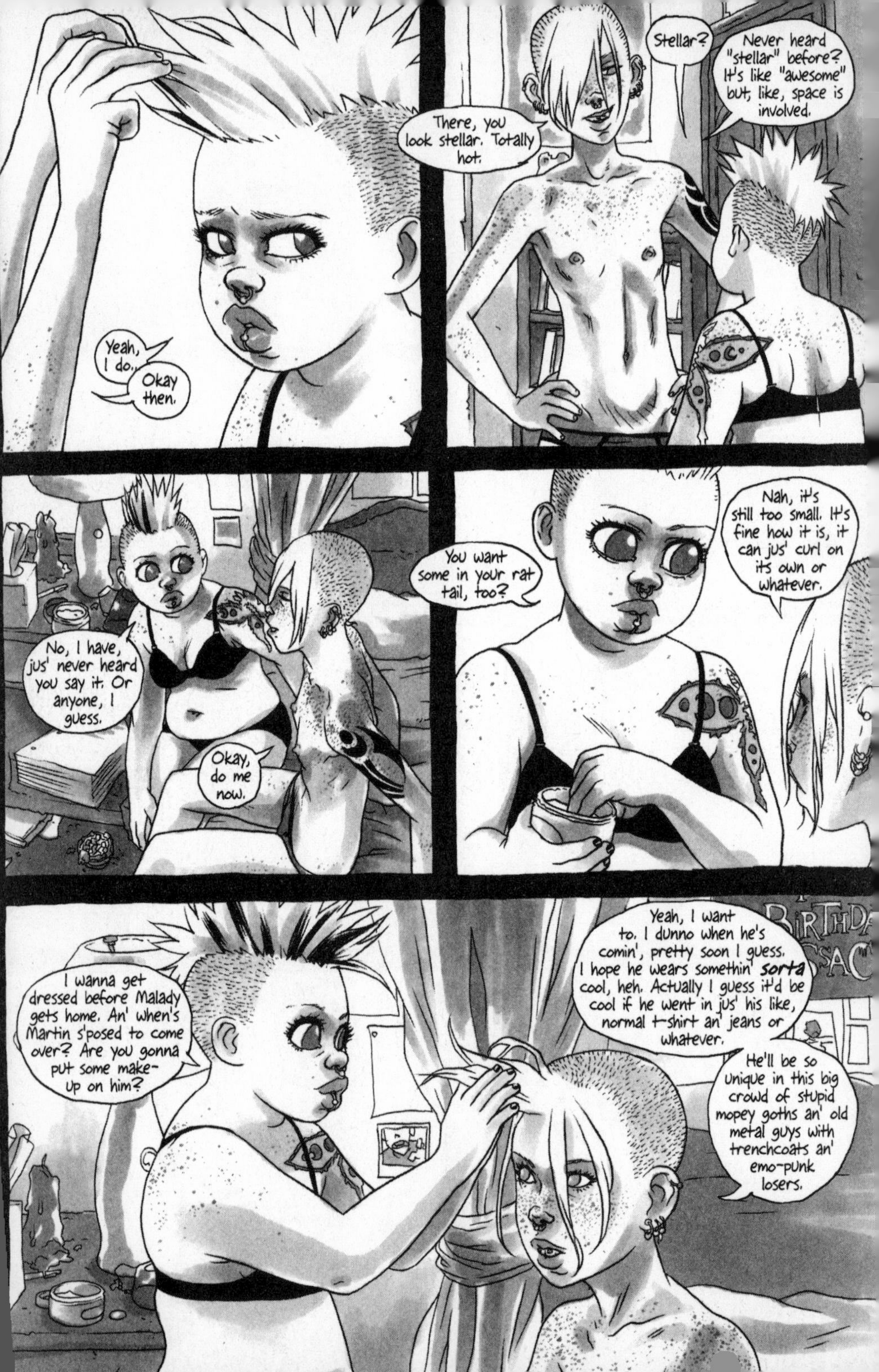

Yeah, I do..
Okay then.
There, you look stellar. Totally hot.
Stellar?
Never heard "stellar" before? It's like "awesome" but, like, space is involved.
No, I have, jus' never heard you say it. Or anyone, I guess.
Okay, do me now.
You want some in your rat tail, too?
Nah, it's still too small. It's fine how it is, it can jus' curl on its own or whatever.
I wanna get dressed before Malady gets home. An' when's Martin s'posed to come over? Are you gonna put some make-up on him?
Yeah, I want to. I dunno when he's comin', pretty soon I guess. I hope he wears somethin' **sorta** cool, heh. Actually I guess it'd be cool if he went in jus' his like, normal t-shirt an' jeans or whatever.
He'll be so unique in this big crowd of stupid mopey goths an' old metal guys with trenchcoats an' emo-punk losers.

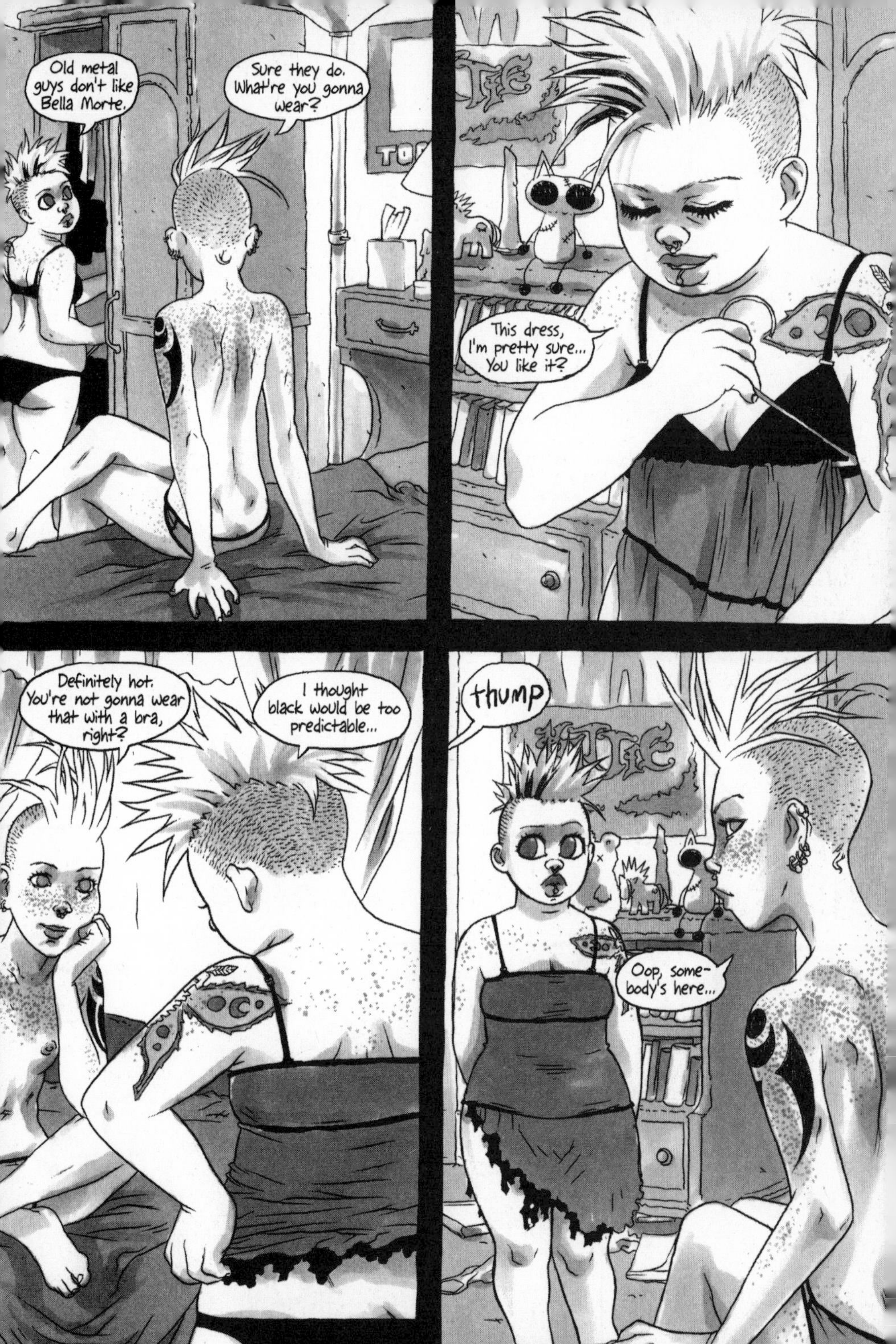
Old metal guys don't like Bella Morte.
Sure they do. What're you gonna wear?
This dress, I'm pretty sure... You like it?
Definitely hot. You're not gonna wear that with a bra, right?
I thought black would be too predictable...
thump
Oop, some-body's here...

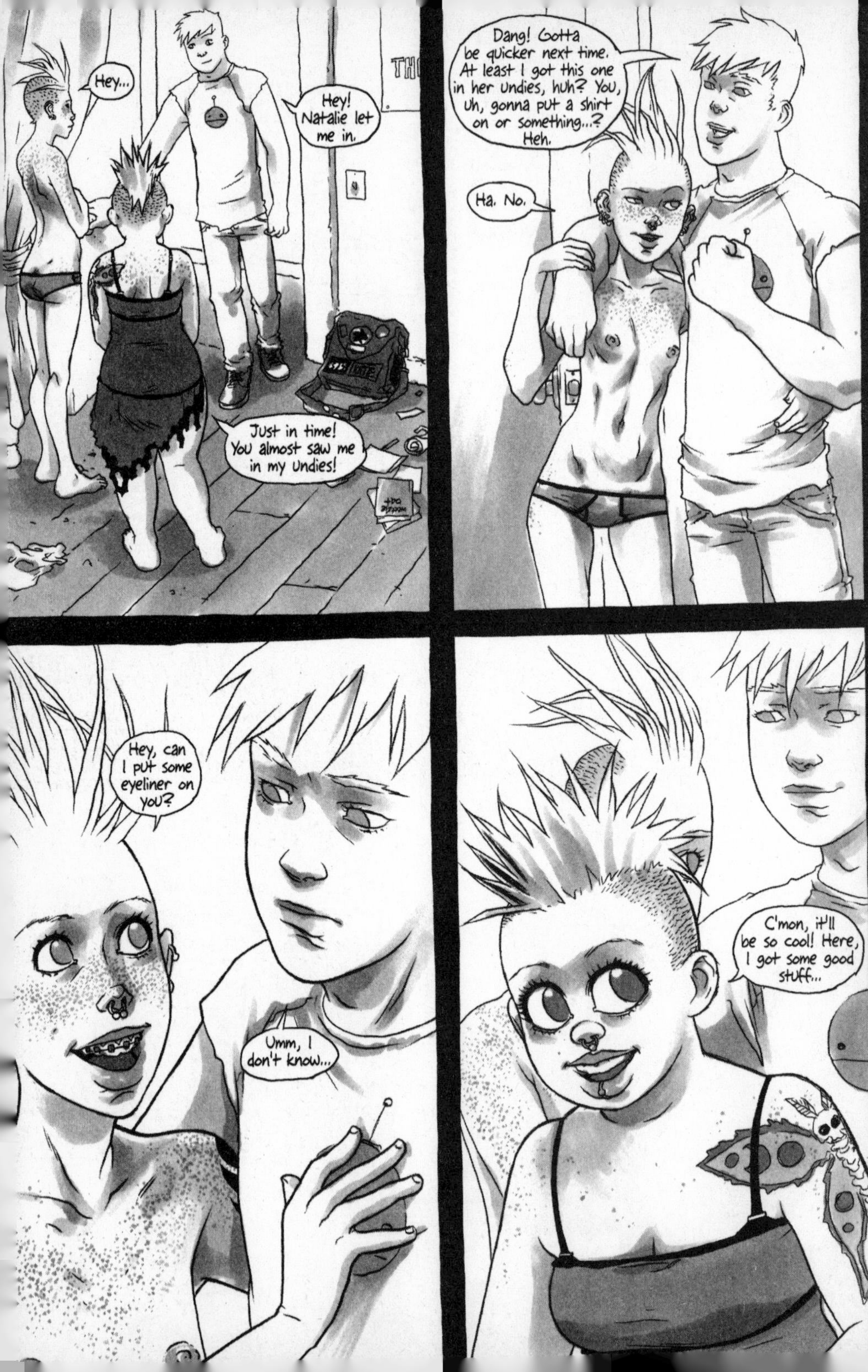
Hey...
Hey! Natalie let me in.
Just in time! You almost saw me in my undies!
Dang! Gotta be quicker next time. At least I got this one in her undies, huh? You, uh, gonna put a shirt on or something...? Heh.
Ha. No.
Hey, can I put some eyeliner on you?
Umm, I don't know...
C'mon, it'll be so cool! Here, I got some good stuff...

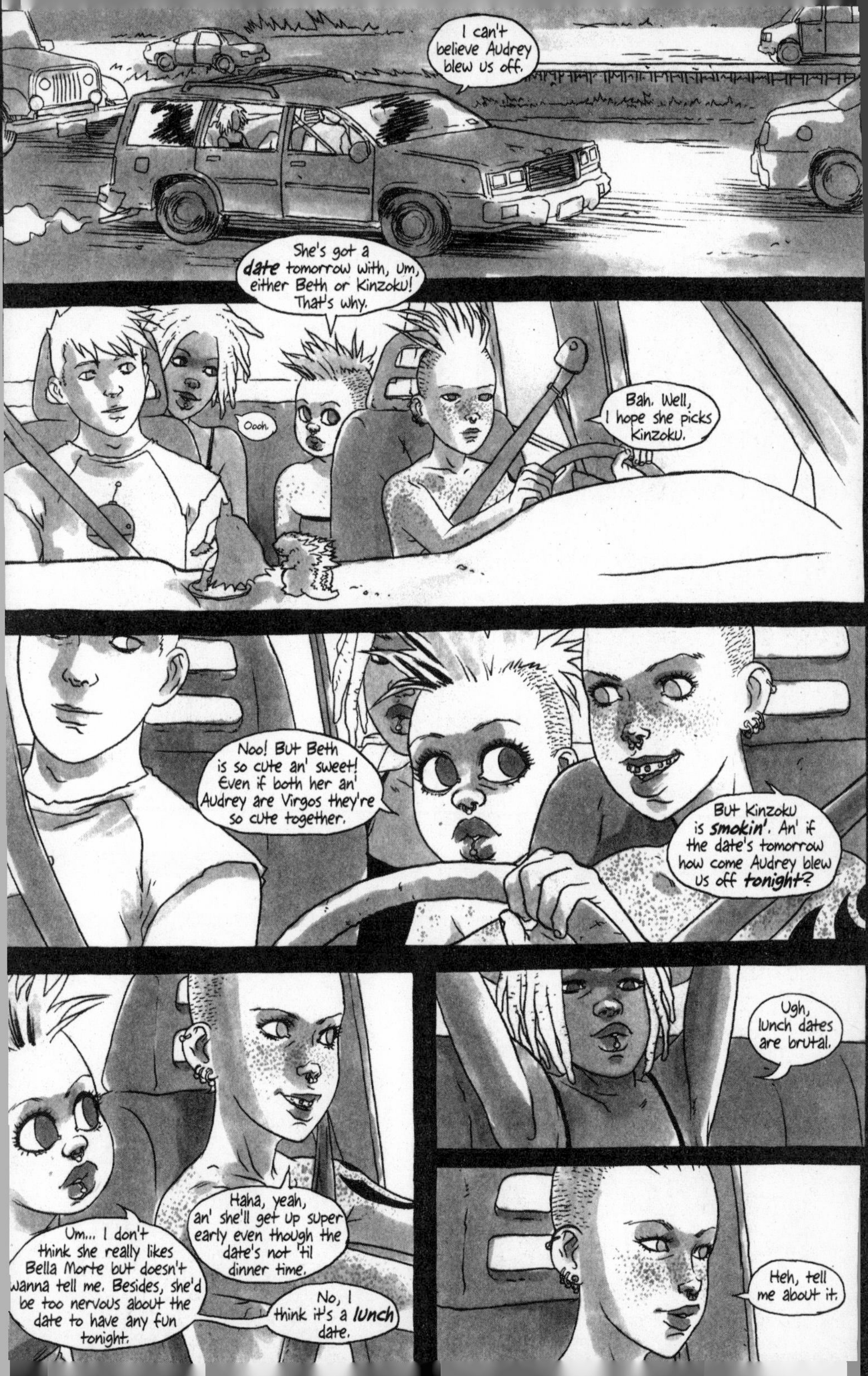

I can't believe Audrey blew us off.
She's got a date tomorrow with, um, either Beth or Kinzoku! That's why.
Oooh.
Bah. Well, I hope she picks Kinzoku.
Noo! But Beth is so cute an' sweet! Even if both her an' Audrey are Virgos they're so cute together.
But Kinzoku is smokin'. An' if the date's tomorrow how come Audrey blew us off tonight?
Um... I don't think she really likes Bella Morte but doesn't wanna tell me. Besides, she'd be too nervous about the date to have any fun tonight.
Haha, yeah, an' she'll get up super early even though the date's not 'til dinner time.
No, I think it's a lunch date.
Ugh, lunch dates are brutal.
Heh, tell me about it.

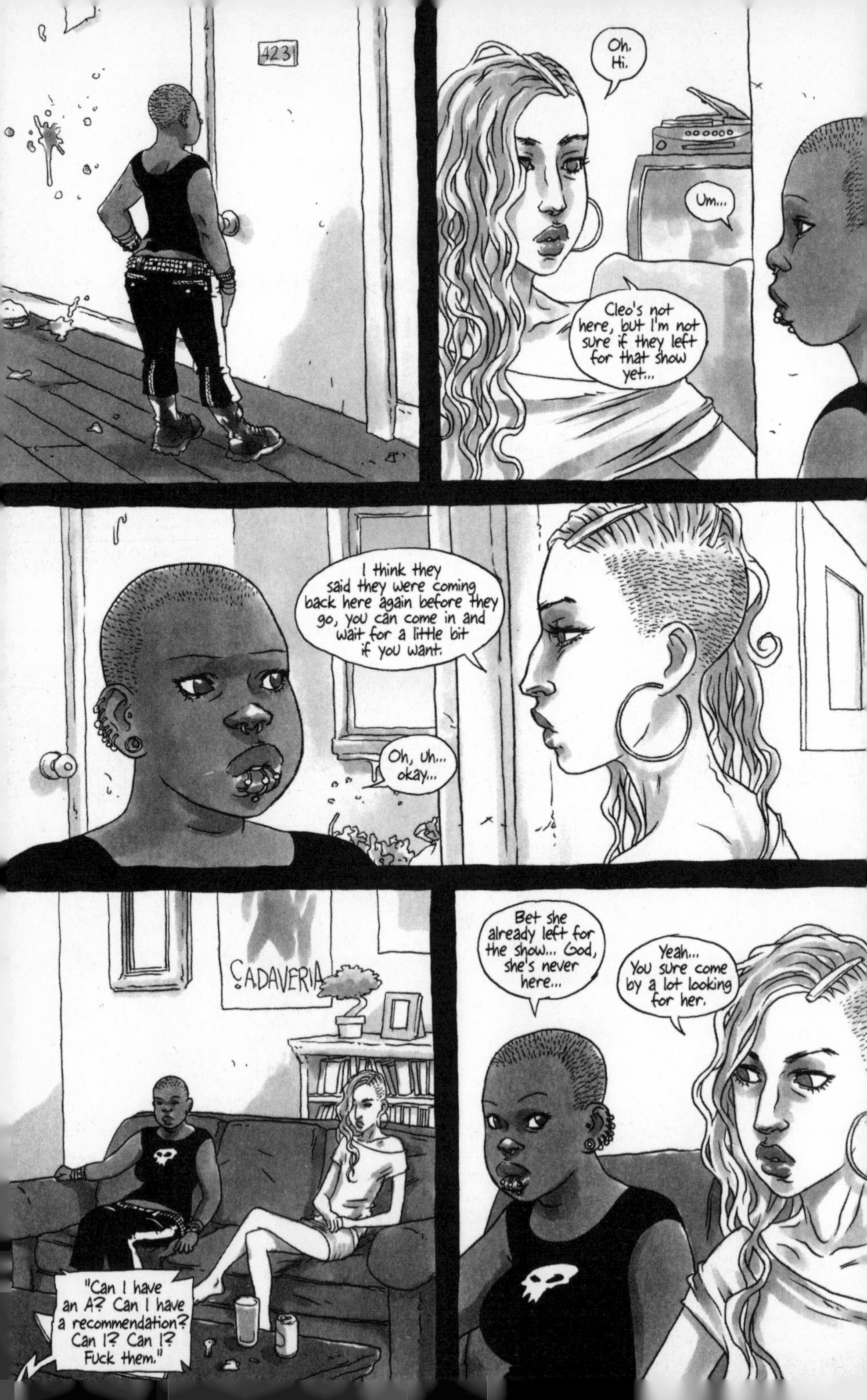

4231
Oh. Hi.
Um...
Cleo's not here, but I'm not sure if they left for that show yet...
I think they said they were coming back here again before they go, you can come in and wait for a little bit if you want.
Oh, uh... okay...
CADAVERIA
"Can I have an A? Can I have a recommendation? Can I? Can I? Fuck them."
Bet she already left for the show... God, she's never here...
Yeah... You sure come by a lot looking for her.

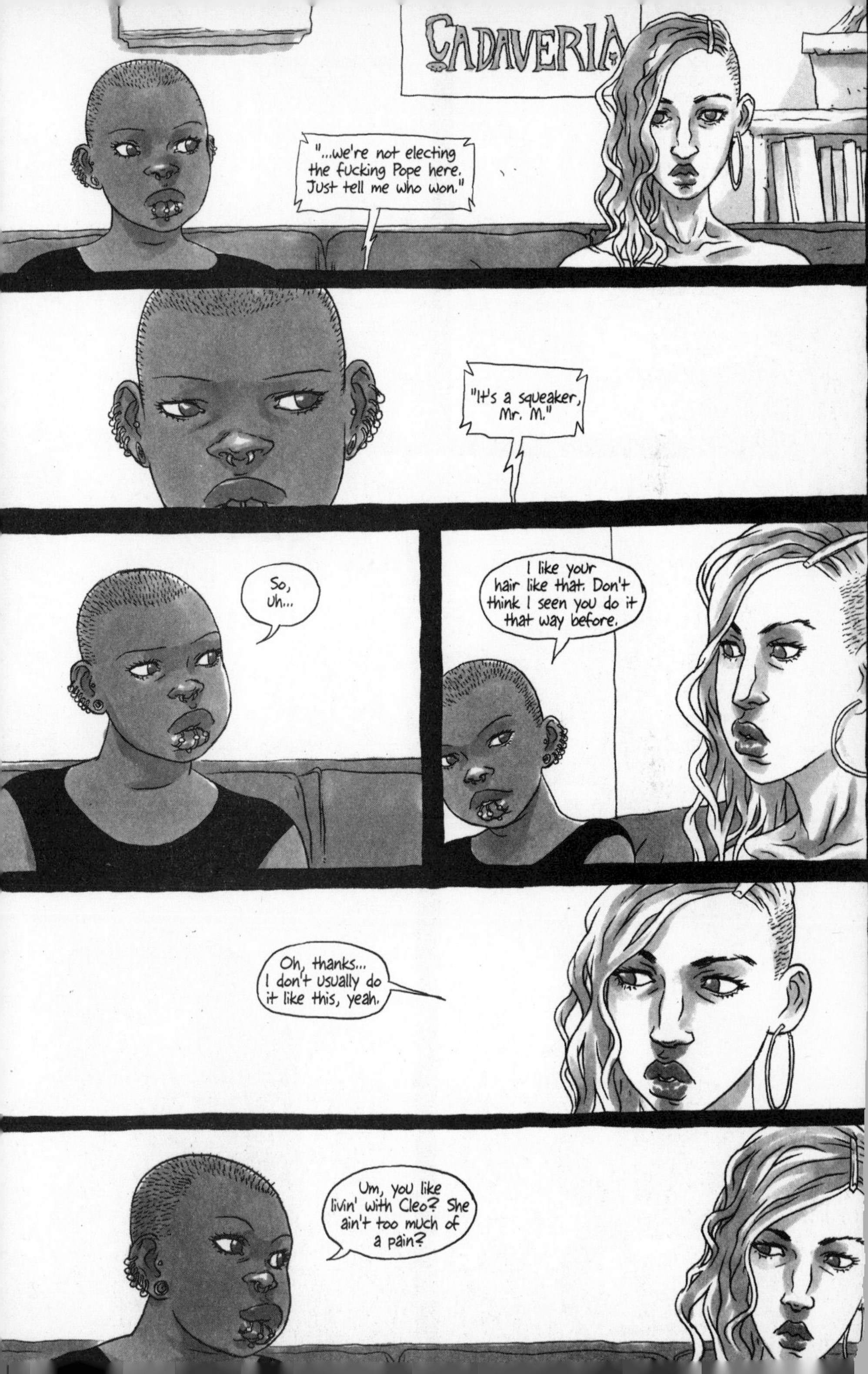
CADAVERIA
"...we're not electing the fucking Pope here. Just tell me who won."
"It's a squeaker, Mr. M."
So, uh...
I like your hair like that. Don't think I seen you do it that way before.
Oh, thanks... I don't usually do it like this, yeah.
Um, you like livin' with Cleo? She ain't too much of a pain?

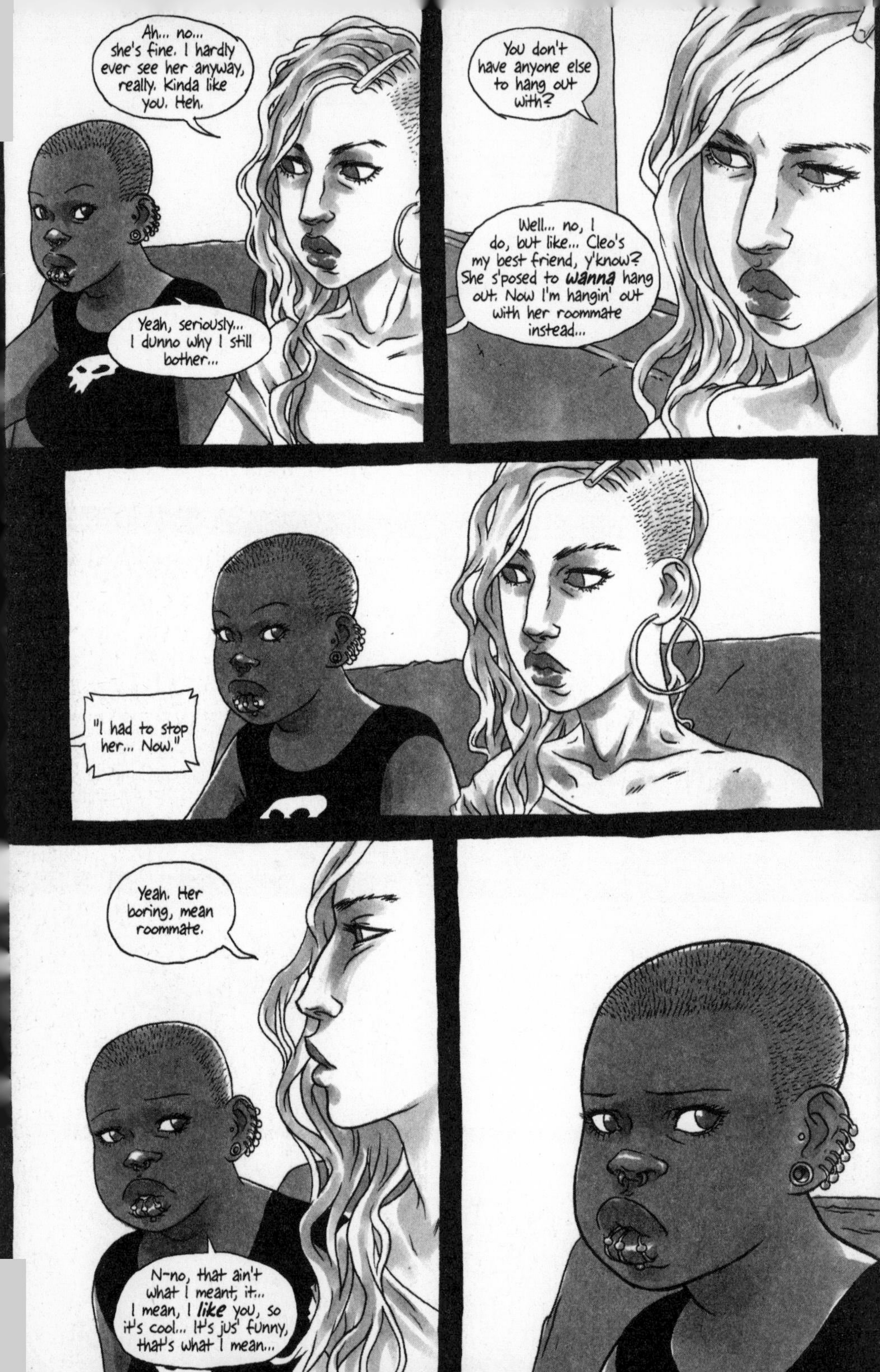
Ah... no... she's fine. I hardly ever see her anyway, really. Kinda like you. Heh.
Yeah, seriously... I dunno why I still bother...
You don't have anyone else to hang out with?
Well... no, I do, but like... Cleo's my best friend, y'know? She s'posed to *wanna* hang out. Now I'm hangin' out with her roommate instead...
"I had to stop her... Now."
Yeah. Her boring, mean roommate.
N-no, that ain't what I meant, it... I mean, I *like* you, so it's cool... It's jus' funny, that's what I mean...

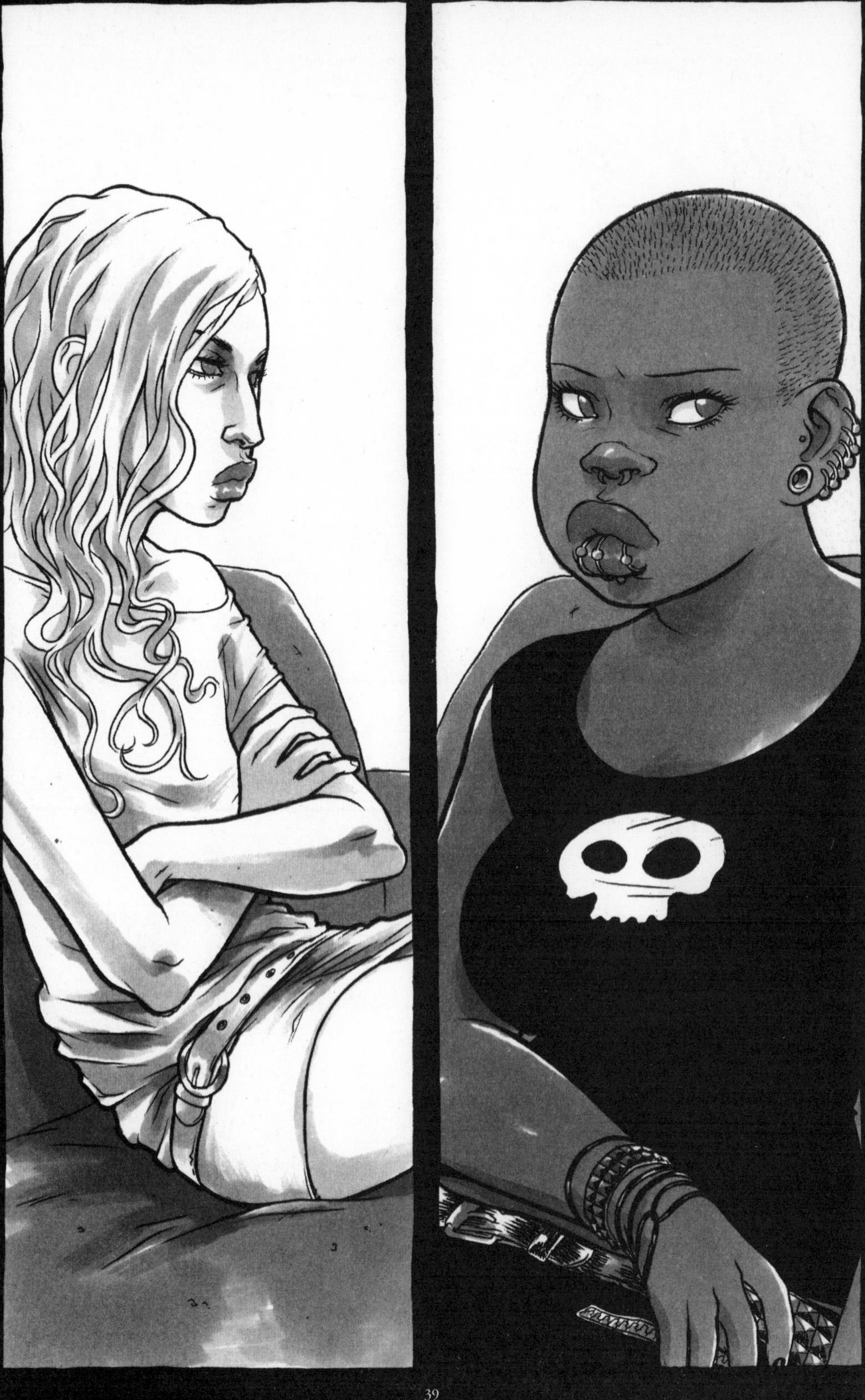

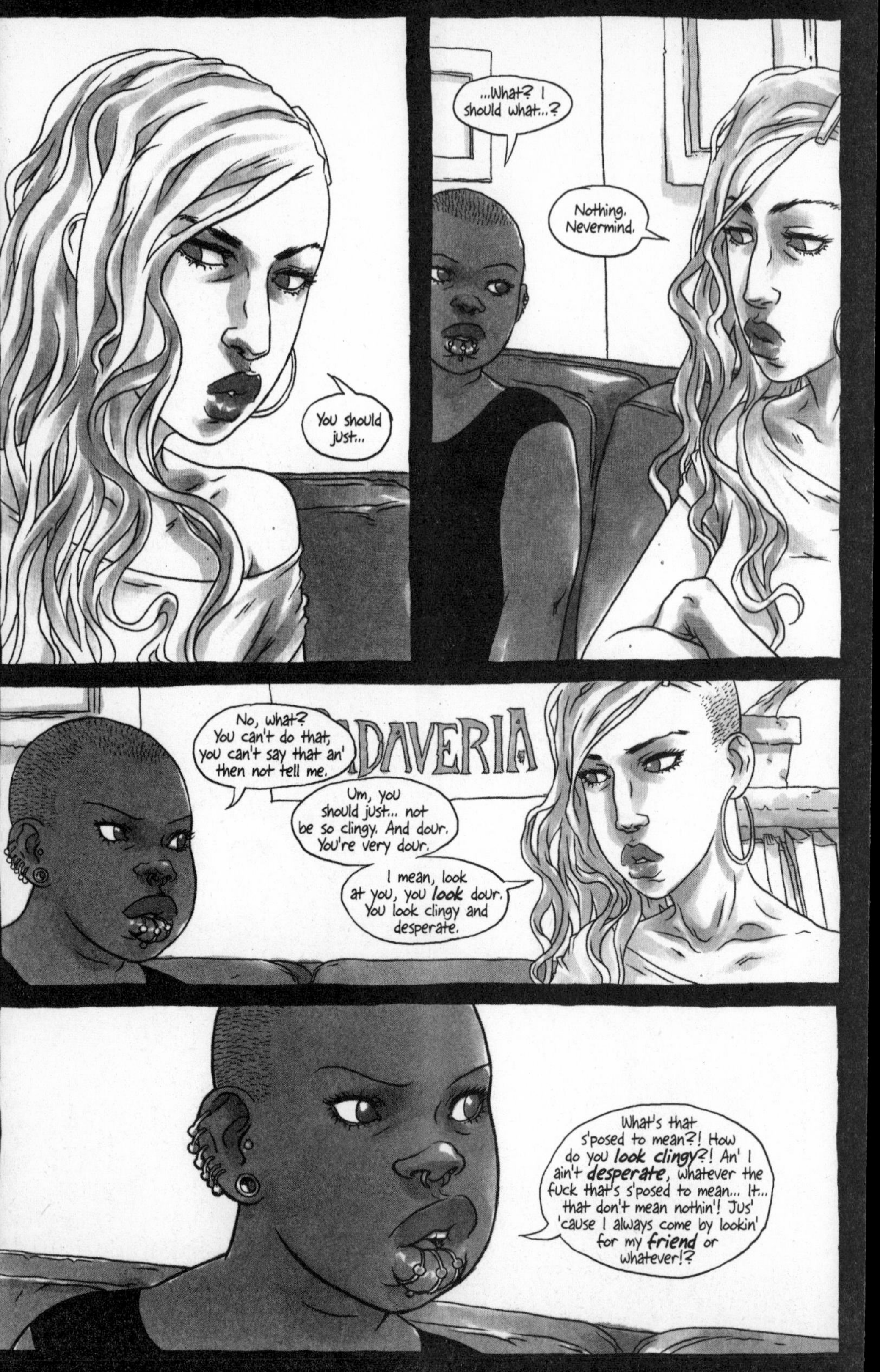
You should just...
...What? I should what...?
Nothing. Nevermind.
No, what? You can't do that, you can't say that an' then not tell me.
ADAVERIA
Um, you should just... not be so clingy. And dour. You're very dour.
I mean, look at you, you look dour. You look clingy and desperate.
What's that s'posed to mean?! How do you look clingy?! An' I ain't desperate, whatever the fuck that's s'posed to mean... It... that don't mean nothin'! Jus' 'cause I always come by lookin' for my friend or whatever!?

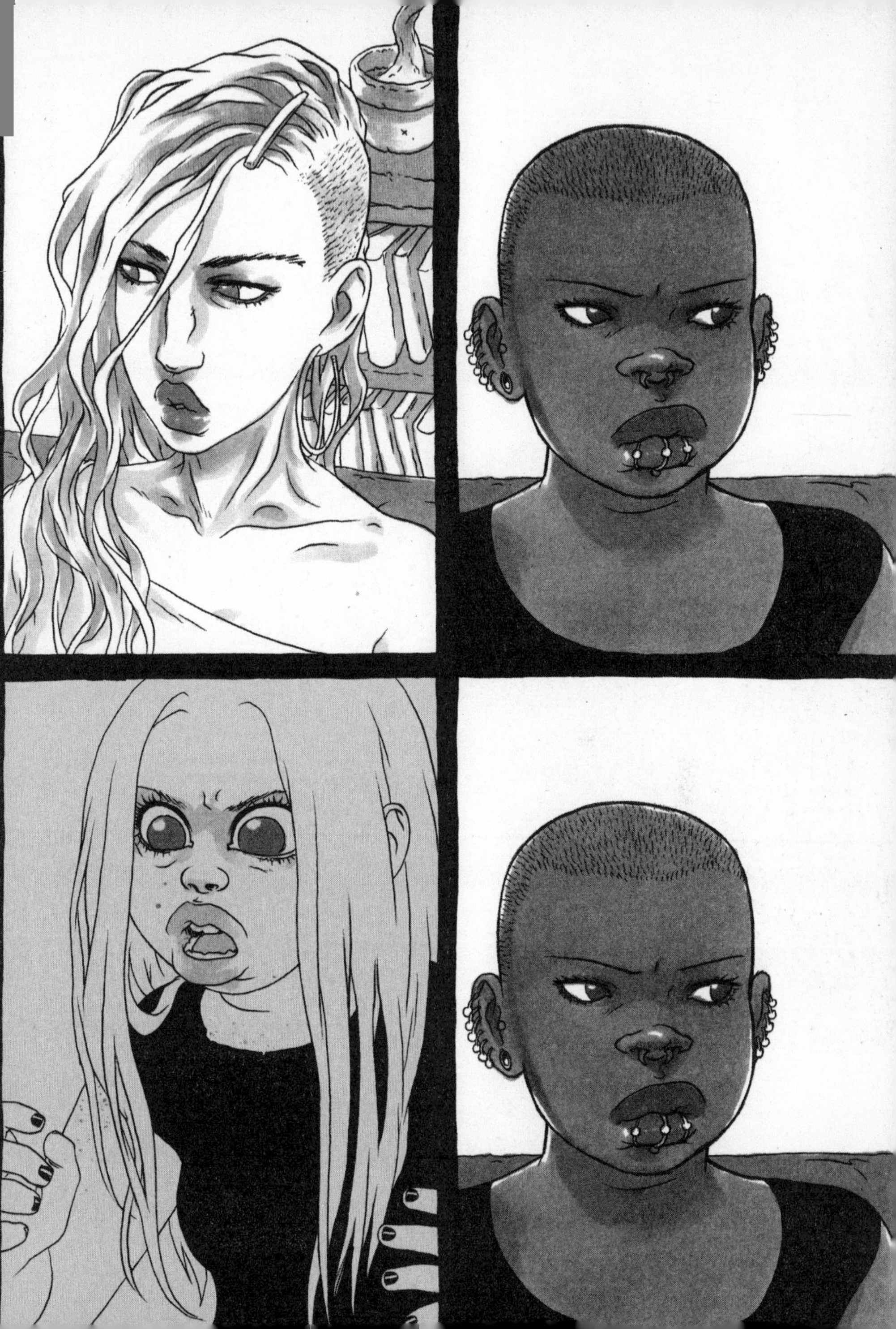

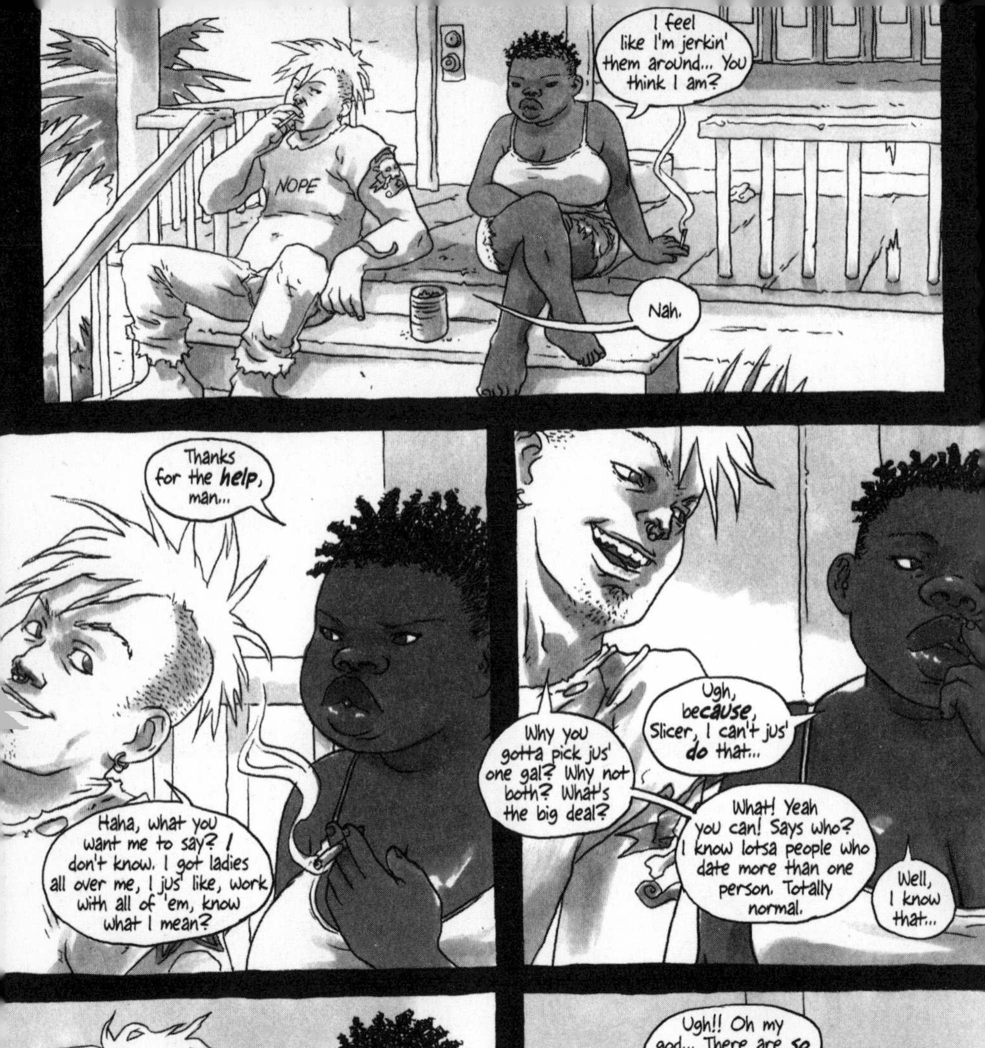

NOPE
I feel like I'm jerkin' them around... You think I am?
Nah.
Thanks for the help, man...
Haha, what you want me to say? I don't know. I got ladies all over me, I jus' like, work with all of 'em, know what I mean?
Why you gotta pick jus' one gal? Why not both? What's the big deal?
Ugh, because, Slicer, I can't jus' do that...
What! Yeah you can! Says who? I know lotsa people who date more than one person. Totally normal.
Well, I know that...
NOPE
But these girls... They're very strong presences. I can't have 'em both. I ain't into that.
Welp, if ya ask me, go Asian. They're always repressed an' love venting in the best possible ways. I've had a good chance to test out all the crayons in the box, an' Yellow Fever is my favorite color by far, heh. C'mon, take it from me, babe.
Ugh!! Oh my god... There are so many things wrong with you...
Bwahaha.

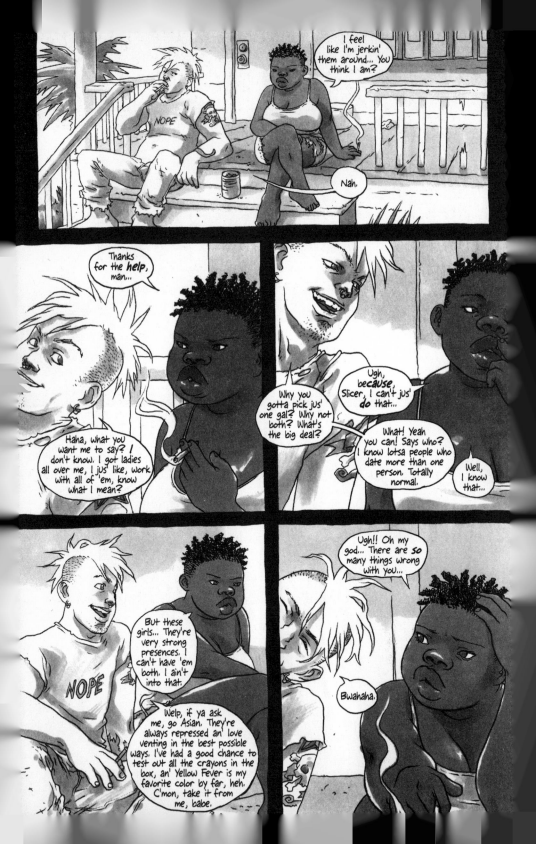

mara's journal

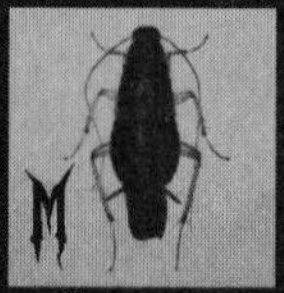

profile

October 11th, 3:23am

I'M MY ENEMY

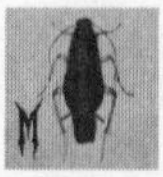

today probably one of the most awkward things that has ever happened to me happened. not only am i completly embarassed now to go over to Cleo's dumb dorm because she's never there but now her stuck-up roomate Natalie thinks i'm the biggest douche on the planet. i always show up there and Cleo is never home so this girl Natalie answers the door and tells me Cleo isn't home every fucking time. then today she told me to wait inside for Cleo so i did, whatever, seemed like a good thing to do. Cleo's gotta come home sometime, right? so i waited with Natalie on the couch, watching some Matthew Broderick movie, the Ferris Bueller guy except now he's old but still looks oddly the same. Reese Witherspoon was in it too. anyway, so we sat there watching this movie, and it's really awkward and totally weird, and then she said like "don't you have anyone else to hang out with?" like i don't have any other friends. of course i do, bitch. who has just ONE friend? well no, i guess some people must have, but she's obviously seen me with other people like Trilby and Audrey, even though Trilby's been seriously pissing me off recently. that's a whole other entry.

anyway, then she goes to say something but stops herself and says "oh, nevermind." i fucking hate it when people do that. especially online. because online, you have all this time to think about what your going to type and you have to hit enter to send what you type, so it doesn't make any sense when people do that shit on MSN, but people still do it. it's all really just to get the other person, in this case me, to go "no, what? tell me!" and beg the person to tell them. the person just does it to have this fucked up kind of control over the other person, like withholding information that the other person obviously is going to want to hear. well normally i'd say fuck that, i don't want to hear your fucking information and play your games, my interest is not piqued, except that's exactly what i did. i go "no, what? tell me!" and she does, of course, and she tells me i look dour and desperate and clingy what the fuck does that mean. i'm glad that i look dour, dour is cool, but i don't look desperate. i don't know, who cares. but so after that i obviously didn't stay, Cleo would never show up anyways, so i just ignored her after that and fucking left. i couldn't stop thinking about her and what she said, it was like eating my brain, so i went for a walk and stopped in at Arcana and found this old copy of *Nightlust* by Edward Lee, so that was cool. i heard it's pretty bad but i'm still interested, and it's tough to find his really old stuff so i had to get it. i'm still in the middle of his book *Portrait of the Psychopath as a Young Woman* and so far it's awesome. i don't know what i'm going to do about Cleo and Natalie. i don't want to be like this.

mood: sad
current music: hocico - spirits of crime

[0 comments | leave a comment]

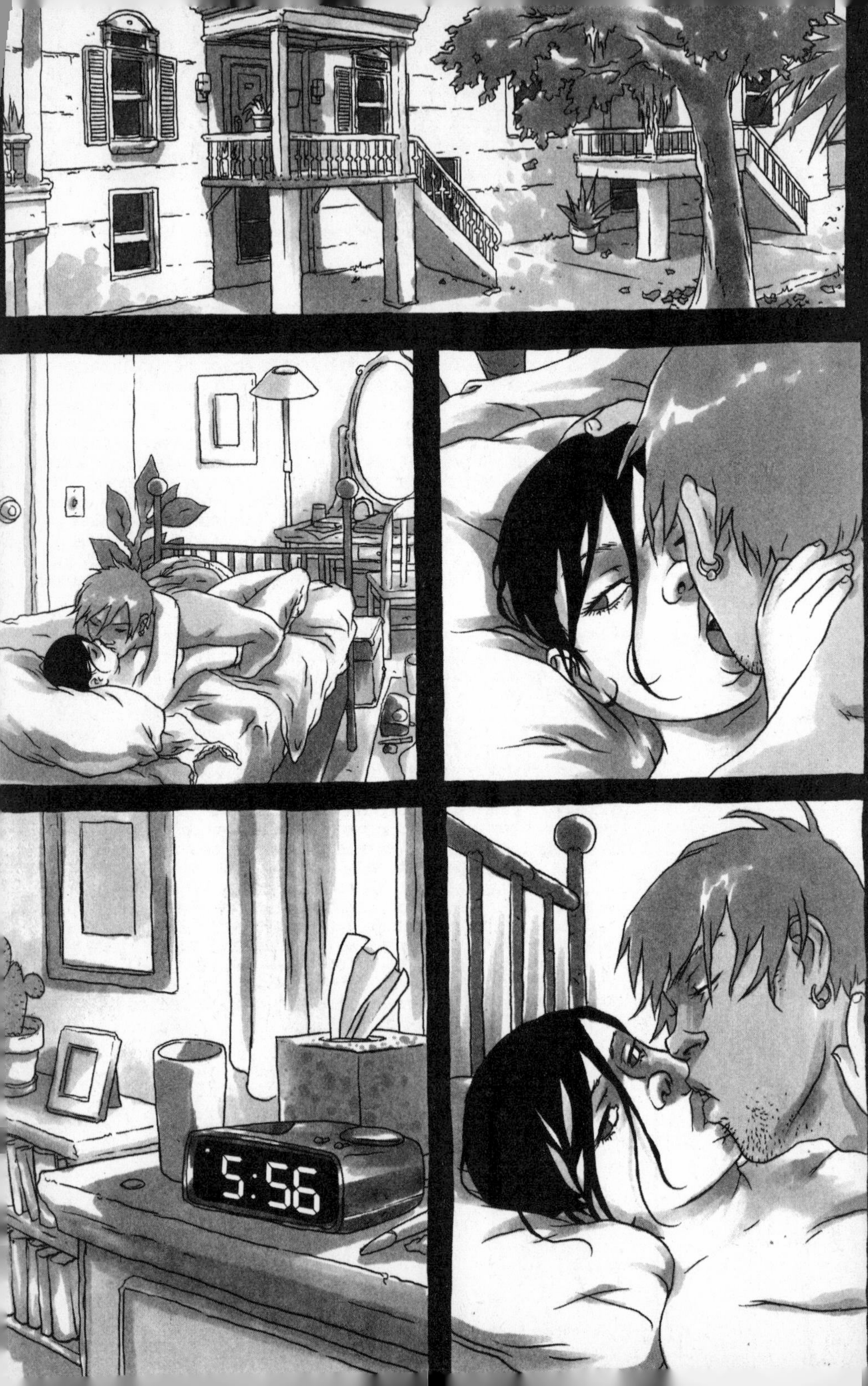
5:56

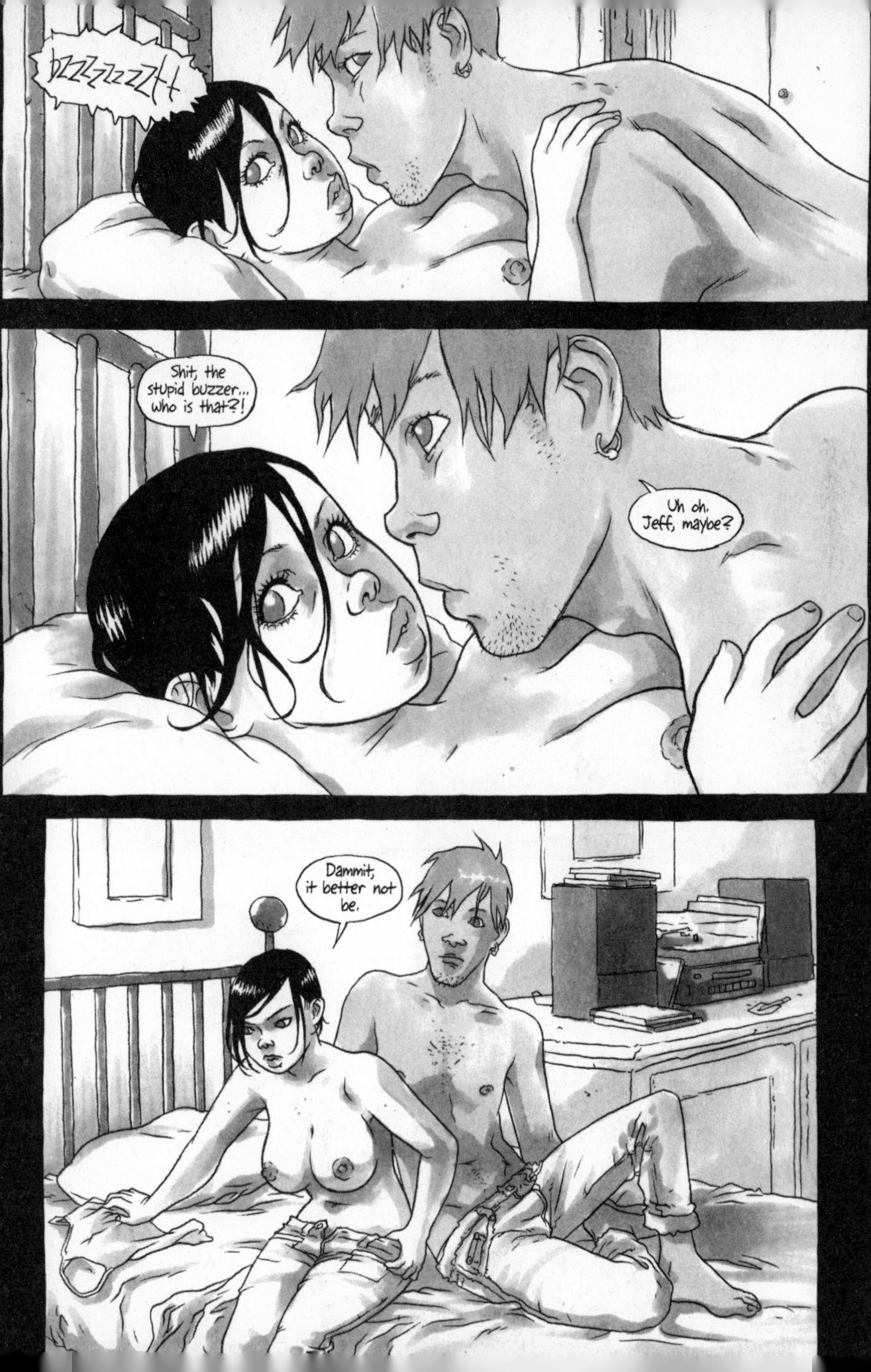
bzzzzzzzzt
Shit, the stupid buzzer... who is that?!
Uh oh. Jeff, maybe?
Dammit, it better not be.

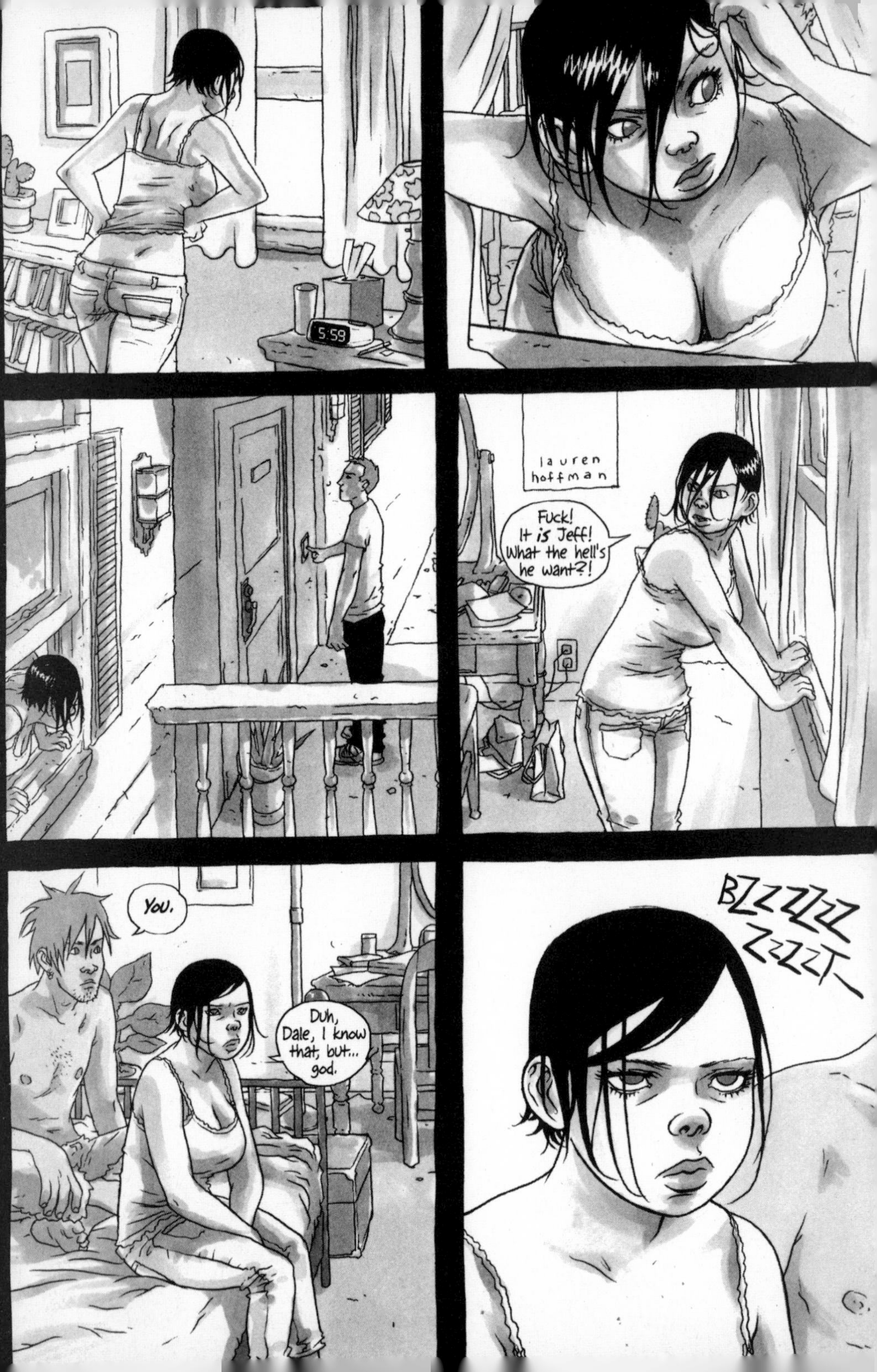
5:59
lauren hoffman
Fuck! It *is* Jeff! What the hell's he want?!
You.
Duh, Dale, I know that, but... god.
BZZZZZZ ZZZZZT

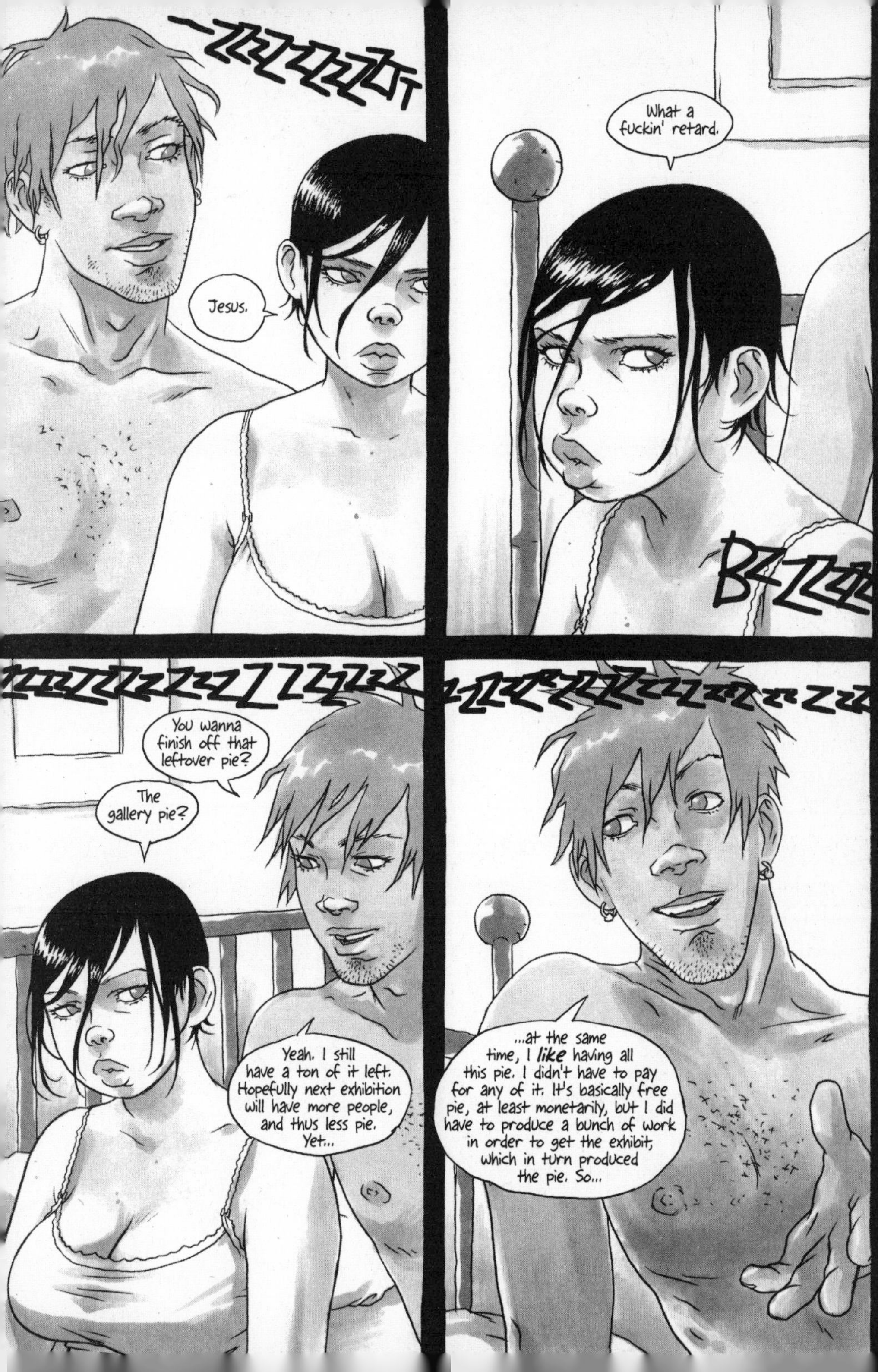

Jesus.
What a fuckin' retard.
You wanna finish off that leftover pie?
The gallery pie?
Yeah. I still have a ton of it left. Hopefully next exhibition will have more people, and thus less pie. Yet...
...at the same time, I *like* having all this pie. I didn't have to pay for any of it. It's basically free pie, at least monetarily, but I did have to produce a bunch of work in order to get the exhibit, which in turn produced the pie. So...

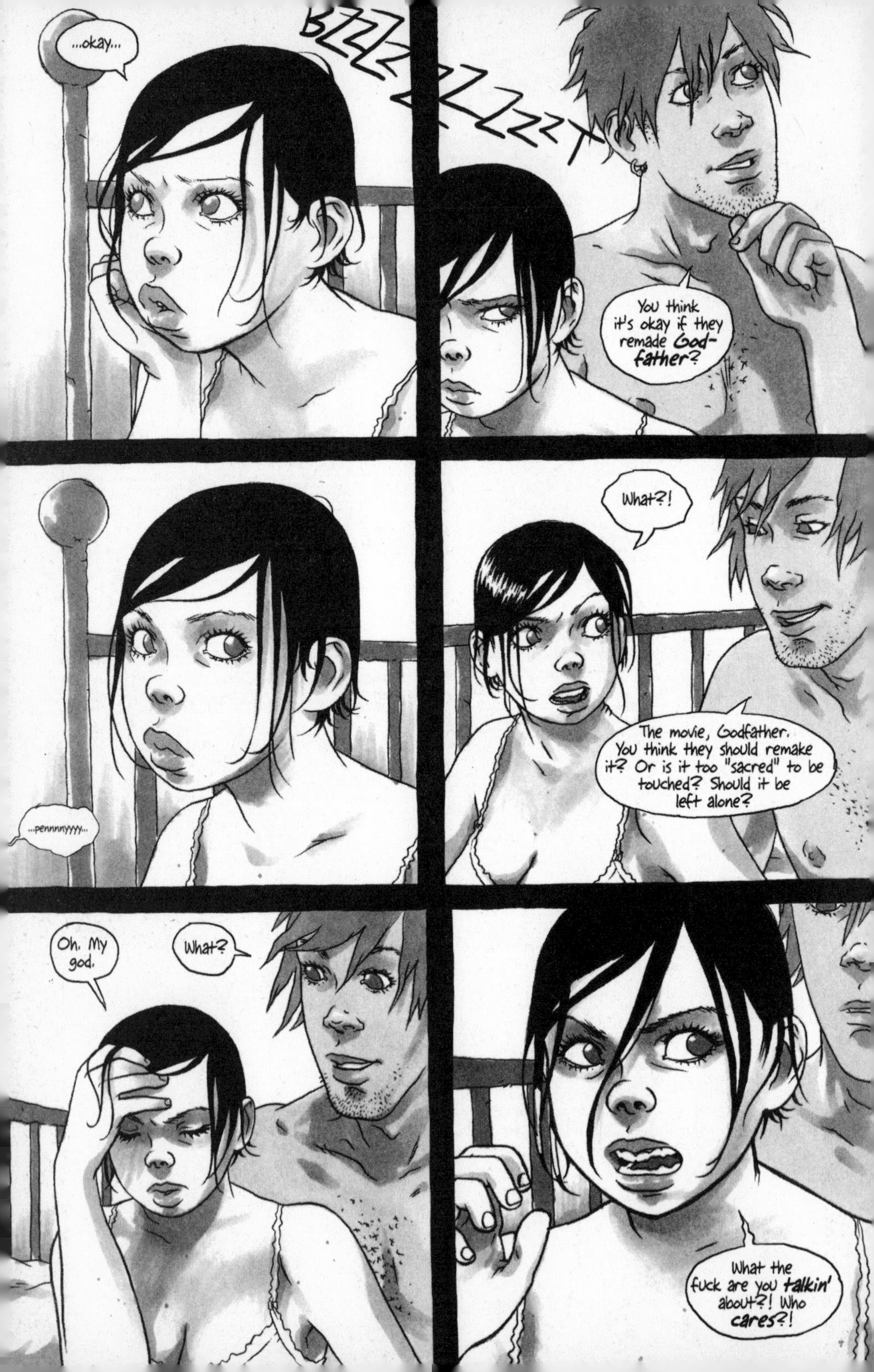
...okay...
BZZZZZZZZZZZZZZZT
You think it's okay if they remade Godfather?
What?!
...pennnnyyyy...
The movie, Godfather. You think they should remake it? Or is it too "sacred" to be touched? Should it be left alone?
Oh. My god.
What?
What the fuck are you talkin' about?! Who cares?!

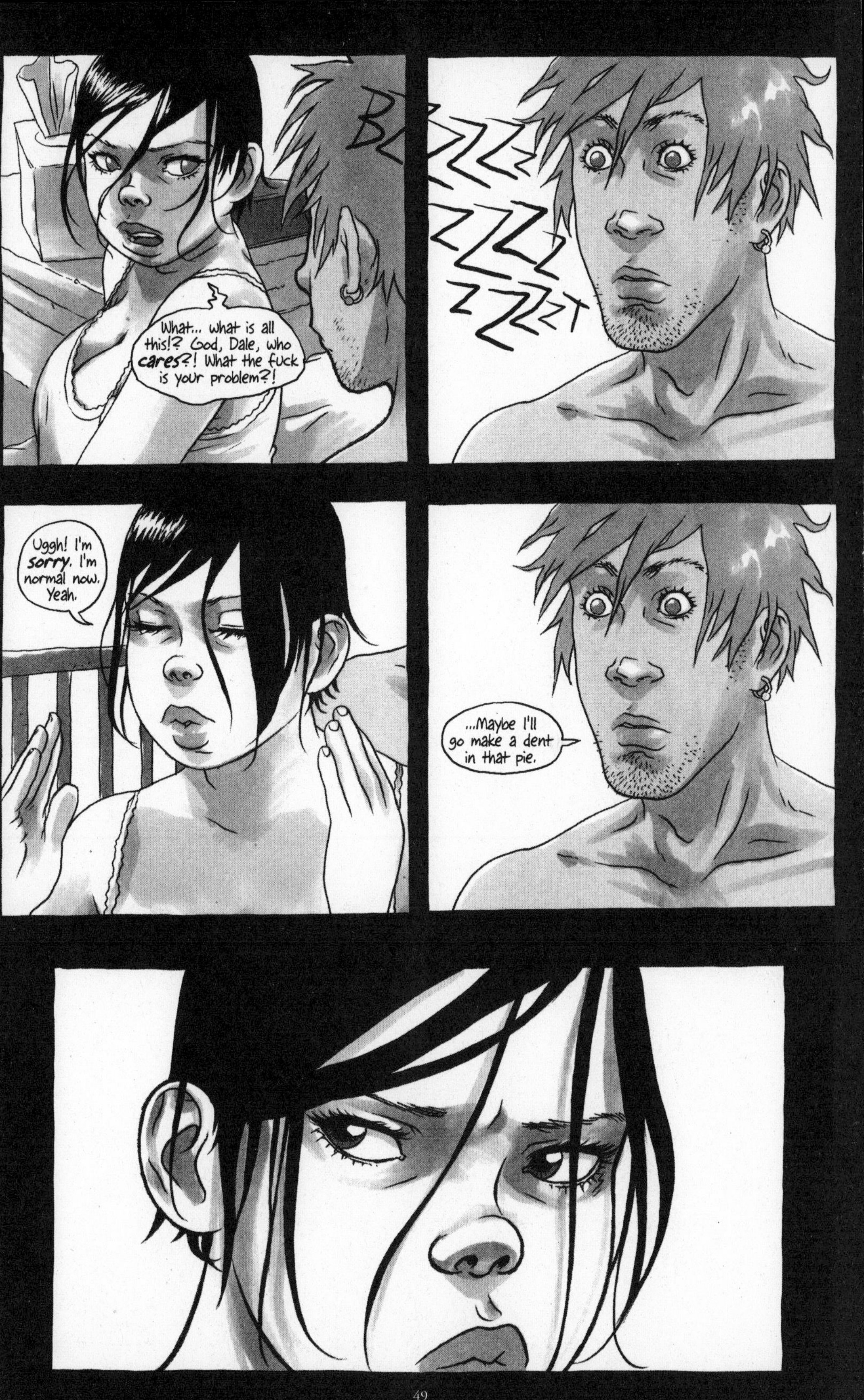
What... what is all this!? God, Dale, who cares?! What the fuck is your problem?!
BZZZZZZZZZZZZZZT
Uggh! I'm sorry. I'm normal now. Yeah.
...Maybe I'll go make a dent in that pie.

12

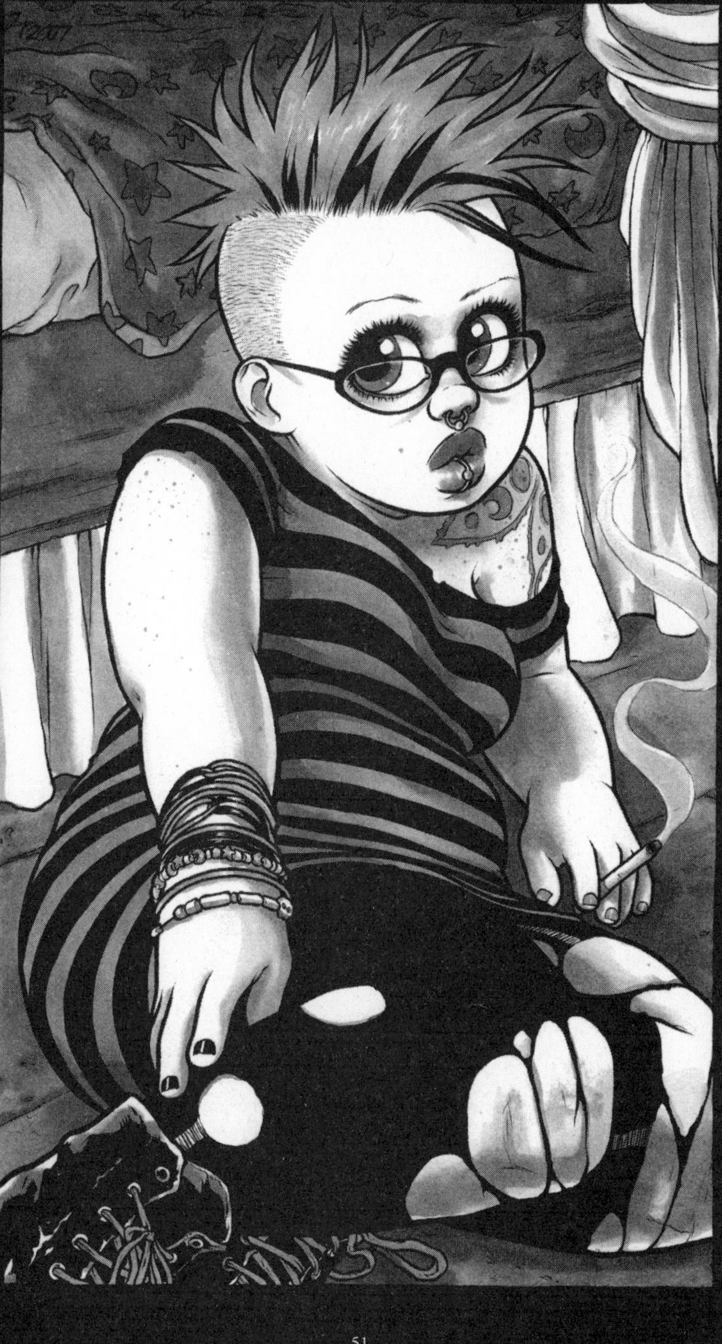

October 12th

I wish Audrey wasn't Miss Big Mouth. I need some [redacted] relationship advice and Audrey is always the best person for it. And because I'm sort of dating a girl. Audrey really does have a big mouth like Trilby says, you can't tell her ANYthing. There was this one time, which I wrote about in my previous diary but I'll write again here, when both me and Tril had a crush on this guy [redacted] Walter, and we both wanted him pretty bad but he asked me out and I didn't know what to do. I really wanted to say yes but I knew Trilby would be upset, so I told Audrey about it thinking maybe she'd give me some advice, but of course like in a matter of hours after that she'd already told Trilby. So the whole thing with Walter got messed up and I never called him back and so neither me or Trilby got with him. I wonder what happened to him.

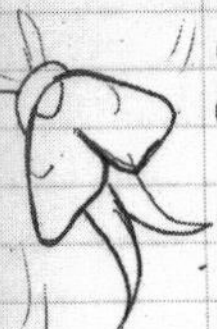

Trilby keeps bugging me to dress up with her for Halloween as a character from a sort of spooky, monstery video game she likes called Darkstalkers. The characters are all real cute but they have tiny, skimpy outfits that I could never wear. Trilby would look adorable, but... I don't think I could do it. Going to the beach in a swimsuit or bikini is one thing, but dressing up all scandalously in a Halloween costume is for some reason totally different. I couldn't pull off that sort of thing. I think I might be lazy this year and just go as a zombie or maybe a mummy. That could be cute, all wrapped up in bandages.

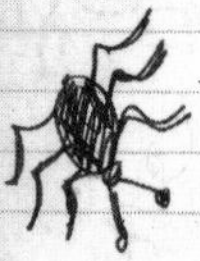

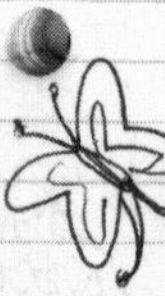

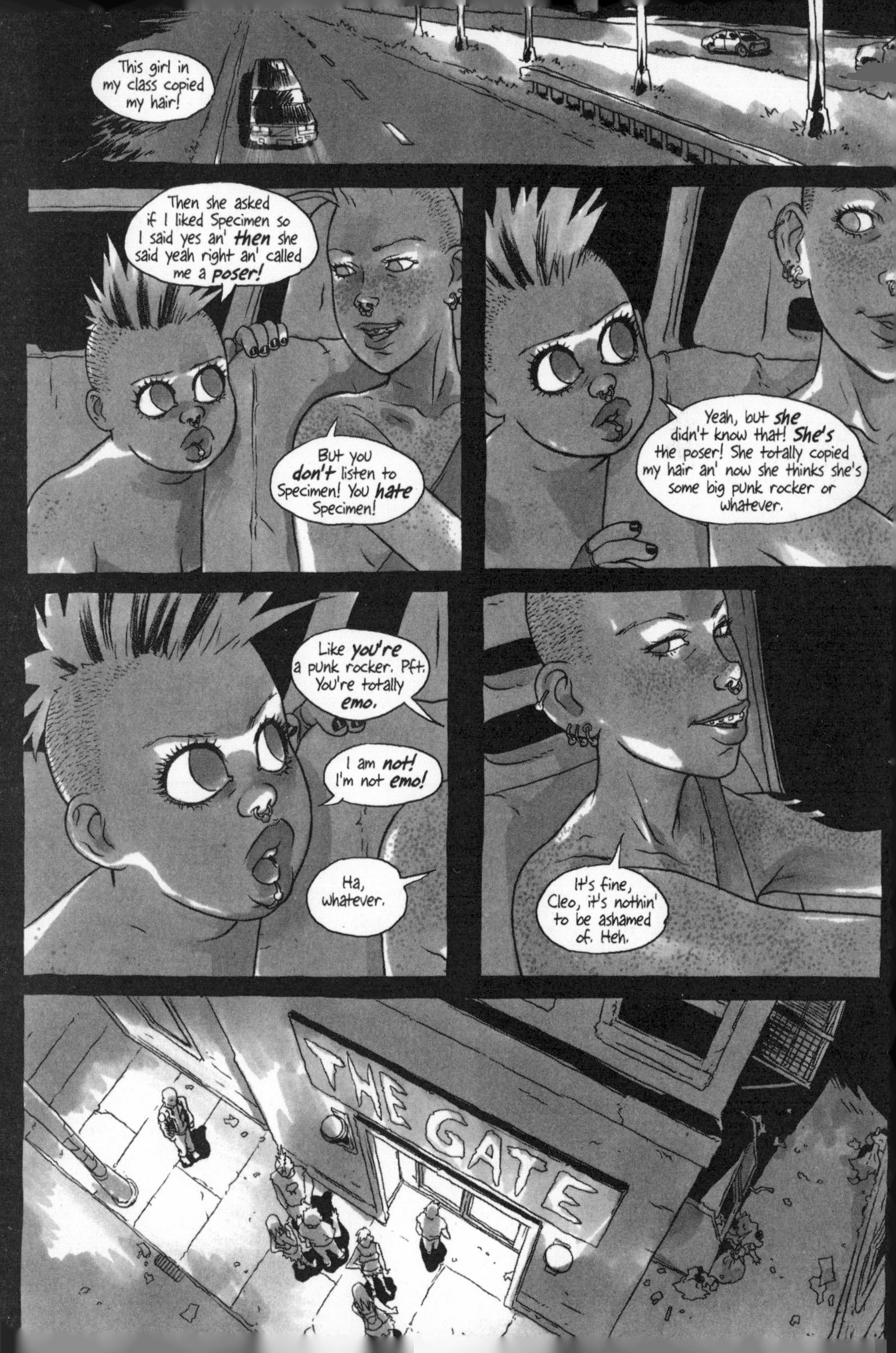
This girl in my class copied my hair!
Then she asked if I liked Specimen so I said yes an' **then** she said yeah right an' called me a **poser!**
But you **don't** listen to Specimen! You **hate** Specimen!
Yeah, but **she** didn't know that! **She's** the poser! She totally copied my hair an' now she thinks she's some big punk rocker or whatever.
Like **you're** a punk rocker. Pft. You're totally **emo.**
I am **not!** I'm not **emo!**
Ha, whatever.
It's fine, Cleo, it's nothin' to be ashamed of. Heh.
THE GATE

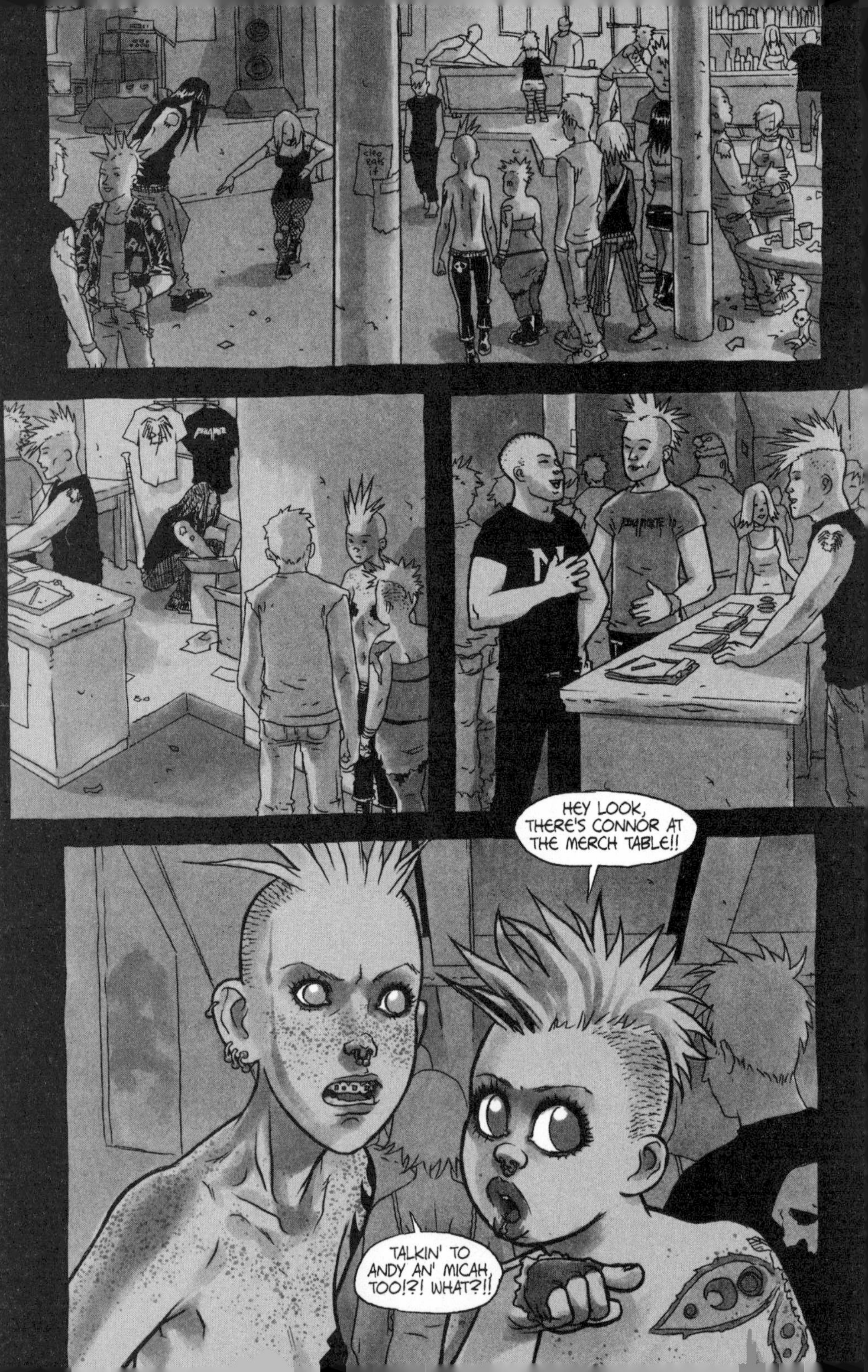
cleo eats it
HEY LOOK, THERE'S CONNOR AT THE MERCH TABLE!!
TALKIN' TO ANDY AN' MICAH, TOO!?! WHAT?!!

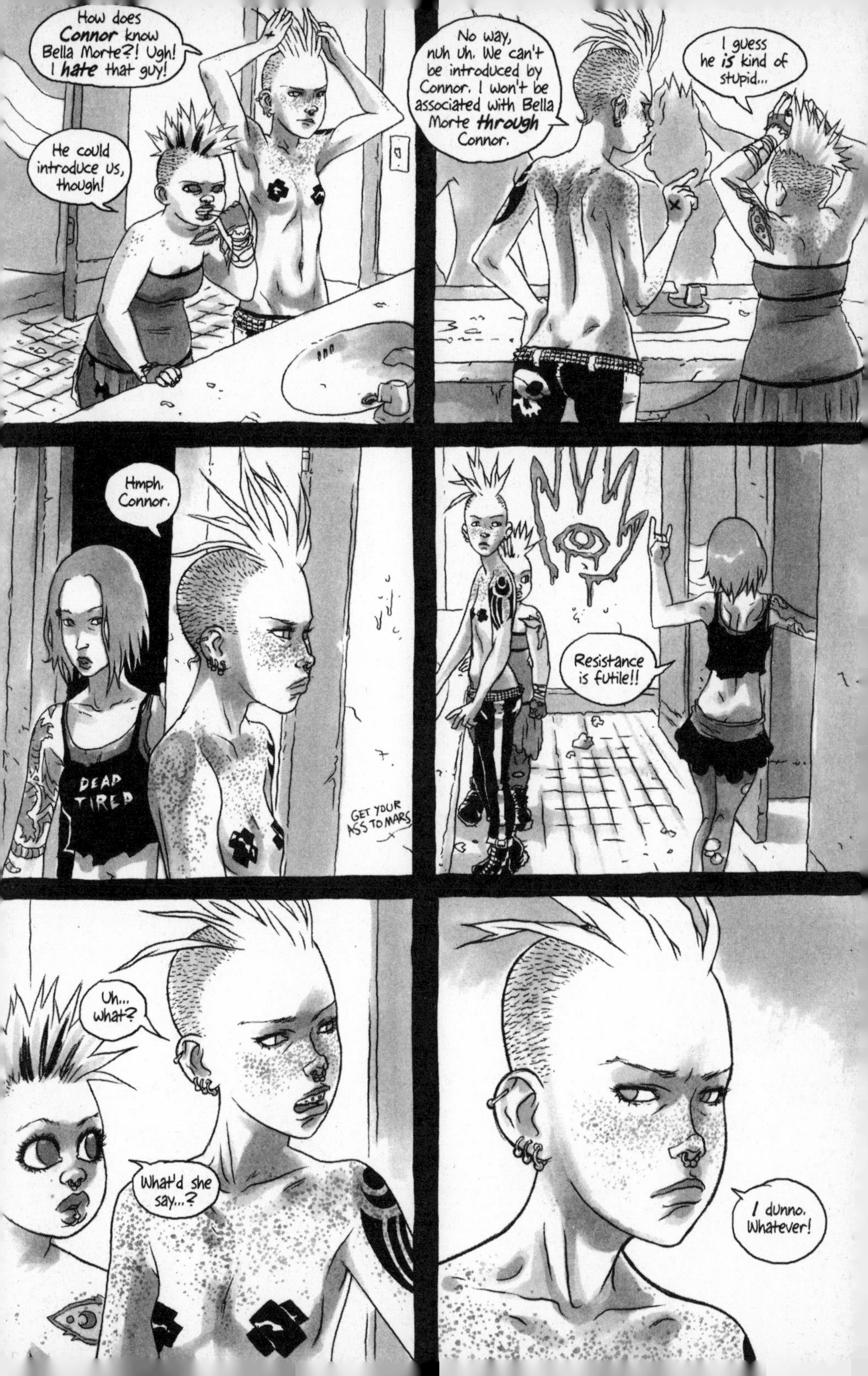
How does Connor know Bella Morte?! Ugh! I hate that guy!
He could introduce us, though!
No way, nuh uh. We can't be introduced by Connor. I won't be associated with Bella Morte through Connor.
I guess he is kind of stupid...
Hmph. Connor.
DEAD TIRED
GET YOUR ASS TO MARS
Resistance is futile!!
Uh... what?
What'd she say...?
I dunno. Whatever!

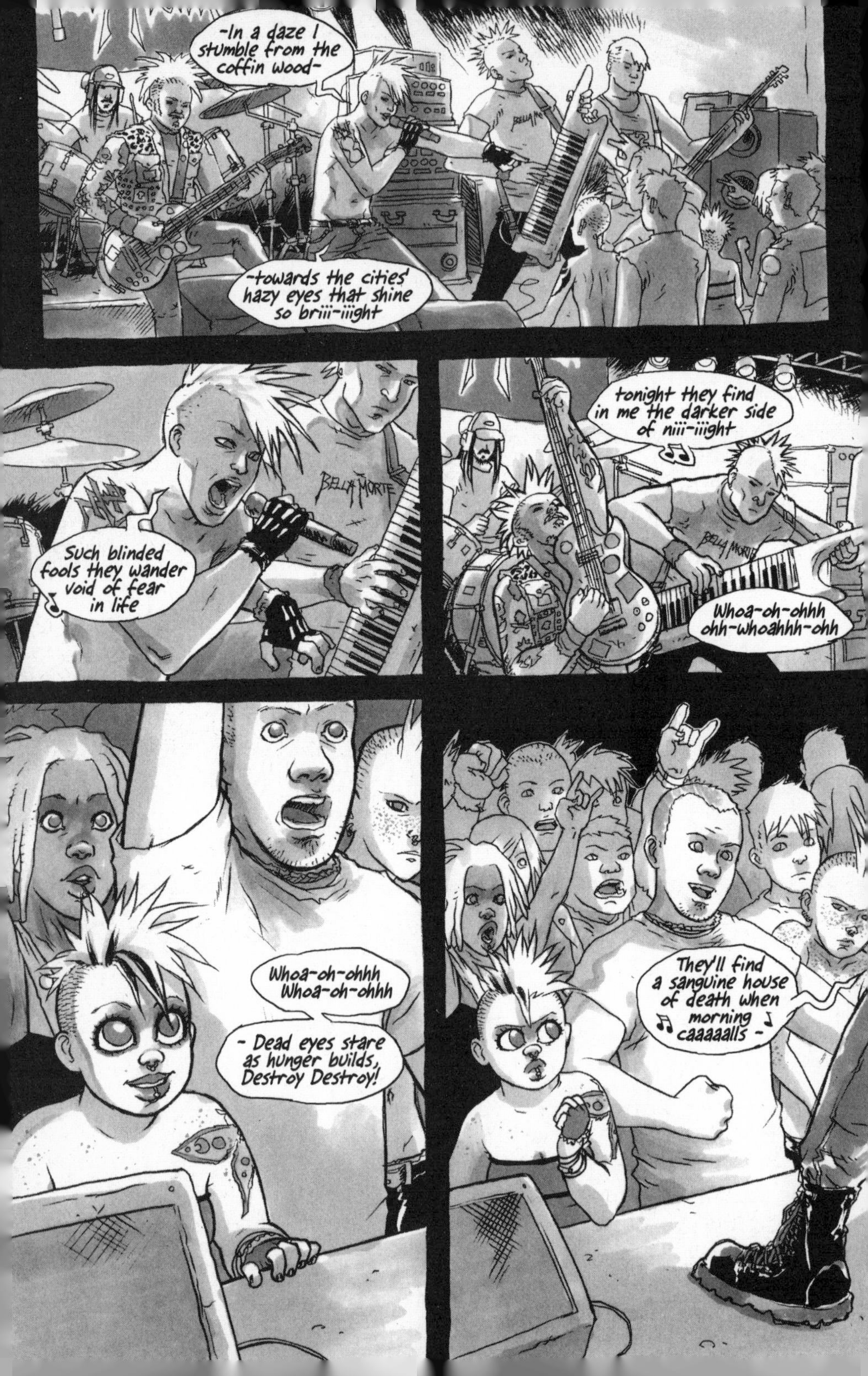
-In a daze I stumble from the coffin wood-
-towards the cities' hazy eyes that shine so briii-iiight
Such blinded fools they wander void of fear in life
tonight they find in me the darker side of niii-iiight
Whoa-oh-ohhh ohh-whoahhh-ohh
Whoa-oh-ohhh Whoa-oh-ohhh
- Dead eyes stare as hunger builds, Destroy Destroy!
They'll find a sanguine house of death when morning caaaaalls -

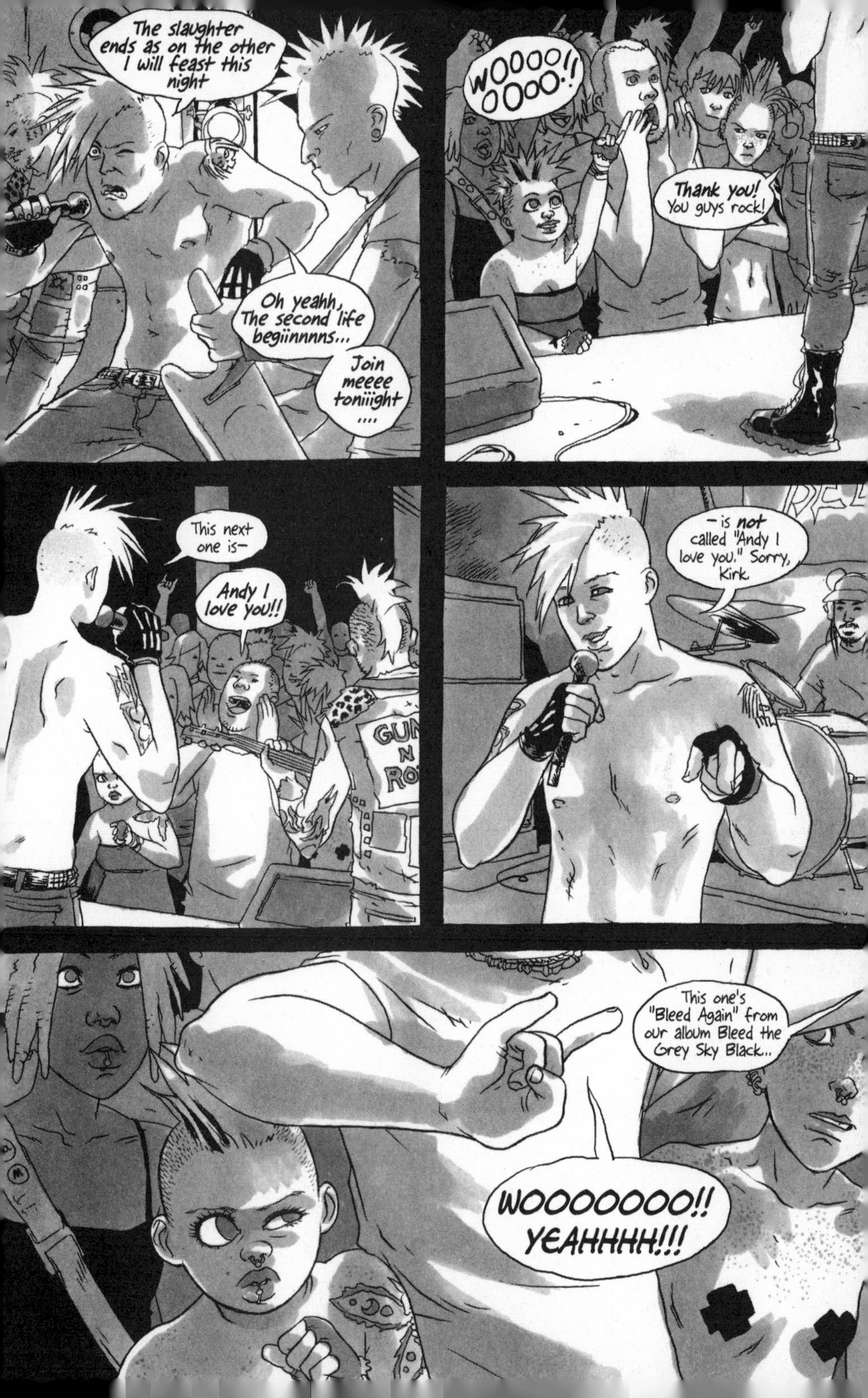
The slaughter ends as on the other I will feast this night
Oh yeahh, The second life begiinnnns...
Join meeee toniiight ....
WOOOO!! OOOO!!
Thank you! You guys rock!
This next one is—
Andy I love you!!
GUN N RO
—is **not** called "Andy I love you." Sorry, Kirk.
This one's "Bleed Again" from our album Bleed the Grey Sky Black...
WOOOOOOO!! YEAHHHH!!!

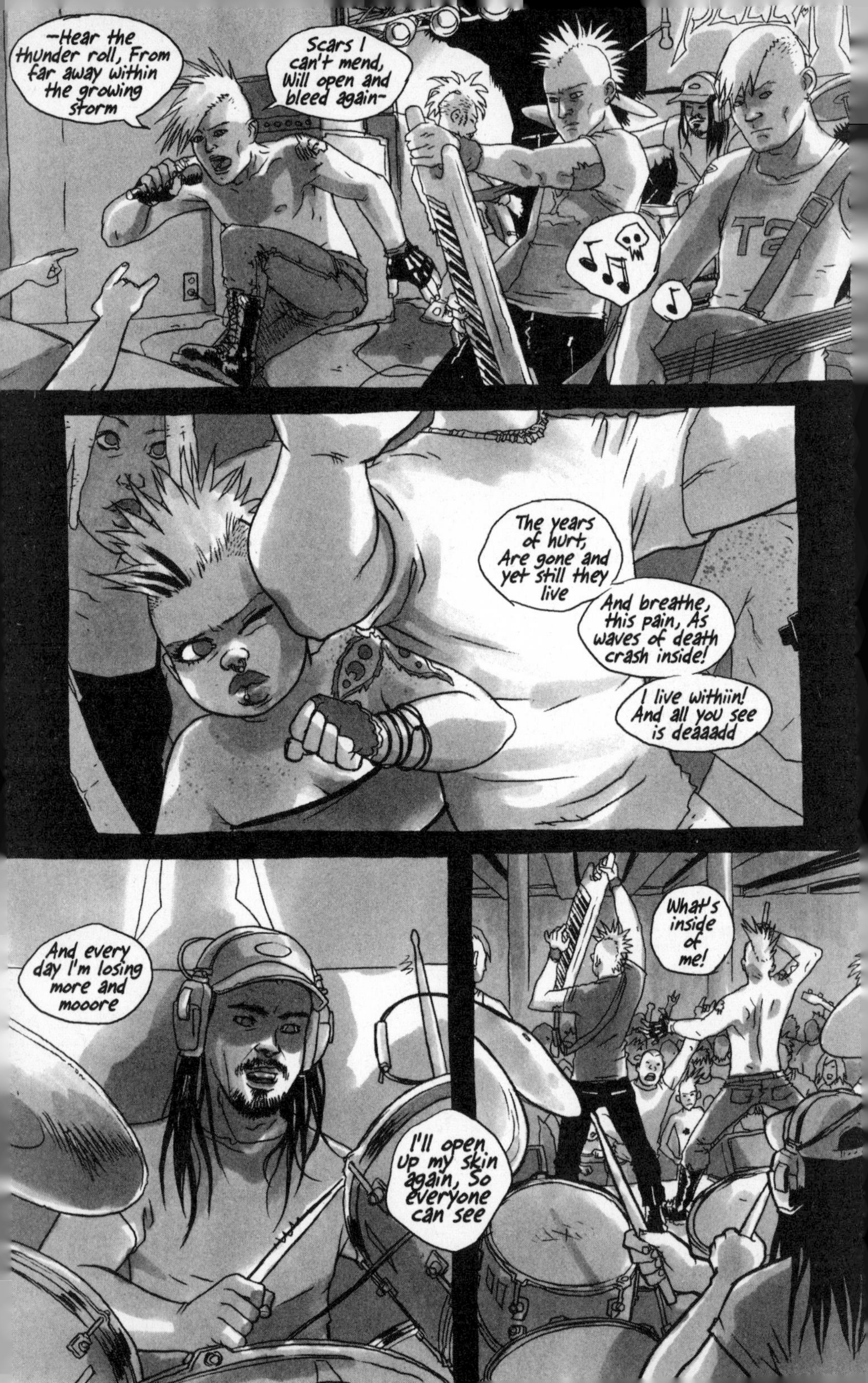

—Hear the thunder roll, From far away within the growing storm
Scars I can't mend, Will open and bleed again—
The years of hurt, Are gone and yet still they live
And breathe, this pain, As waves of death crash inside!
I live withiin! And all you see is deaaadd
And every day I'm losing more and mooore
I'll open up my skin again, So everyone can see
What's inside of me!

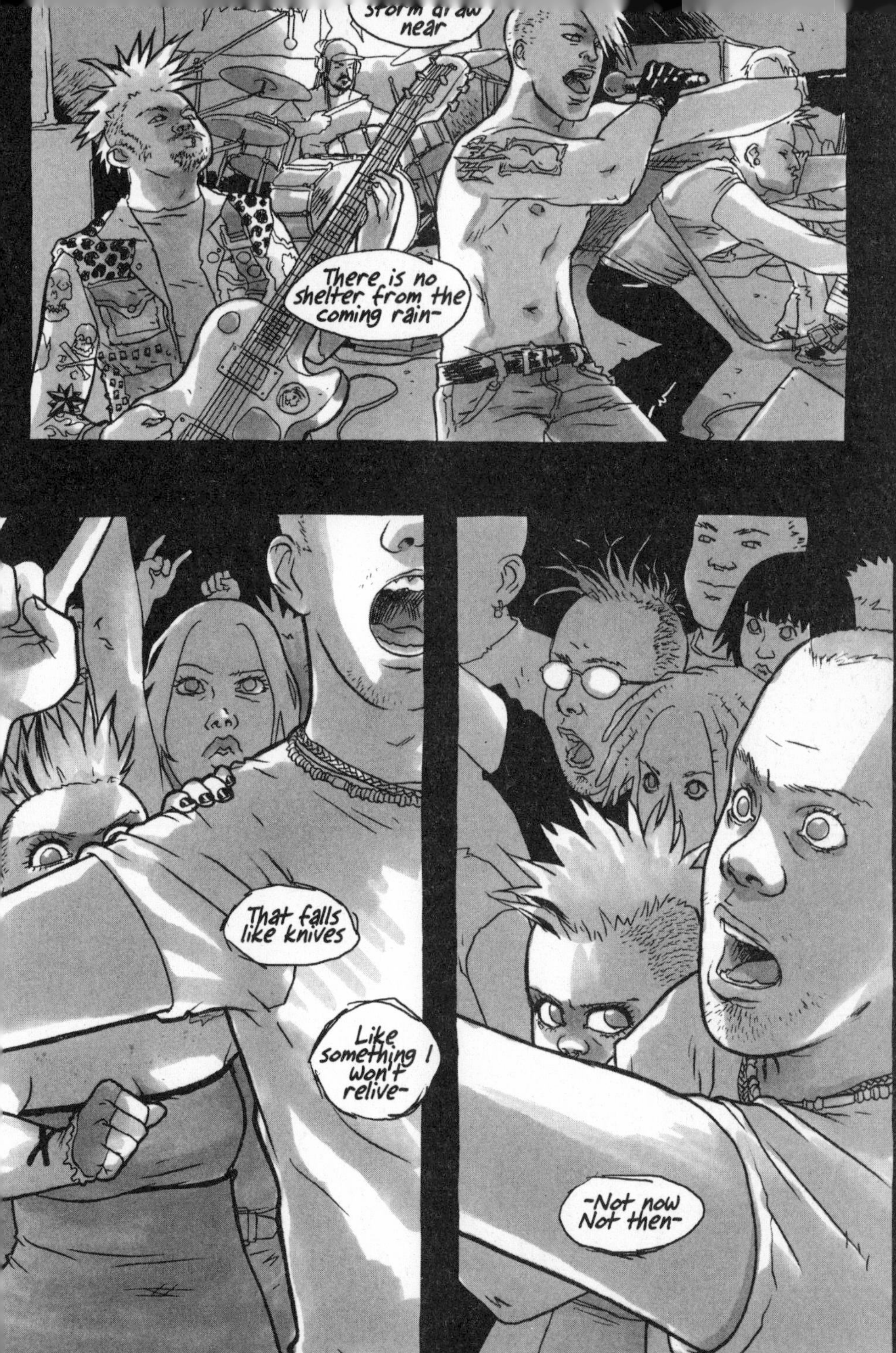
storm draw near
There is no shelter from the coming rain-
That falls like knives
Like something I won't relive-
-Not now Not then-

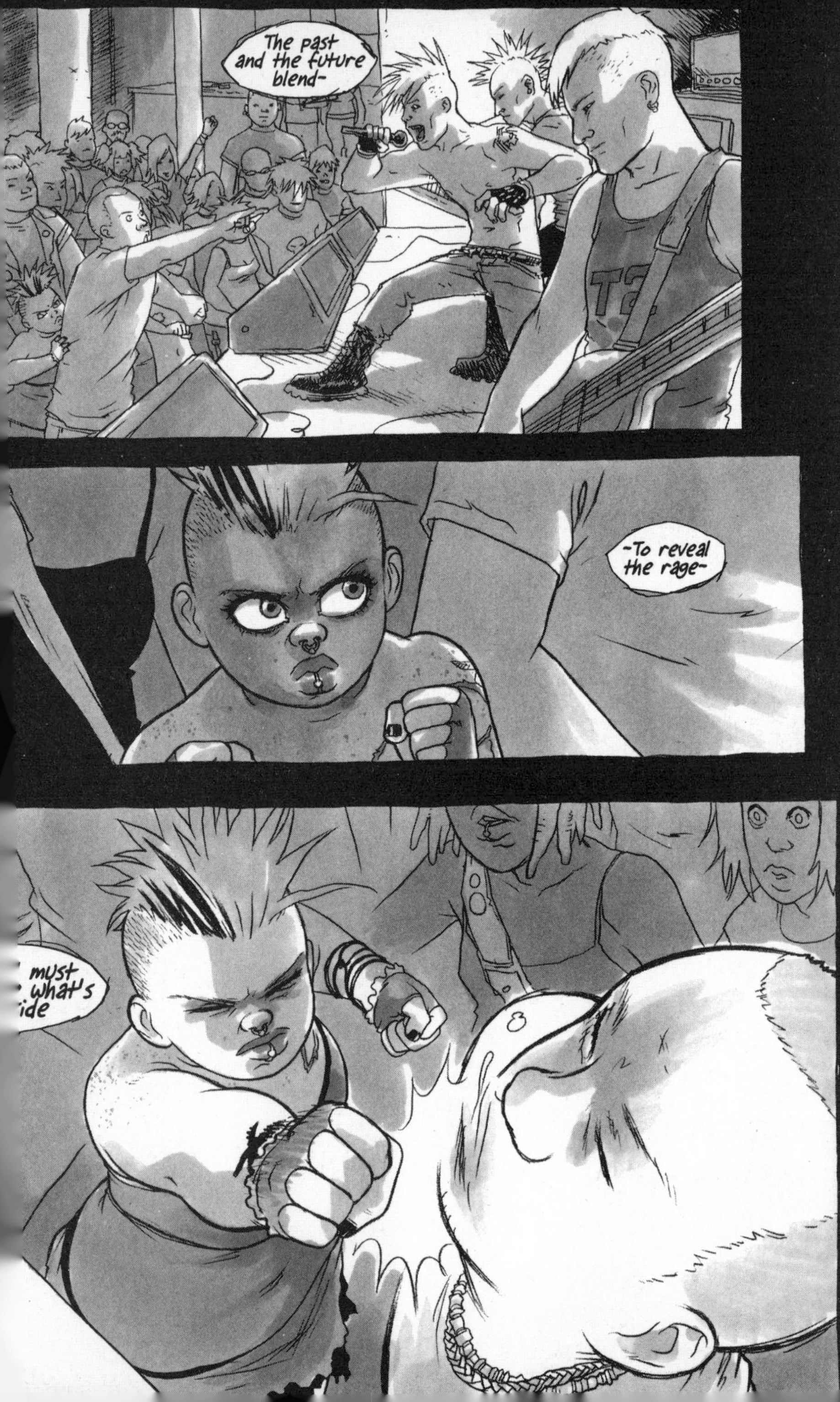
The past and the future blend-
-To reveal the rage-
must what's ide

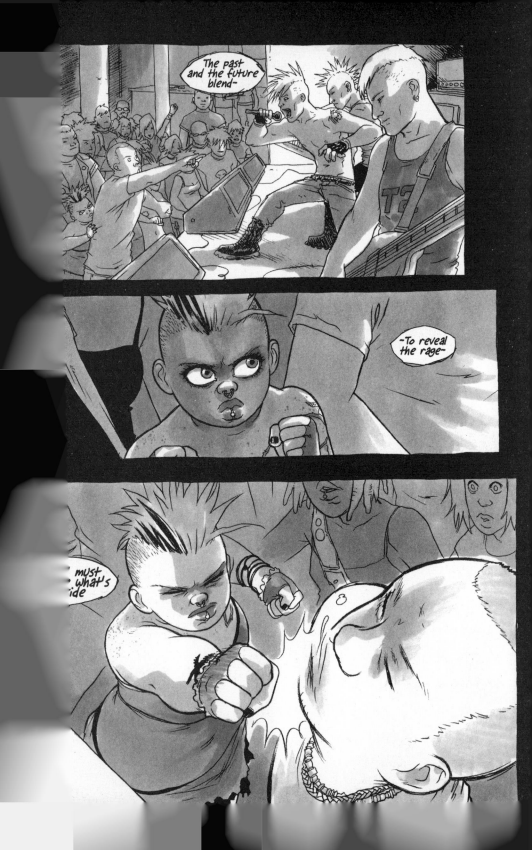

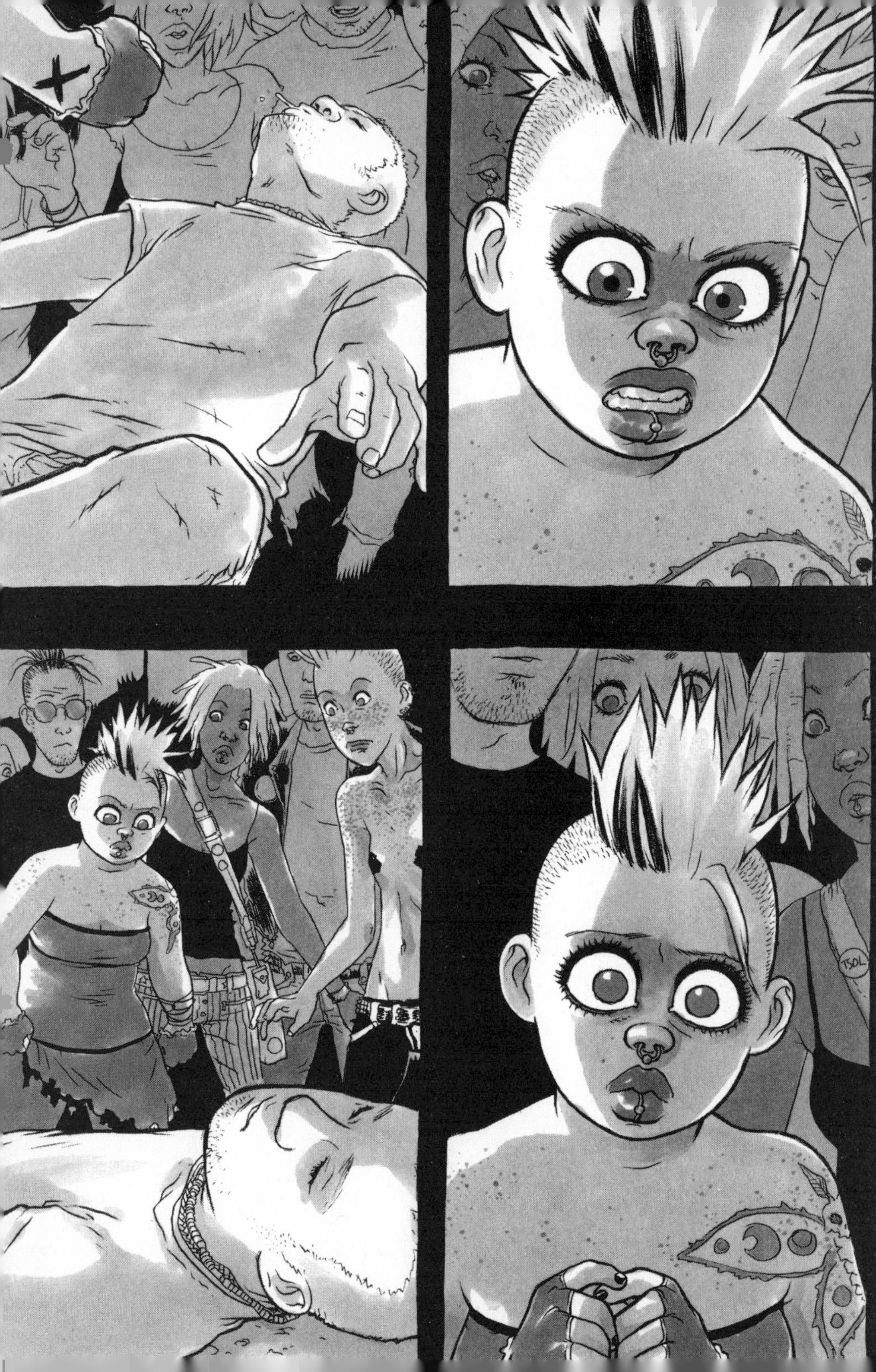
TSOL

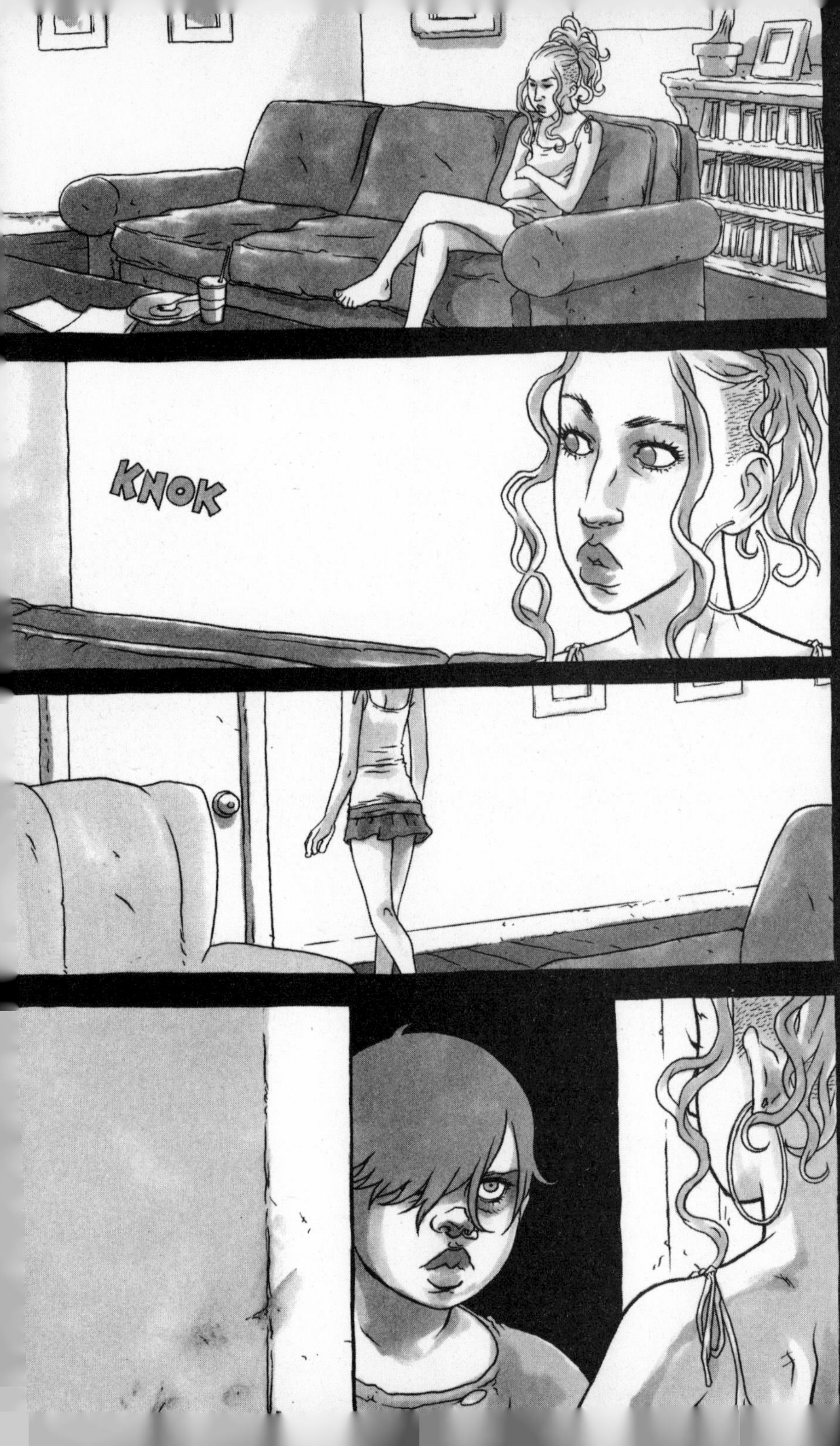
KNOK

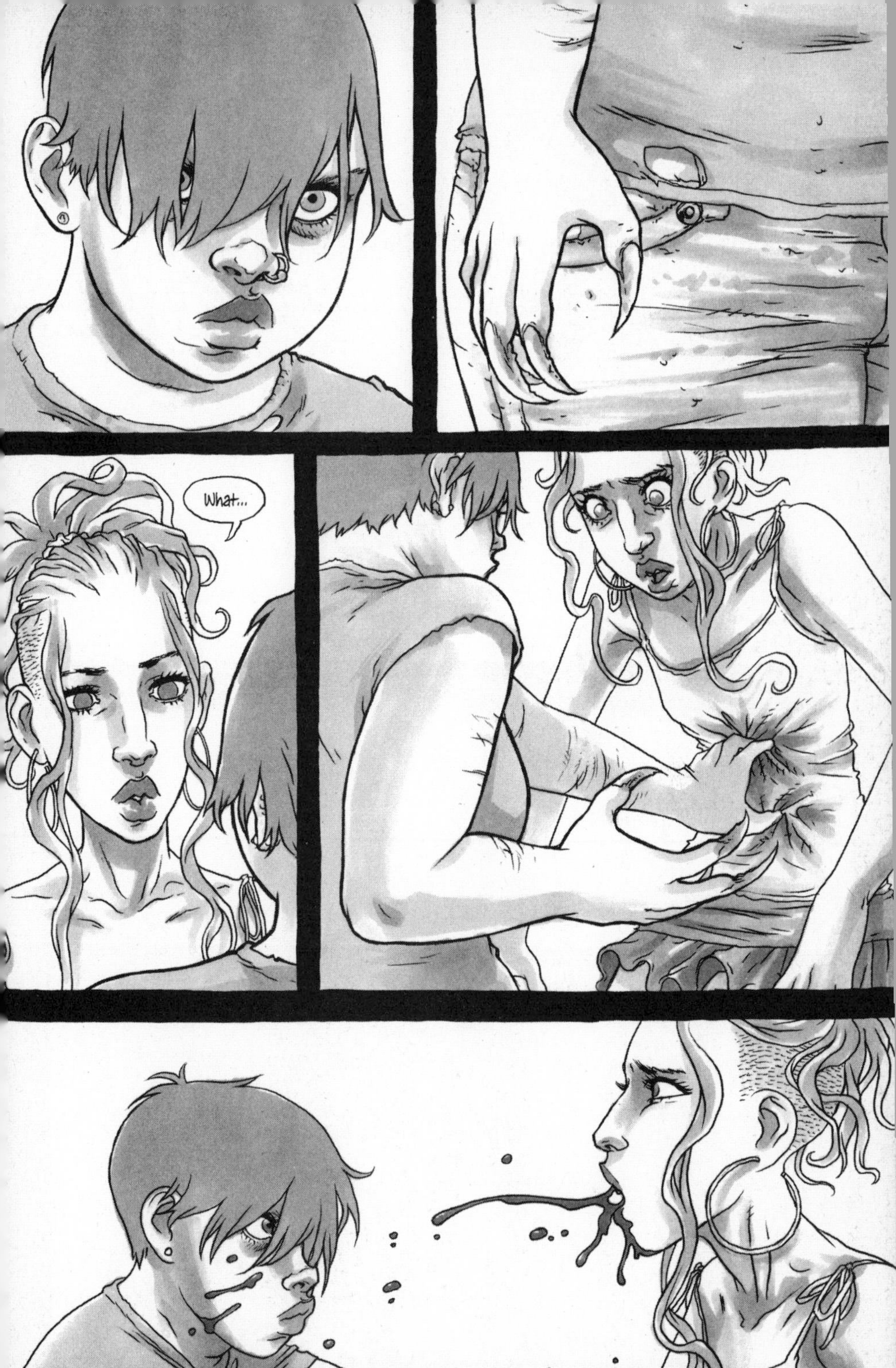
What...

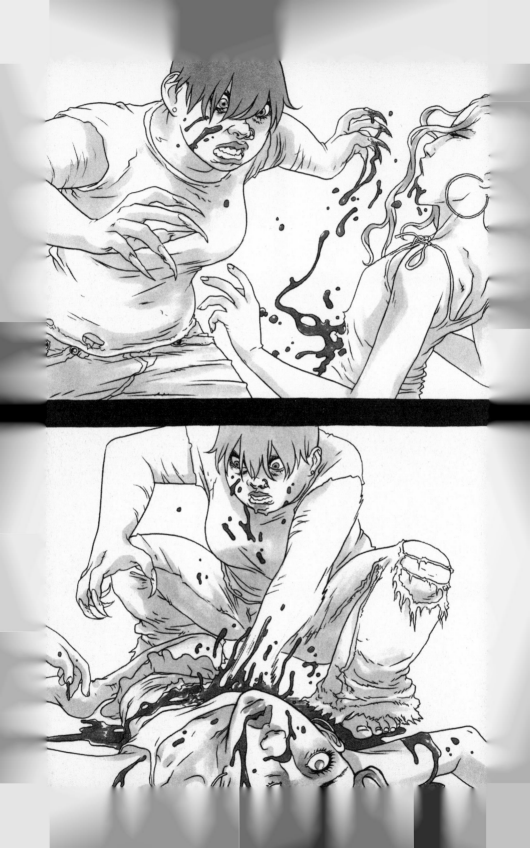

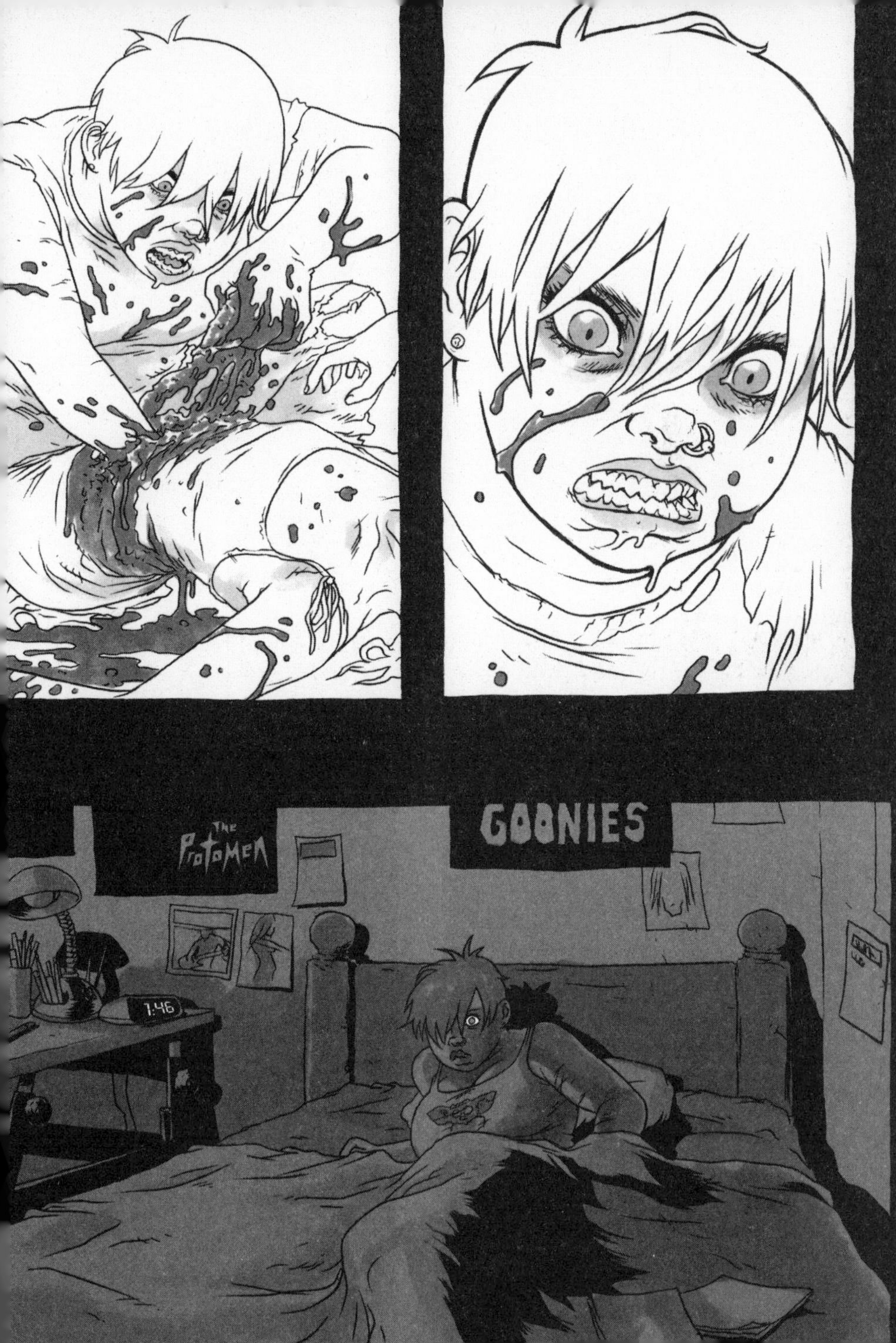
The ProtoMen
GOONIES
1:46

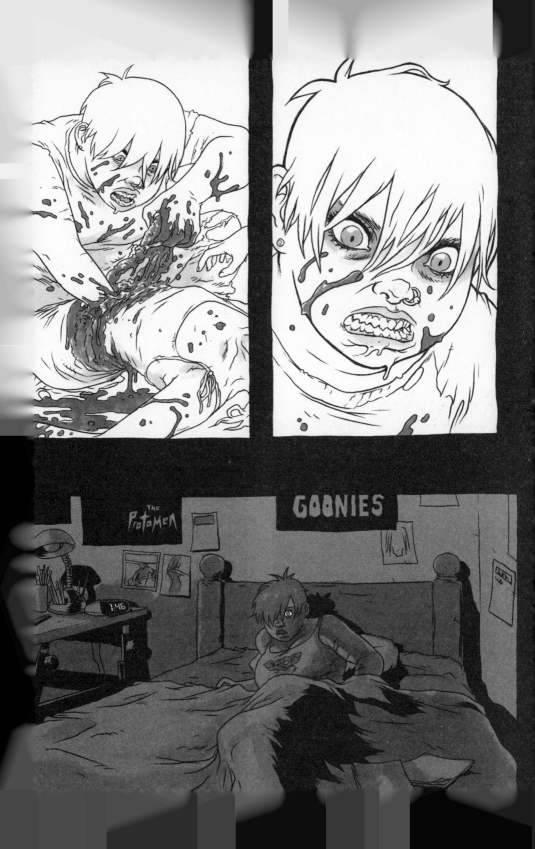

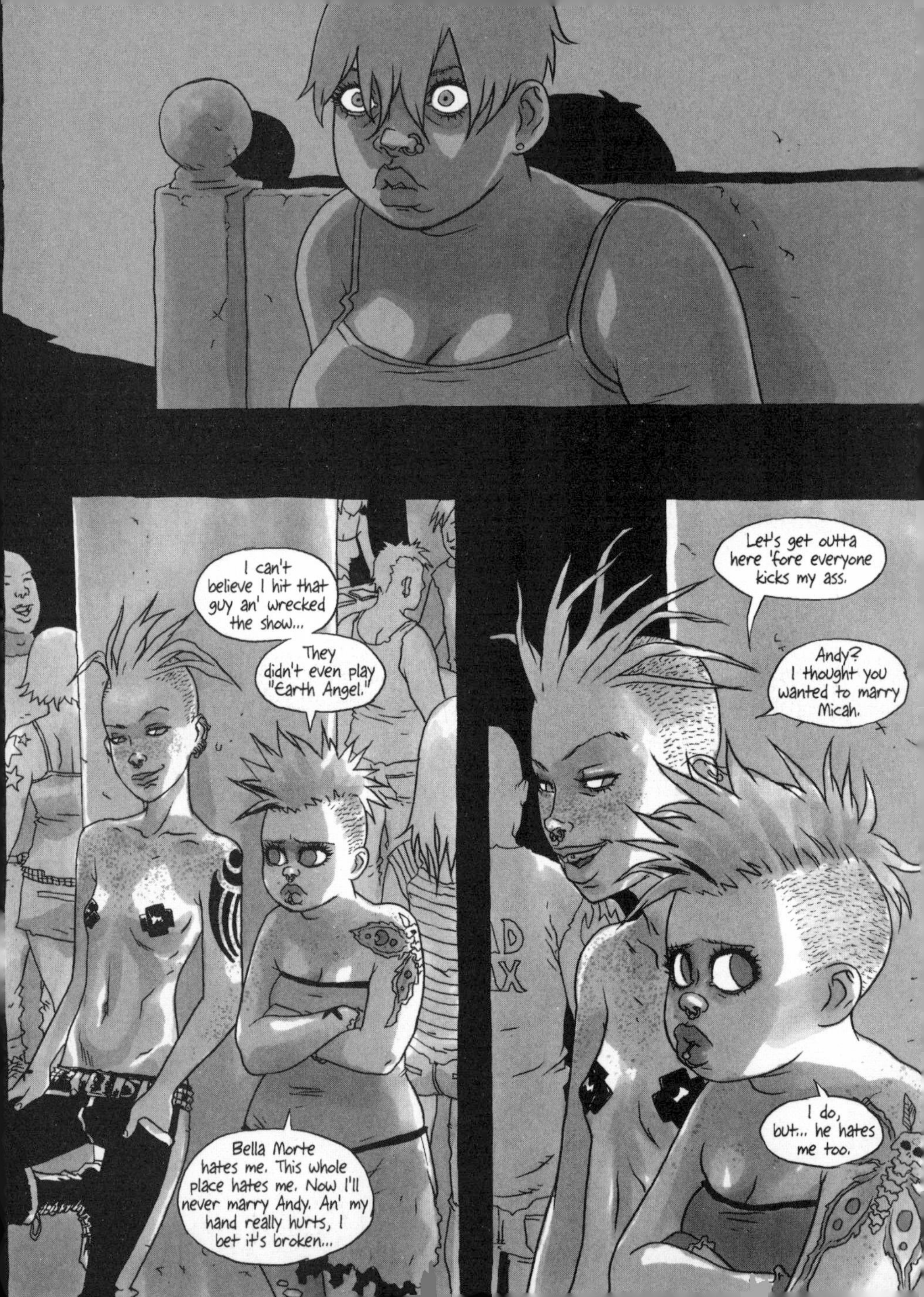

I can't believe I hit that guy an' wrecked the show...
They didn't even play "Earth Angel."
Bella Morte hates me. This whole place hates me. Now I'll never marry Andy. An' my hand really hurts, I bet it's broken...
Let's get outta here 'fore everyone kicks my ass.
Andy? I thought you wanted to marry Micah.
I do, but... he hates me too.

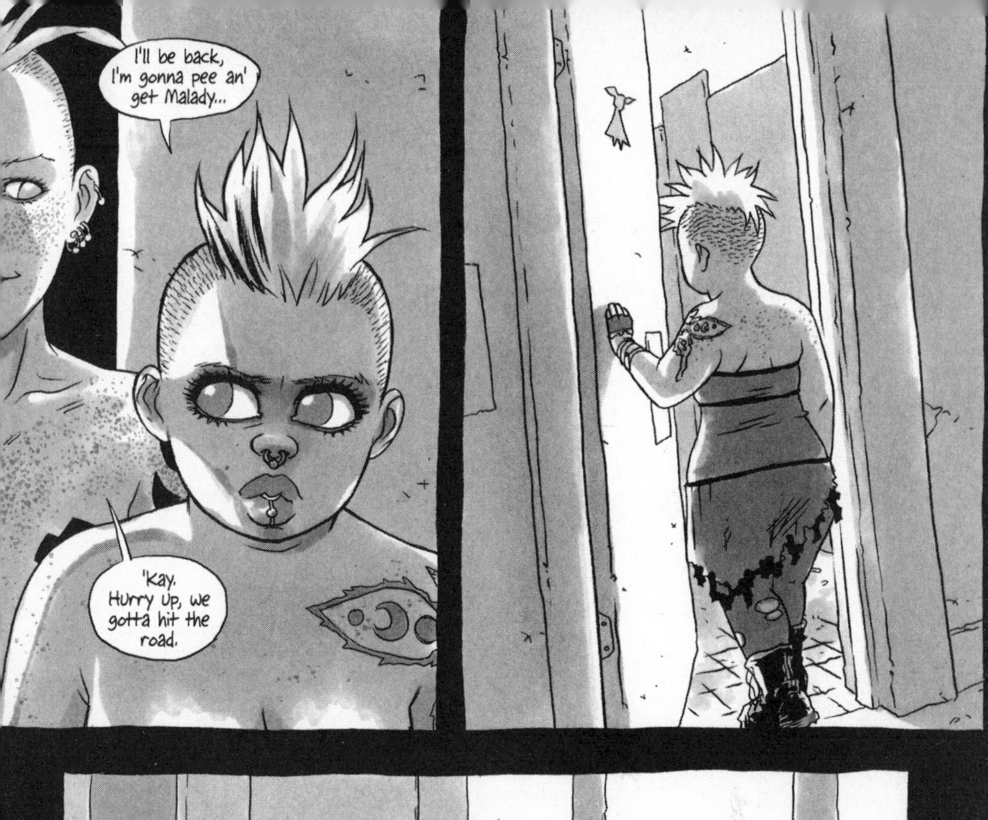
I'll be back, I'm gonna pee an' get Malady...
'Kay. Hurry up, we gotta hit the road.

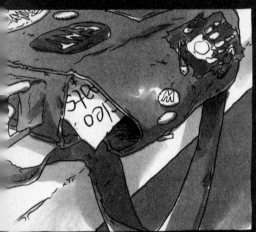

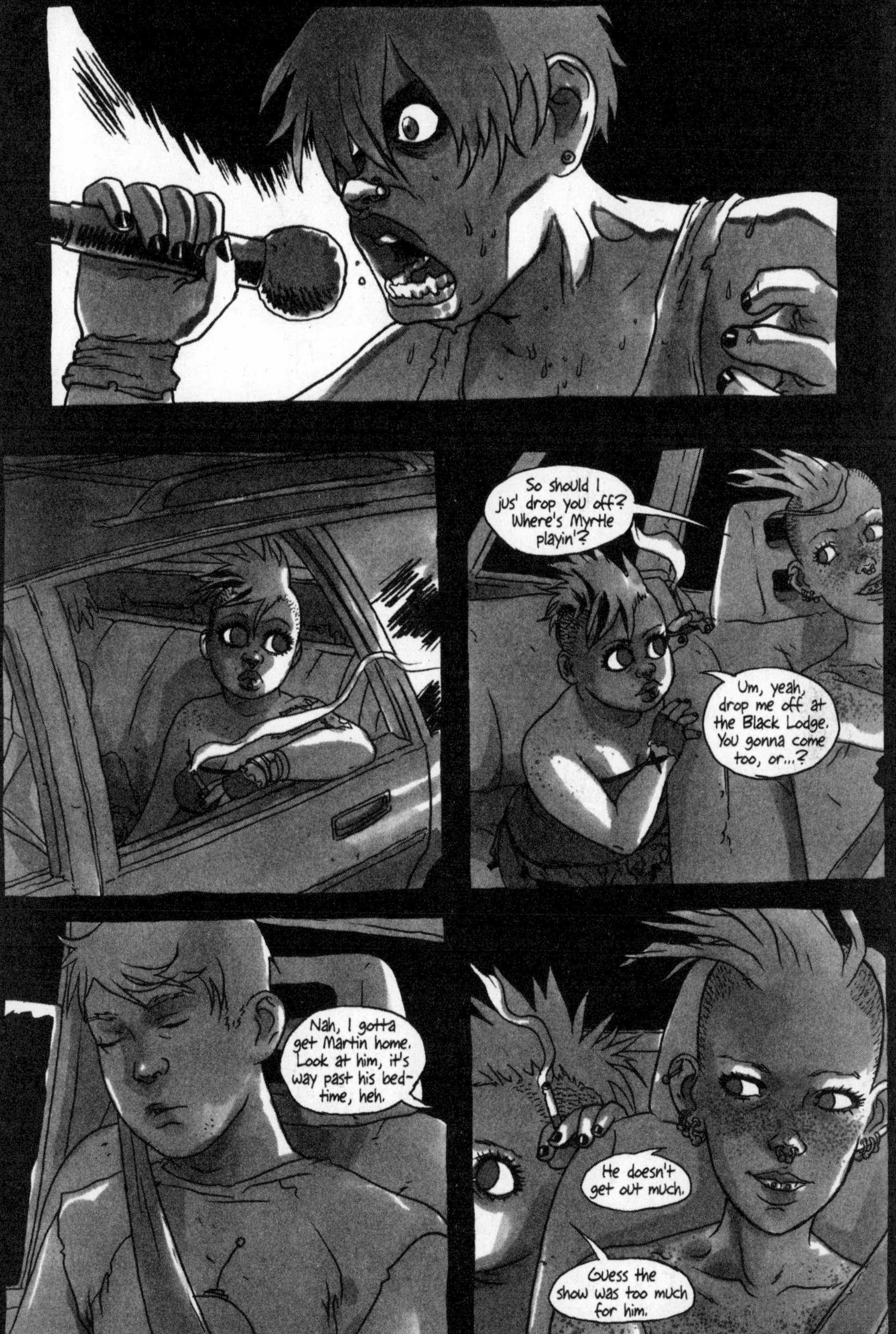
So should I jus' drop you off? Where's Myrtle playin'?
Um, yeah, drop me off at the Black Lodge. You gonna come too, or...?
Nah, I gotta get Martin home. Look at him, it's way past his bed-time, heh.
He doesn't get out much.
Guess the show was too much for him.

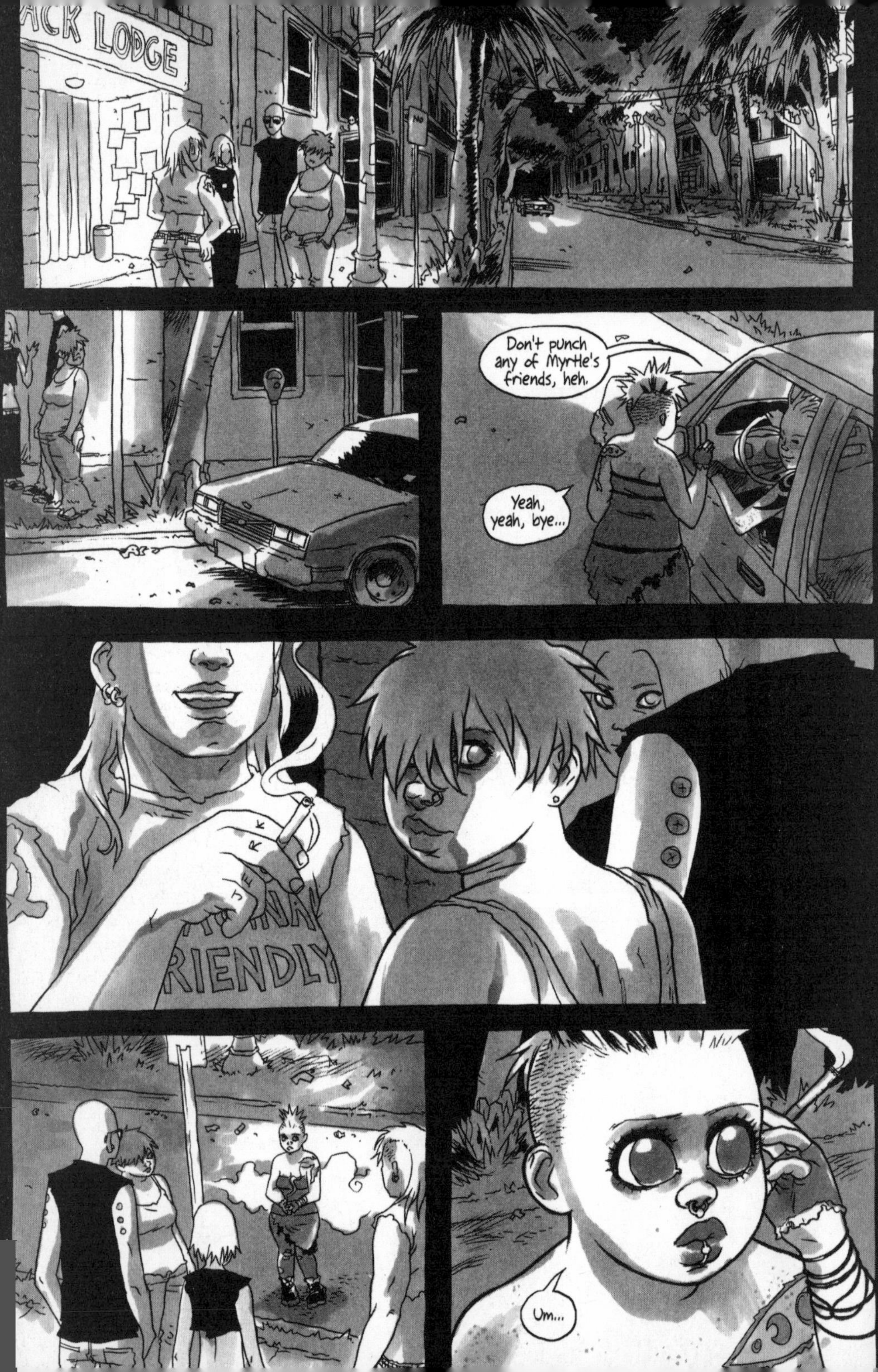
ACK LODGE
Don't punch any of Myrtle's friends, heh.
Yeah, yeah, bye...
RIENDLY
Um...

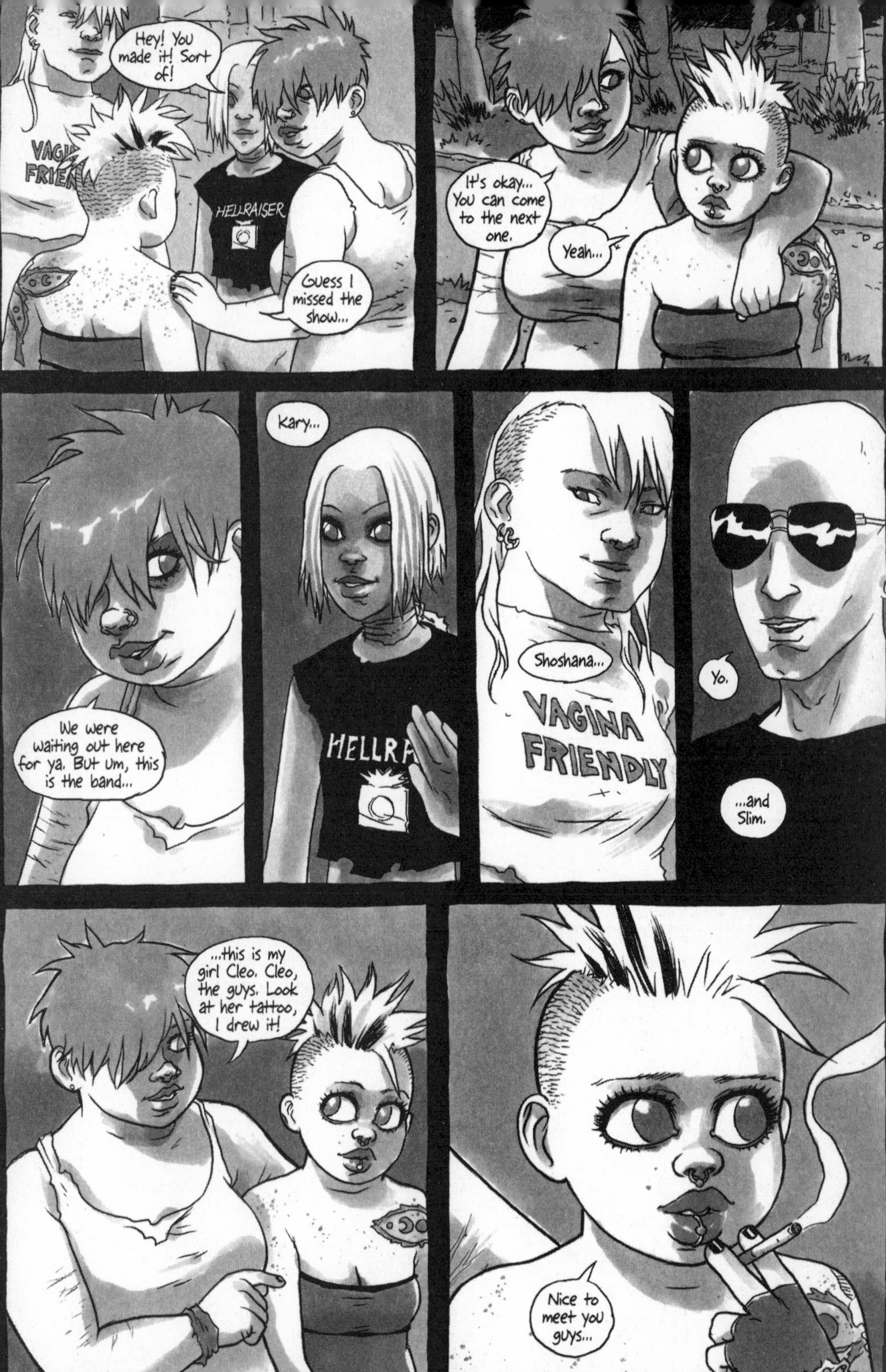
Hey! You made it! Sort of!
VAGINA FRIEN
HELLRAISER
Guess I missed the show...
It's okay... You can come to the next one.
Yeah...
We were waiting out here for ya. But um, this is the band...
Kary...
HELLRA
Shoshana...
VAGINA FRIENDLY
Yo.
...and Slim.
...this is my girl Cleo. Cleo, the guys. Look at her tattoo, I drew it!
Nice to meet you guys...

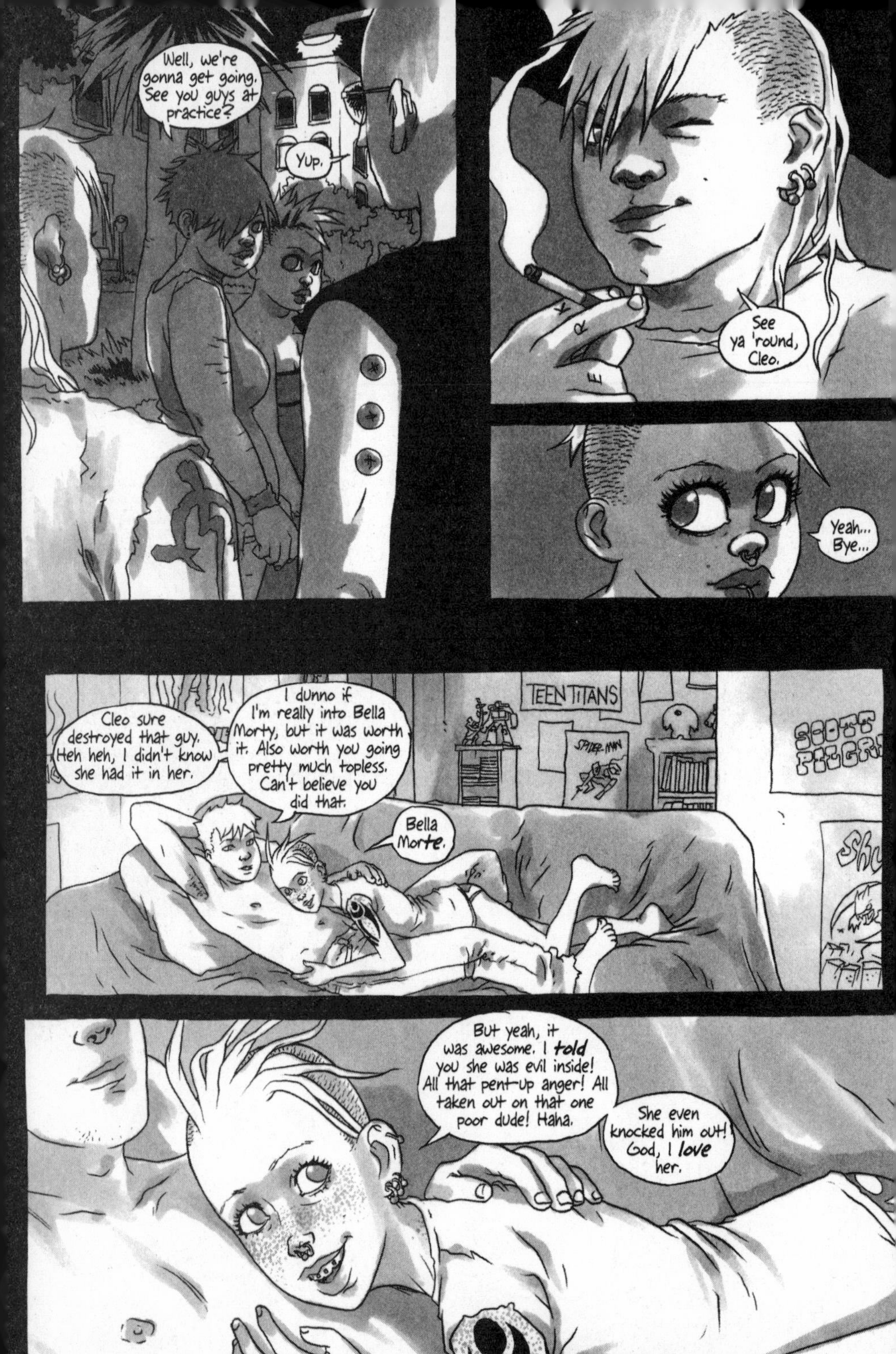
Well, we're gonna get going. See you guys at practice?
Yup.
See ya 'round, Cleo.
Yeah... Bye...
Cleo sure destroyed that guy. Heh heh, I didn't know she had it in her.
I dunno if I'm really into Bella Morty, but it was worth it. Also worth you going pretty much topless. Can't believe you did that.
Bella Morte.
TEEN TITANS
SPIDER-MAN
But yeah, it was awesome. I told you she was evil inside! All that pent-up anger! All taken out on that one poor dude! Haha.
She even knocked him out! God, I love her.

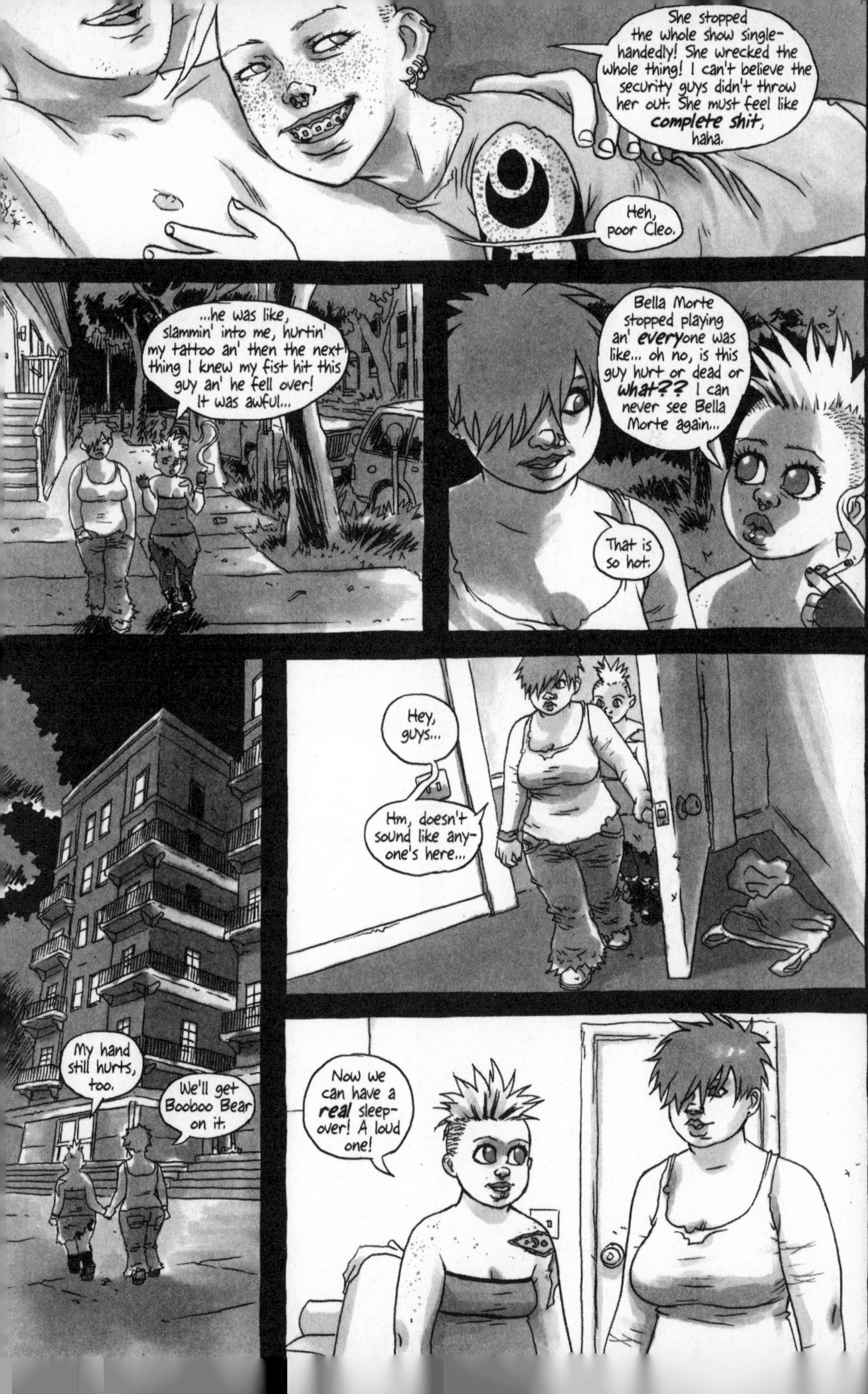
She stopped the whole show single-handedly! She wrecked the whole thing! I can't believe the security guys didn't throw her out. She must feel like **complete shit**, haha.
Heh, poor Cleo.
...he was like, slammin' into me, hurtin' my tattoo an' then the next thing I knew my fist hit this guy an' he fell over! It was awful...
Bella Morte stopped playing an' ***every***one was like... oh no, is this guy hurt or dead or ***what??*** I can never see Bella Morte again...
That is so hot.
My hand still hurts, too.
We'll get Booboo Bear on it.
Hey, guys...
Hm, doesn't sound like any-one's here...
Now we can have a ***real*** sleep-over! A loud one!

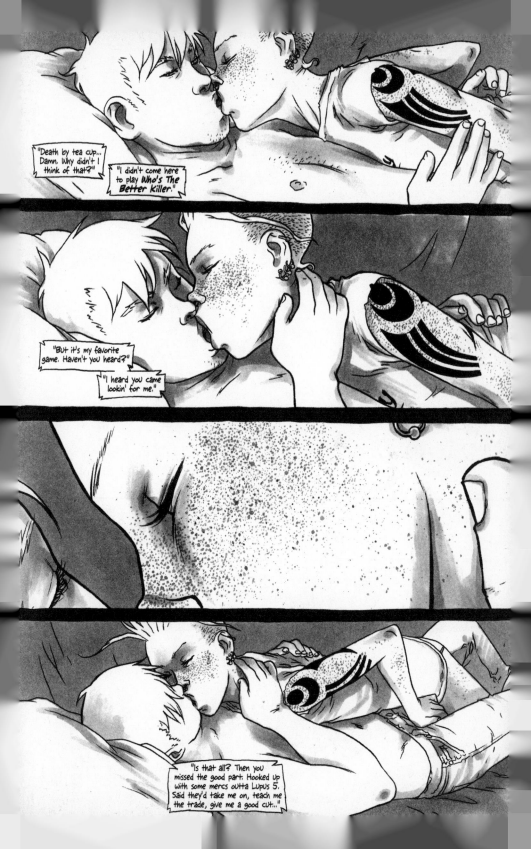

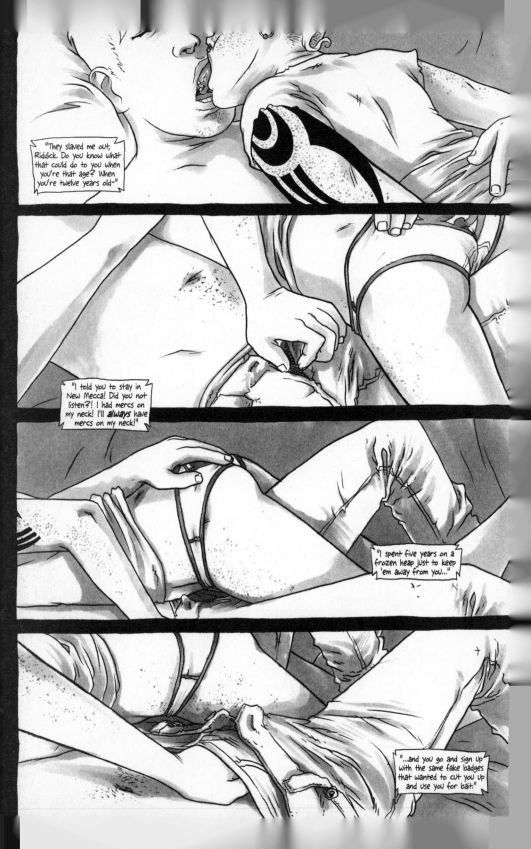

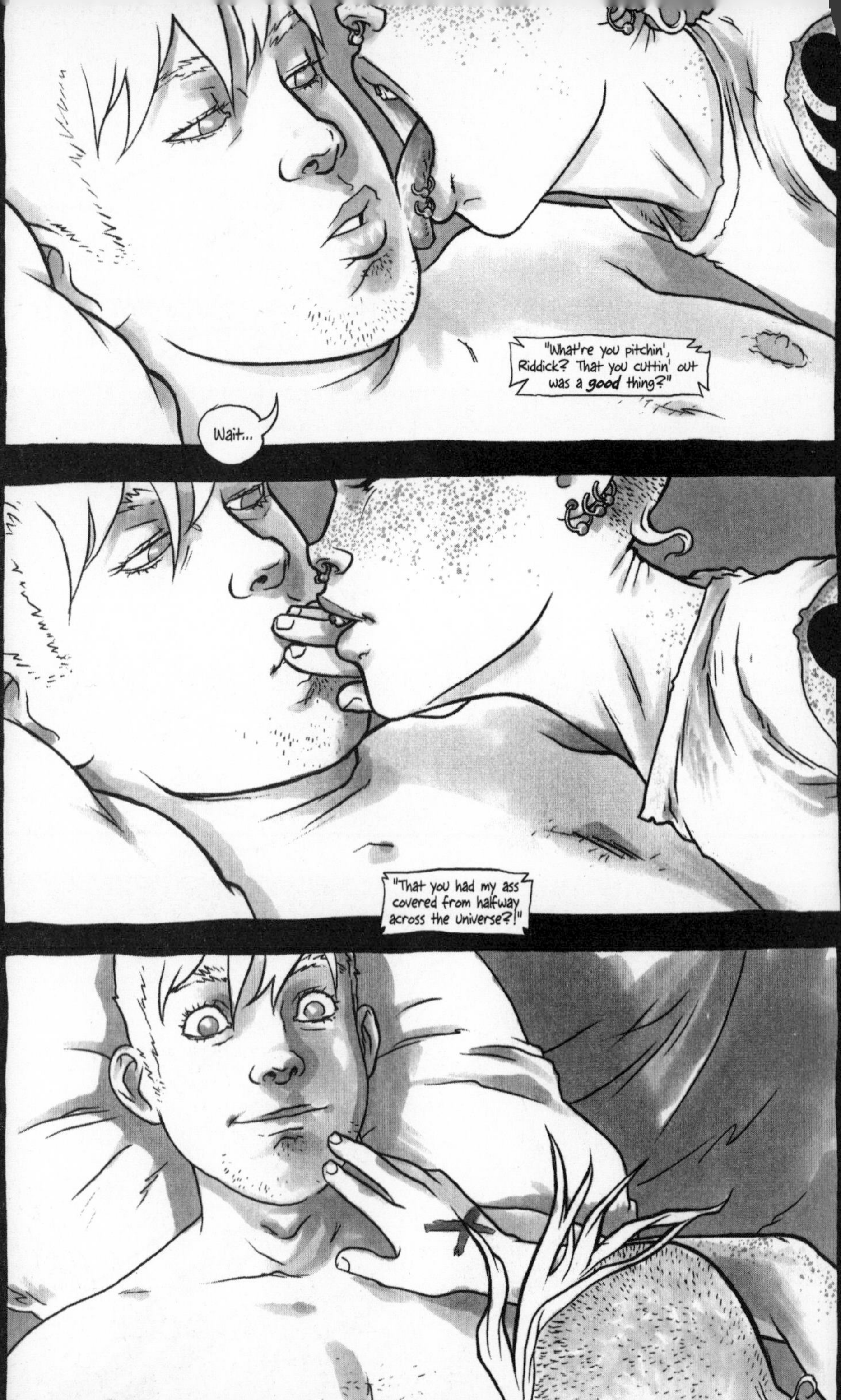
"What're you pitchin', Riddick? That you cuttin' out was a **good** thing?"
Wait...
"That you had my ass covered from halfway across the universe?!"

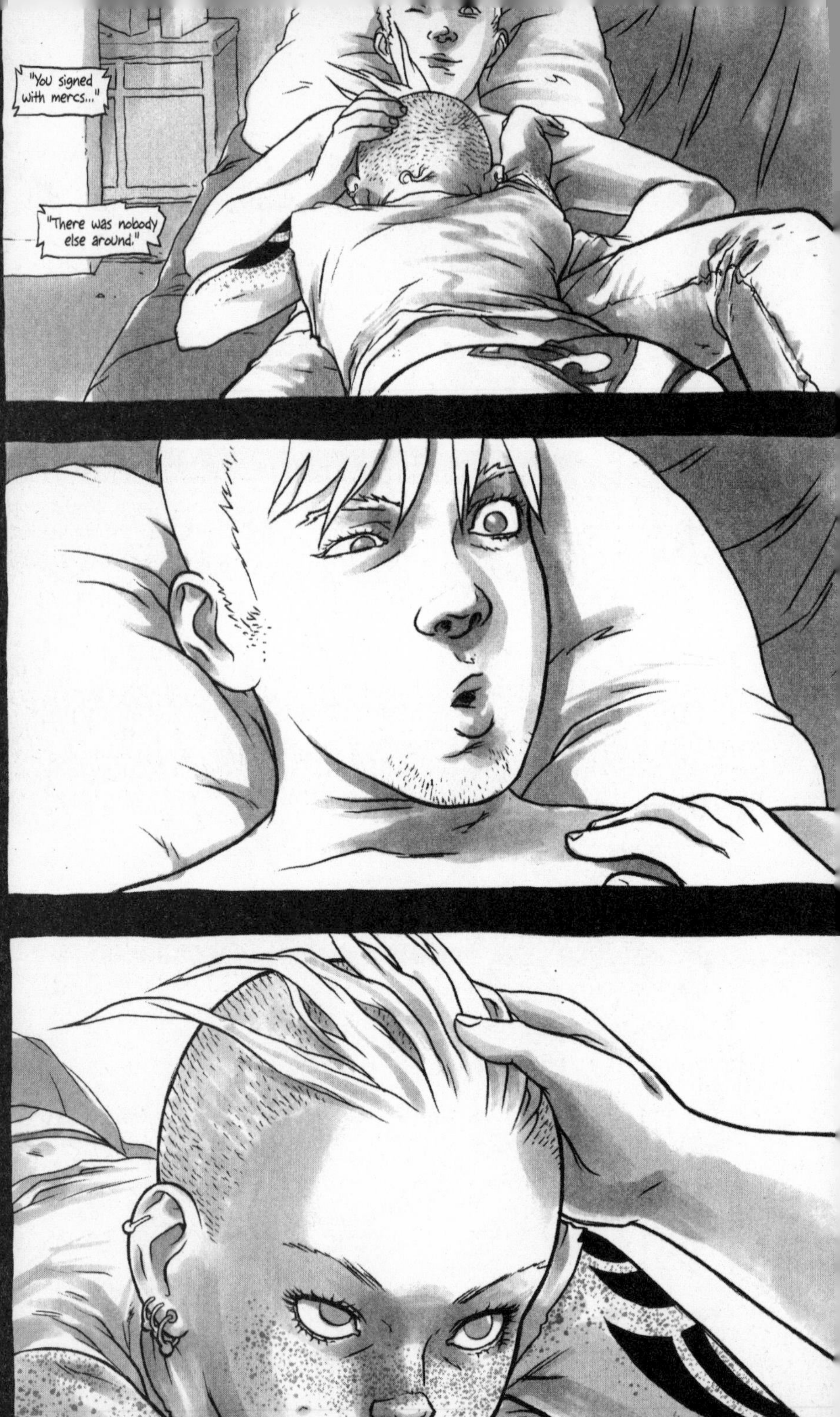
"You signed with mercs..."
"There was nobody else around."

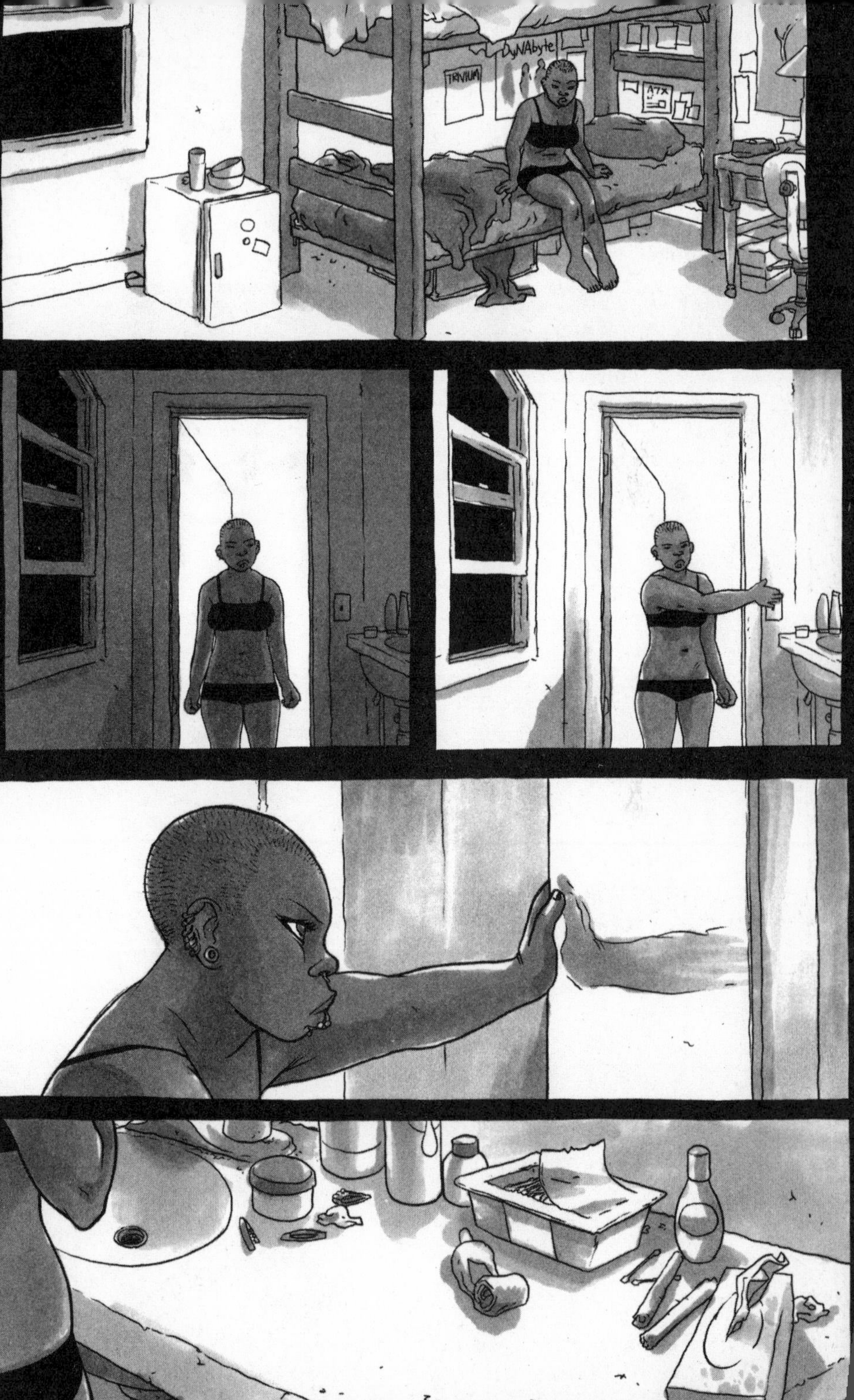
TRIVIUM
DyNAbyte

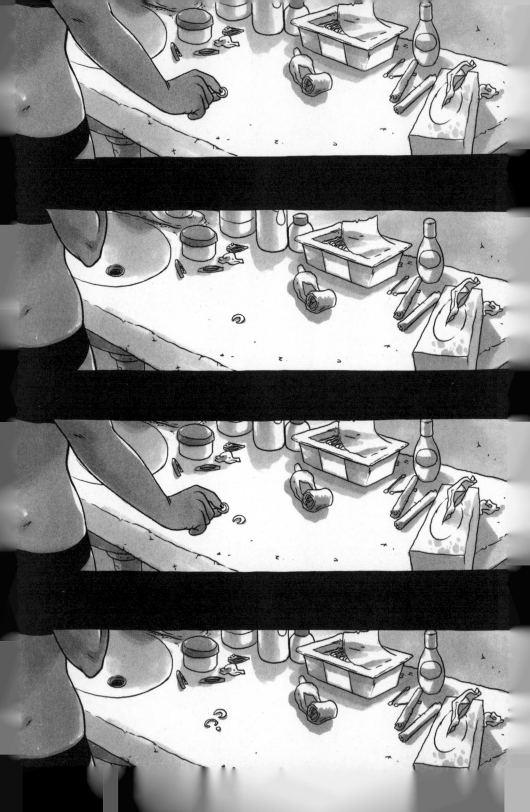

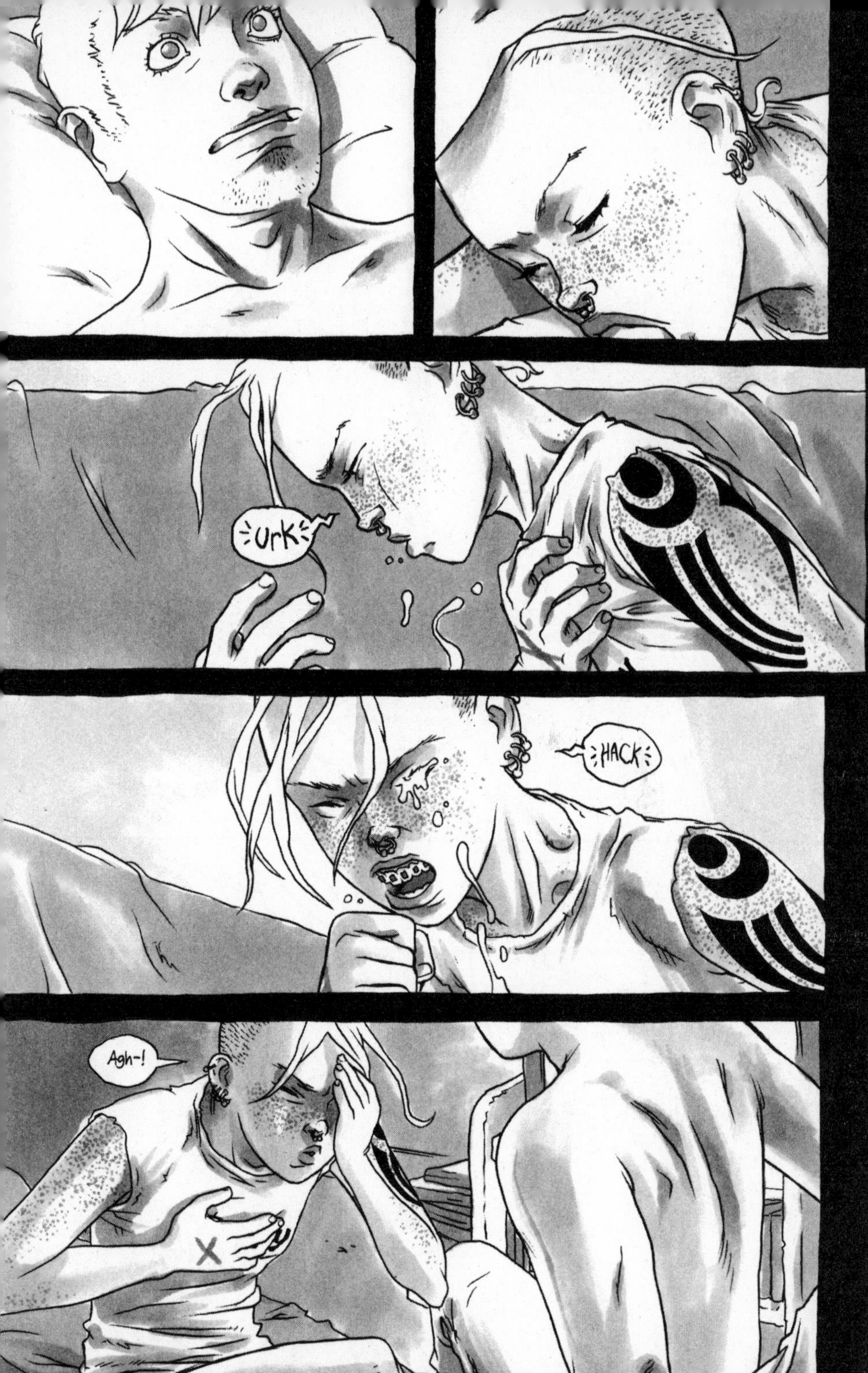

Urk
HACK
Agh-!

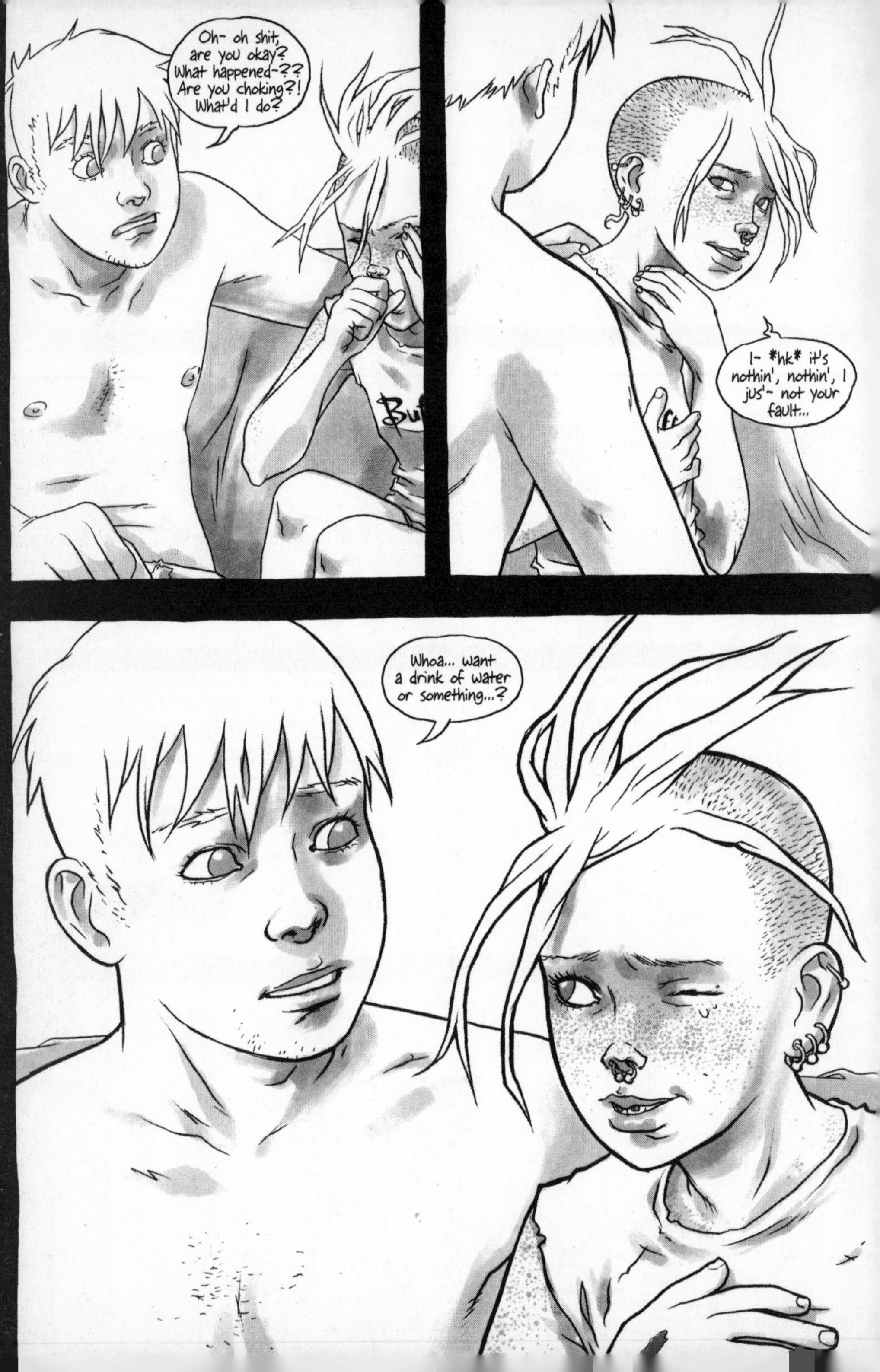
Oh- oh shit, are you okay? What happened-?? Are you choking?! What'd I do?
I- *hk* it's nothin', nothin', I jus'- not your fault...
Whoa... want a drink of water or something...?

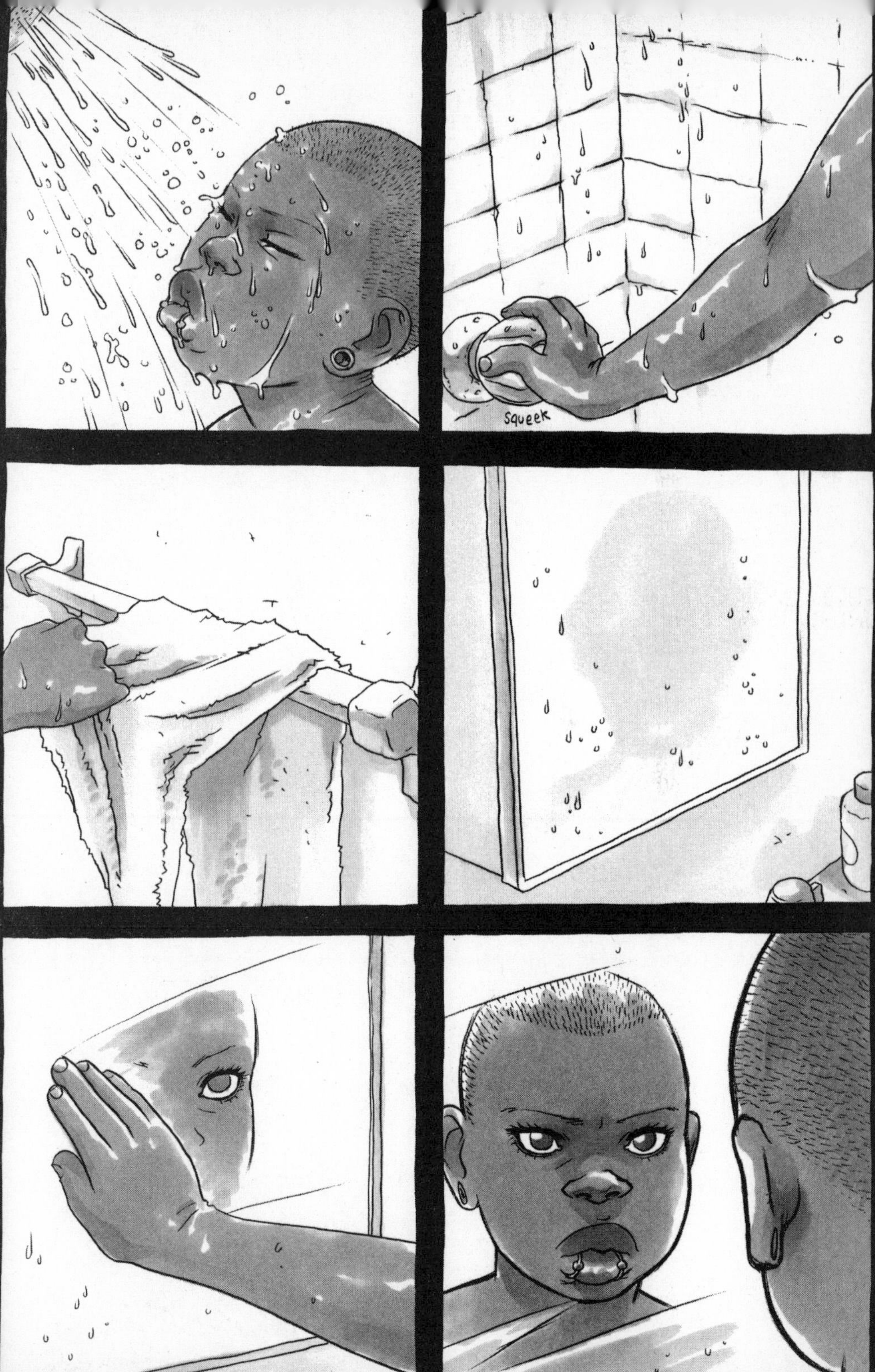
squeek

13

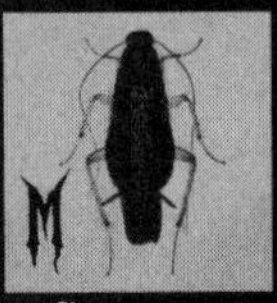

profile

October 13th, 11:32pm

INTRUDER ALERT

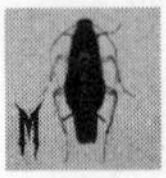

i slept all day. i got up and it was past 10:00pm. i haven't done that in a long time, i used to sleep this late during summer vacation in high school sometimes, but hardly ever anymore. it's a real weird feeling, i can't explain it... it's like you missed something but you don't know what it is and you never will, and you know that you never will, too, so you can't worry about it. and there's something weird but great about after you get up this ridculously late, you take a shower like it's a normal morning. it's both uncomfortable and satisfying at the same time. that's what i just did. i took out a lot of my piercings too, it seemed like the right thing to do, i was getting sick of them... sometimes lately i feel like i don't know who i am anymore. i know that sounds totally lame and emo or whatever, but it's true and i can't lie about it. it seems like once college started, or maybe over the summer after senior year of high school, that everybody started to change real quick except for me. when i think about it, i guess Cleo and Trilby and Audrey are all basically the same, but it doesn't feel like it.

Cleo's been changing a lot in the past few years, so it wasn't a big jump for her, but now i feel like she's all popular or something which is why she's never home. but it's not like she's meeting all these new people, she still hangs out with Trilby, Audrey and Glen and i guess me (sometimes), and i know she doesn't hang out with her roommates, but i guess it's that Myrtle girl who she's always with. it's kind of weird, this whole college thing, because usually you're supposed to go away for school, go away to some other state or at least another city, but all of us stayed in the same town because we had a good school here already that had everything we wanted to do. so instead of being forced to meet entirely new people and make an entirely new group of friends, we don't have to because all our best friends from high school are here with us in college. i wonder if that stunts your growth in some way. is it a natural, necessary thing to go away for college? is it an important learning stage that you should go through? maybe not for all people, but for some people. because a lot of people don't even go to college. and i definately don't think college is necessary, because not everyone knows what they want to do and some people don't have any ambitions that you need a degree for. which is cool. i don't think i need a degree to be a writer either, i think i could do that on my own and become well-known and write for a living without school. i don't know what's going on.

mood: thoughtful
current music: combichrist - lying sack of shit

[0 comments | leave a comment]

October 11th, 3:23am

I'M MY ENEMY

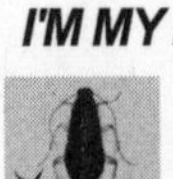

today probably one of the most awkward things that has ever happened to me happened. not only am i completly embarassed now to go over to Cleo's dumb dorm because she's never there but now her stuck-up roomate Natalie thinks i'm the biggest douche on the planet. i always show up there and Cleo is never home so this girl Natalie answers the door and tells me Cleo isn't home every fucking time. then today she told me to wait inside for Cleo so i did, whatever, seemed like a good thing to do. Cleo's gotta come home sometime, right? so i waited with Natalie on the couch, watching some Matthew Broderick movie, the Ferris Bueller guy except now he's old but still looks oddly the same. Reese Witherspoon was in it too. anyway, so we sat there

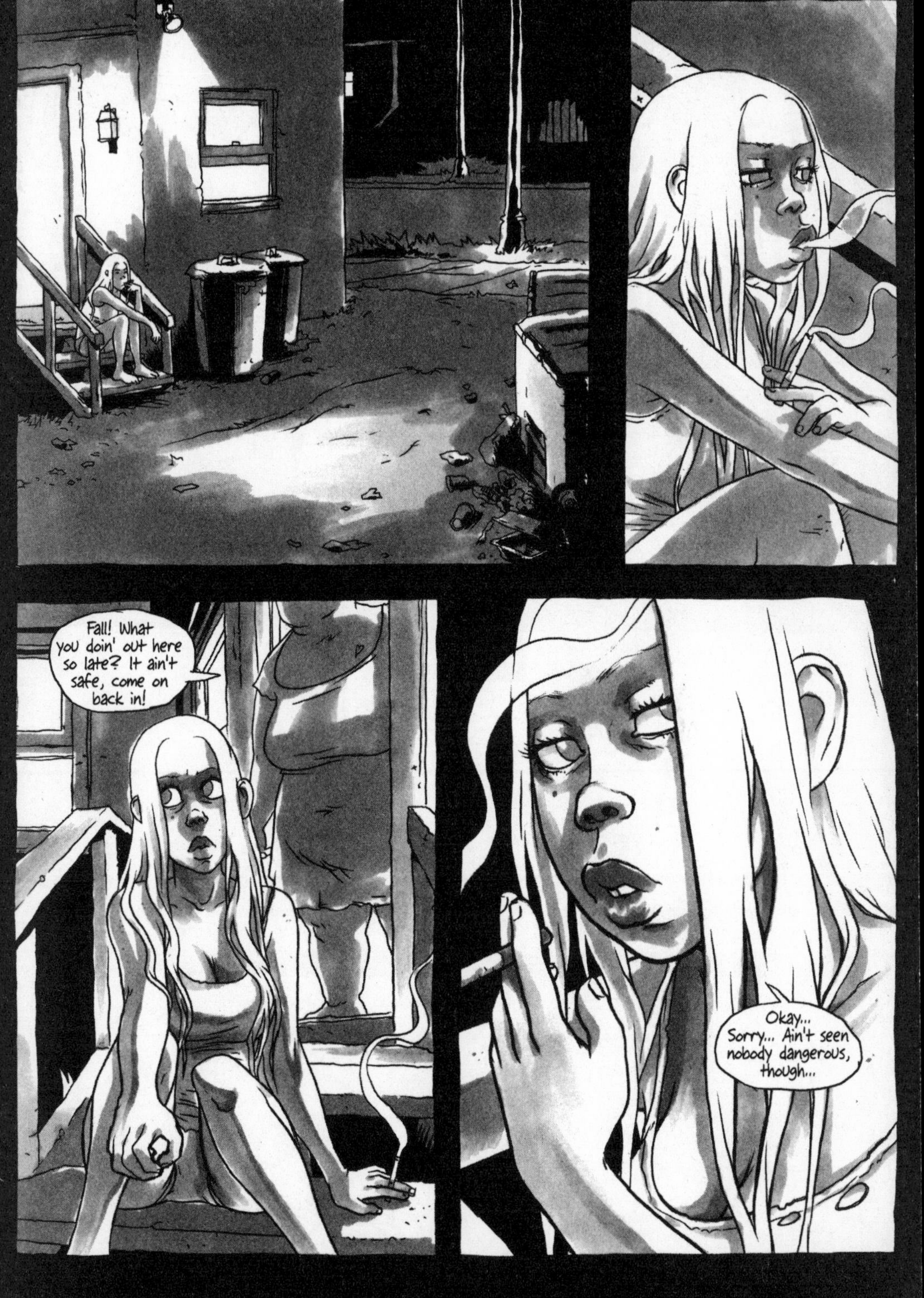
Fall! What you doin' out here so late? It ain't safe, come on back in!
Okay... Sorry... Ain't seen nobody dangerous, though...

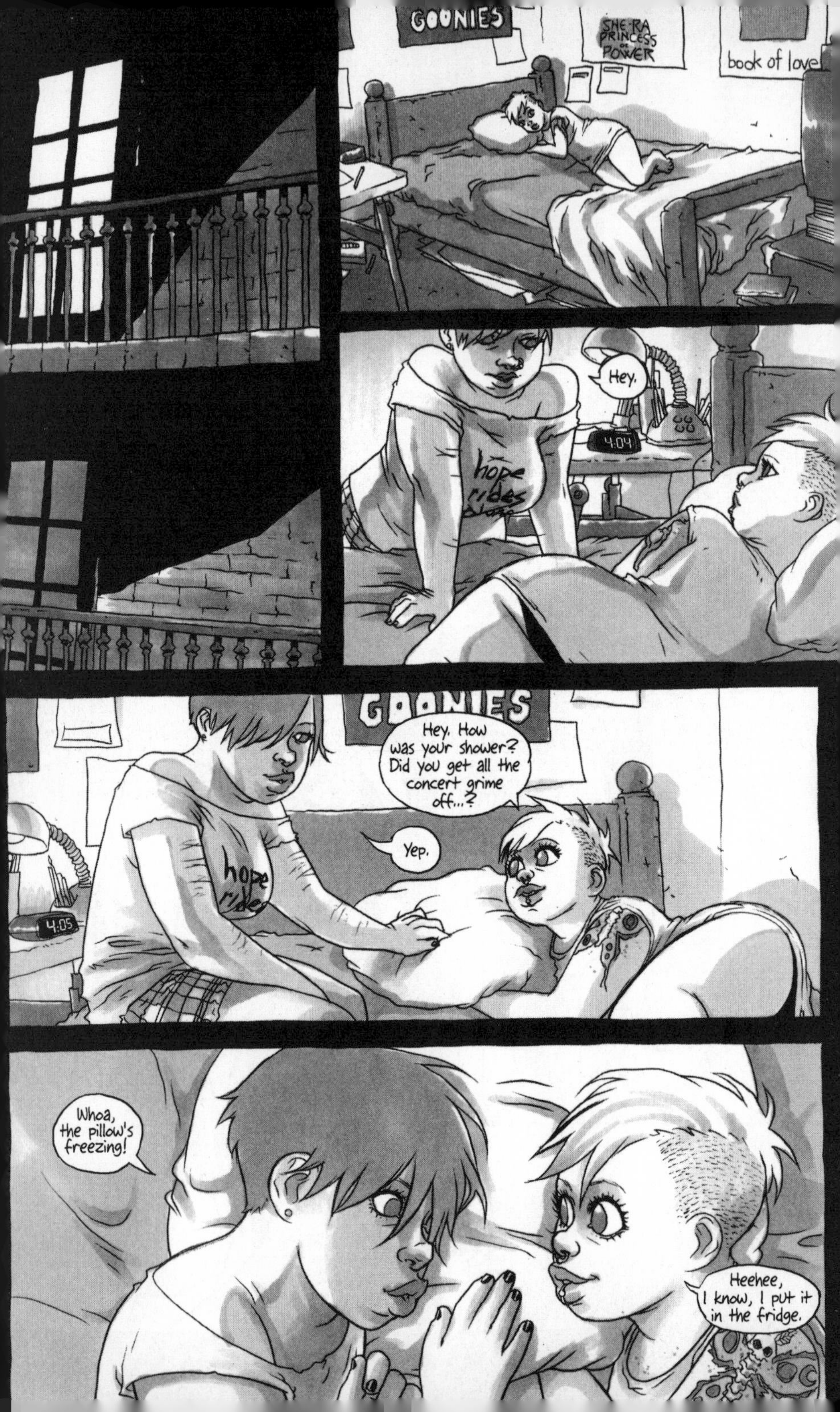
GOONIES
SHE-RA PRINCESS OF POWER
book of love
Hey.
4:04
hope rides
Hey. How was your shower? Did you get all the concert grime off...?
Yep.
4:05
Whoa, the pillow's freezing!
Heehee, I know, I put it in the fridge.

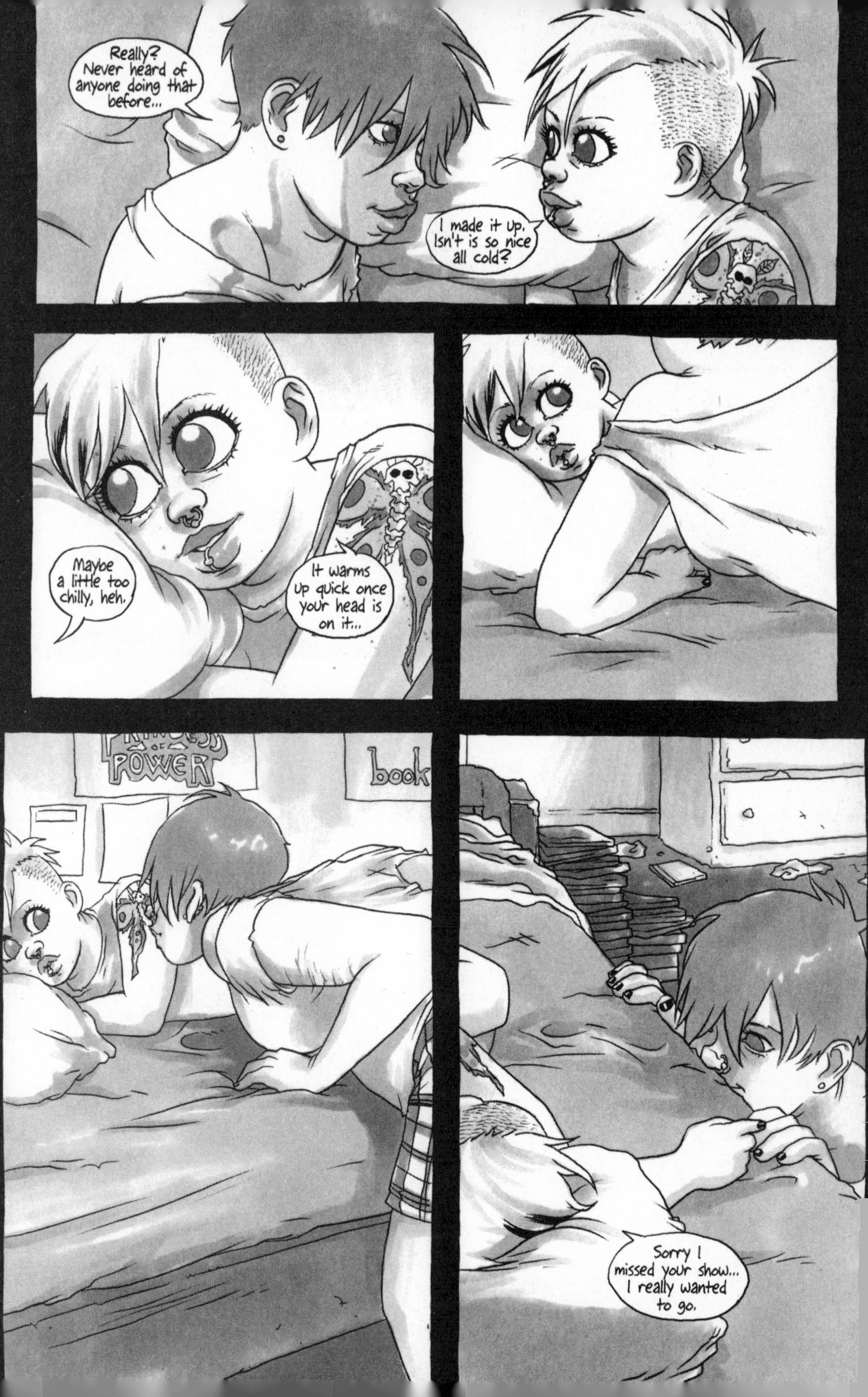
Really? Never heard of anyone doing that before...
I made it up. Isn't is so nice all cold?
Maybe a little too chilly, heh.
It warms up quick once your head is on it...
PRINCESS OF POWER
book
Sorry I missed your show... I really wanted to go.

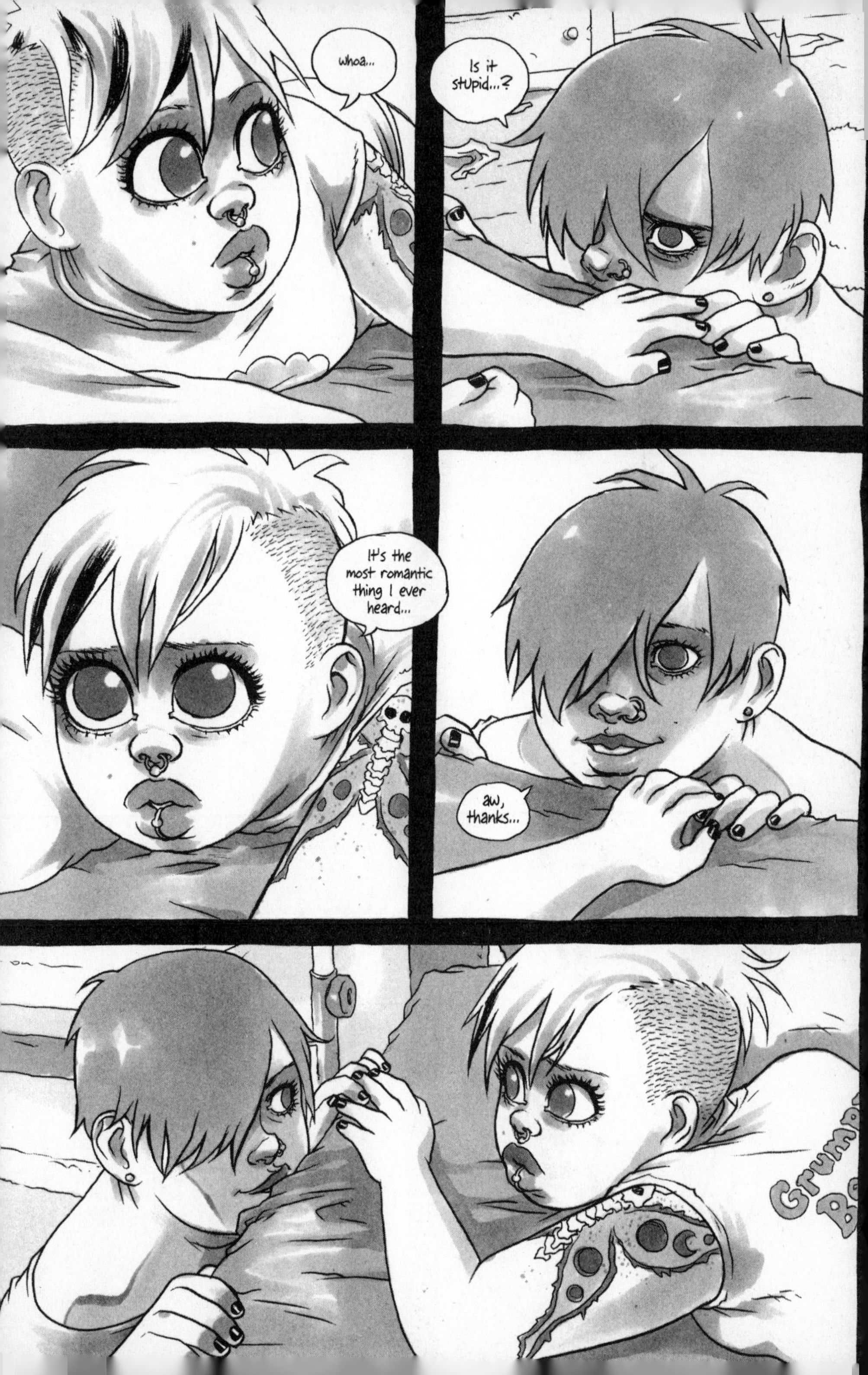
whoa...
Is it stupid...?
It's the most romantic thing I ever heard...
aw, thanks...

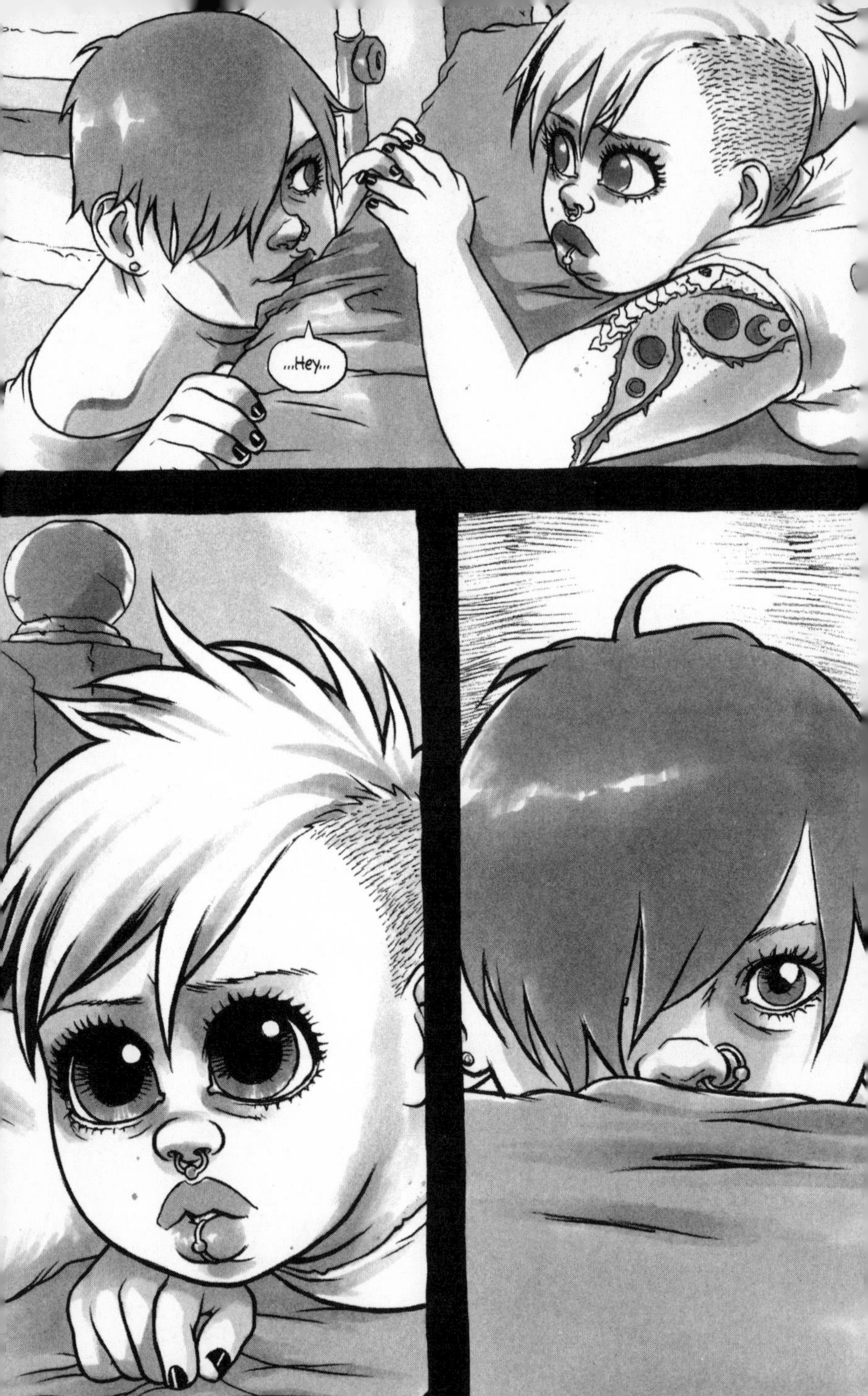
...Hey...

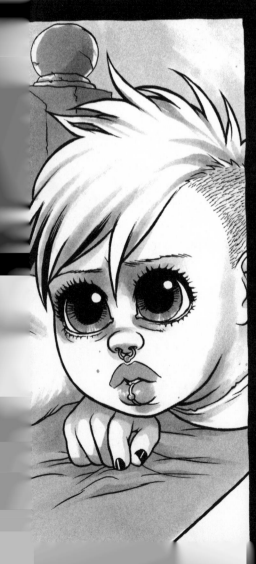

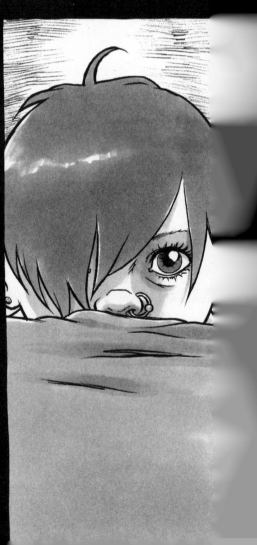

WET MOON
HIGH SCHOOL

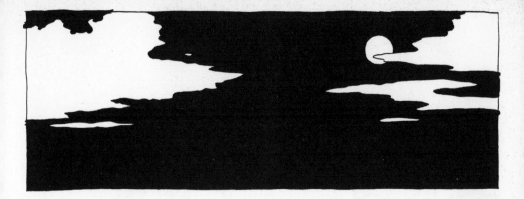

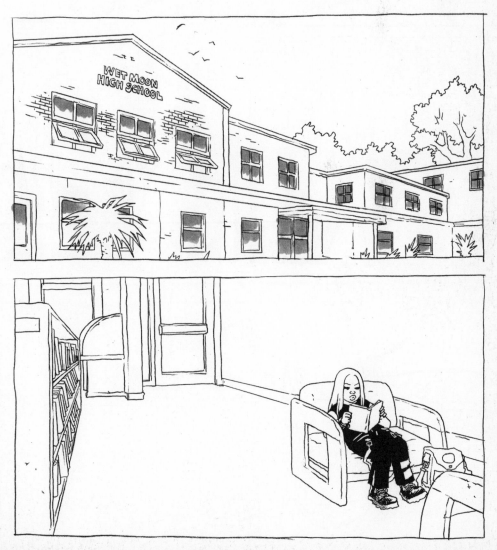

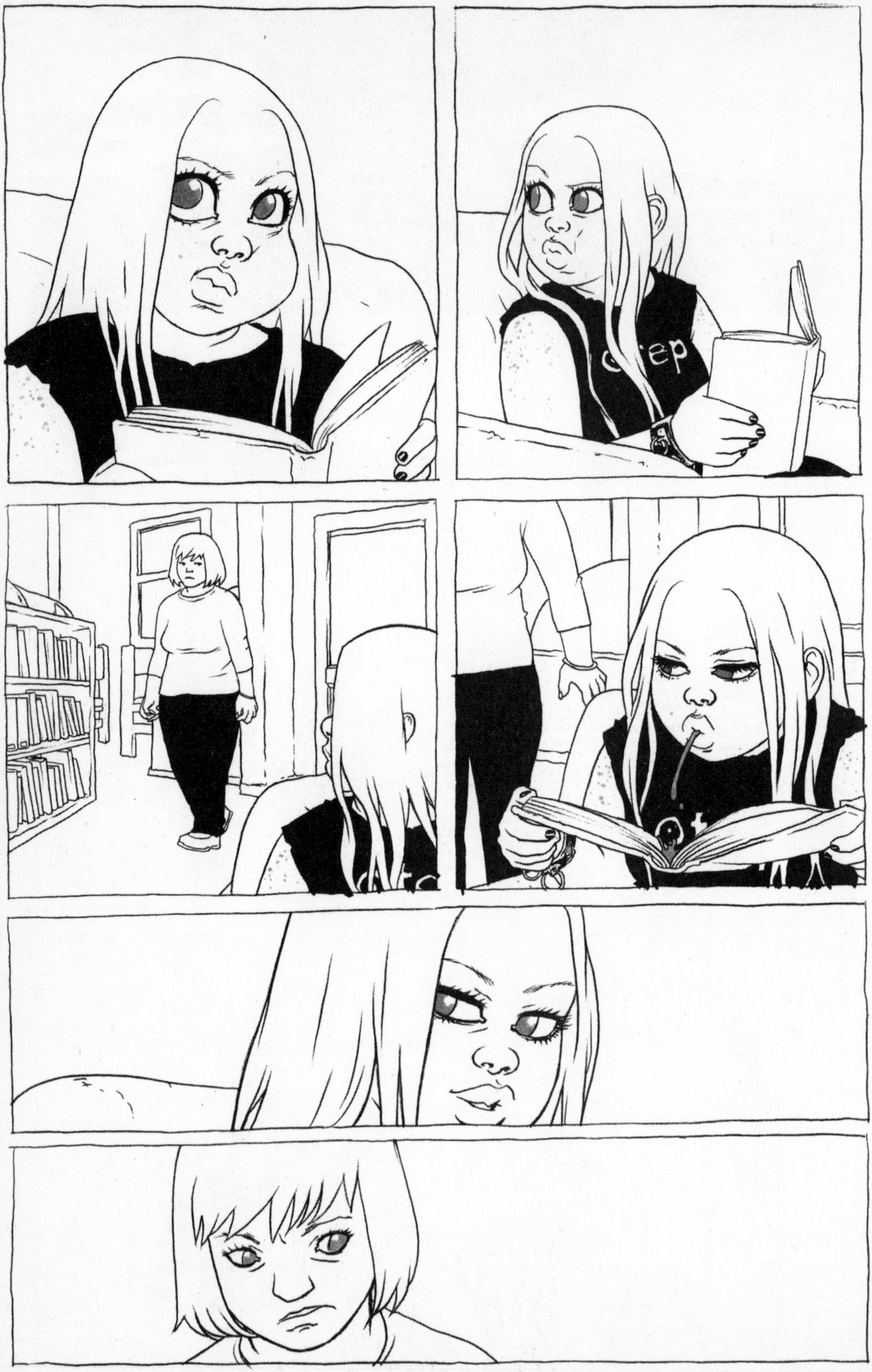

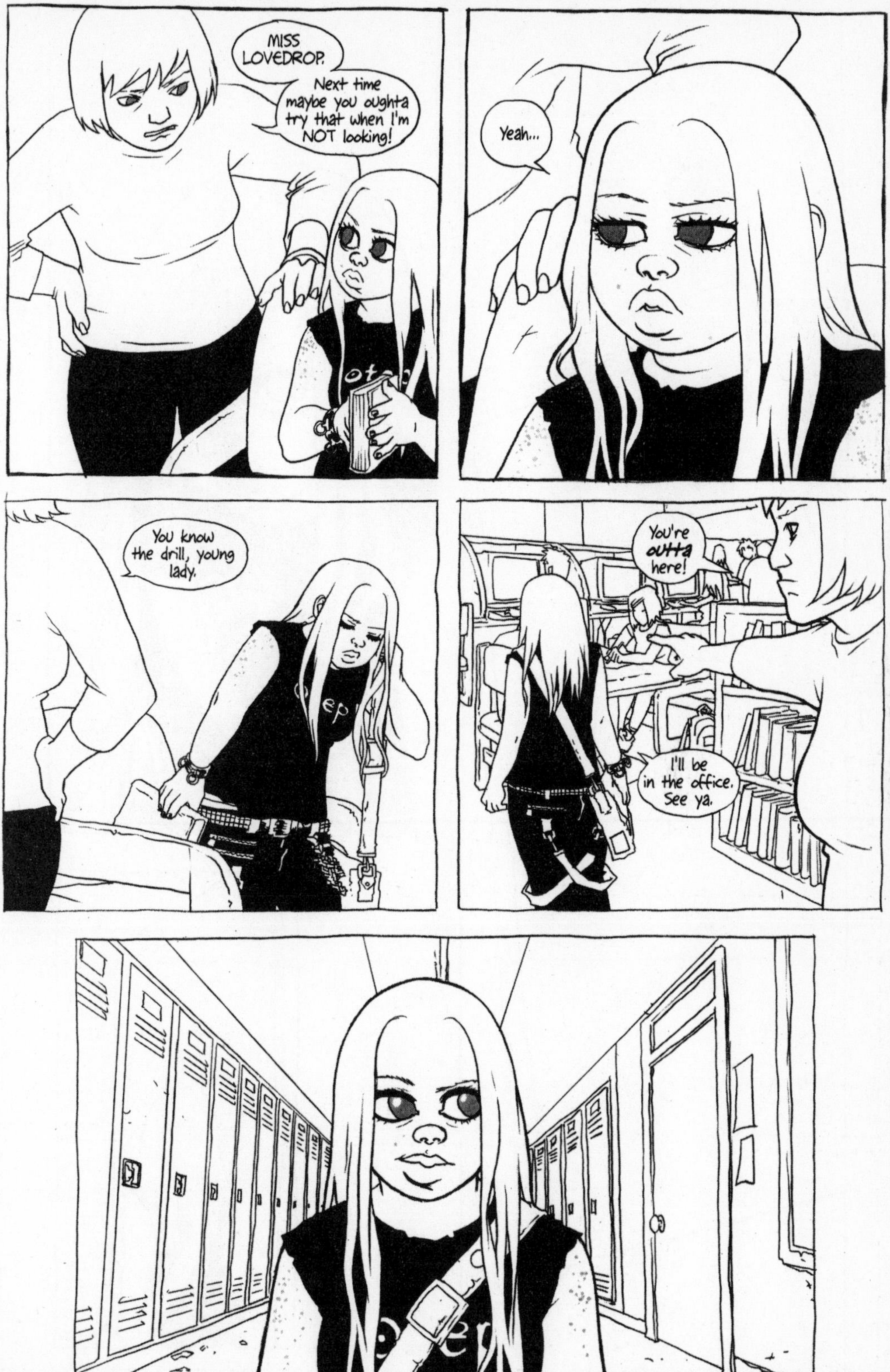
MISS LOVEDROP.
Next time maybe you oughta try that when I'm NOT looking!
Yeah...
You know the drill, young lady.
You're outta here!
I'll be in the office. See ya.

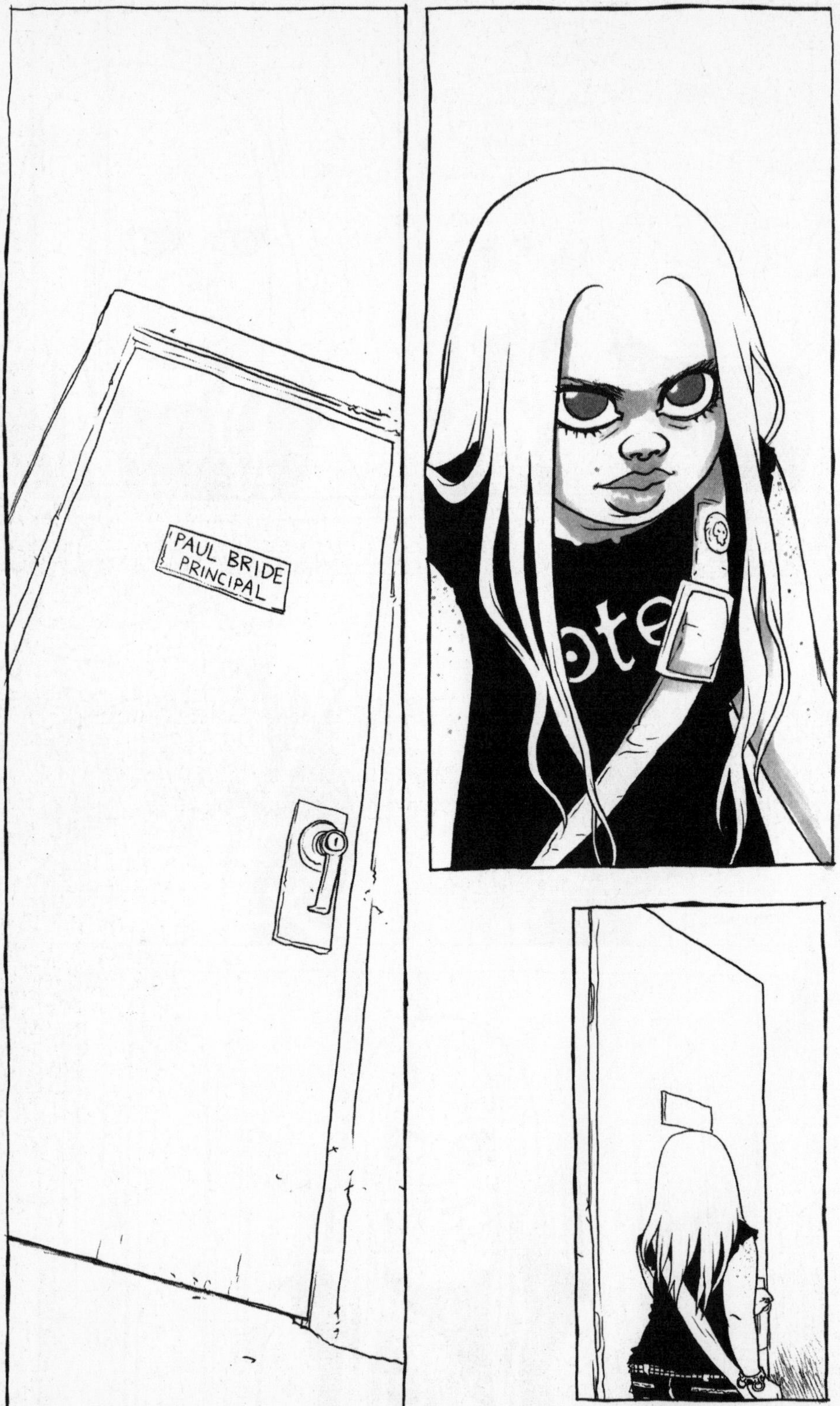
PAUL BRIDE
PRINCIPAL

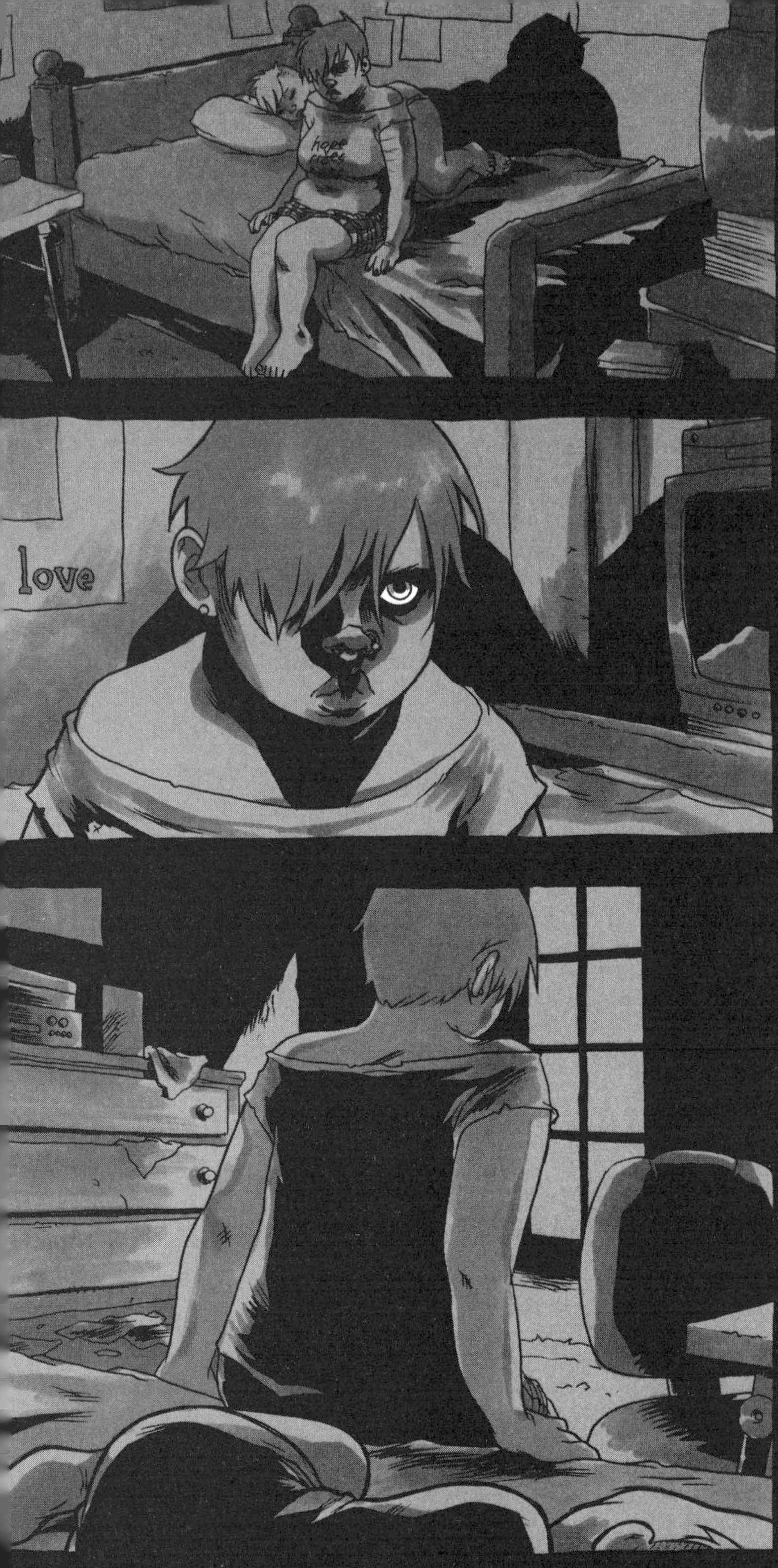
love

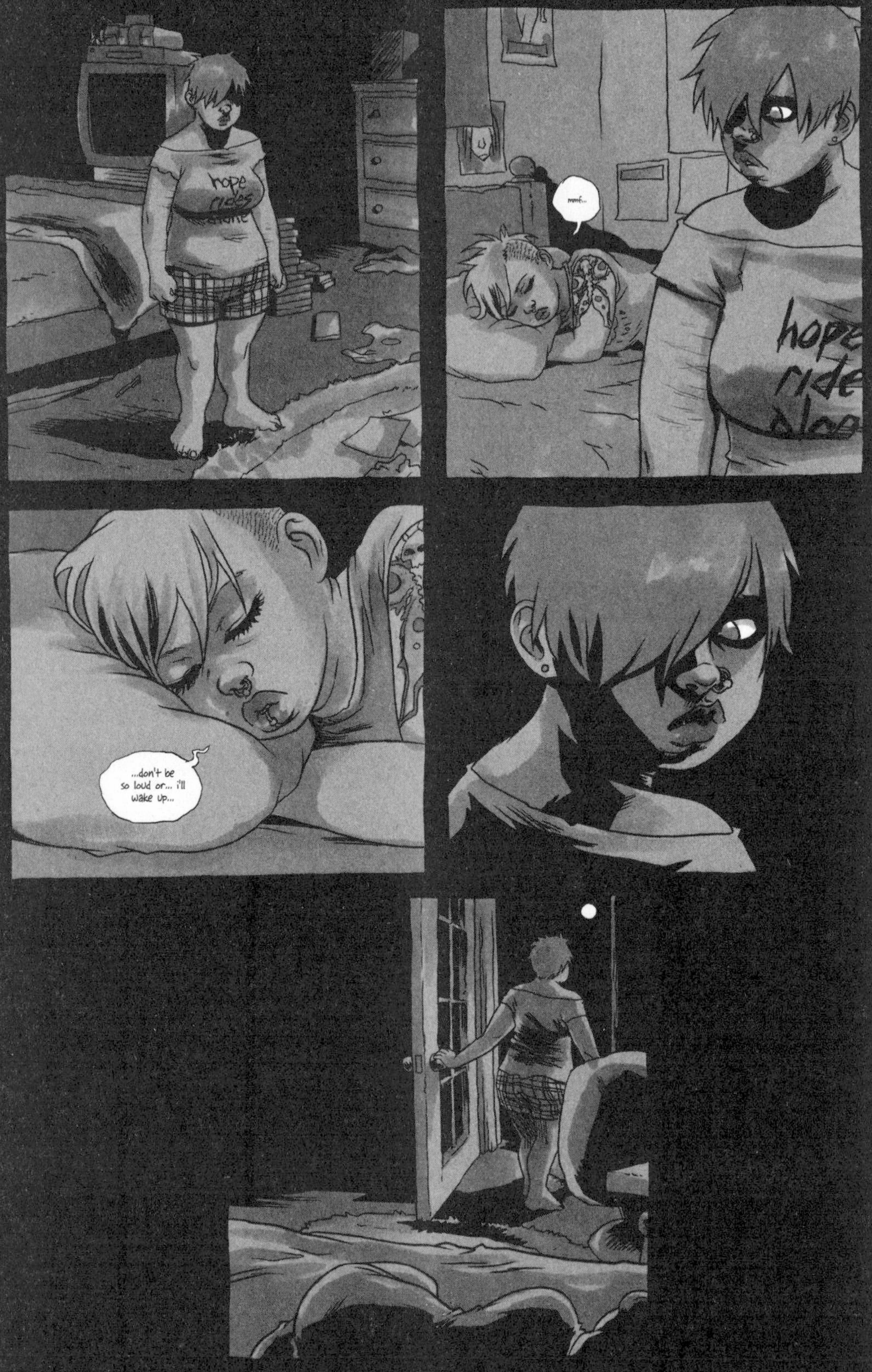
hope rides alone
mmf...
...don't be so loud or... i'll wake up...

October 14th

Myrtle called me her girl!! I guess that means girlfriend. I don't know. That's cool, though, I think I like that. She's doing a song for me!! Wow, so romantic! I can hardly even stand it when I think about it! It takes so much to write a song, it's not like writing a poem or drawing a picture, when you write a song you have to write a poem (the lyrics), and write every layer of music, then get your band to learn the parts, then get everyone together, then play the whole thing and make sure it records the way it's supposed to, or if you're playing a live show make sure not to screw it up because everyone's watching... It seems like such an undertaking! Nobody's ever done anything like this for me before! God what if Myrtle is totally in LOVE with me or something?? I don't know, this could be really serious. Trilby is weird. She says she wants me to get with Myrtle, which I guess I did, but I know that if I told her that she'd make fun of me

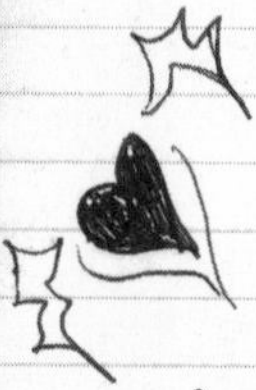

myrtle

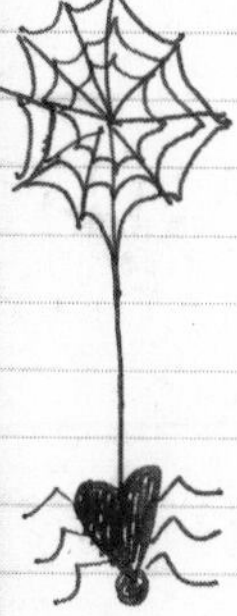

or tease me or whatever it doesn't make any sense. Trilby's never really made sense, though, ever since I met her. Maybe I don't make sense, either.

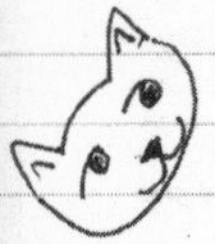

I still can't believe I punched that guy. I feel so bad about it, I wish I could contact him somehow and apologize when he's not unconscious. I really need to get my own computer so I don't have to go to the lab every time. I'm almost <u>positive</u> that Malady must be writing the "Cleo eats it" flyers!! Well, maybe, but at the show I took a peek in her bag in the bathroom and I saw a flyer in there! I know she was collecting them for me, but... it seemed weird that she didn't show me <u>this</u> one... why would she keep this one a secret? Maybe she wrote it and planned to put it up somewhere in secret at the show venue before we left. Oh god, how could it be her? I thought we were friends! I don't know, I'll have to do more investigating before I decide... I guess

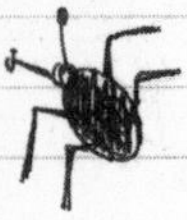

besides the punching thing the show was cool. Bella Marte do such a great show, and they're all so cute... I bet they all have girlfriends, though, or they could all be gay, maybe with each other. That would be hot. Now I don't think I'll ever get to see them play again, I just know they'll remember me: the girl who punched a guy and ruined the show. And I think they were friends with that guy, too. Andy said something to him during the show but I can't remember what his name was. But that's so even worse, because I punched their friend. Maybe I could do my hair different and wear contacts or dark sunglasses like a mask and wear a big coat, maybe then they wouldn't recognize me. I could be Daray Wilcox, from Kentucky.

Speaking of Daray, I haven't written any on my novel in almost two weeks. School is making me super busy, it feels like I hardly have time for anything else. I have a big

paper to write for my satirical literature class that I haven't even started yet and it's due like next week!

SCHOOLBUS
WORMLIZARDS
FCS

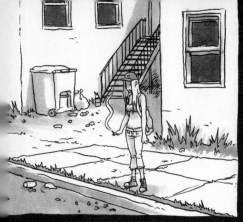

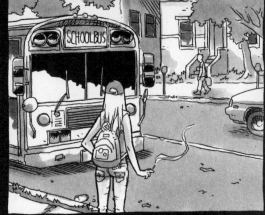

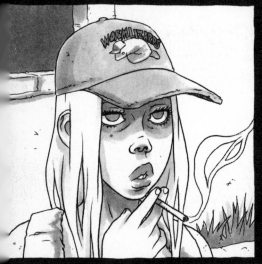

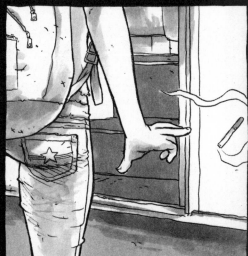

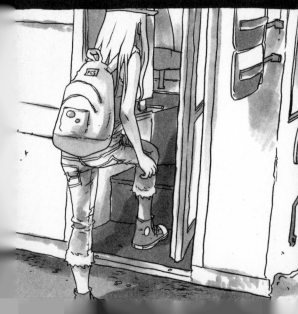

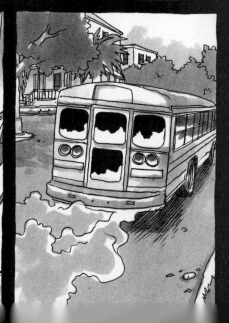

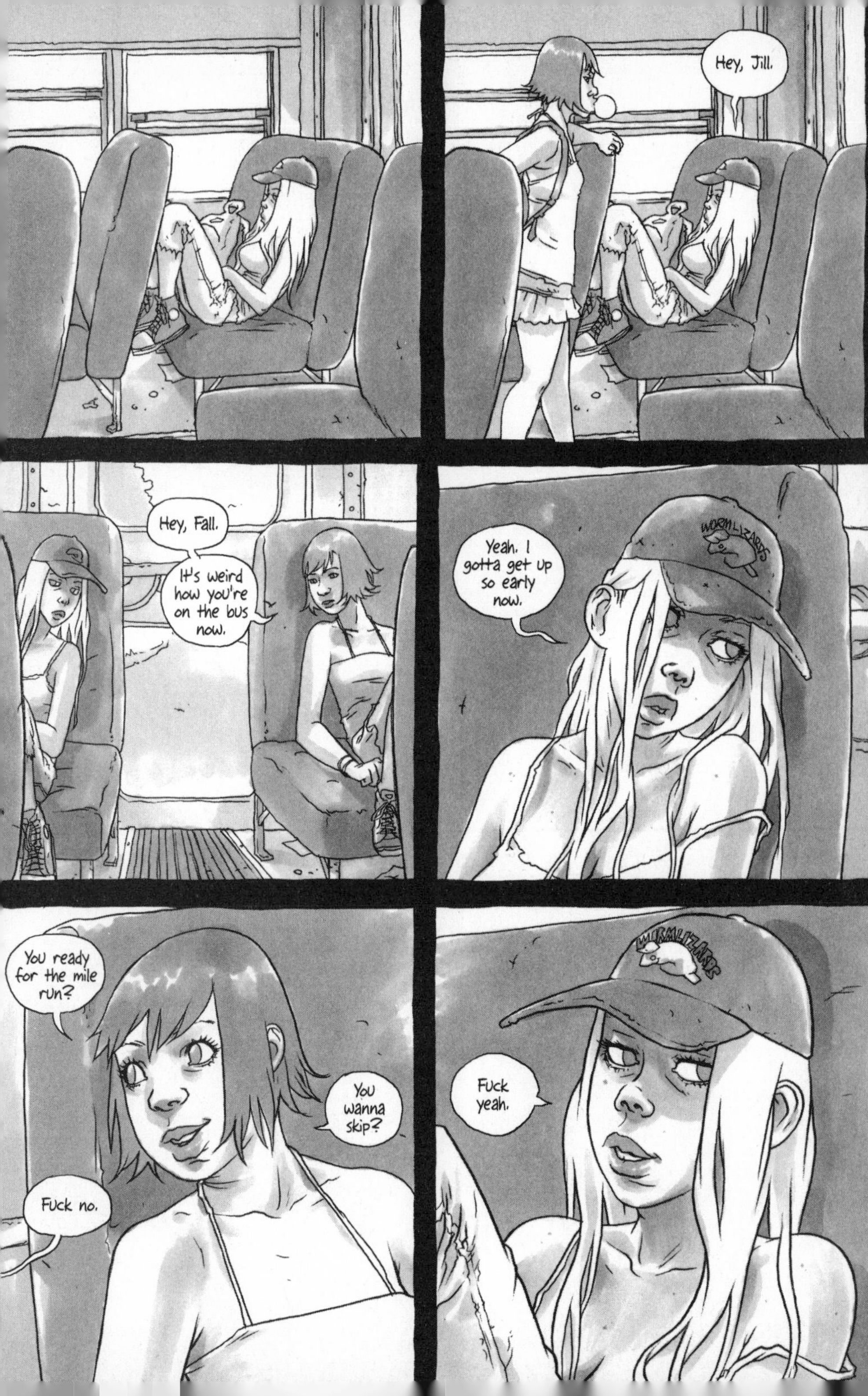
Hey, Jill.
Hey, Fall.
It's weird how you're on the bus now.
Yeah. I gotta get up so early now.
WORM-LIZARDS
You ready for the mile run?
You wanna skip?
Fuck no.
WORMLIZARDS
Fuck yeah.

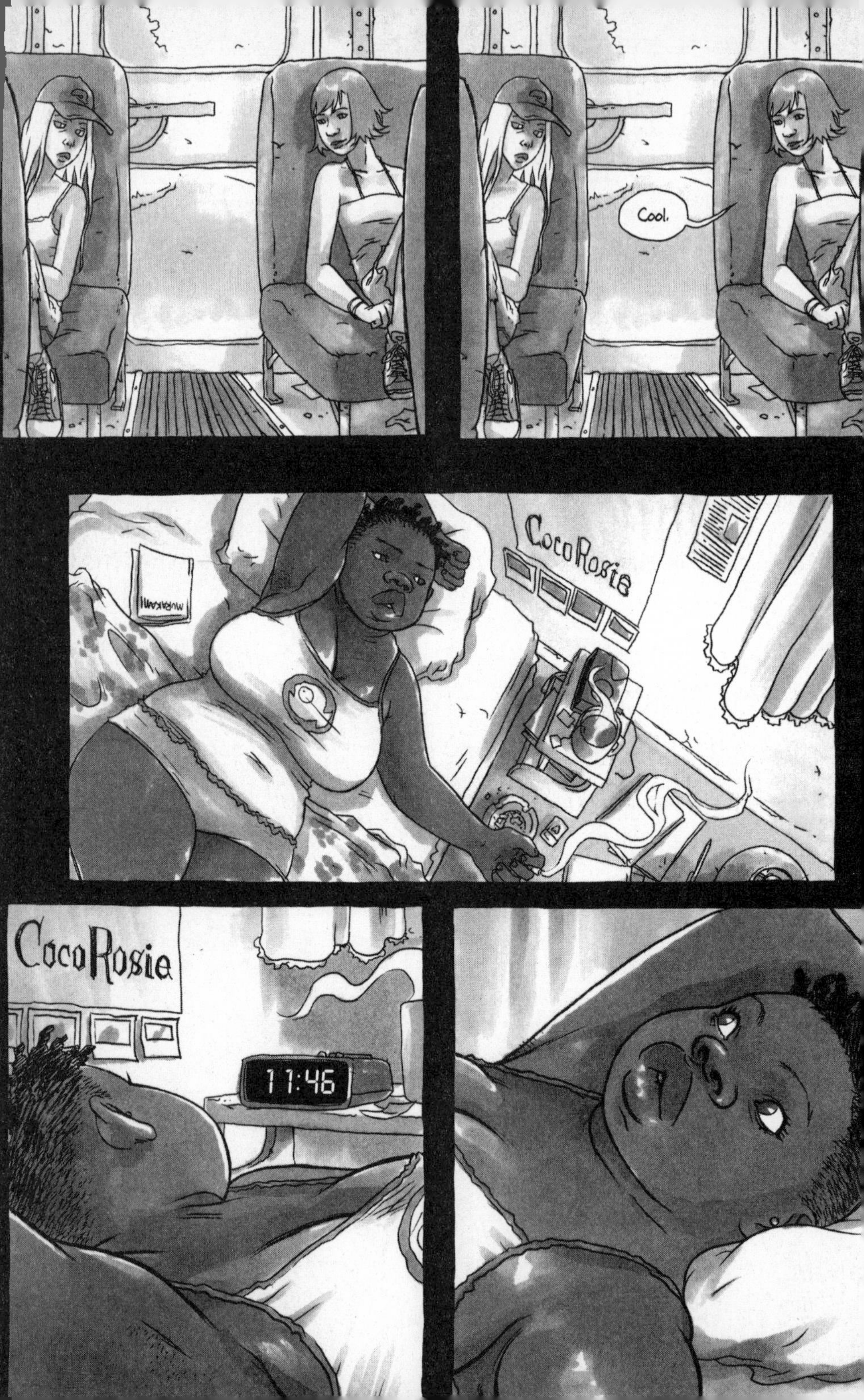
Cool.
MURAKAMI
CocoRosie
CocoRosie
11:46

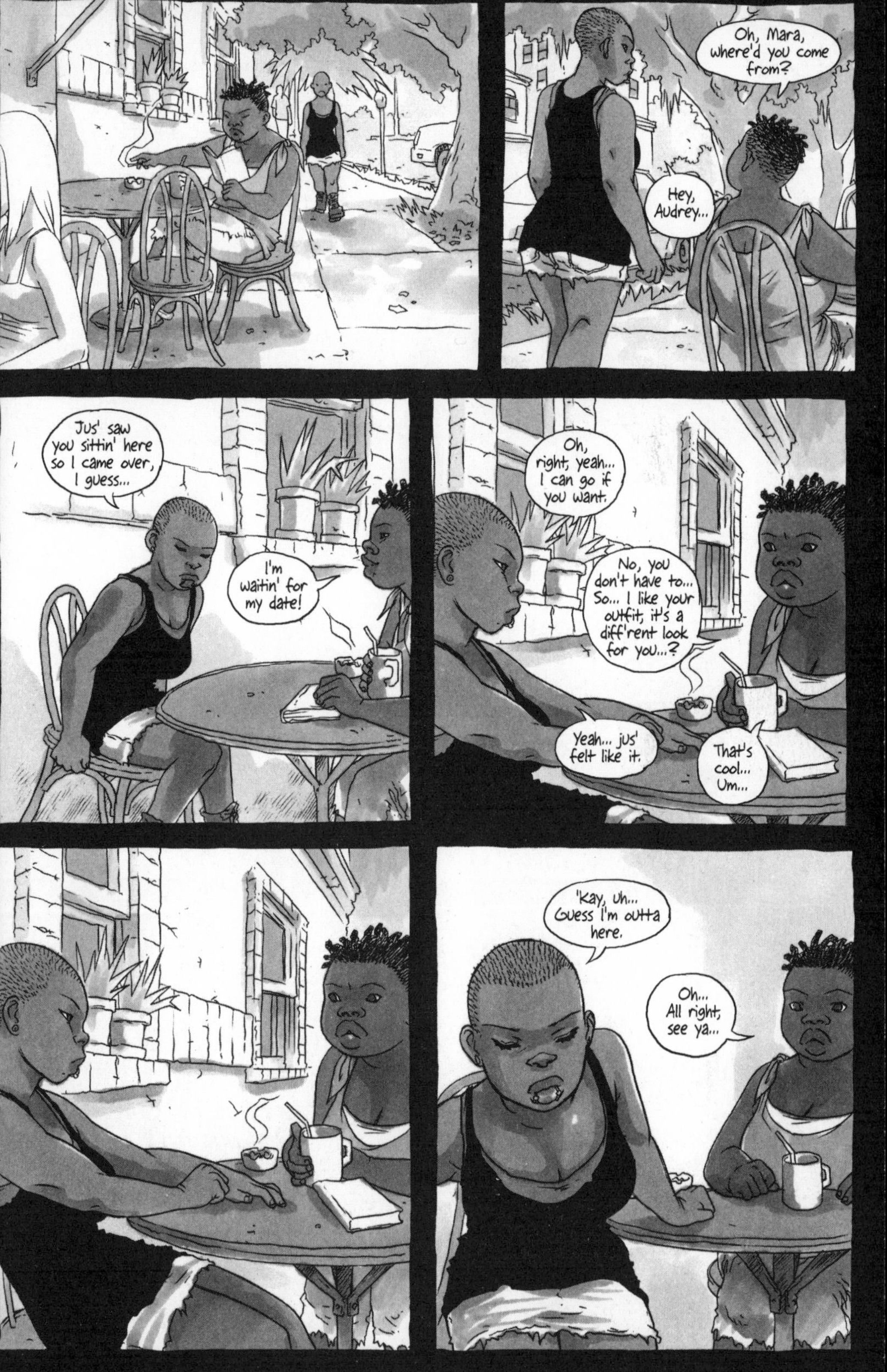
Oh, Mara, where'd you come from?
Hey, Audrey...
Jus' saw you sittin' here so I came over, I guess...
I'm waitin' for my date!
Oh, right, yeah... I can go if you want.
No, you don't have to... So... I like your outfit, it's a diff'rent look for you...?
Yeah... jus' felt like it.
That's cool... Um...
'Kay, uh... Guess I'm outta here.
Oh... All right, see ya...

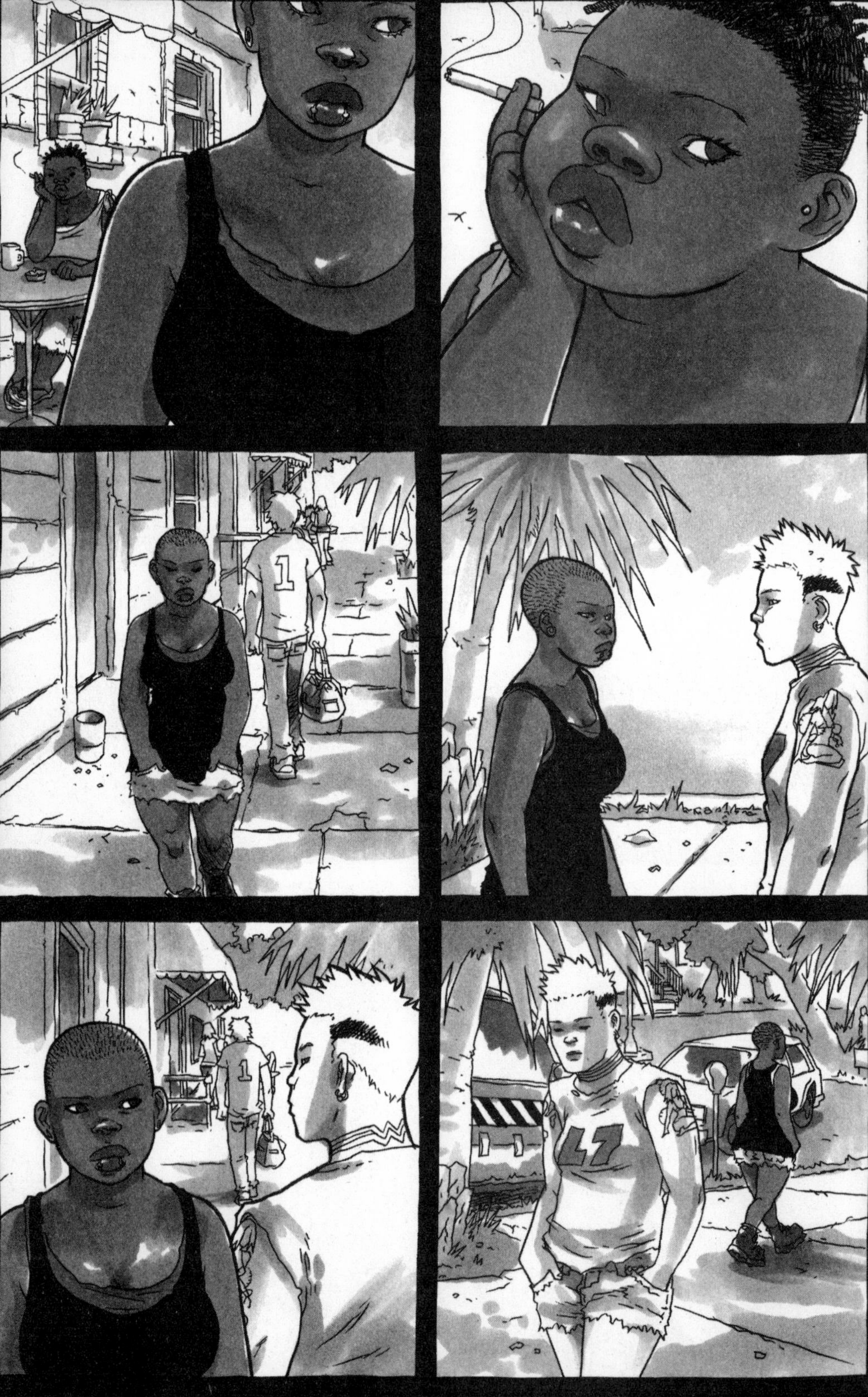

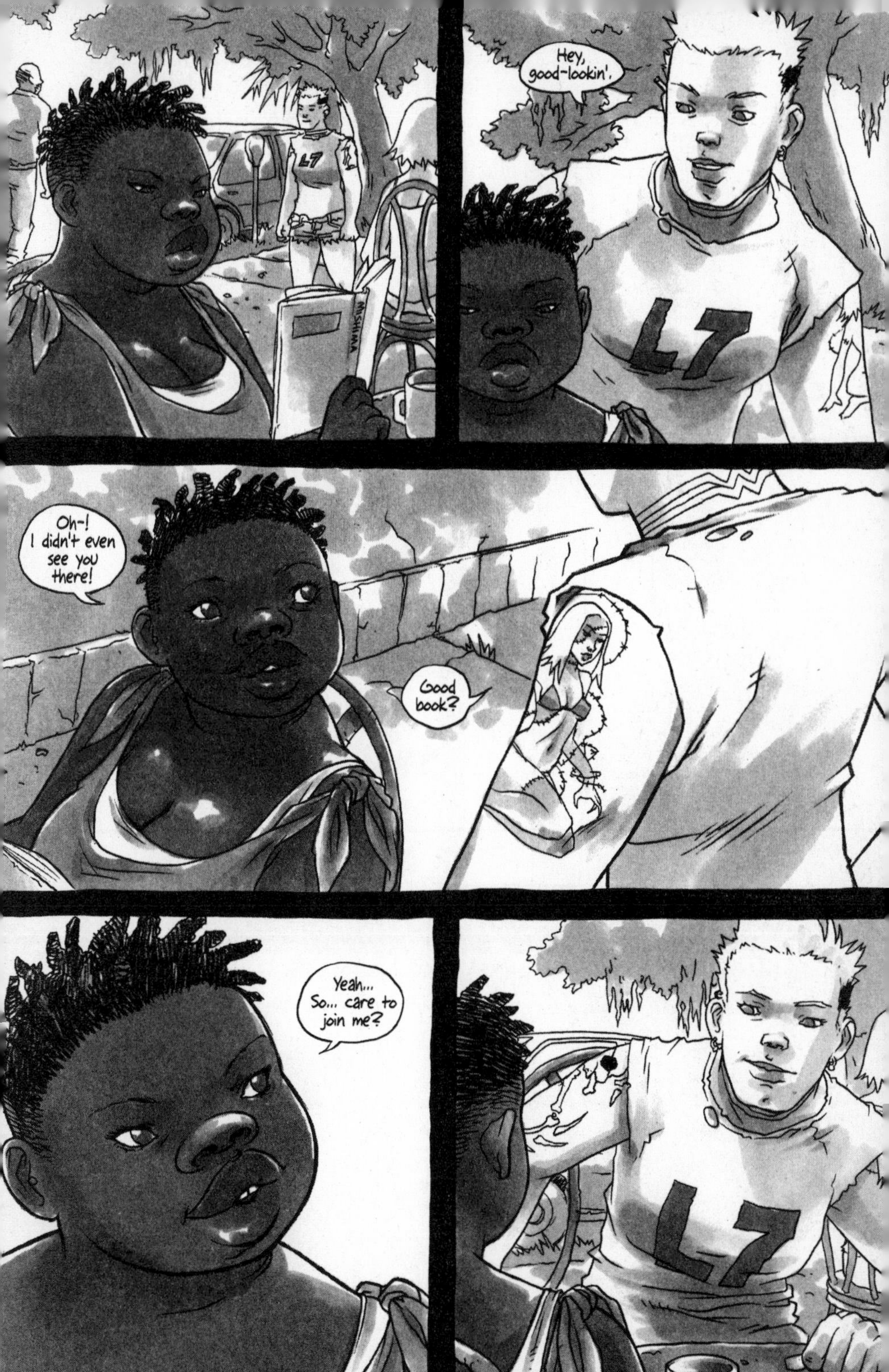
MISHIMA
Hey, good-lookin'.
Oh-! I didn't even see you there!
Good book?
Yeah... So... care to join me?

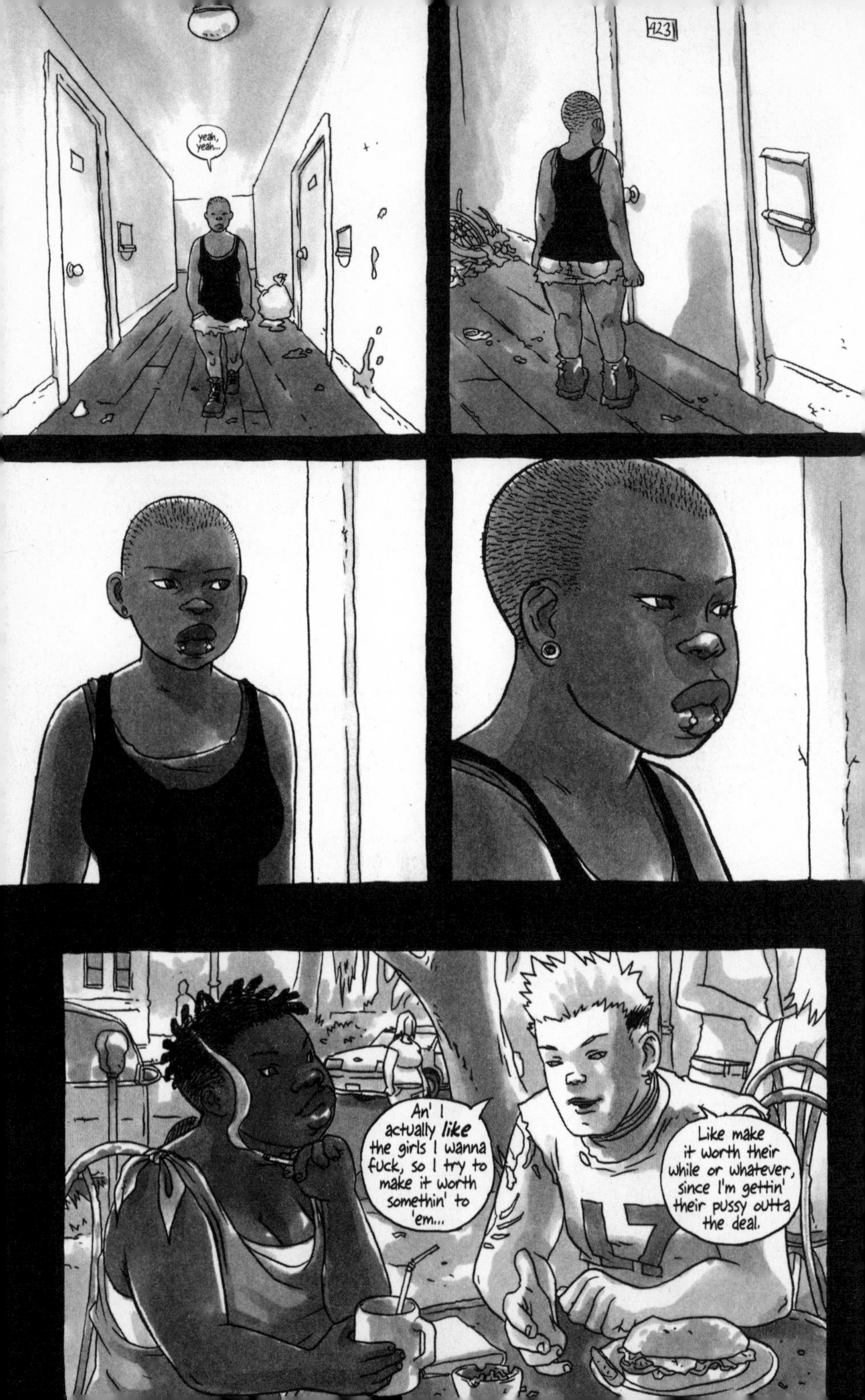
yeah, yeah...
423
An' I actually *like* the girls I wanna fuck, so I try to make it worth somethin' to 'em...
Like make it worth their while or whatever, since I'm gettin' their pussy outta the deal.

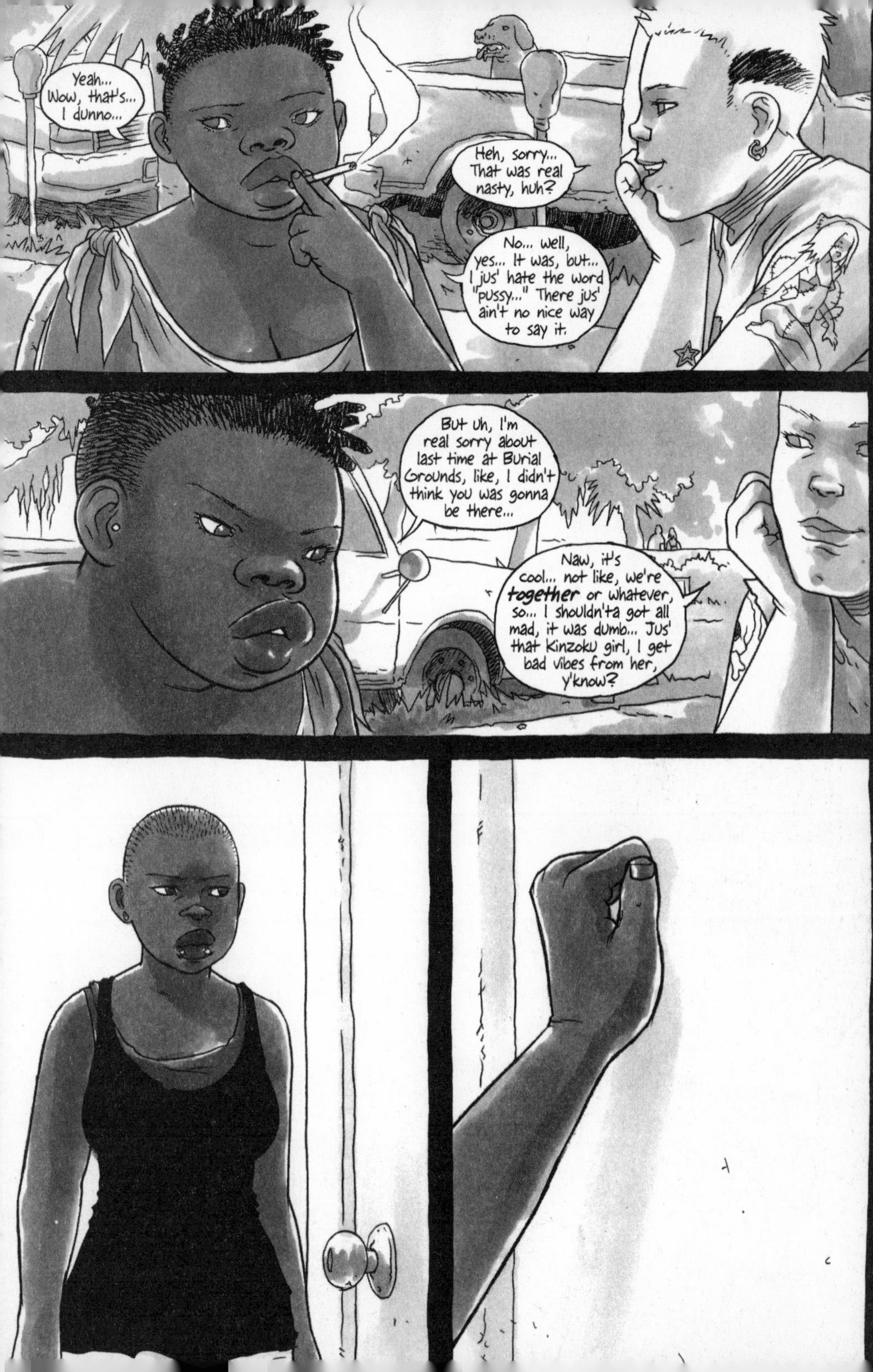
Yeah... Wow, that's... I dunno...
Heh, sorry... That was real nasty, huh?
No... well, yes... It was, but... I jus' hate the word "pussy..." There jus' ain't no nice way to say it.
But uh, I'm real sorry about last time at Burial Grounds, like, I didn't think you was gonna be there...
Naw, it's cool... not like, we're **together** or whatever, so... I shouldn'ta got all mad, it was dumb... Jus' that Kinzoku girl, I get bad vibes from her, y'know?

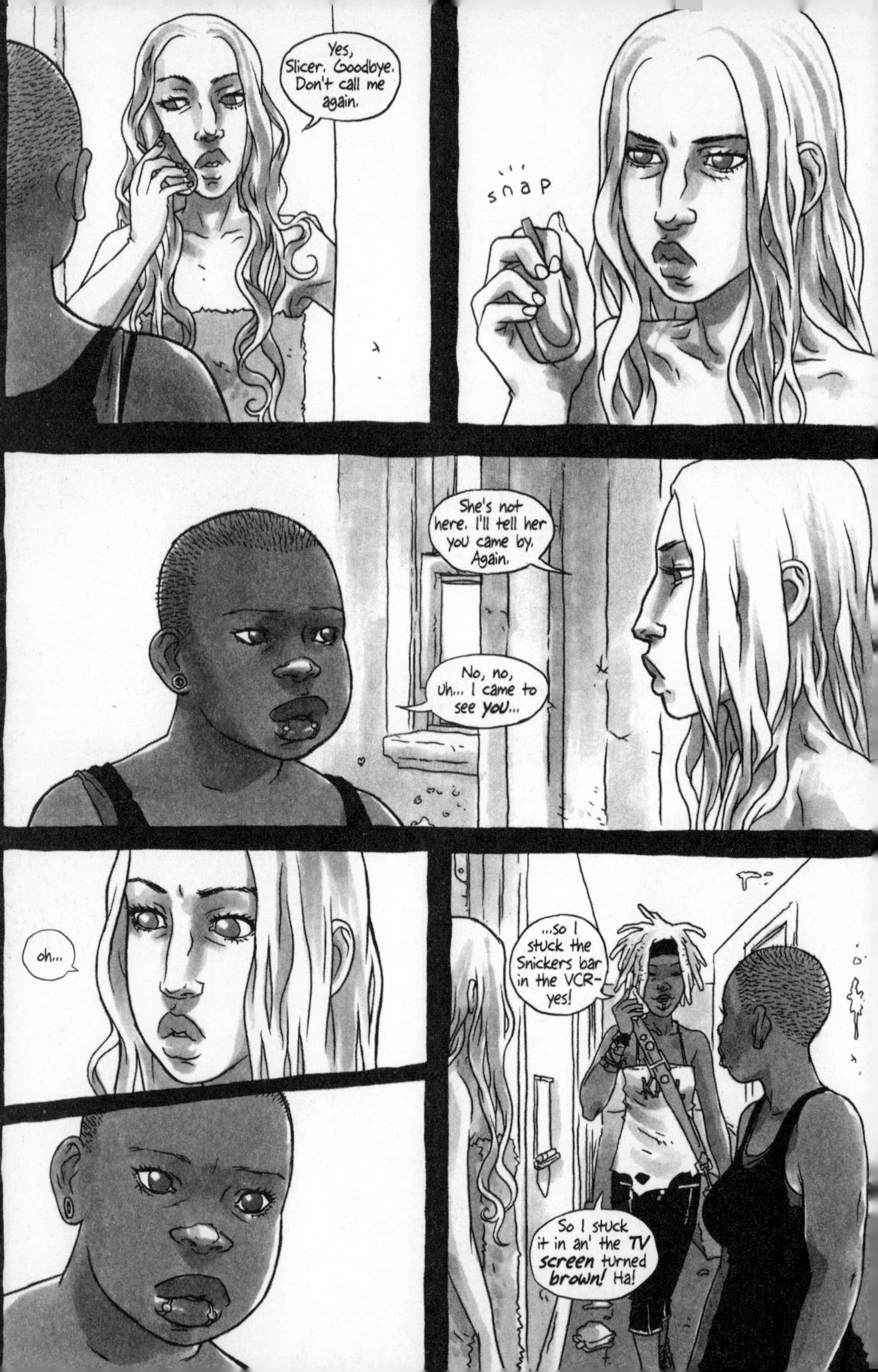
Yes, Slicer. Goodbye. Don't call me again.
snap
She's not here. I'll tell her you came by. Again.
No, no, uh... I came to see *you*...
oh...
...so I stuck the Snickers bar in the VCR-yes!
So I stuck it in an' the **TV screen** turned **brown!** Ha!

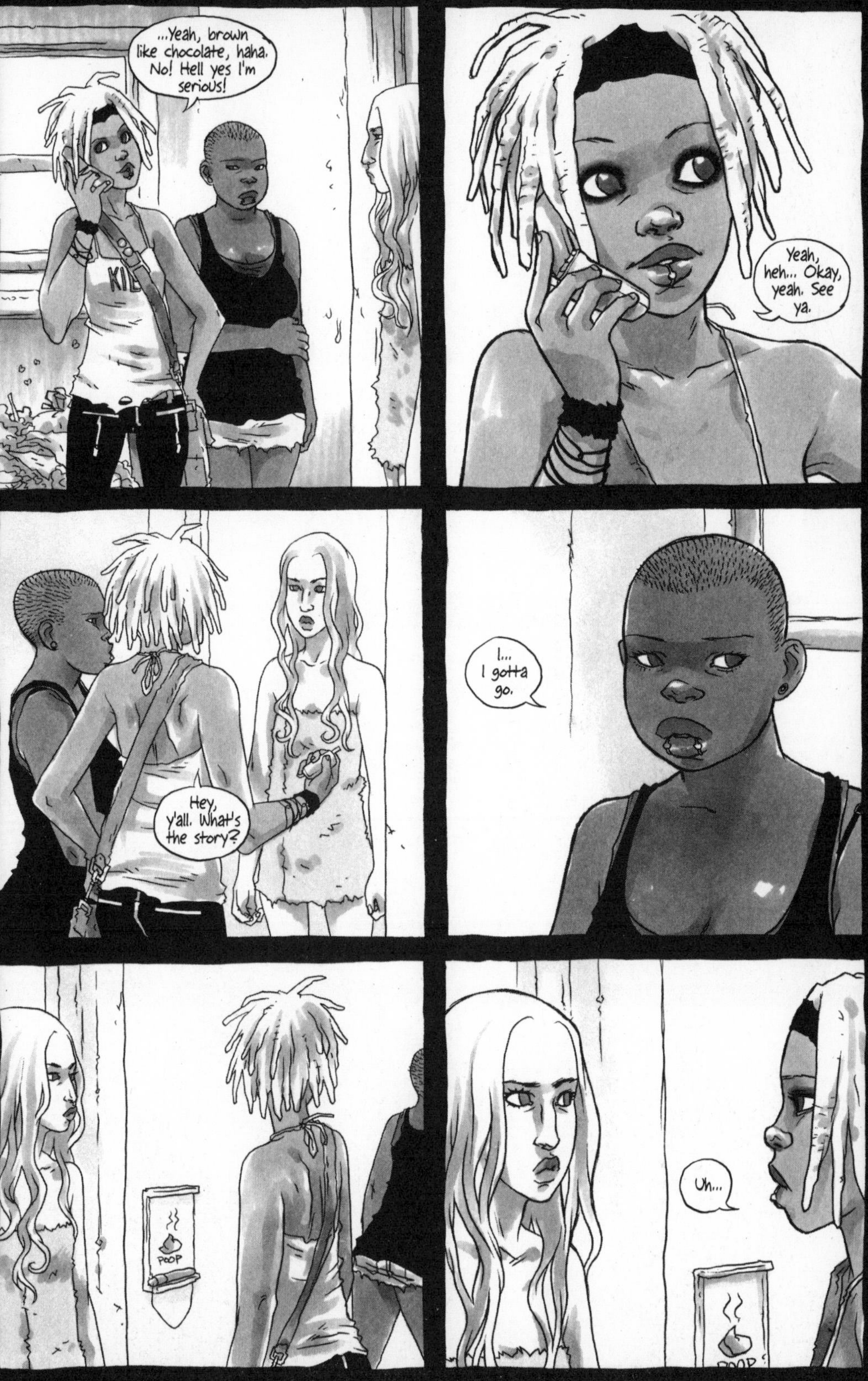

...Yeah, brown like chocolate, haha. No! Hell yes I'm serious!
Yeah, heh... Okay, yeah. See ya.
Hey, y'all. What's the story?
I... I gotta go.
POOP
Uh...

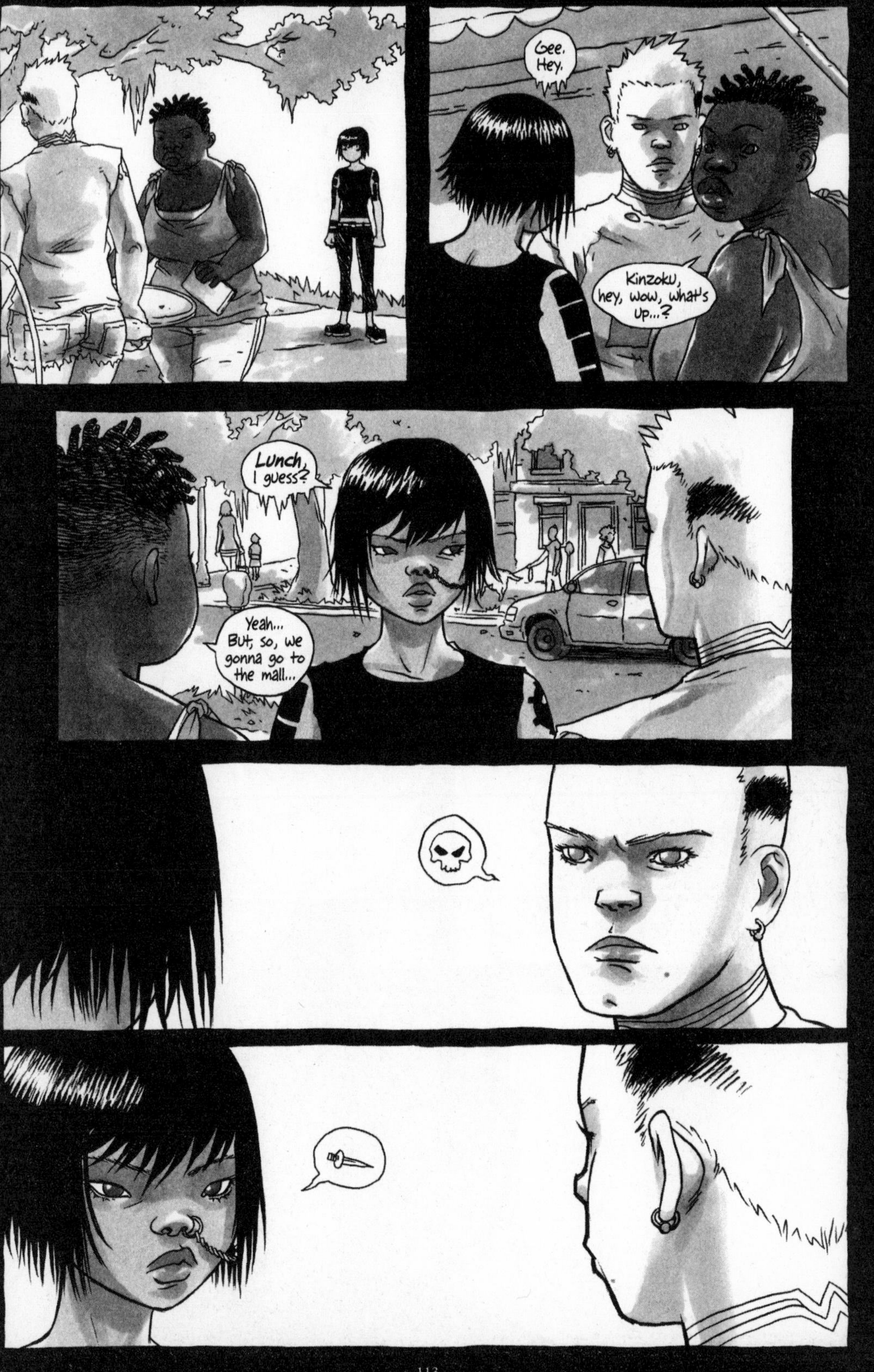
Gee. Hey.
Kinzoku, hey, wow, what's up...?
Lunch, I guess?
Yeah... But, so, we gonna go to the mall...

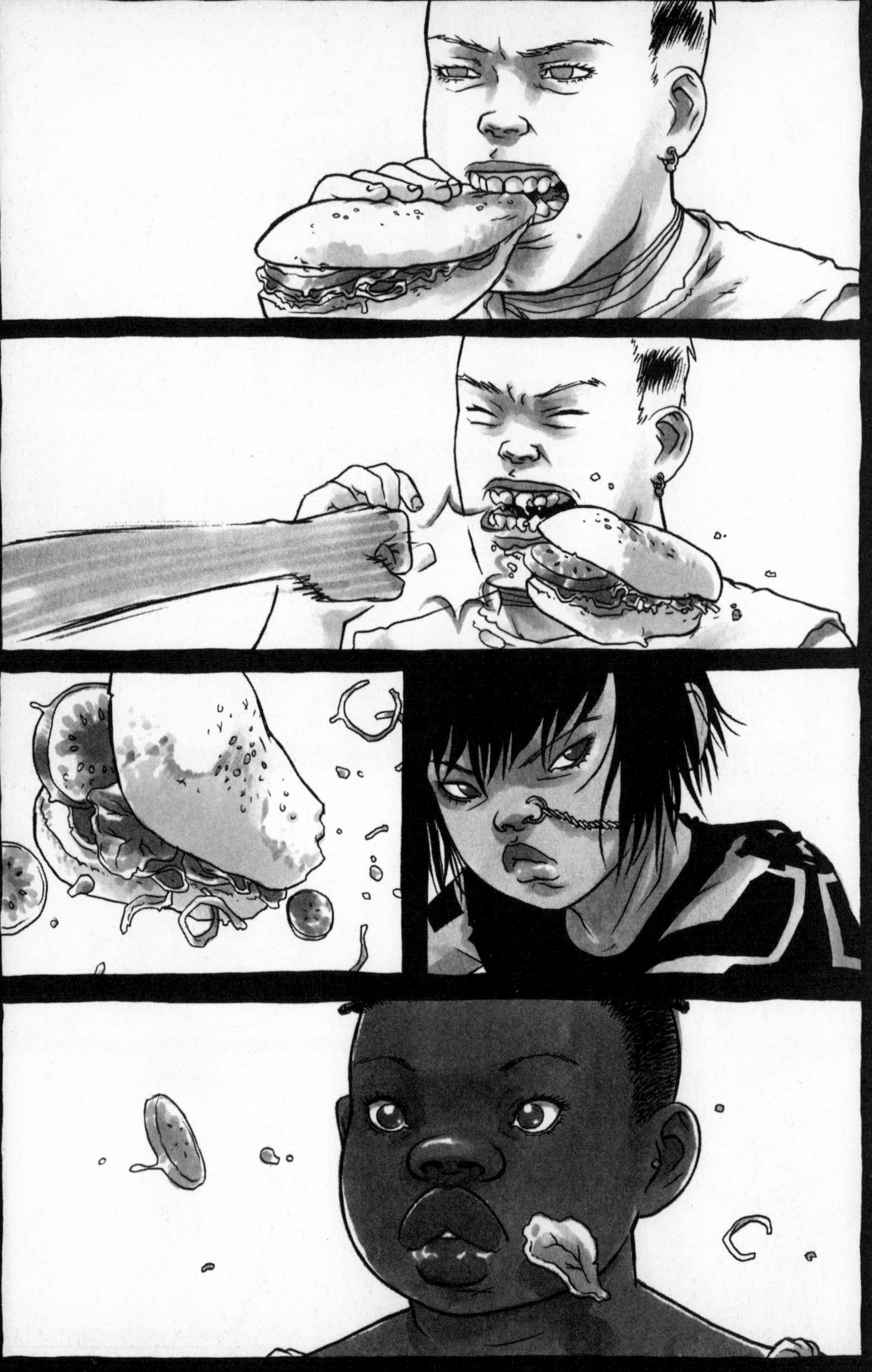

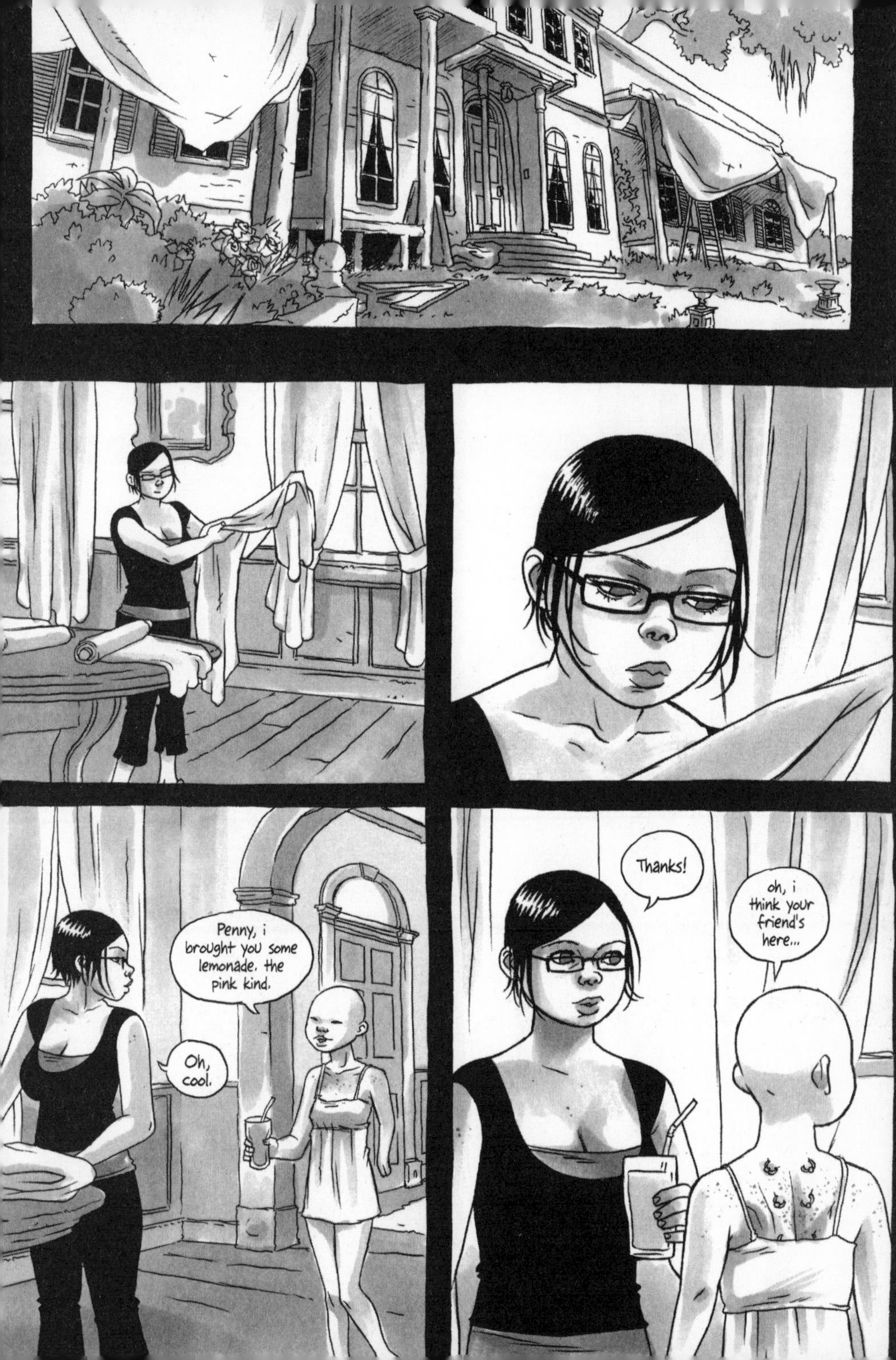
Penny, i brought you some lemonade. the pink kind.
Oh, cool.
Thanks!
oh, i think your friend's here...

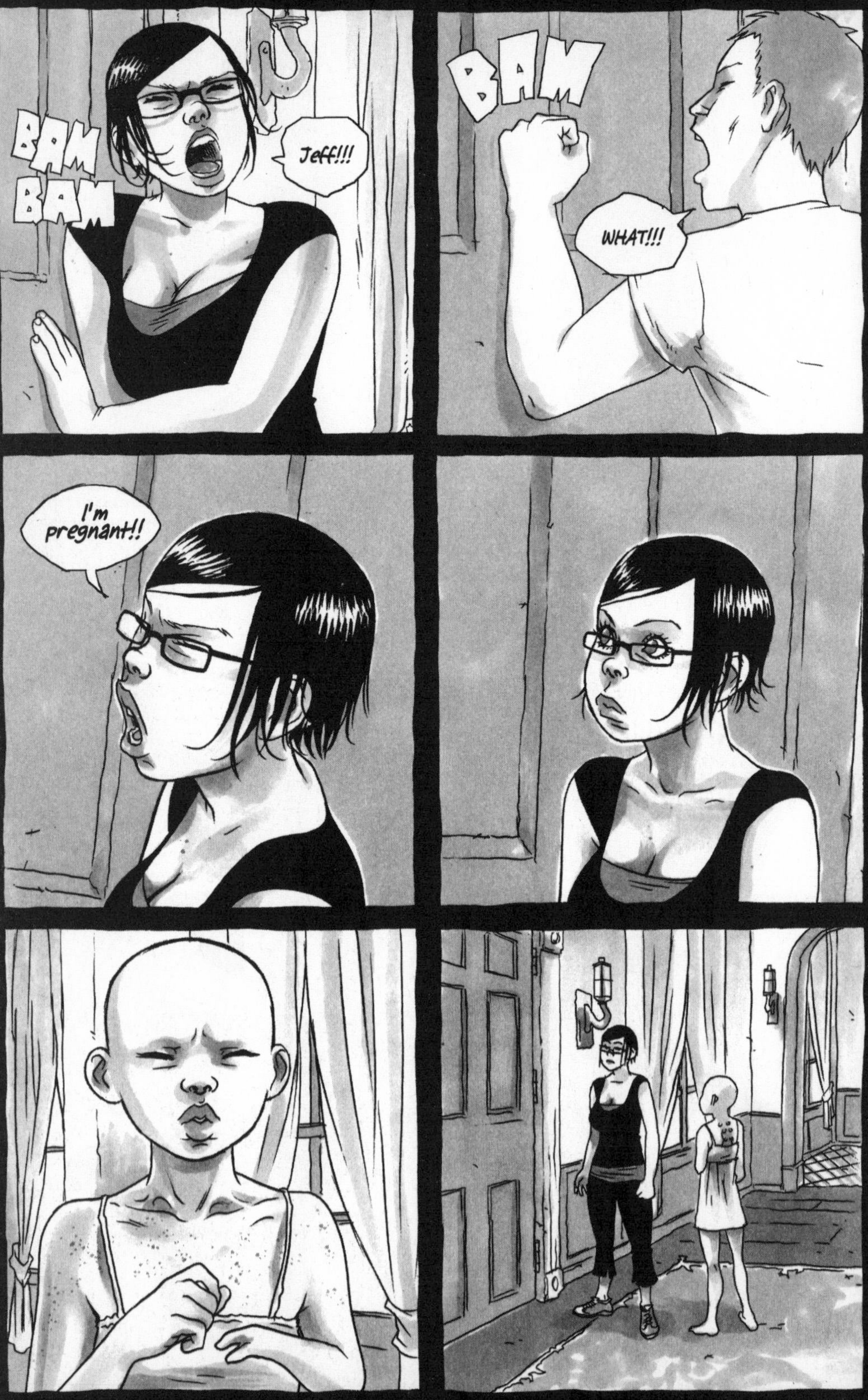
BAM BAM
Jeff!!!
BAM
WHAT!!!
I'm pregnant!!

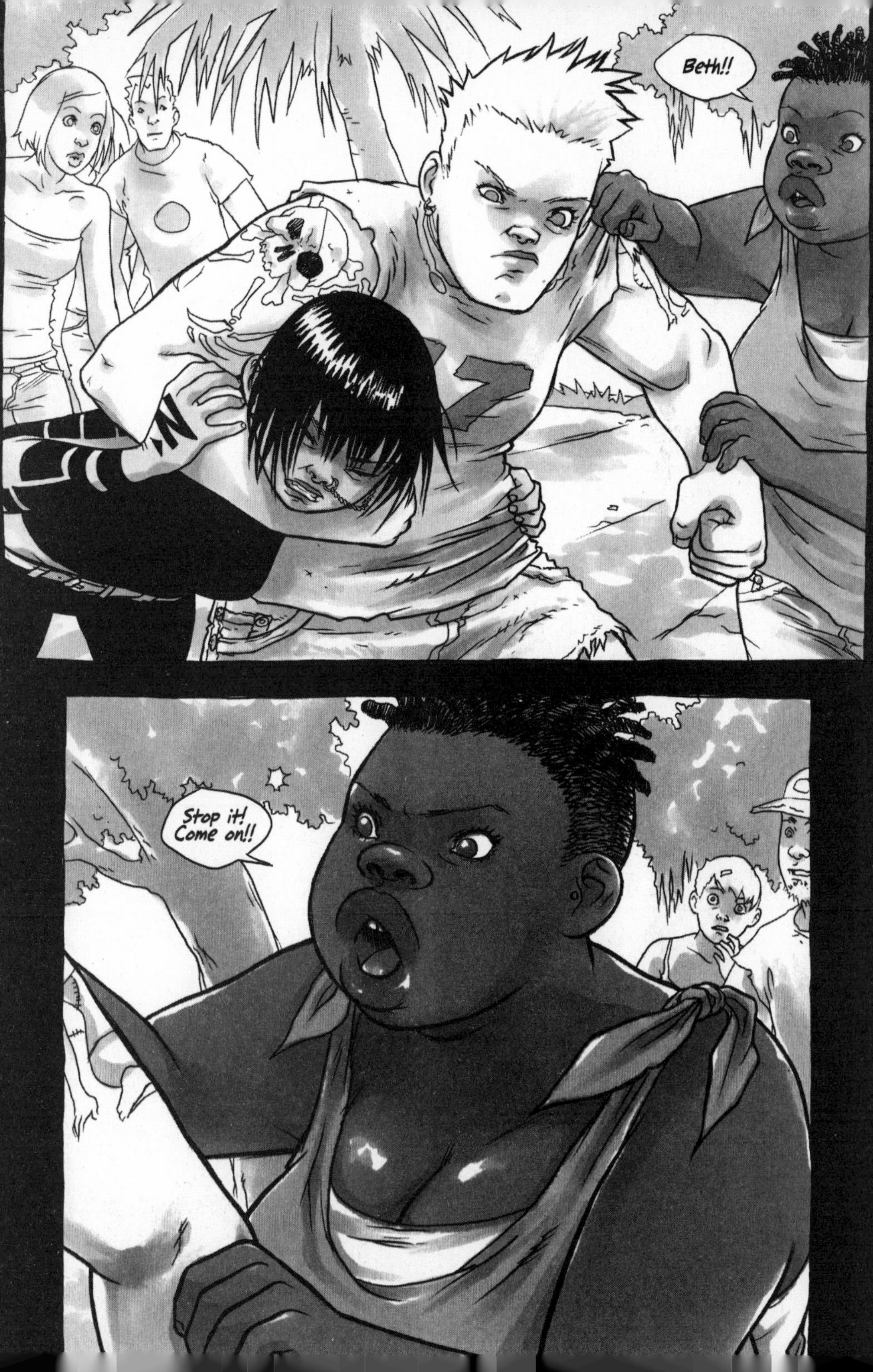
Beth!!
Stop it! Come on!!

14

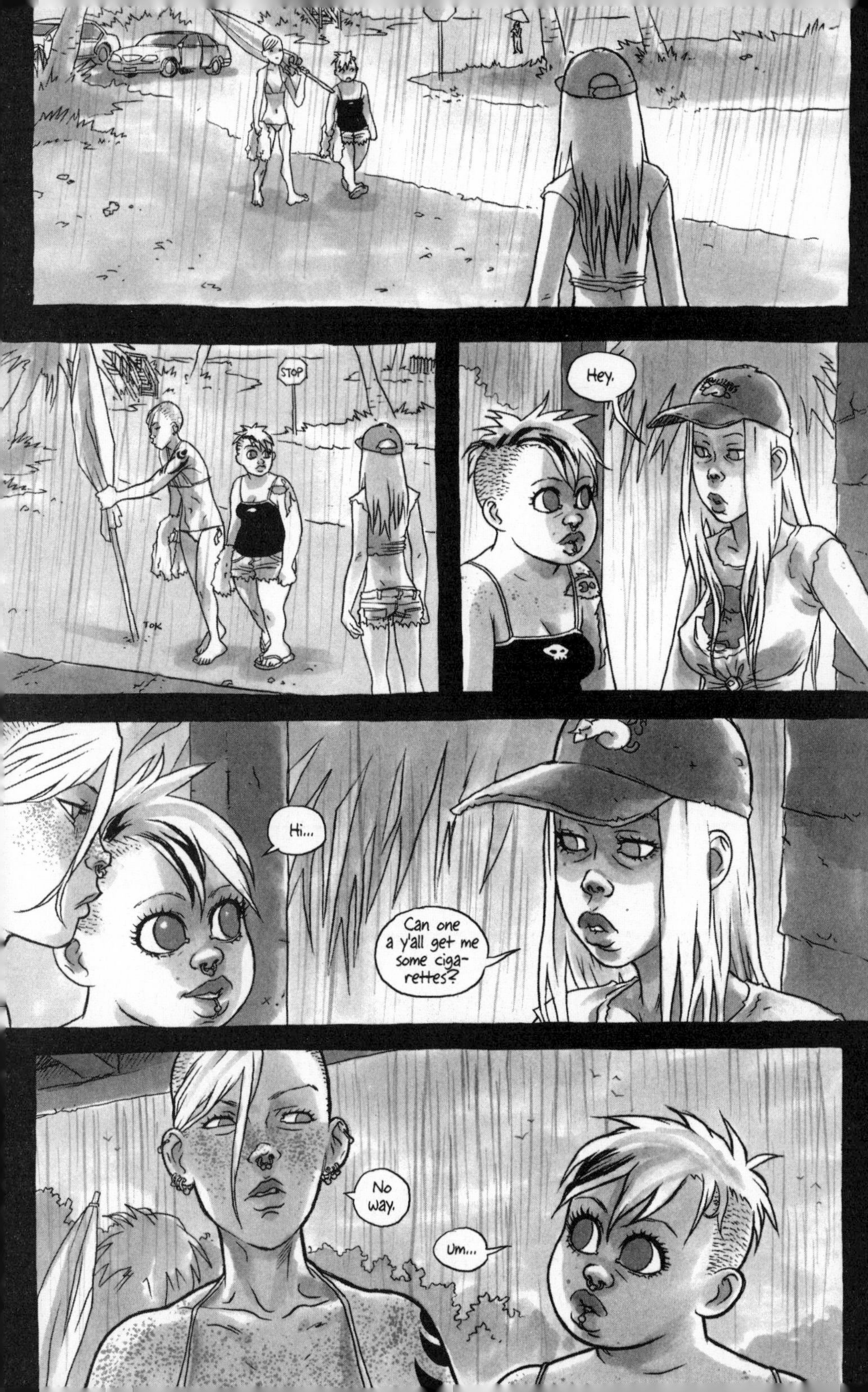
STOP
TOK
Hey.
Hi...
Can one a y'all get me some ciga-rettes?
No way.
Um...

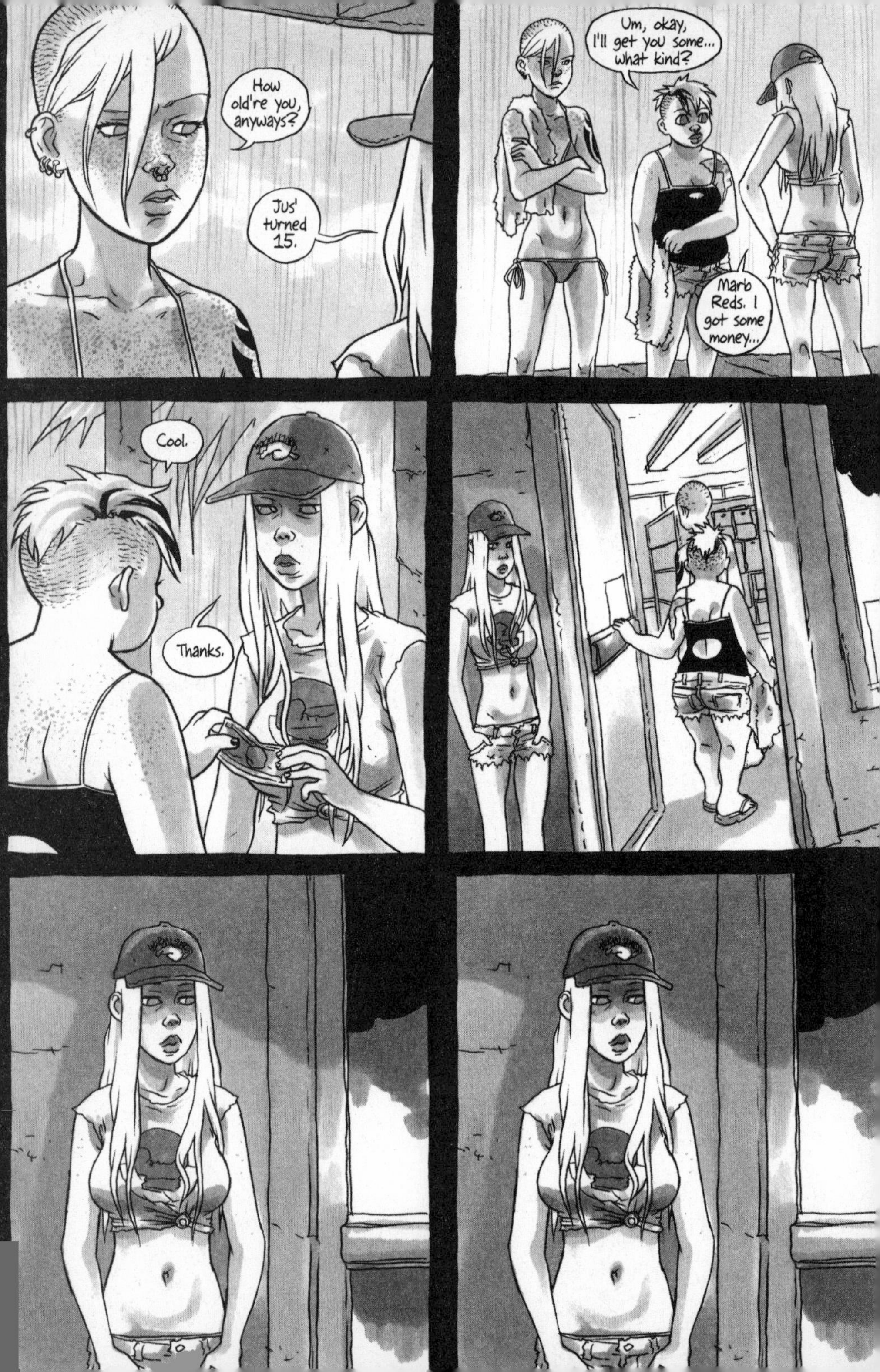
How old're you, anyways?
Jus' turned 15.
Um, okay, I'll get you some... what kind?
Marb Reds. I got some money...
Cool.
Thanks.

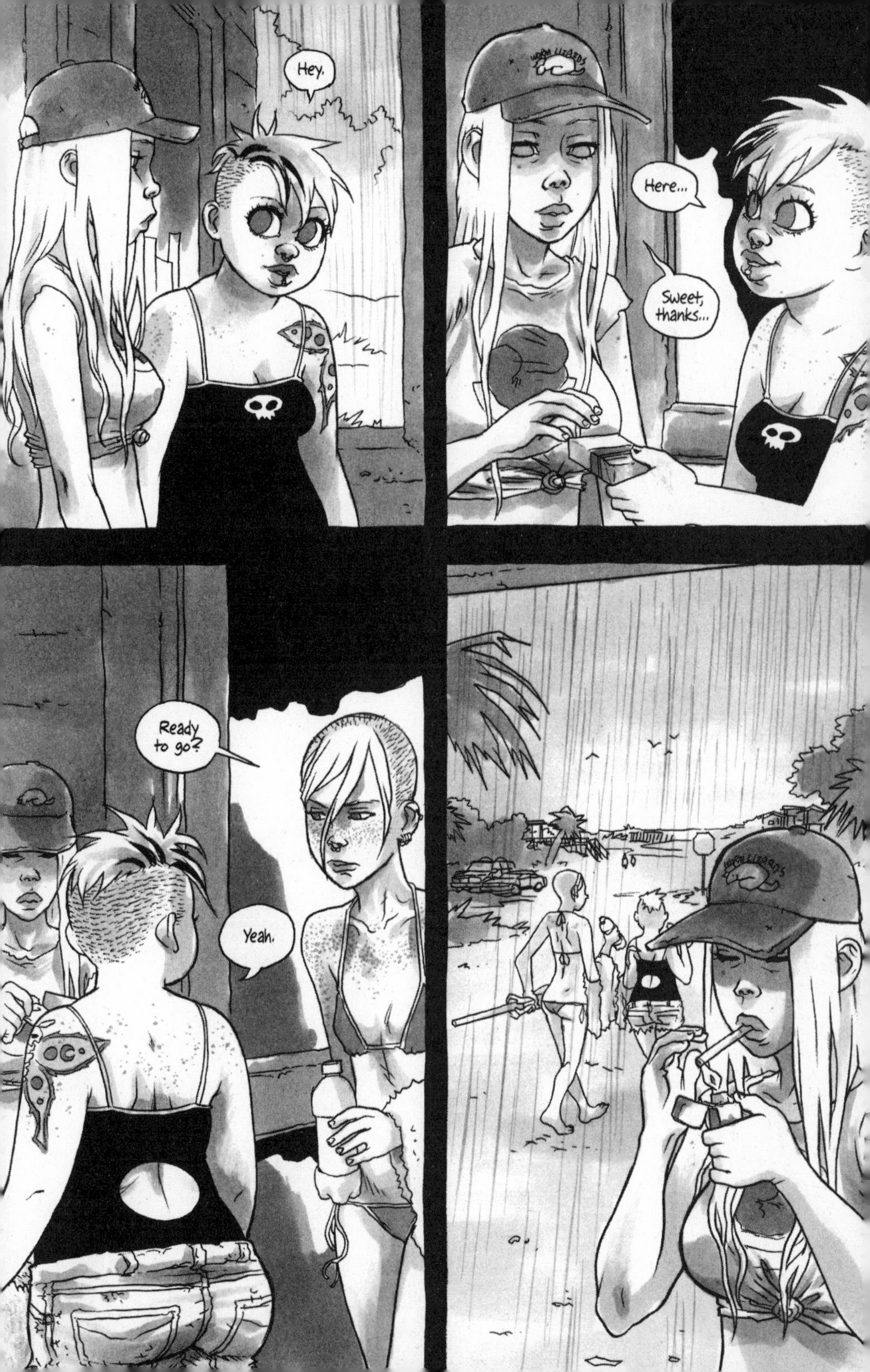
Hey.
Here...
Sweet, thanks...
Ready to go?
Yeah.

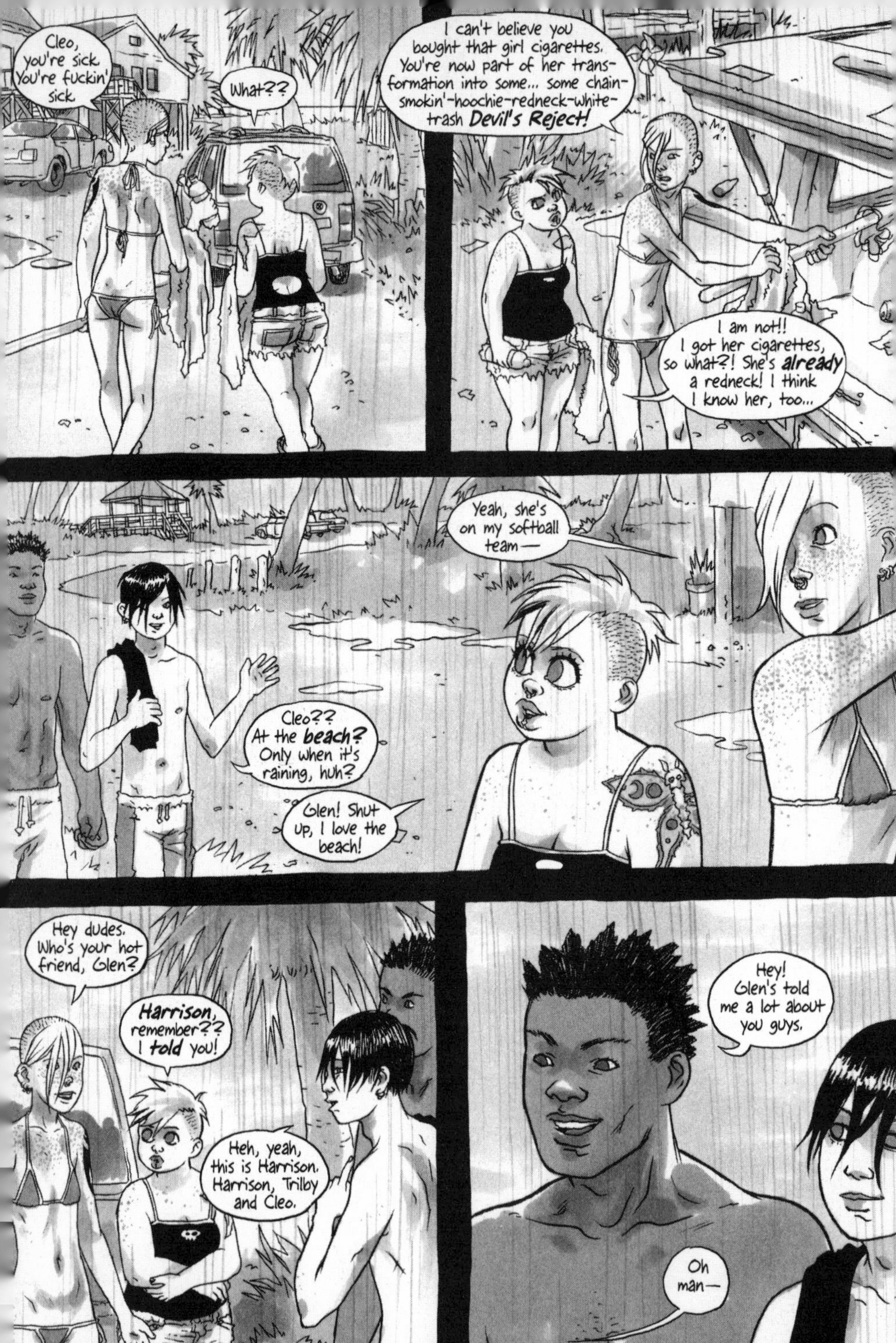
Cleo, you're sick. You're fuckin' sick.
What??
I can't believe you bought that girl cigarettes. You're now part of her transformation into some... some chain-smokin'-hoochie-redneck-white-trash **Devil's Reject!**
I am not!! I got her cigarettes, so what?! She's **already** a redneck! I think I know her, too...
Yeah, she's on my softball team—
Cleo?? At the **beach?** Only when it's raining, huh?
Glen! Shut up, I love the beach!
Hey dudes. Who's your hot friend, Glen?
Harrison, remember?? I **told** you!
Heh, yeah, this is Harrison. Harrison, Trilby and Cleo.
Hey! Glen's told me a lot about you guys.
Oh man—

129

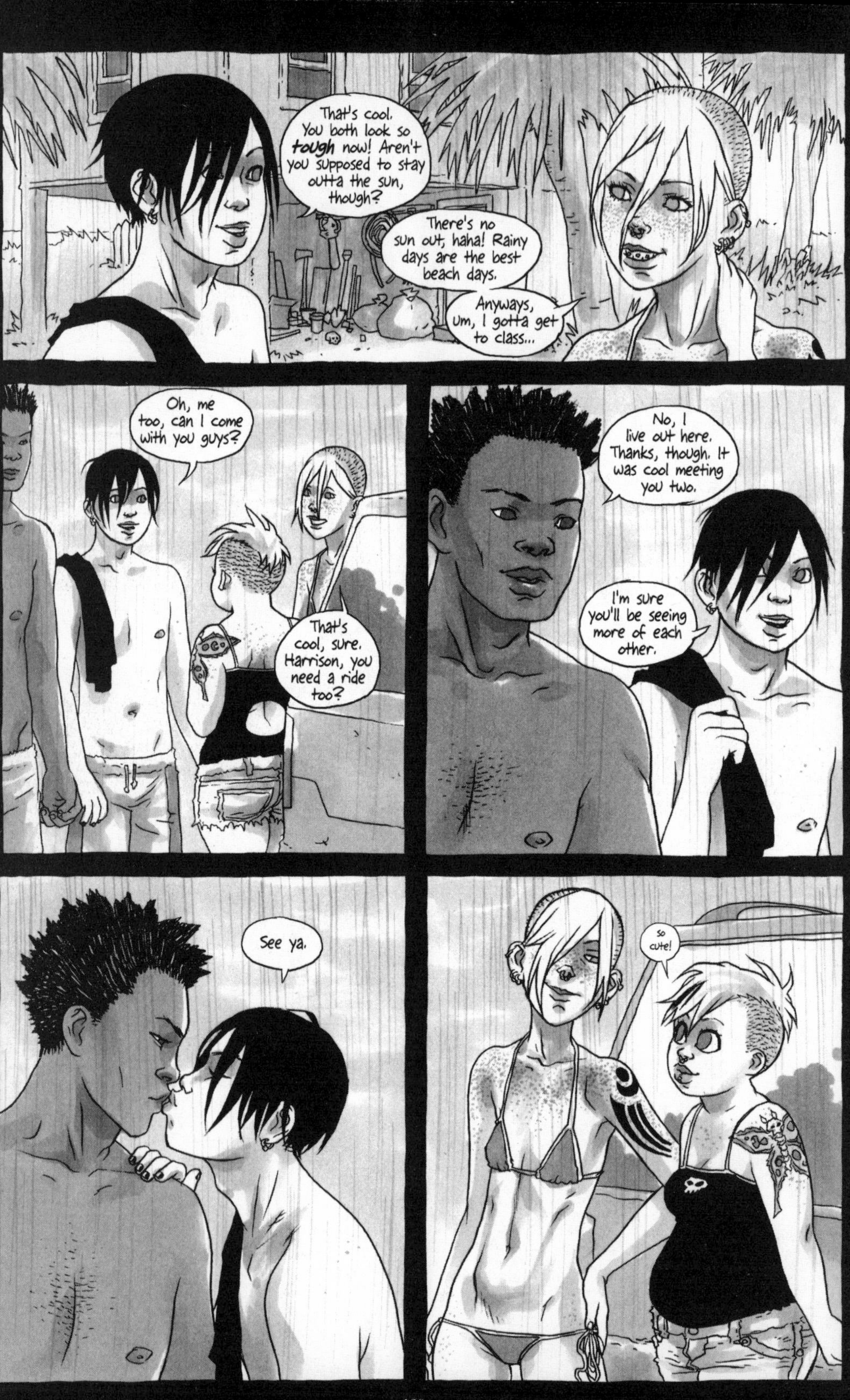
That's cool. You both look so **tough** now! Aren't you supposed to stay outta the sun, though?
There's no sun out, haha! Rainy days are the best beach days.
Anyways, um, I gotta get to class...
Oh, me too, can I come with you guys?
That's cool, sure. Harrison, you need a ride too?
No, I live out here. Thanks, though. It was cool meeting you two.
I'm sure you'll be seeing more of each other.
See ya.
so cute!

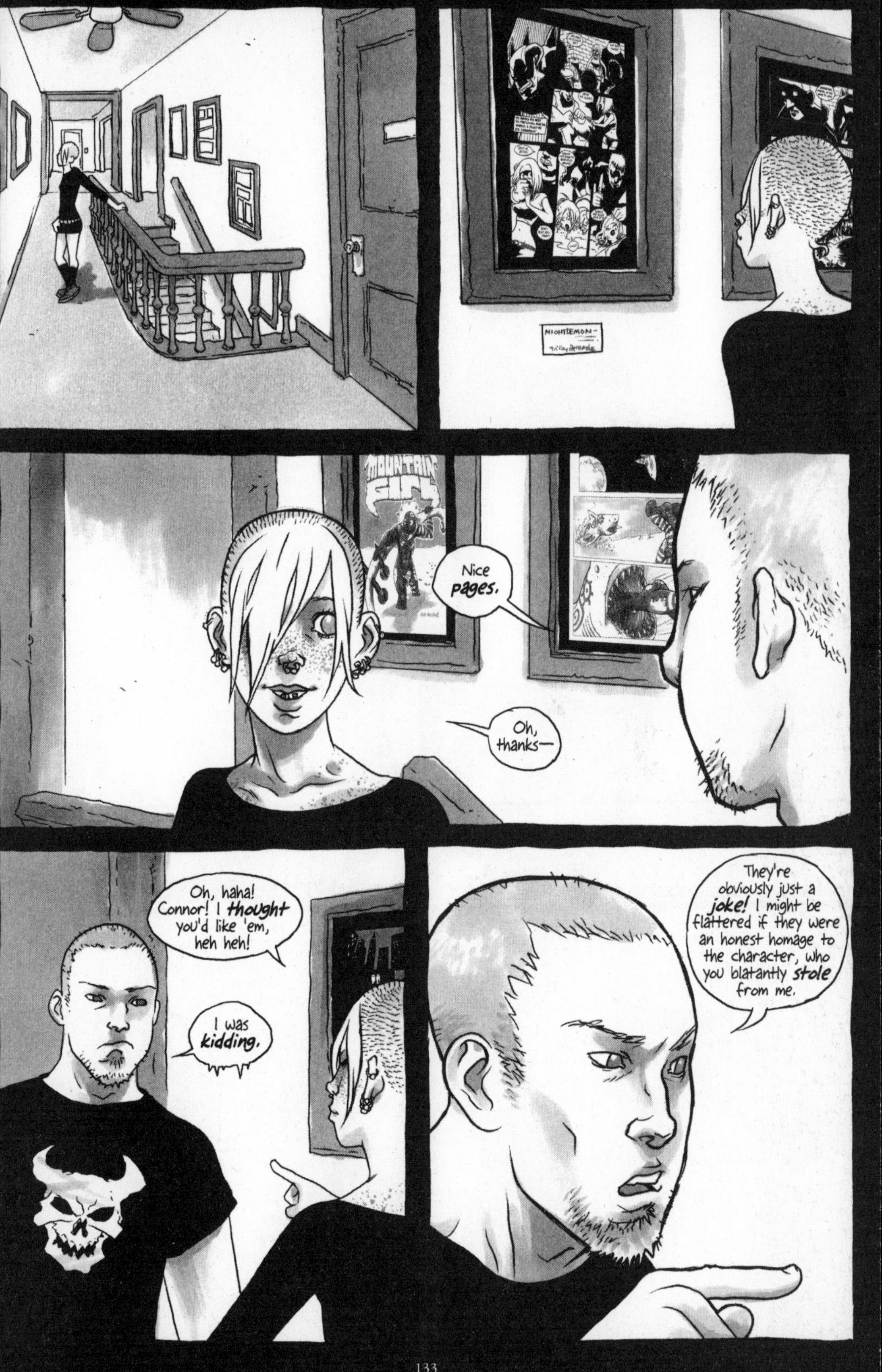
Nice pages.
Oh, thanks—
Oh, haha! Connor! I thought you'd like 'em, heh heh!
I was kidding.
They're obviously just a joke! I might be flattered if they were an honest homage to the character, who you blatantly stole from me.

PFt! I made him **cool**. What're you **doin'** here anyways? Go back to your **ILLUSTRATION** buddies 'fore you get pounded fuckin' Justice League style by a mob of Sequential nerds!

Ha! I'm gonna tell Bella Morte never to let you and your friend Chloe into one of their shows again! Especially after she fucked up the entire show the other night!

You're **blacklisted!**

Yeah right, douchebag! They're nice guys! I **KNOW** too nice to **blacklist** people! **'Specially** two hot girls!

An' that's **Cleo!** Not **Chloe!** It's short for **Cleopatra!** There's no **Chloepatra**, asshole!

Well, whatever her name is, I don't know.

You **should** know! You're the one who tried to put the moves on her with that stupid Nightdemon drawing she **HATED!**

Oh... she... she really didn't like it...?

Duh! Girls don't like demons or superheroes an' shit, stupid! You gotta draw their **portrait** if you wanna get in their pants!

But **you're** a girl, **you** like superheroes! You like **Star Trek**, too, I saw at the show you had a Borg tattoo!

Yeah, well, I meant like **real** girls or whatever— fuck, it's— it's not a **Borg** tattoo, okay?! It...

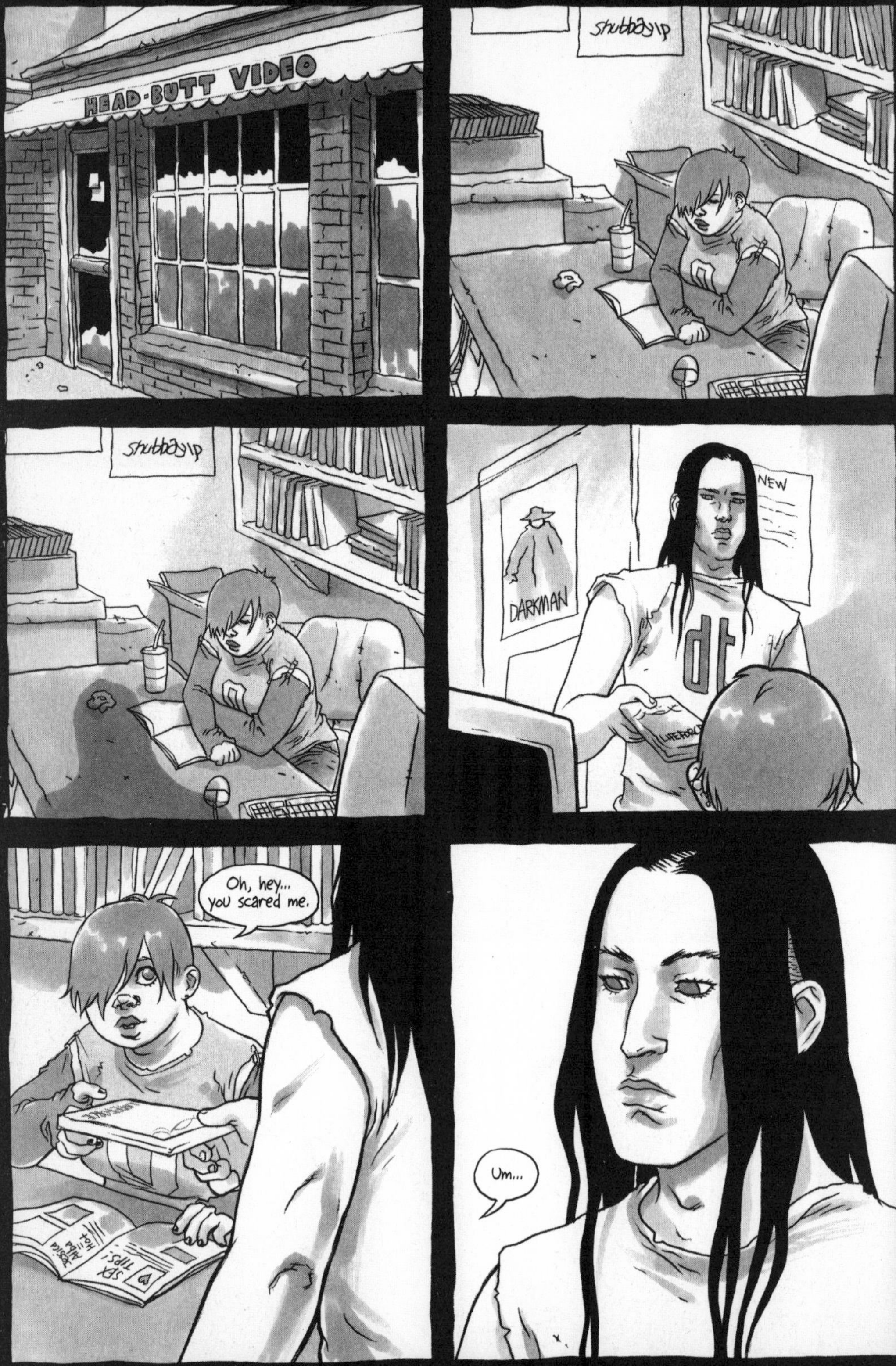
HEAD-BUTT VIDEO
NEW
DARKMAN
Oh, hey... you scared me.
SEX TIPS!
Um...

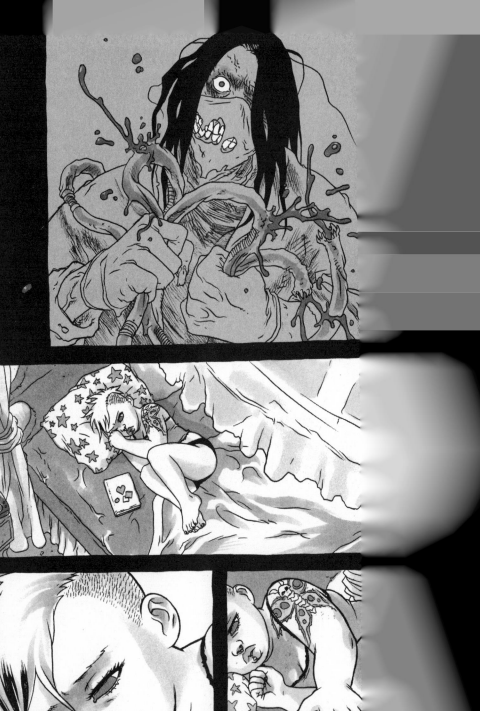

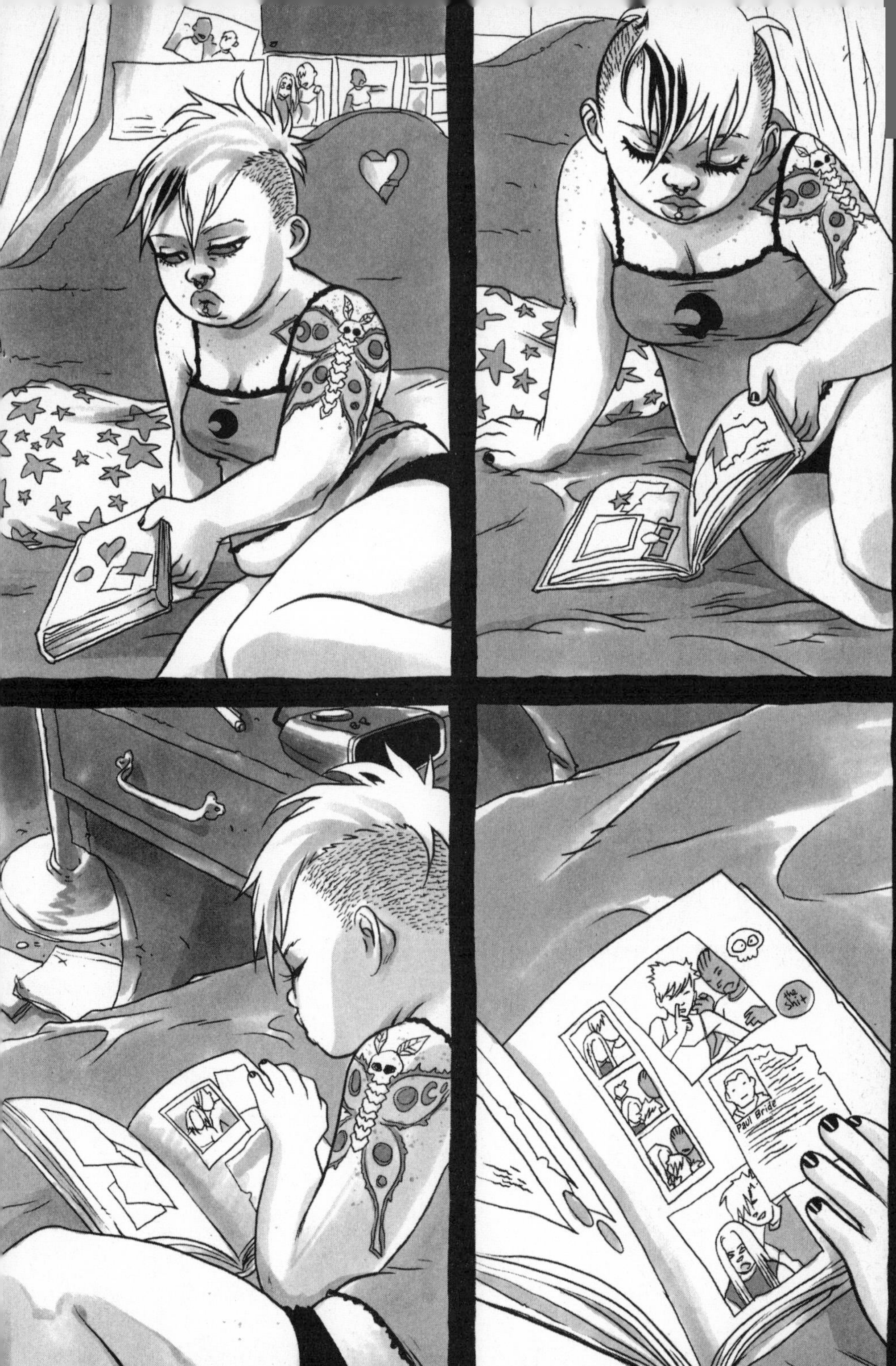
the shit
Paul Bride

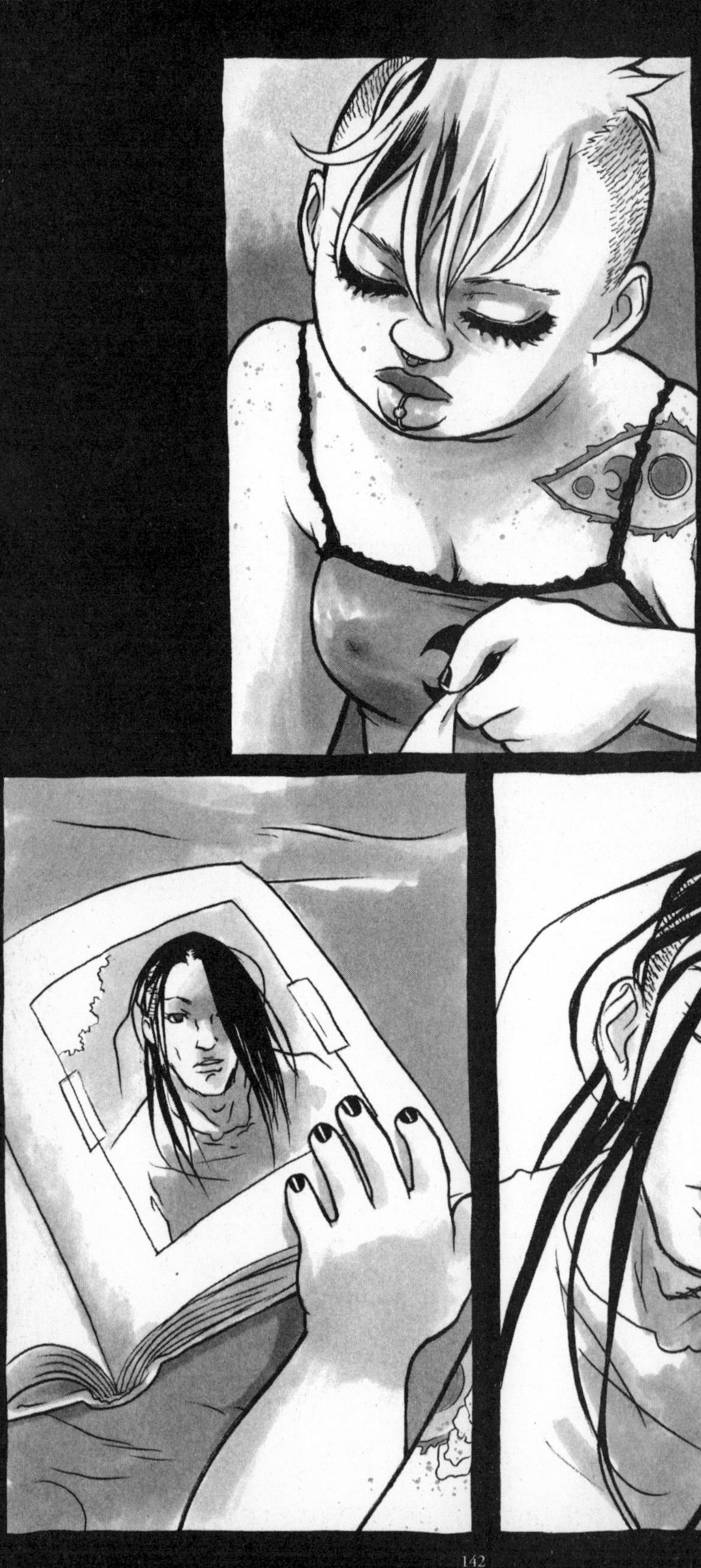

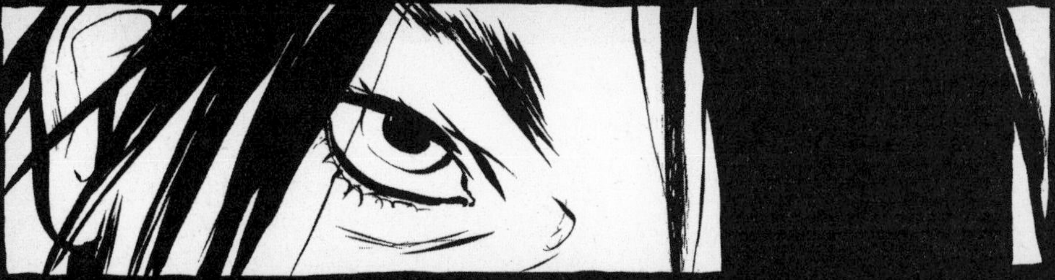

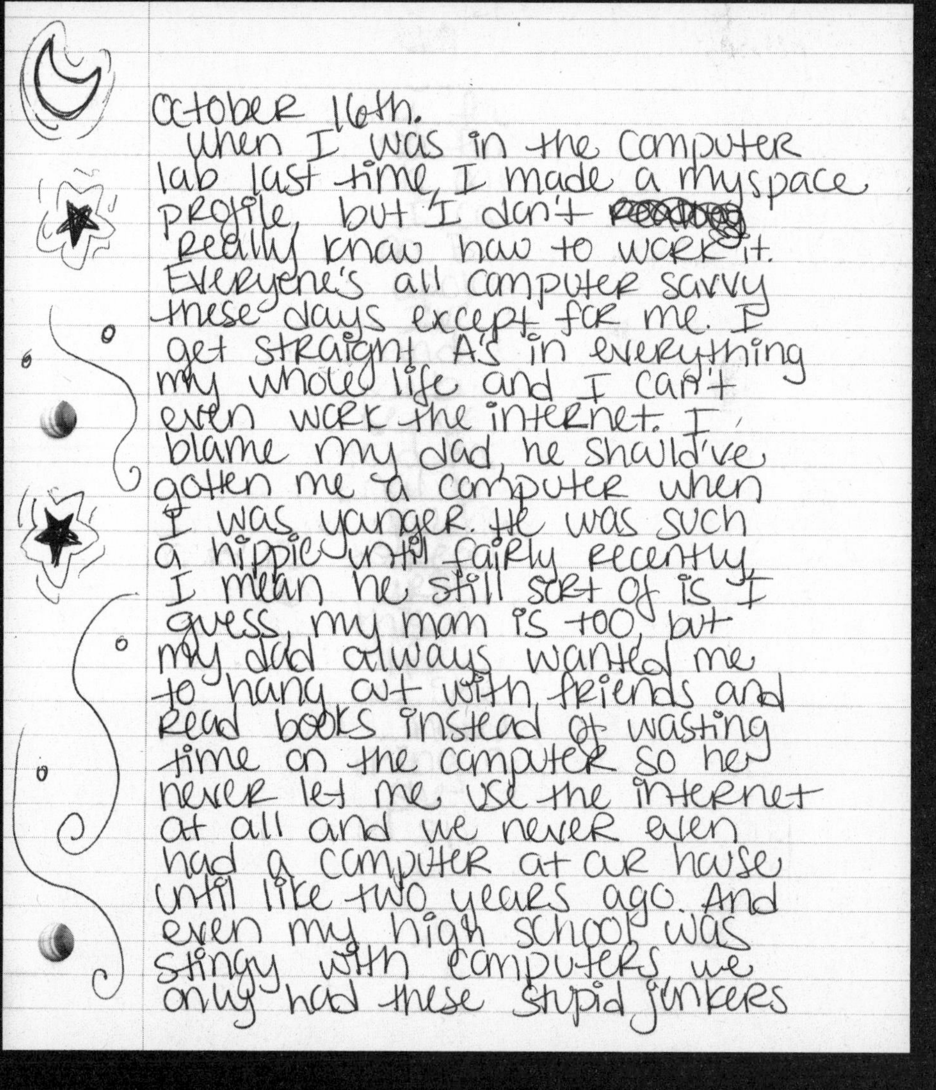

October 16th.
When I was in the computer lab last time, I made a myspace profile, but I don't really know how to work it. Everyone's all computer savvy these days except for me. I get straight A's in everything my whole life and I can't even work the internet. I blame my dad, he should've gotten me a computer when I was younger. He was such a hippie until fairly recently. I mean he still sort of is I guess, my mom is too, but my dad always wanted me to hang out with friends and read books instead of wasting time on the computer so he never let me use the internet at all and we never even had a computer at our house until like two years ago. And even my high school was stingy with computers we only had these stupid junkers

from the 70's or something. I'm so stunted. I'm probably the only person under 25 who ~~XXXXXXXX~~ doesn't know this shit. But I'm figuring it out really fast, so I'll be savvy in no time, too. I pretty much only made my profile so I could leave comments on Bella Morte's page and apologize for wrecking their show. I've left a cuple comments and even sent them a message but there's been no response yet...

Trilby told me Mara has a livejournal but it's "friends only" so you have to be on her list to read it! I wonder what she writes about... Probably ~~XXXX~~ all this amazing ~~XXXX~~ secret stuff that she doesn't tell anyone. She's such a private person. She hardly even tells me anything anymore. But I think if she knew I read her journal she'd stop writing in it.

I have so much fun with Myrtle. She reminds me of Tril sometimes, since she's sort of bouncy and fun like Trilby is, but in a different way. She makes a lot of jokes but they're not usually at the expense of others and her sense of humor is really different. She also has this darkness to her that I can't put my finger on, but I like it. Even though she seems happy and smiley most of the time, she has a slight sadness to her. I don't want her to be sad, but when I see her show this under-the-surface sadness, it makes me smile. I smile when I think about it, too. I'm not sure if that's bad, since I suppose it's me smiling about somebody being sad, ~~and that's~~ and that's mean, but I don't think it's like that... It's not really a happy smile. I guess even though I am happy when she's around and everything, but it's just that I like that aspect of her and I think it's cute. It makes me want to hug her or something, and then me hugging her because of the

subtle sadness and I also can't help but smile about that.

I'm taking Myrtle home on Friday to have a late breakfast (brunch?) with dad and Penny. I'm half scared and half excited. I hope Phyllis doesn't act crazy. I hope my dad doesn't tell horrible stories about me, but I know he will so I'm prepared for the worst. I don't know if this is one of those times where your significant other meets your family and it's a big deal. things with Myrtle are strange. Actually I think I'm more excited than scared.

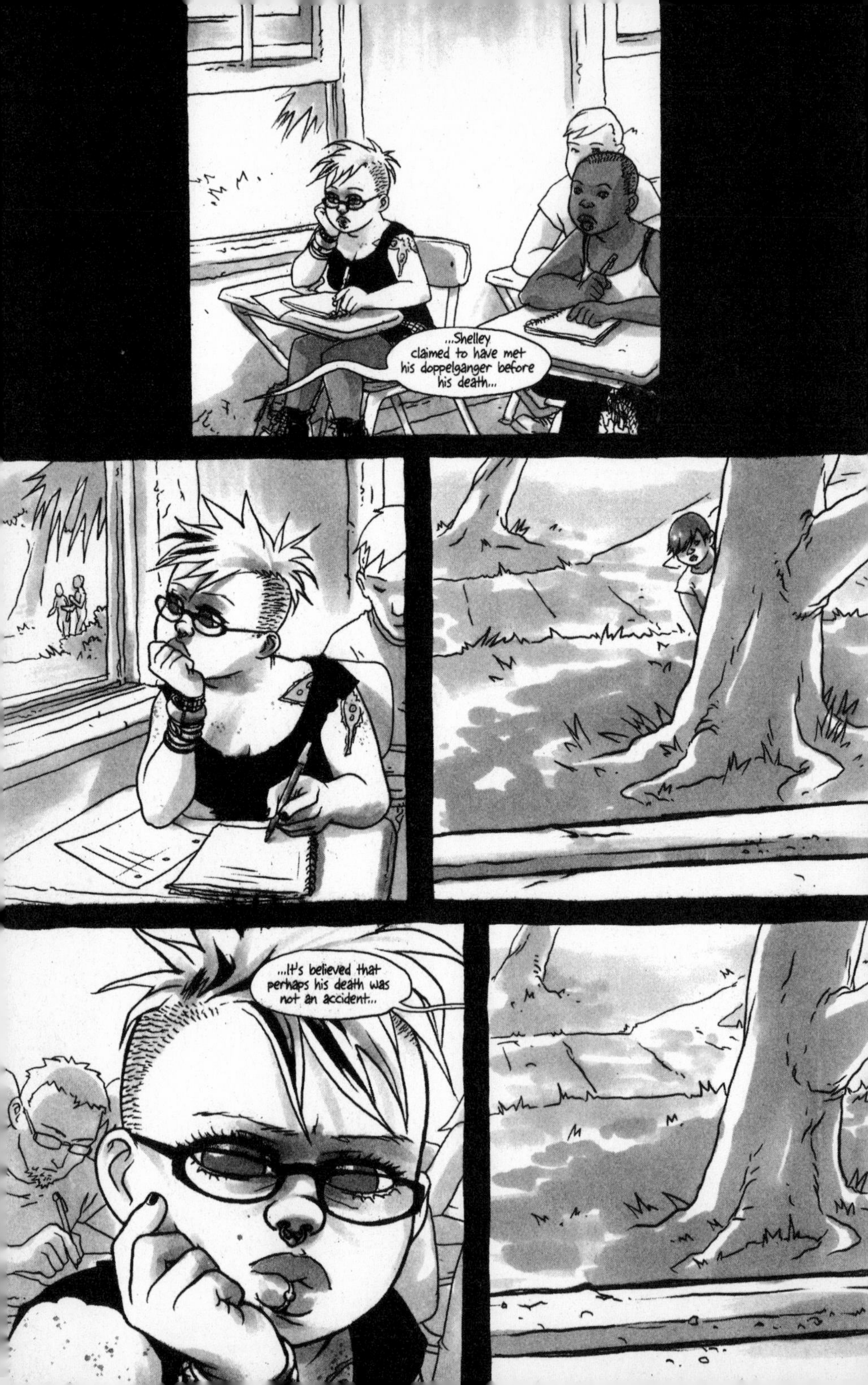
...Shelley
claimed to have met
his doppelganger before
his death...
...It's believed that
perhaps his death was
not an accident...

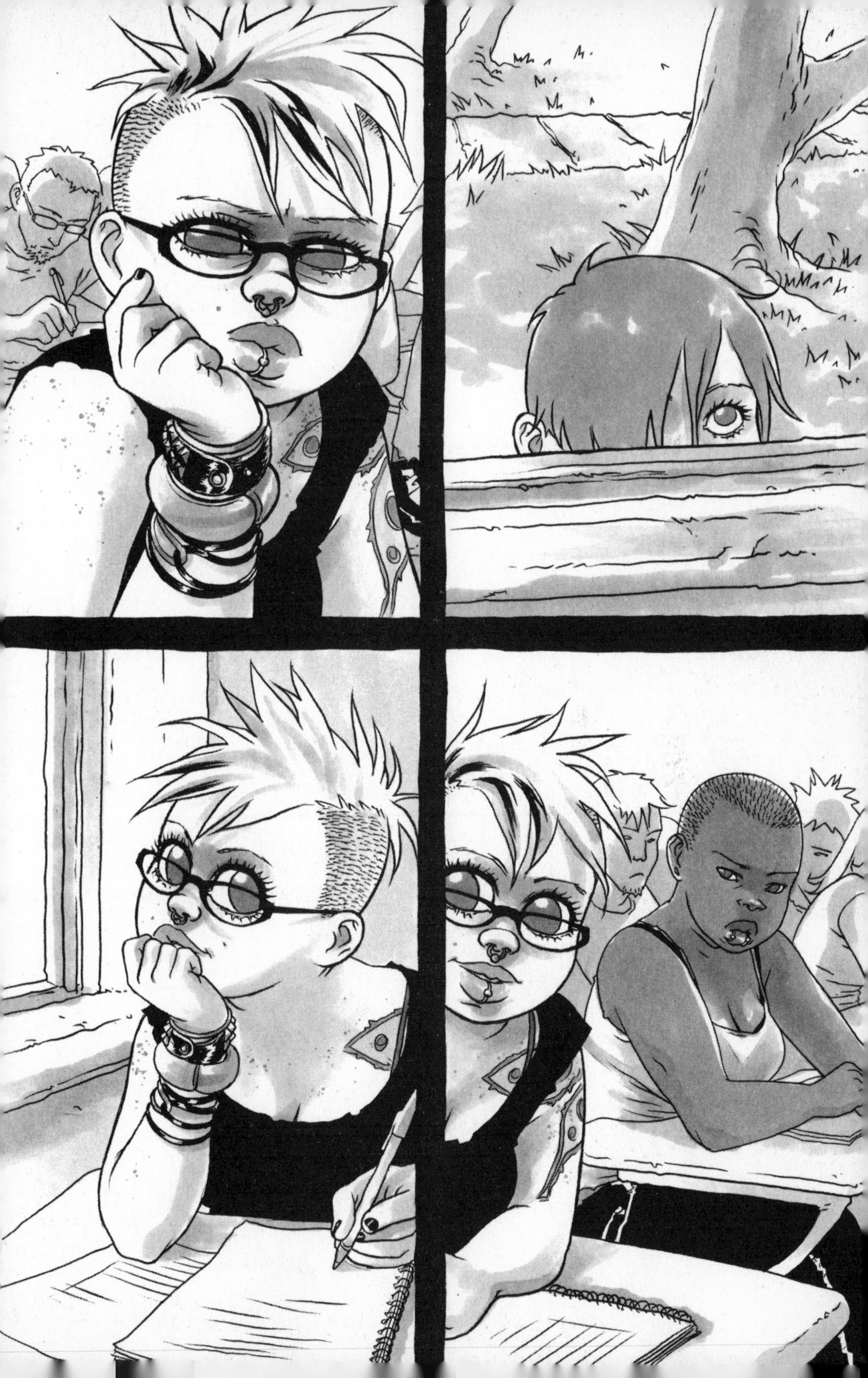

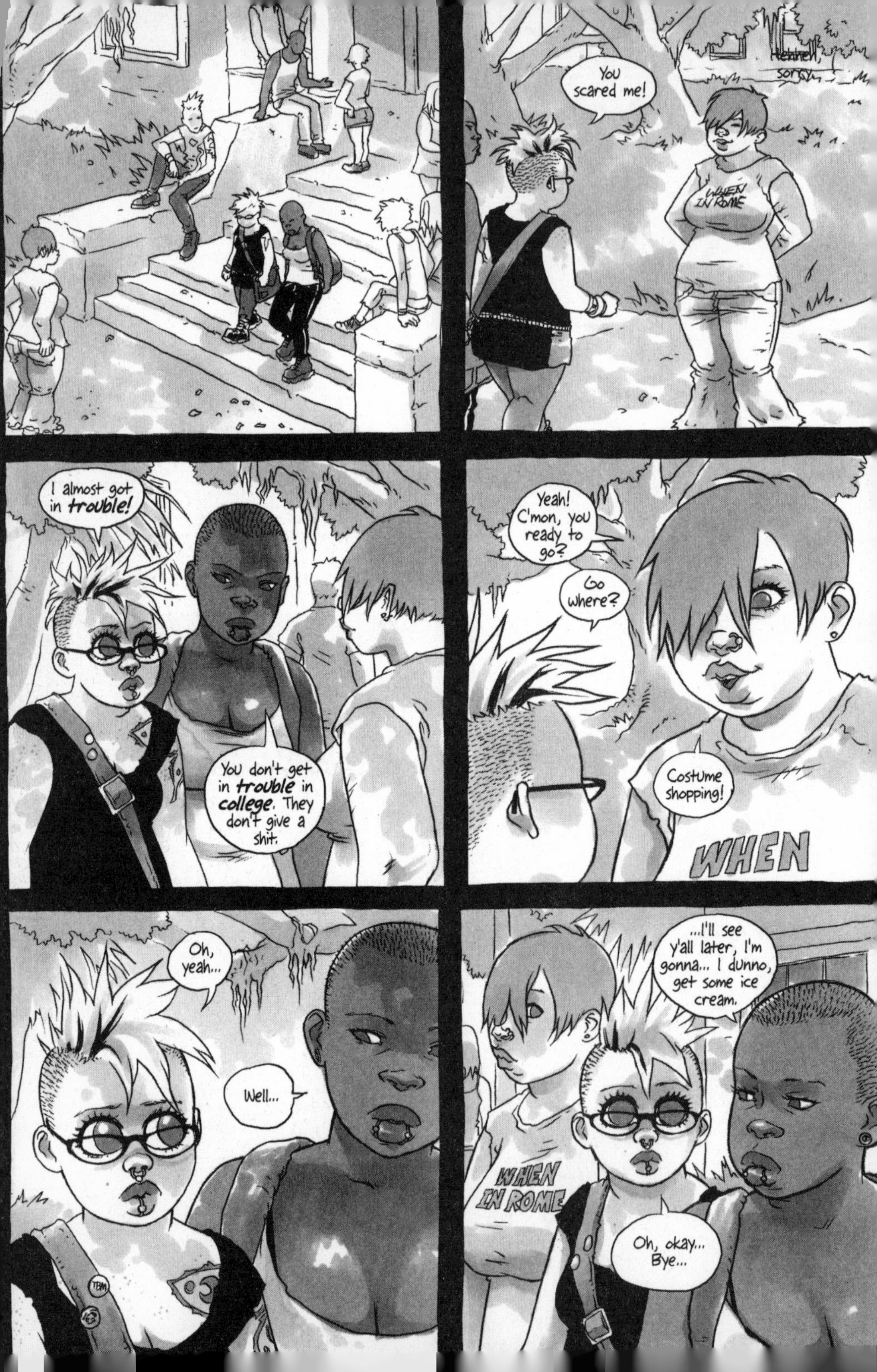
Hehheh, sorry.
You scared me!
I almost got in trouble!
You don't get in trouble in college. They don't give a shit.
Yeah! C'mon, you ready to go?
Go where?
Costume shopping!
WHEN
Oh, yeah...
Well...
...I'll see y'all later, I'm gonna... I dunno, get some ice cream.
WHEN IN ROME
Oh, okay... Bye...

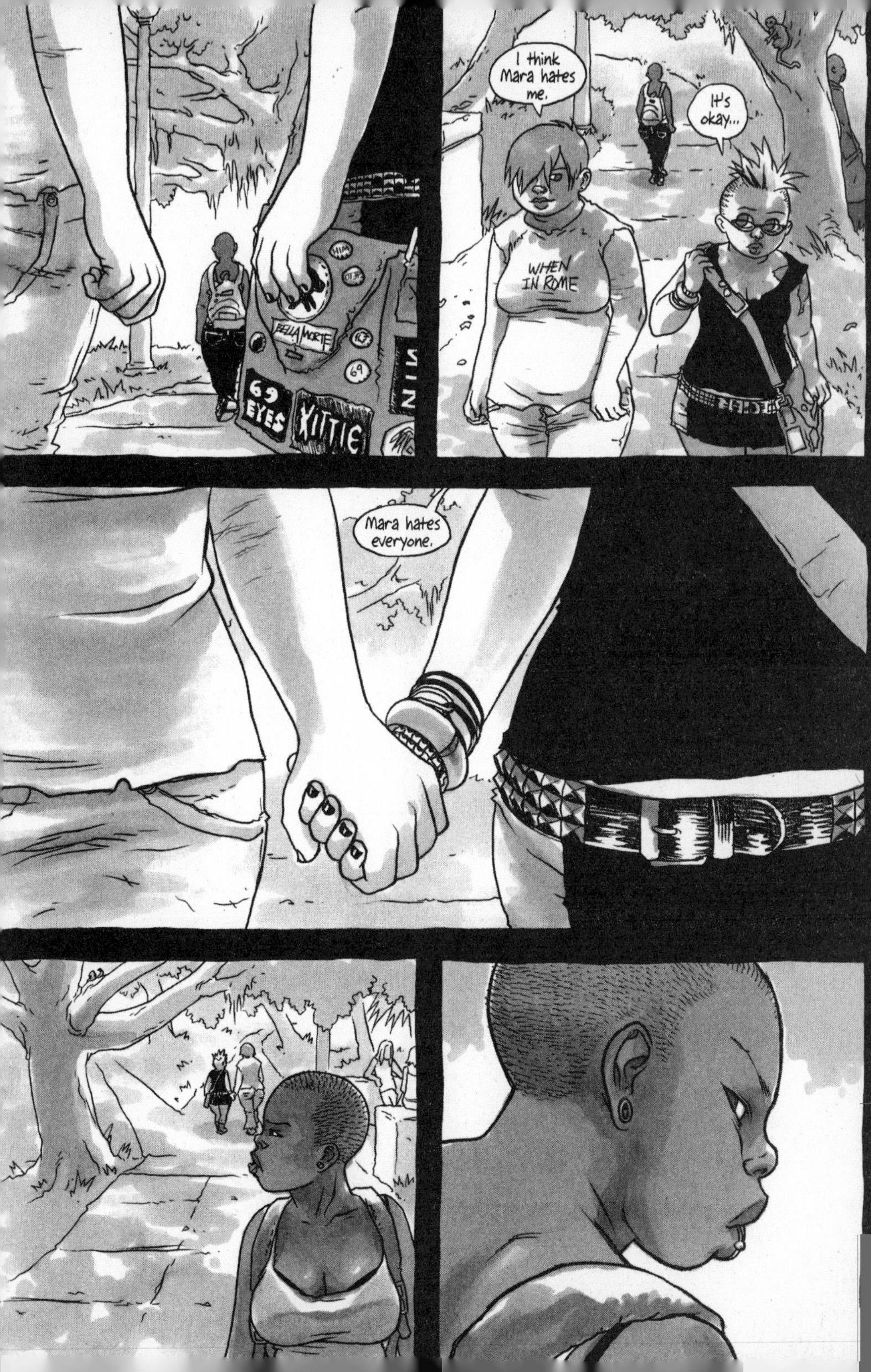

BELLA MORTE
69 EYES
I think Mara hates me.
It's okay...
WHEN IN ROME
Mara hates everyone.

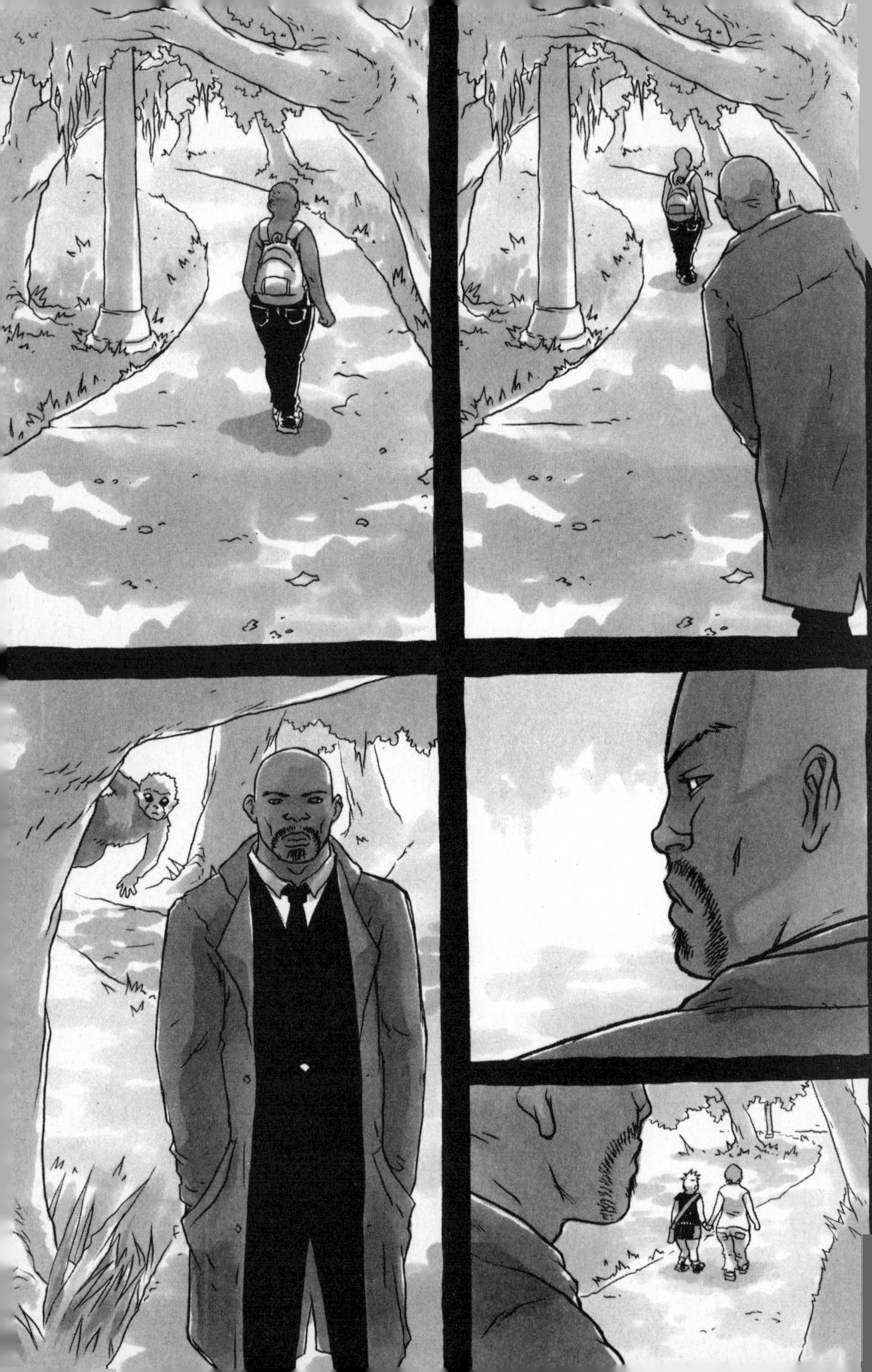

15

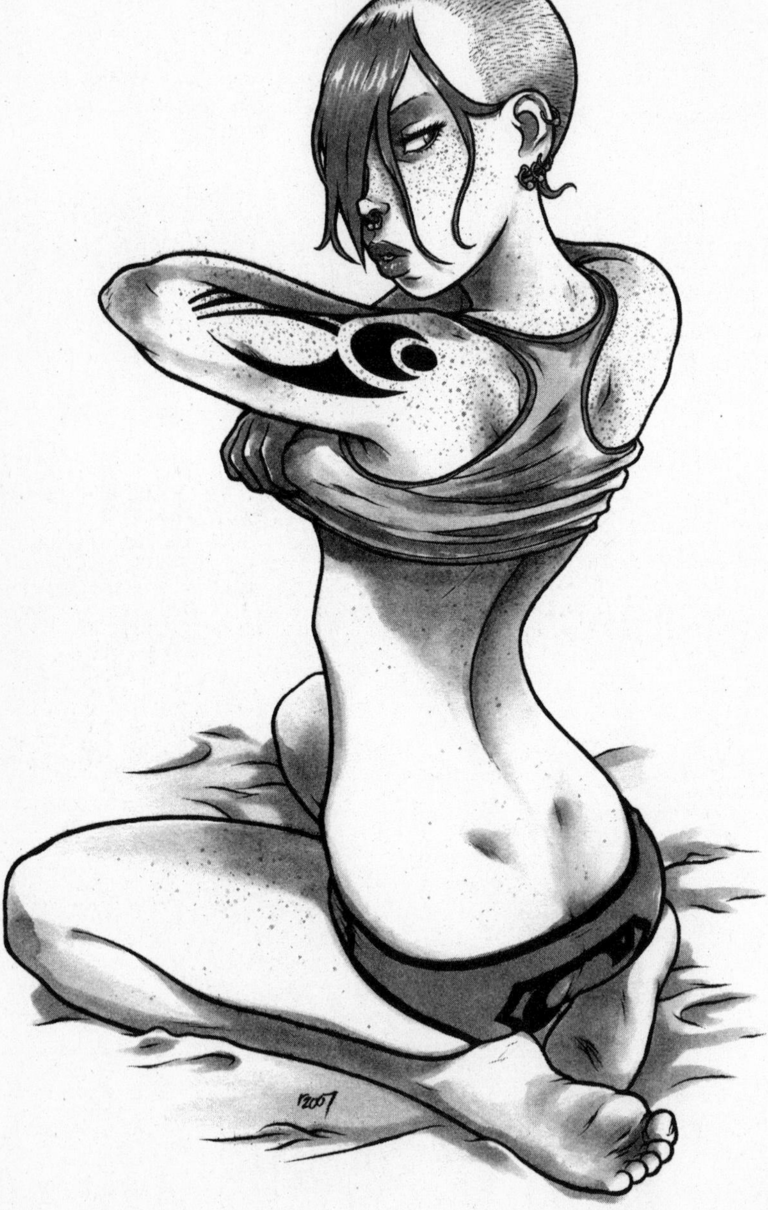

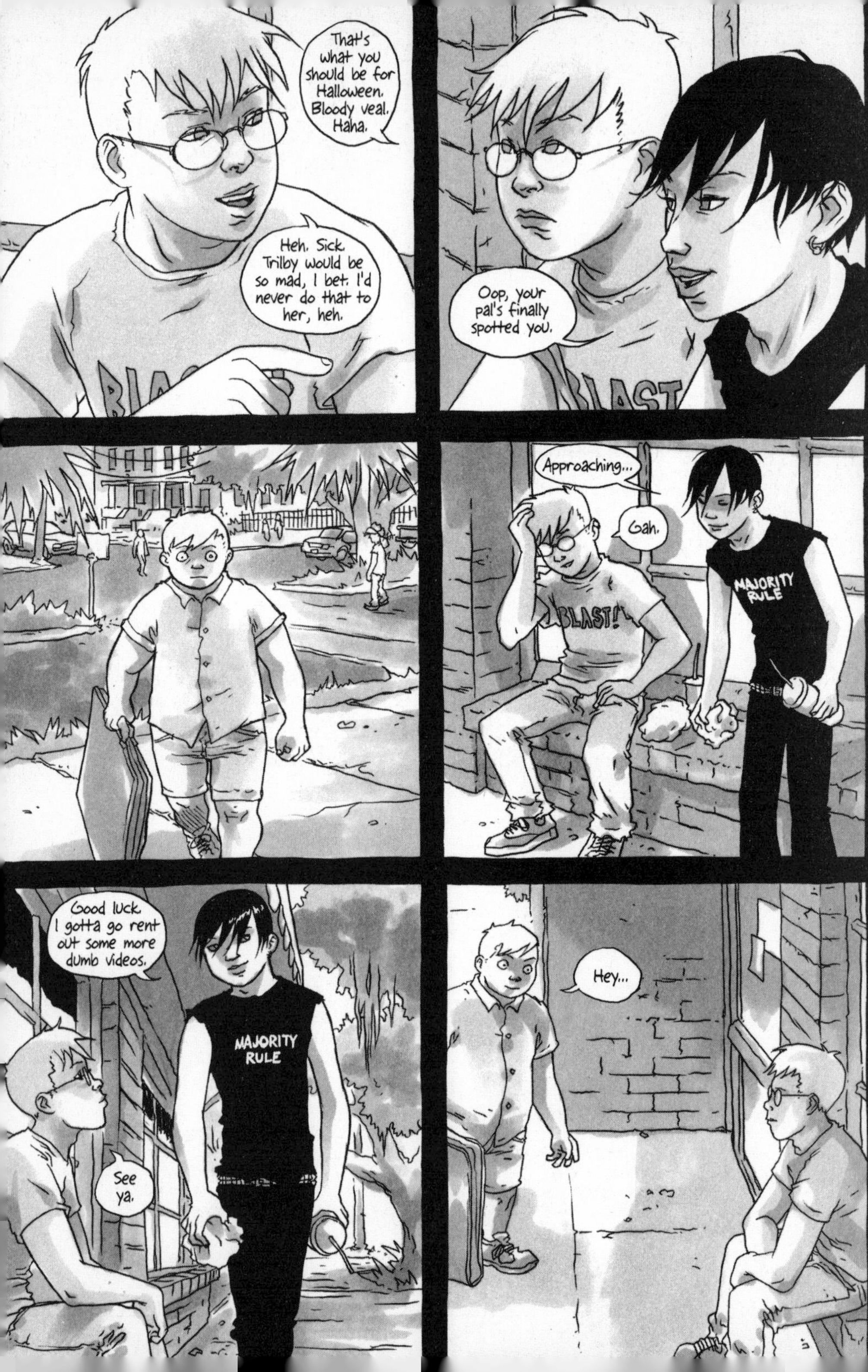
That's what you should be for Halloween. Bloody veal. Haha.
Heh. Sick. Trilby would be so mad, I bet. I'd never do that to her, heh.
BLAST
Oop, your pal's finally spotted you.
BLAST
Approaching...
Gah.
BLAST!
MAJORITY RULE
Good luck. I gotta go rent out some more dumb videos.
MAJORITY RULE
See ya.
Hey...

The Wonders At Your Feet

[friendtoroaches@gmail.com]

Recent Entries Archive Friends User Info

mara's journal

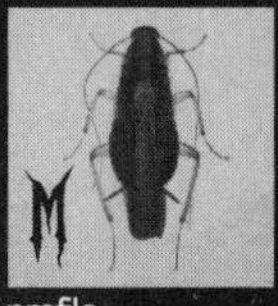
M

profile

October 16th, 3:47pm

THIS RIVER BANK HOLDS SECRETS

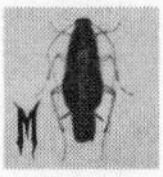
M

today i got up around 2pm, that's a good start. Cleo is seeing this girl Myrtle, i've mentioned her before. i didn't really think about it at first but i'm pretty much positive now that it's a romantic thing between them. Myrtle actually came up to the window in our European Romanticism class to bug Cleo. who does that? then after that i saw them holding hands. i guess it's cool. i think i'm going to start playing softball again. i walked past the field today and i got all nostalgic and remembering when i used to play. me and Trilby both played and i know Trilby still does so that might be weird with her on the team too. but i know i should really do this, i'm going to tryouts next week. i used to hit some killer home runs. it'll be great to be playing for the Wet Moon Worm Lizards again. maybe this means i'll have to stop smoking.

Trilby being with Martin, Cleo with Myrtle and Audrey with Beth sort of half makes me want to be with someone too, like this subconscious, passive peer pressure. nobody's actively trying to get me to do anything, but it's this presence that's still there. i like being the one single girl though, there's something appealing about it. when all my friends are off with their significant others i'm pretty much left alone, and while i sort of know my roomate Claire i don't really have anyone else to hang out with but i kind of like that, being forced to be by myself and entertain myself. it gives me a lot of time to do things i'd never normally do or read things i wouldn't normally think of to read. there's something also really cool about going out to eat by yourself. either in a restaurant or the dining hall. or even getting takeout alone is cool. i can't imagine myself dating anyone right now anyway, i can't imagine how anyone could really pull me out of this. everyone always rubs me the wrong way or i piss them off and everything goes down the shitter so i might as well keep to myself for now.

mood: nostalgic
current music: thismeansyou - river

[0 comments | leave a comment]

October 13th, 11:32pm

INTRUDER ALERT

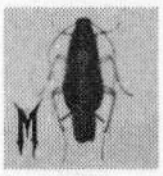
M

i slept all day. i got up and it was past 10 o'clock. i haven't done that in a long time, i used to sleep this late during summer vacation in high school sometimes, but hardly ever anymore. it's a real weird feeling, i can't explain it... it's like you missed something but you don't know what it is and you never will, and you know that you never will, too, so you can't worry about it. and there's something weird but great about after you get up this ridculously late, you take a shower like it's a normal morning. it's both uncomfortable and satisfying at the same time. that's what i just did. i took out a lot of my piercings too, it seemed like the right thing to do, i was getting sick of them... sometimes lately i feel like i don't know who i am anymore. i know that sounds totally lame and emo or whatever, but it's true and i can't lie about it. it seems like once college started, or maybe over the summer after senior year of high school, that everybody started to change real quick except for me. when i think about it, i guess Cleo and Trilby and Audrey are all basically the same, but it doesn't feel like it.

Cleo's been changing a lot in the past few years, so it wasn't a big jump for her, but now i feel like she's all popular or something which is why she's never home. but it's not like she's meeting all these new people, she still hangs out with Trilby,

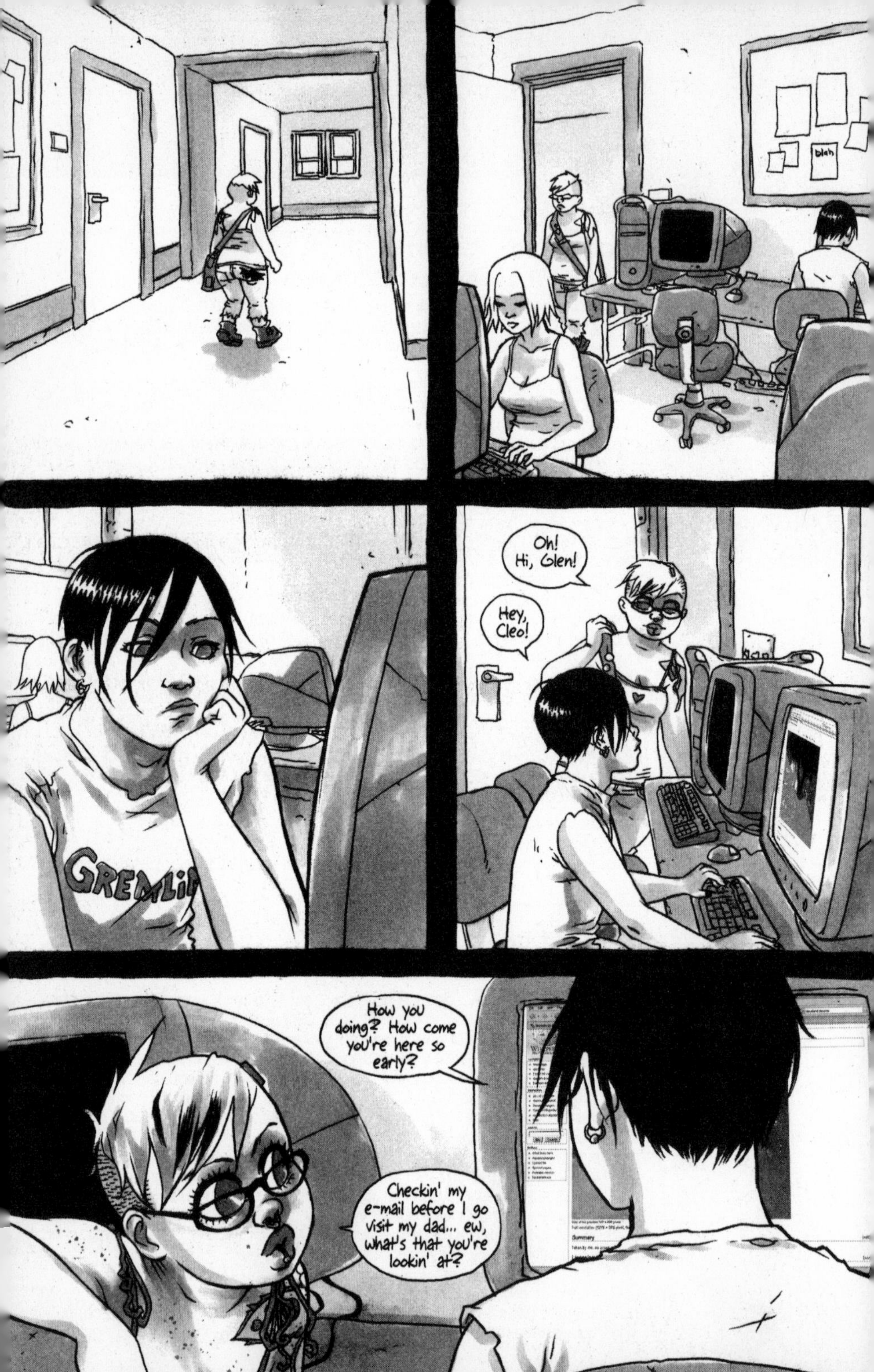

blah
Oh! Hi, Glen!
Hey, Cleo!
How you doing? How come you're here so early?
Checkin' my e-mail before I go visit my dad... ew, what's that you're lookin' at?

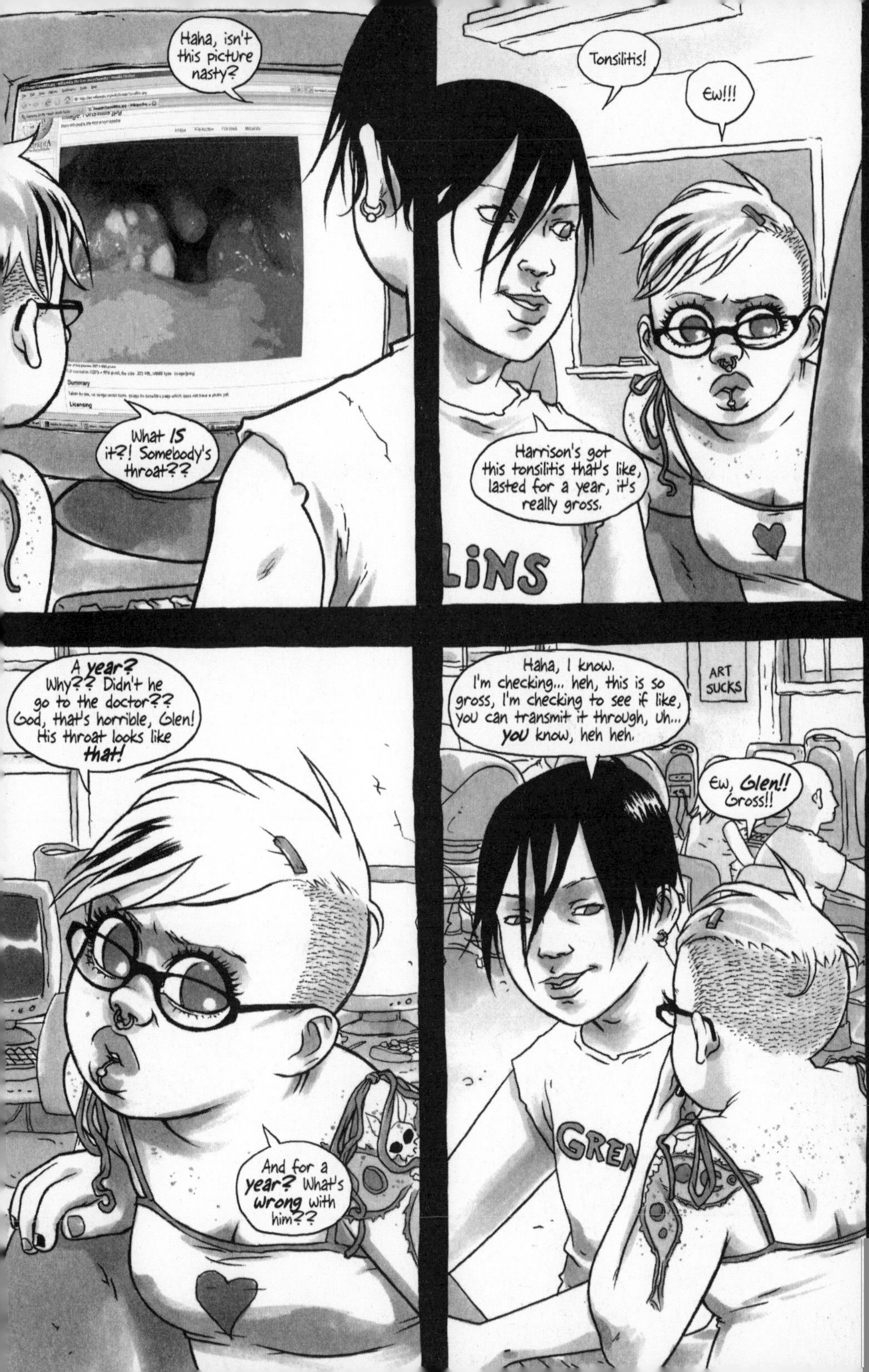
Haha, isn't this picture nasty?
What IS it?! Somebody's throat??
Tonsilitis!
Ew!!!
Harrison's got this tonsilitis that's like, lasted for a year, it's really gross.
LINS
A year? Why?? Didn't he go to the doctor?? God, that's horrible, Glen! His throat looks like that!
And for a year? What's wrong with him??
Haha, I know. I'm checking... heh, this is so gross, I'm checking to see if like, you can transmit it through, uh... you know, heh heh.
ART SUCKS
Ew, Glen!! Gross!!
GREN

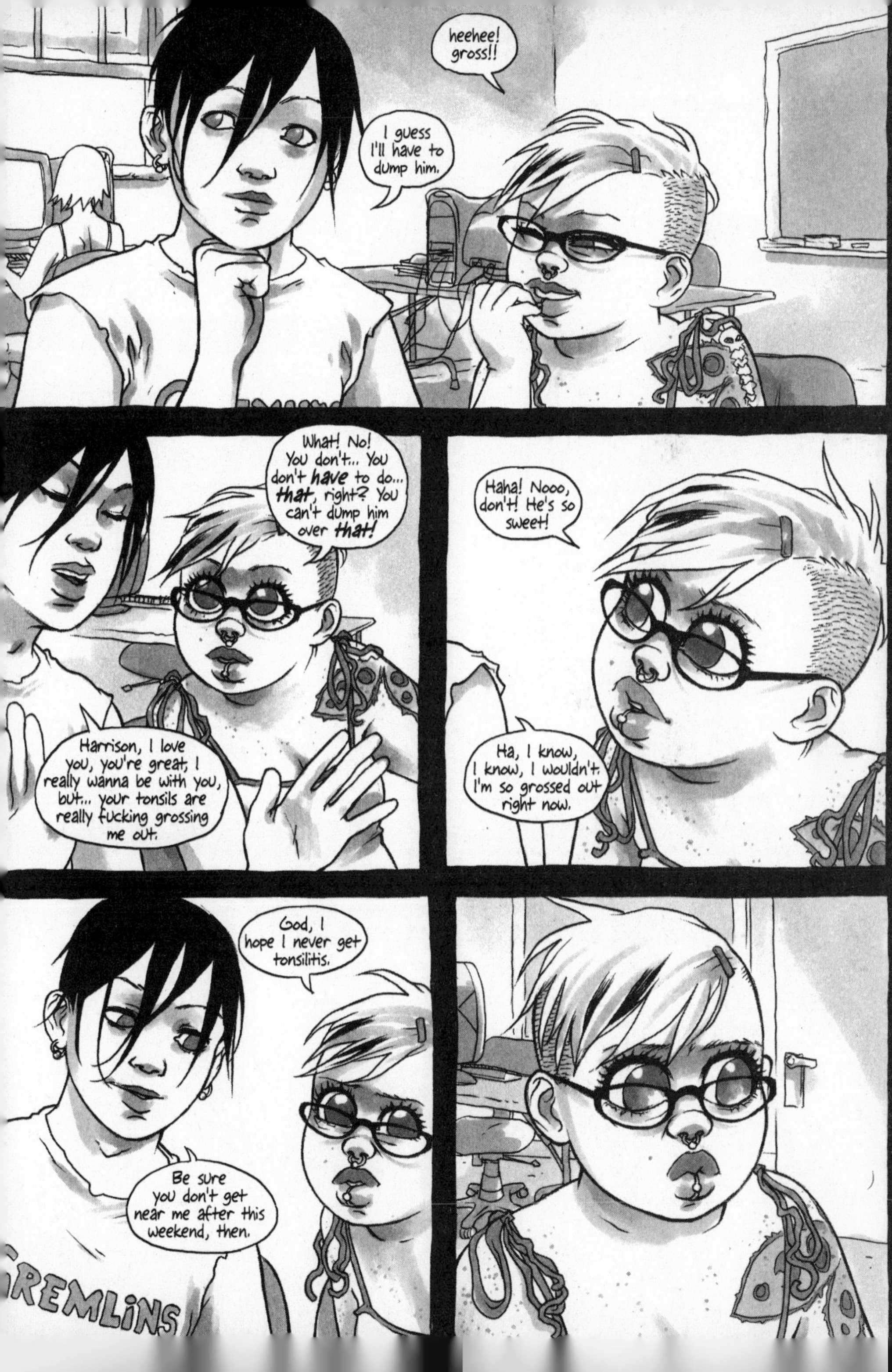
heehee! gross!!
I guess I'll have to dump him.
What! No! You don't... You don't have to do... that, right? You can't dump him over that!
Harrison, I love you, you're great, I really wanna be with you, but... your tonsils are really fucking grossing me out.
Haha! Nooo, don't! He's so sweet!
Ha, I know, I know, I wouldn't. I'm so grossed out right now.
God, I hope I never get tonsilitis.
Be sure you don't get near me after this weekend, then.
GREMLINS

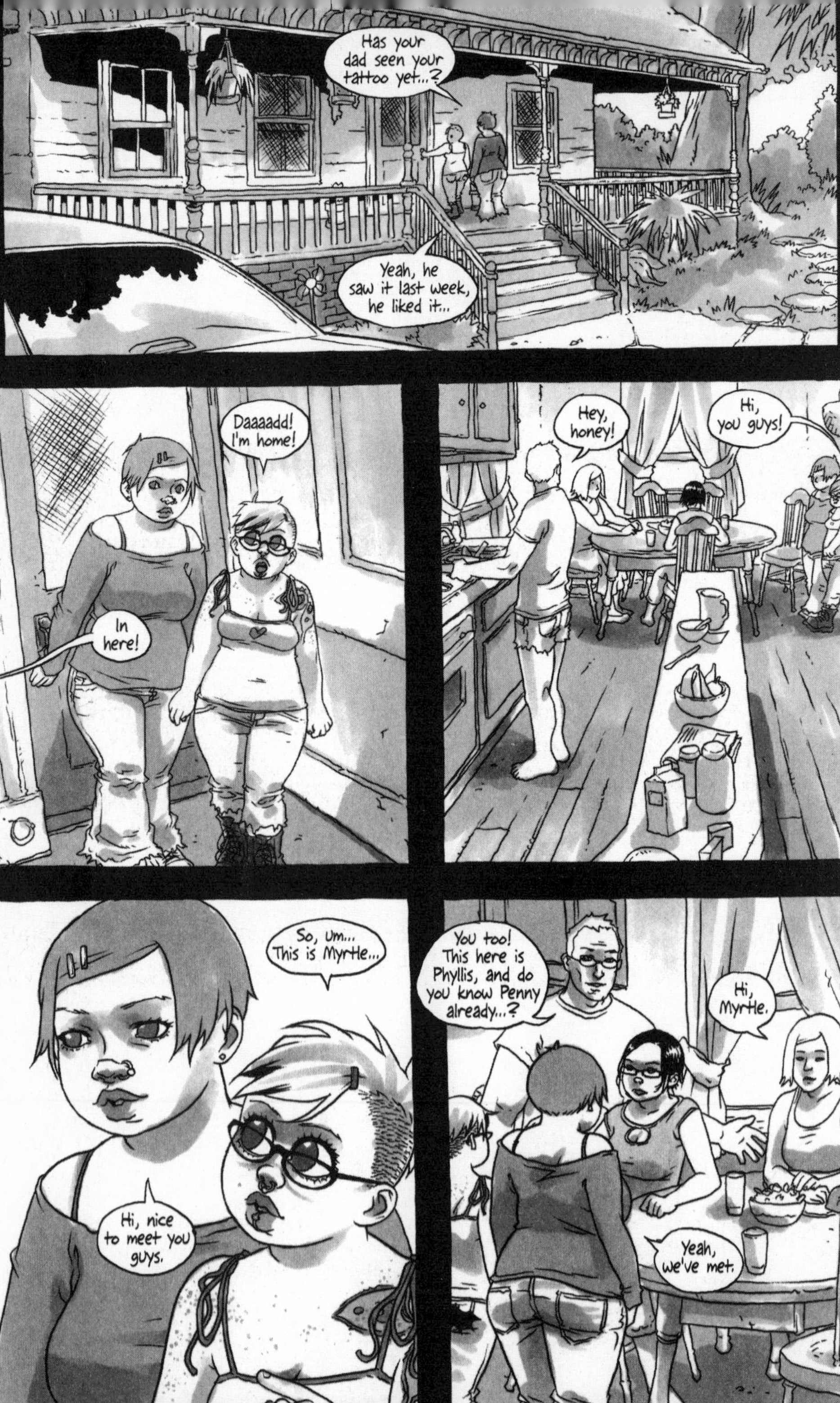
Has your dad seen your tattoo yet...?
Yeah, he saw it last week, he liked it...
Daaaadd! I'm home!
In here!
Hey, honey!
Hi, you guys!
So, um... This is Myrtle...
Hi, nice to meet you guys.
You too! This here is Phyllis, and do you know Penny already...?
Hi, Myrtle.
Yeah, we've met.

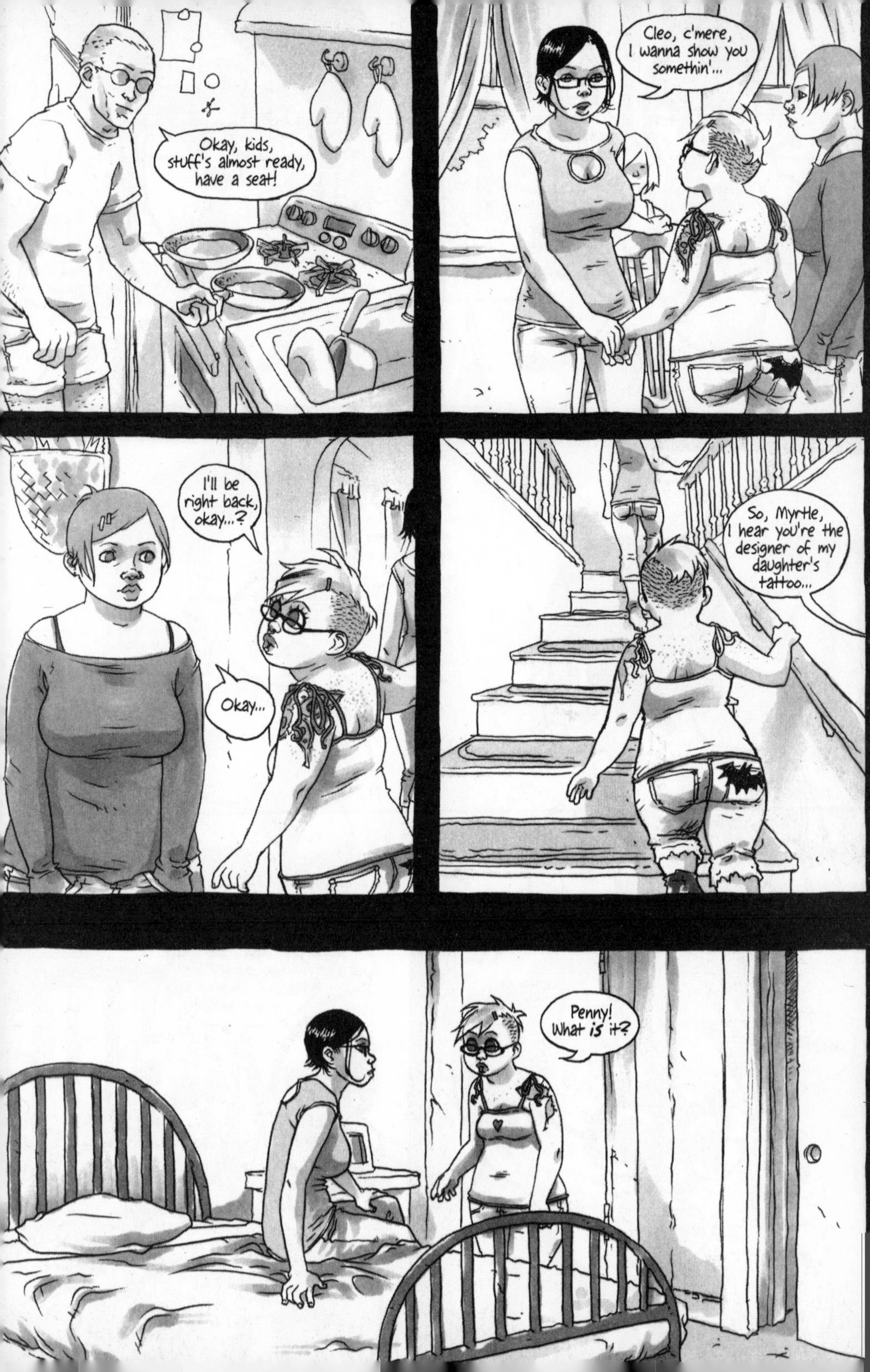
Okay, kids, stuff's almost ready, have a seat!
Cleo, c'mere, I wanna show you somethin'...
I'll be right back, okay...?
Okay...
So, Myrtle, I hear you're the designer of my daughter's tattoo...
Penny! What *is* it?

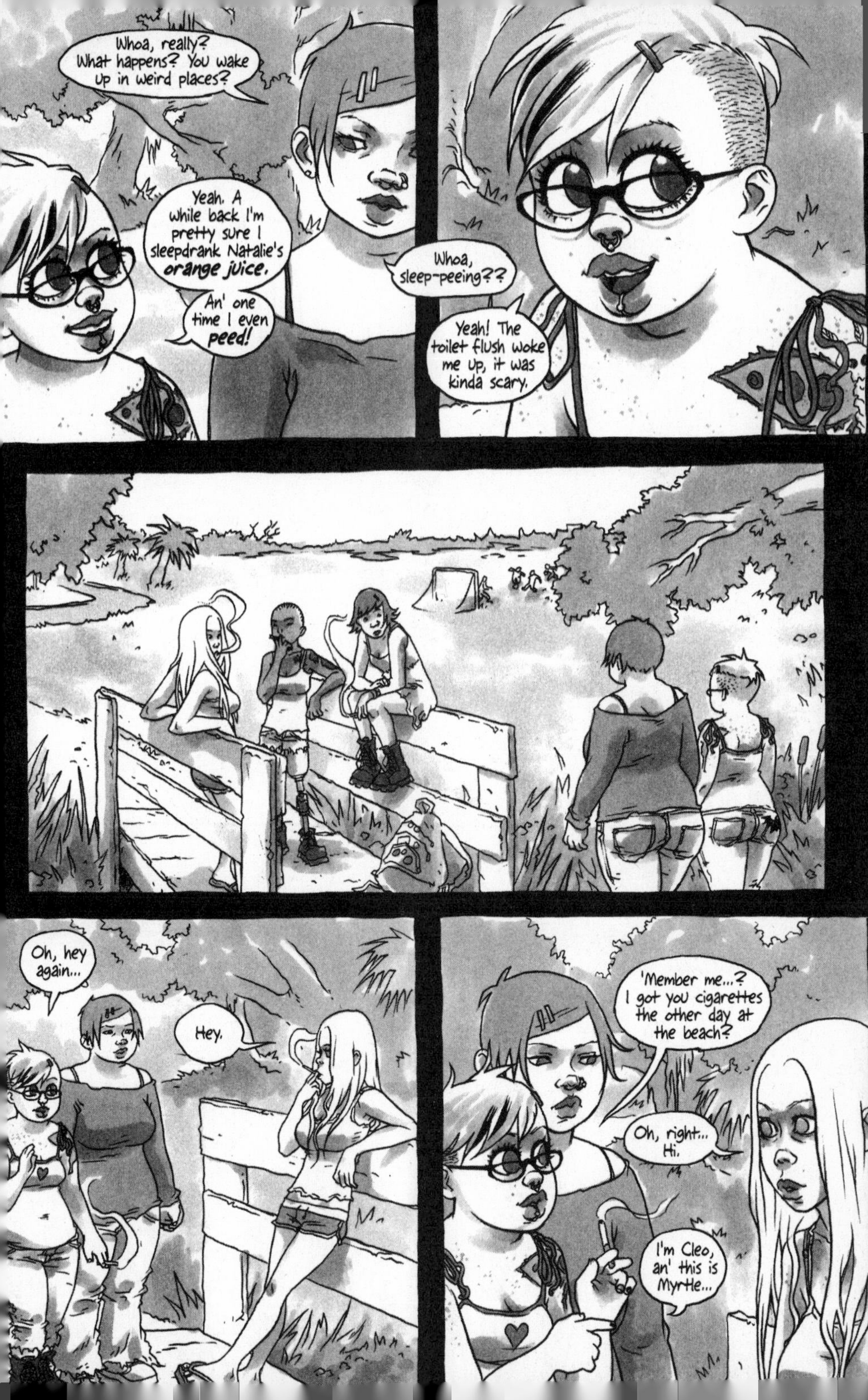
Whoa, really? What happens? You wake up in weird places?
Yeah. A while back I'm pretty sure I sleepdrank Natalie's **orange juice.**
An' one time I even **peed!**
Whoa, sleep-peeing??
Yeah! The toilet flush woke me up, it was kinda scary.
Oh, hey again...
Hey.
'Member me...? I got you cigarettes the other day at the beach?
Oh, right... Hi.
I'm Cleo, an' this is Myrtle...

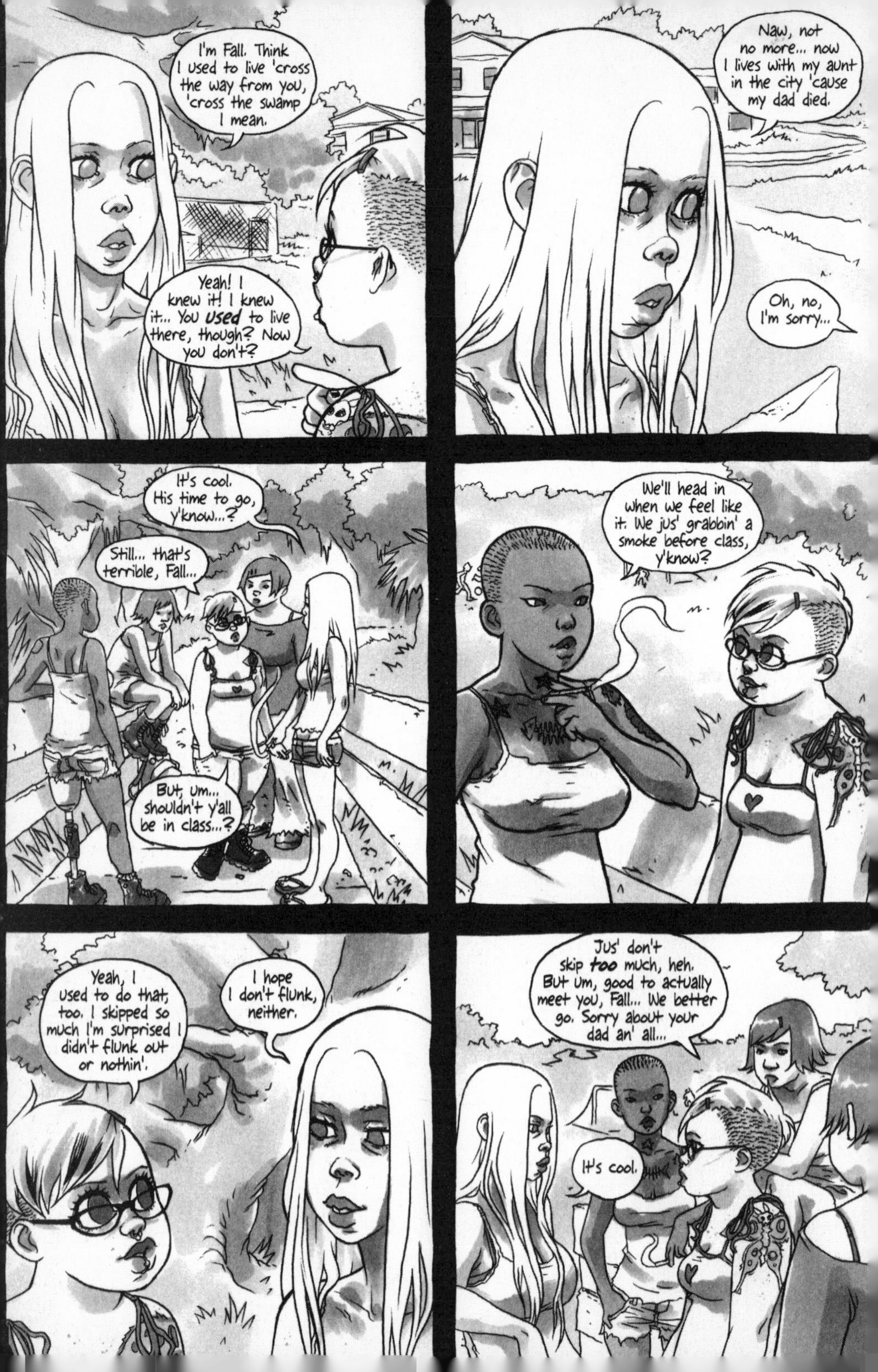
I'm Fall. Think I used to live 'cross the way from you, 'cross the swamp I mean.
Yeah! I knew it! I knew it... You *used* to live there, though? Now you don't?
Naw, not no more... now I lives with my aunt in the city 'cause my dad died.
Oh, no, I'm sorry...
It's cool. His time to go, y'know...?
Still... that's terrible, Fall...
But, um... shouldn't y'all be in class...?
We'll head in when we feel like it. We jus' grabbin' a smoke before class, y'know?
Yeah, I used to do that, too. I skipped so much I'm surprised I didn't flunk out or nothin'.
I hope I don't flunk, neither.
Jus' don't skip *too* much, heh. But um, good to actually meet you, Fall... We better go. Sorry about your dad an' all...
It's cool.

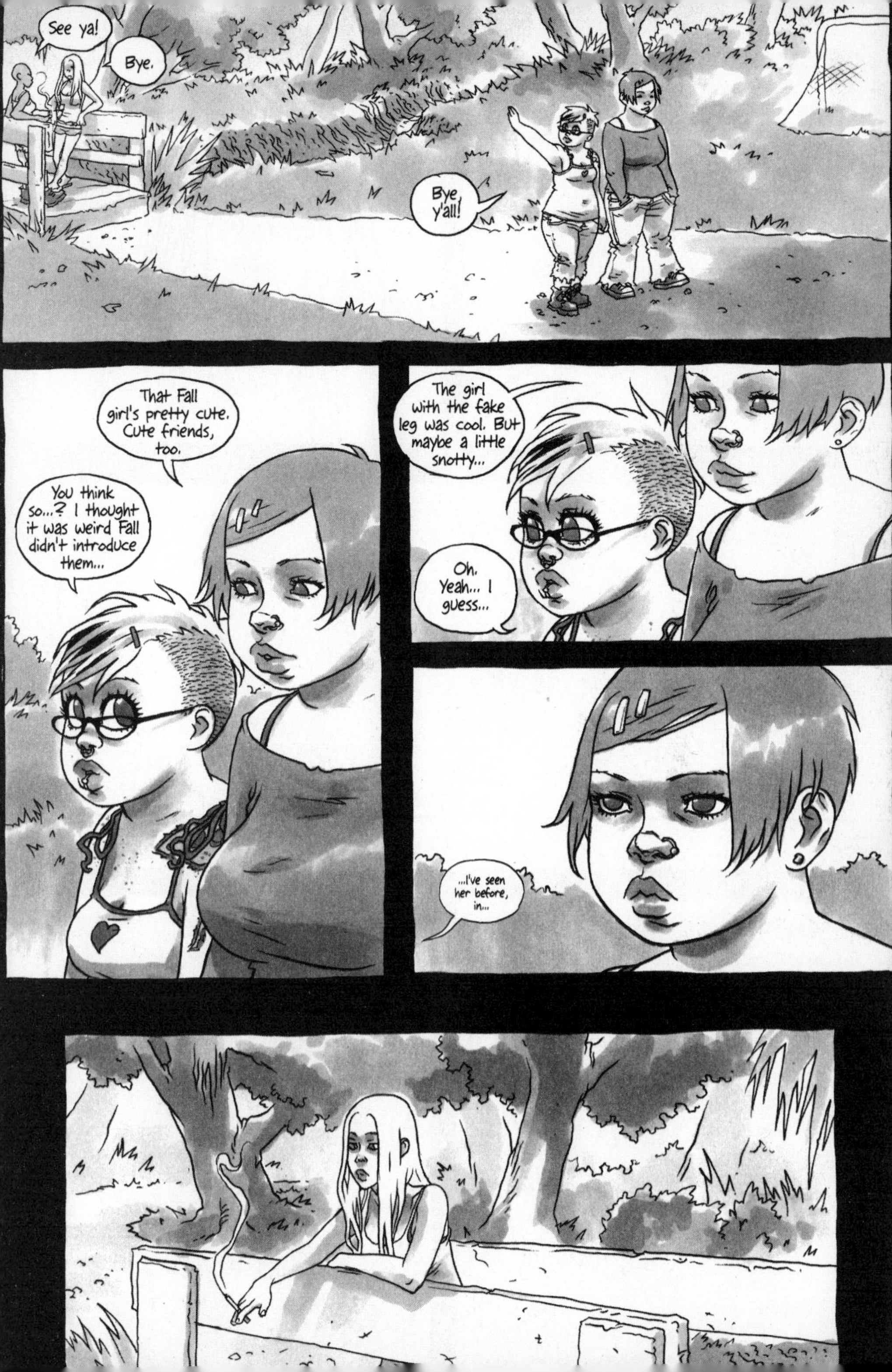
See ya!
Bye.
Bye, y'all!
That Fall girl's pretty cute. Cute friends, too.
You think so...? I thought it was weird Fall didn't introduce them...
The girl with the fake leg was cool. But maybe a little snotty...
Oh. Yeah... I guess...
...I've seen her before, in...

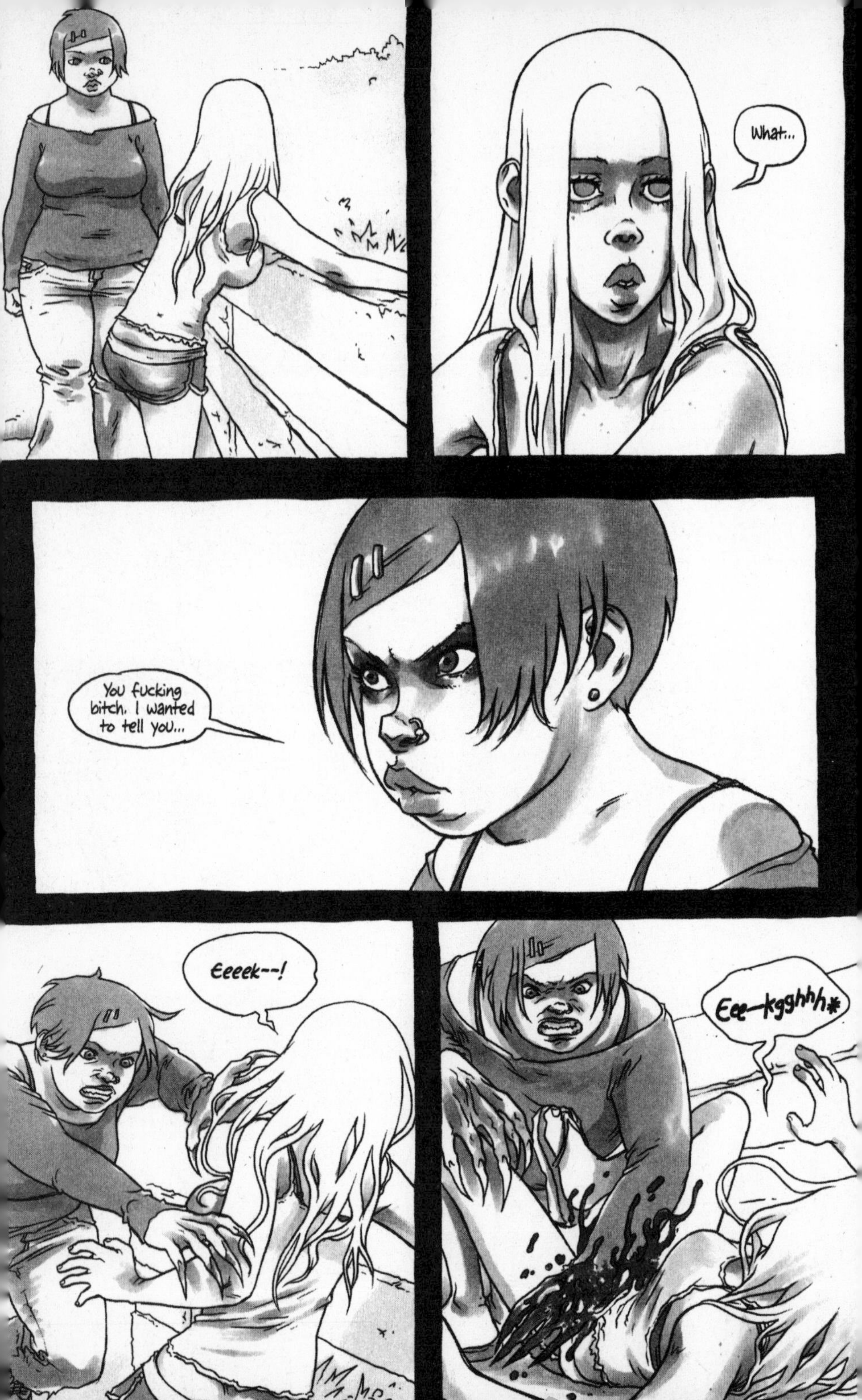
What...
You fucking bitch. I wanted to tell you...
Eeeek--!
Eee-kgghhh*

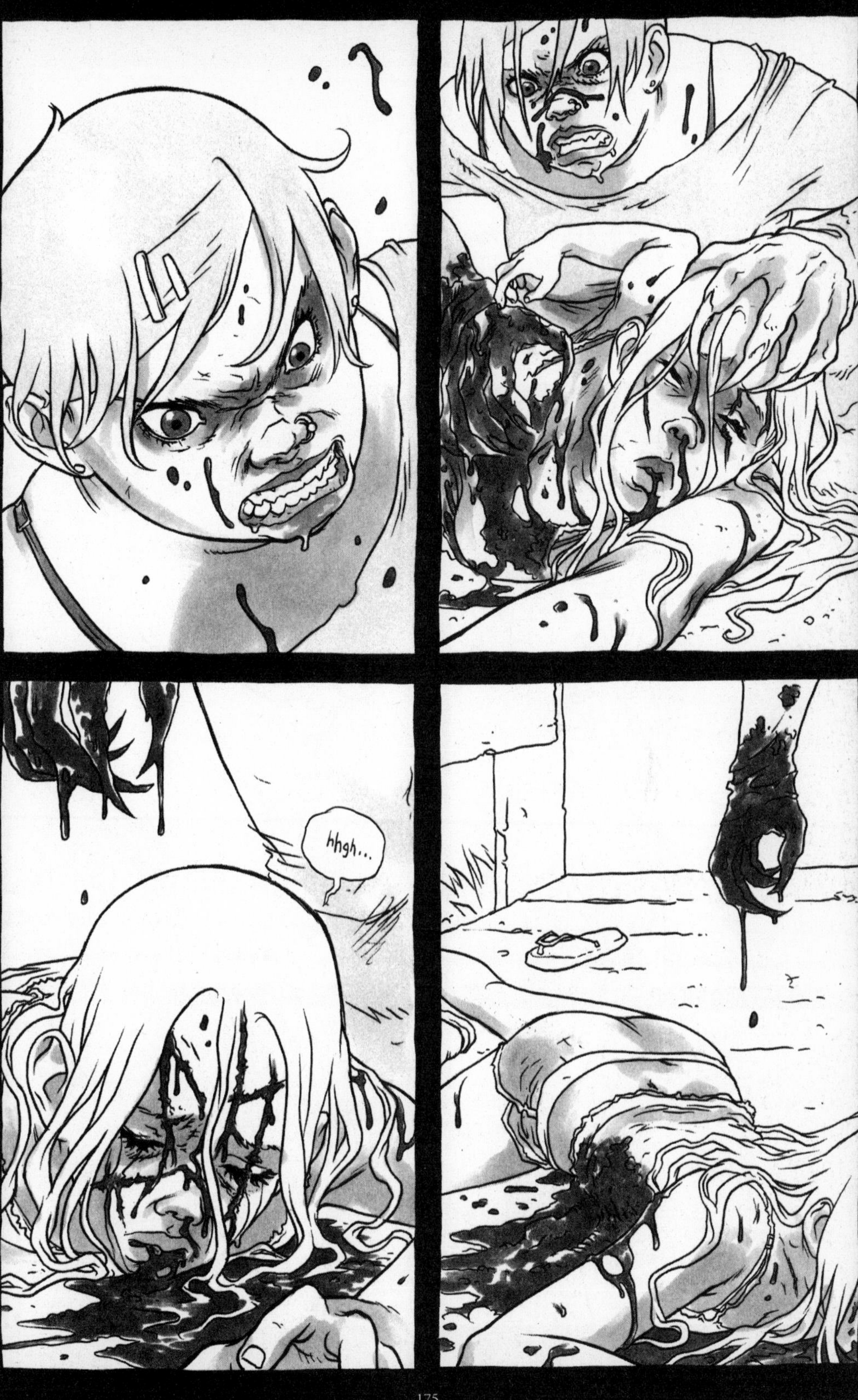
hhgh...

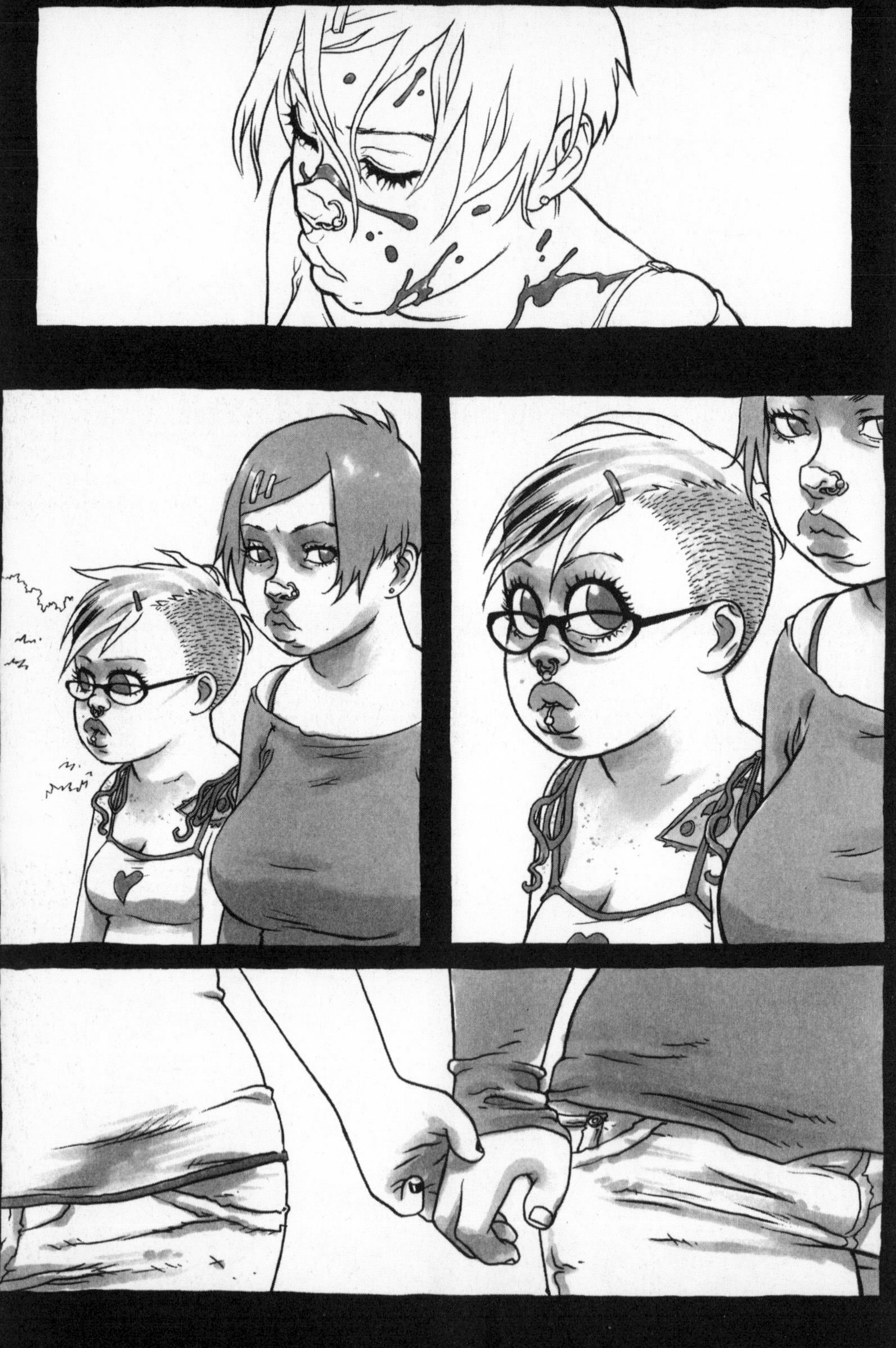

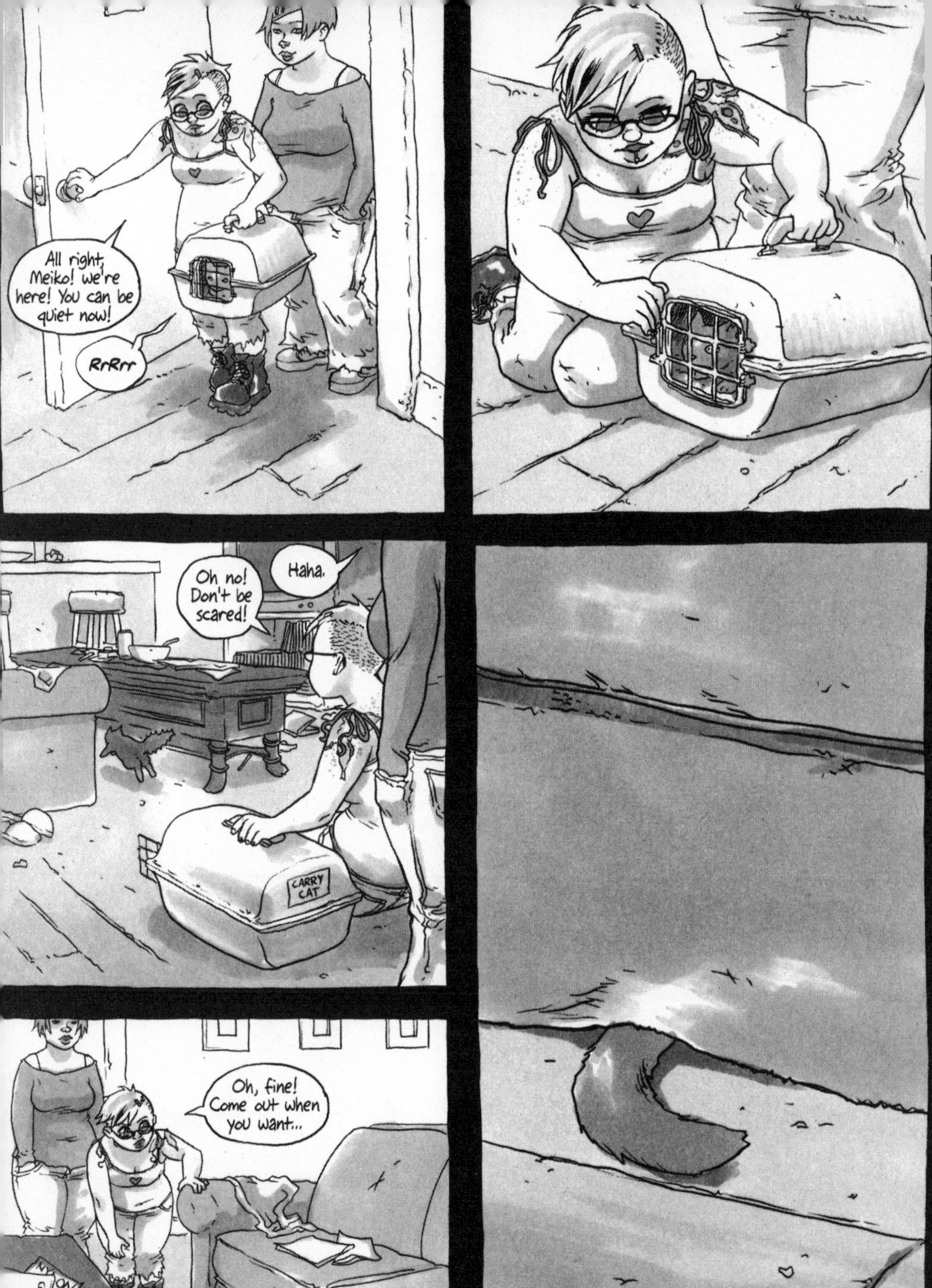

All right, Meiko! We're here! You can be quiet now!
RrRrr
Oh no! Don't be scared!
Haha.
CARRY CAT
Oh, fine! Come out when you want...

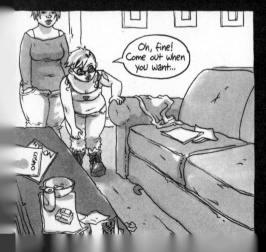

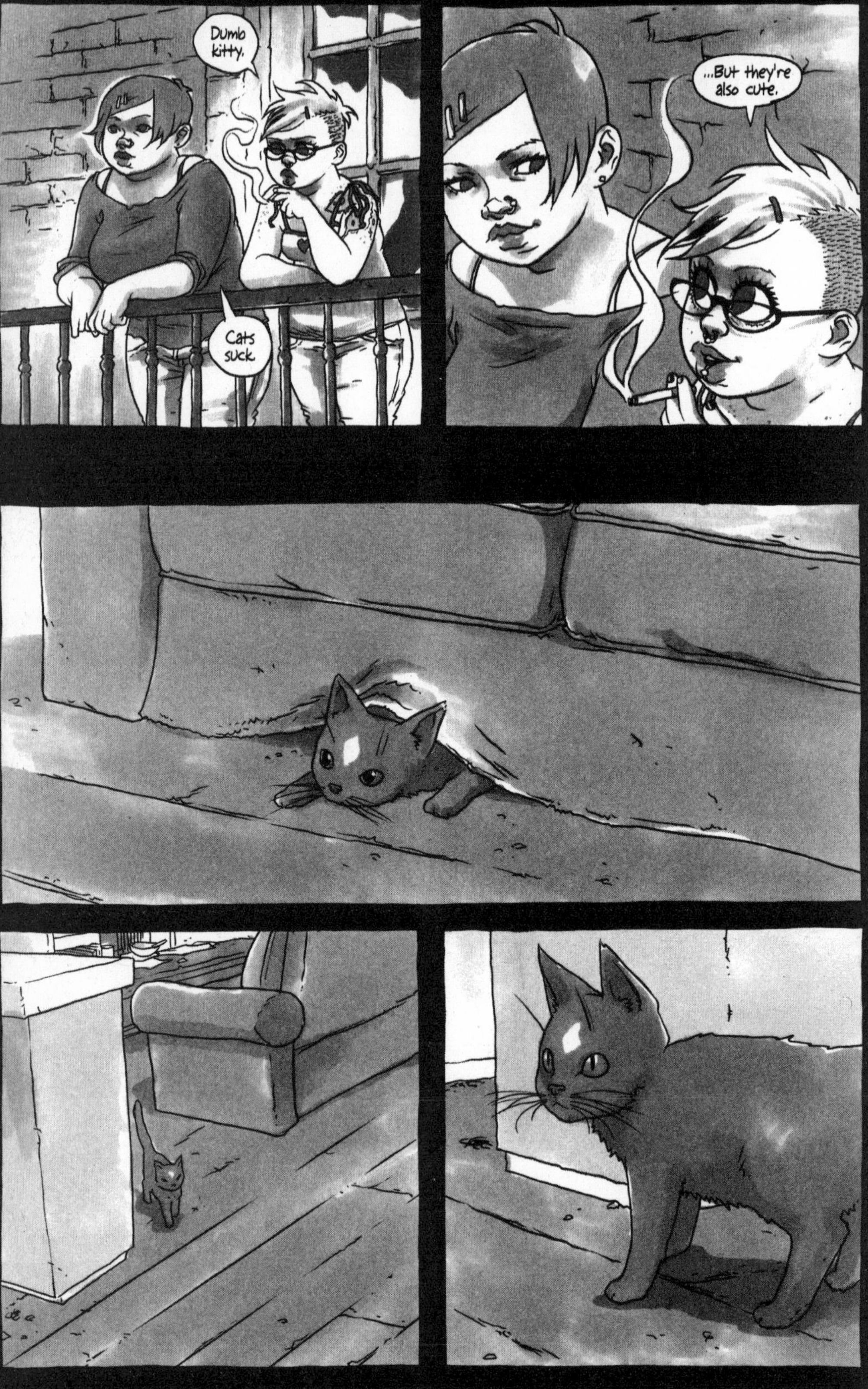
Dumb kitty.
Cats suck.
...But they're also cute.

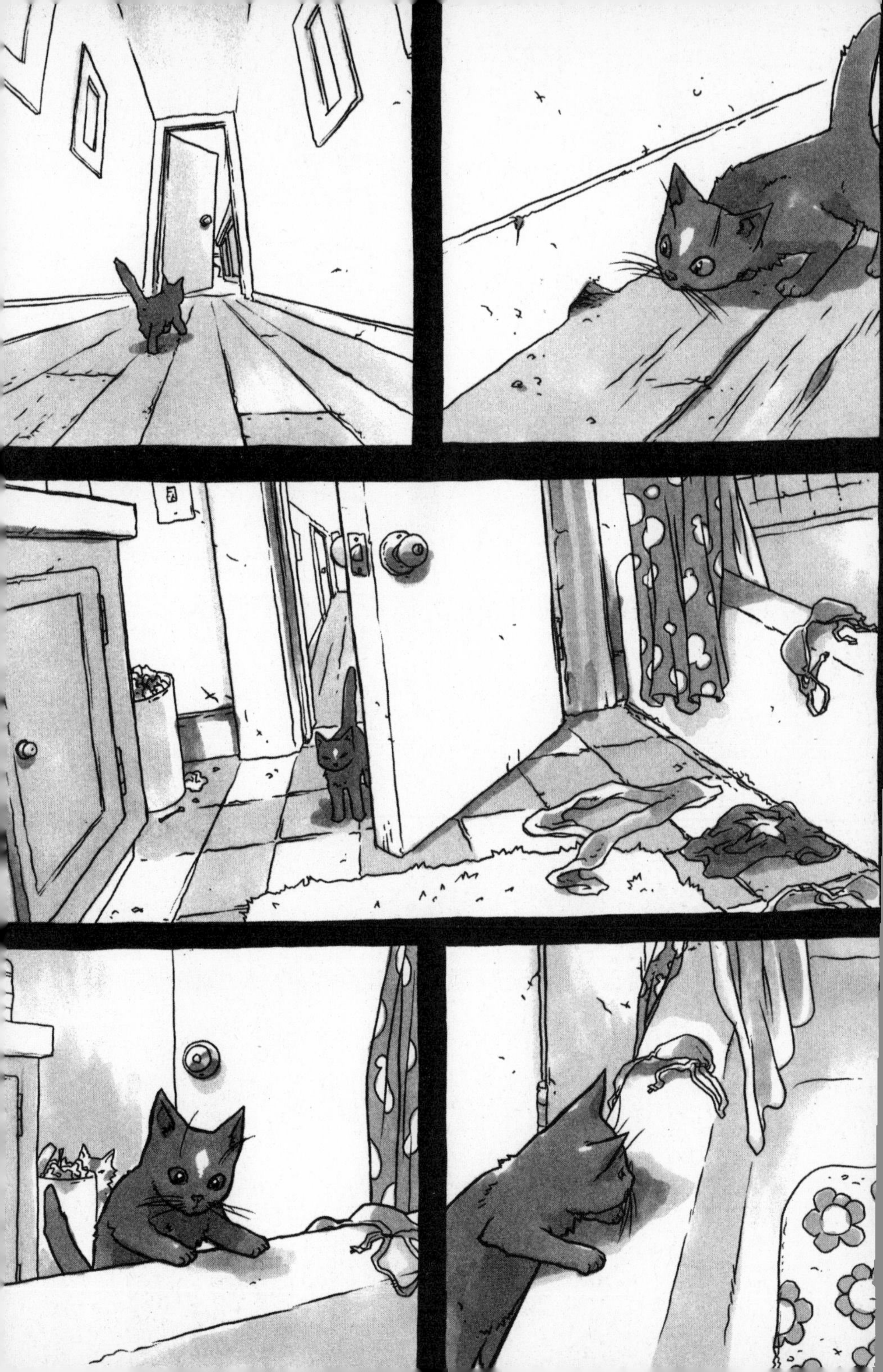

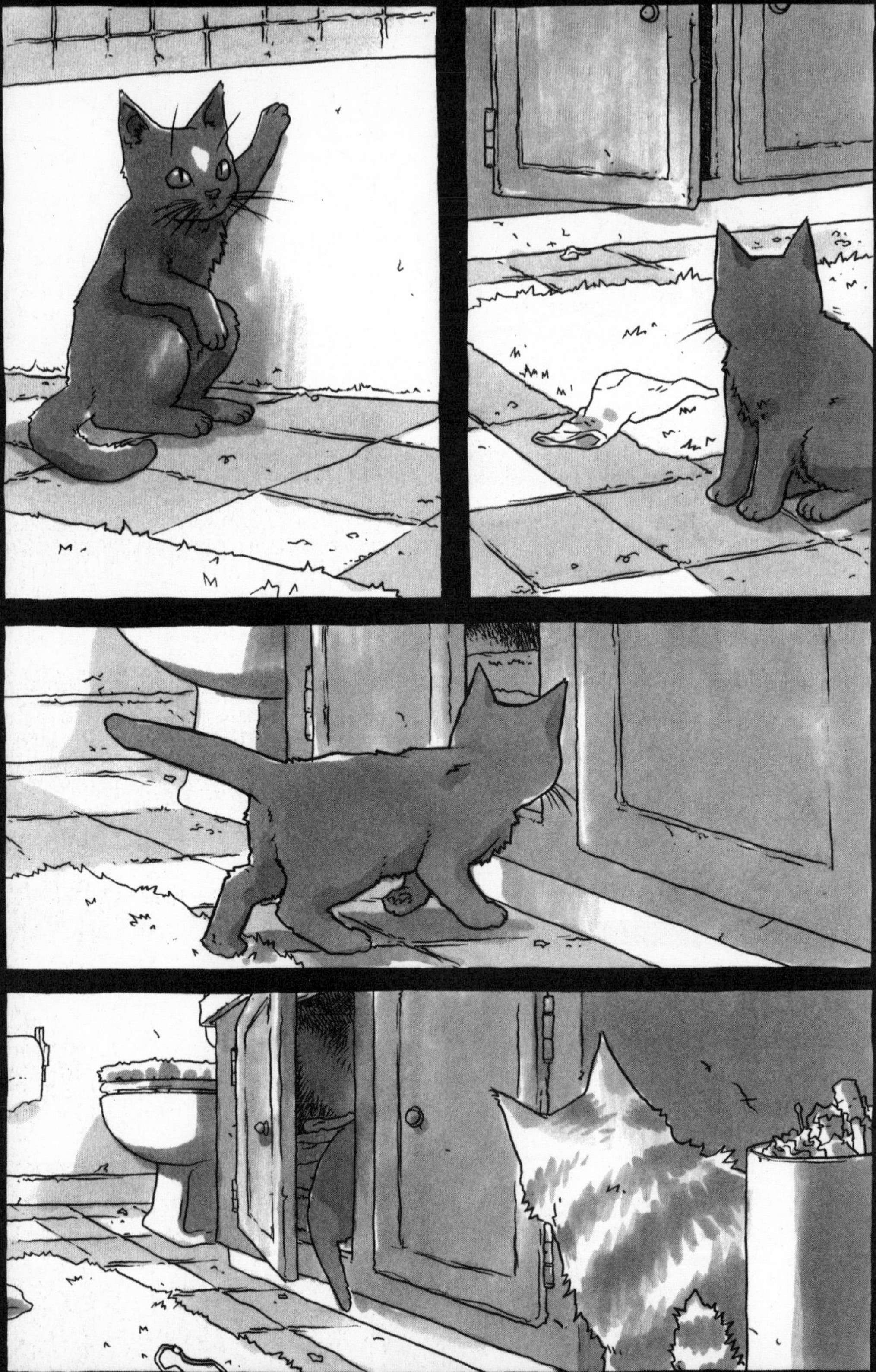

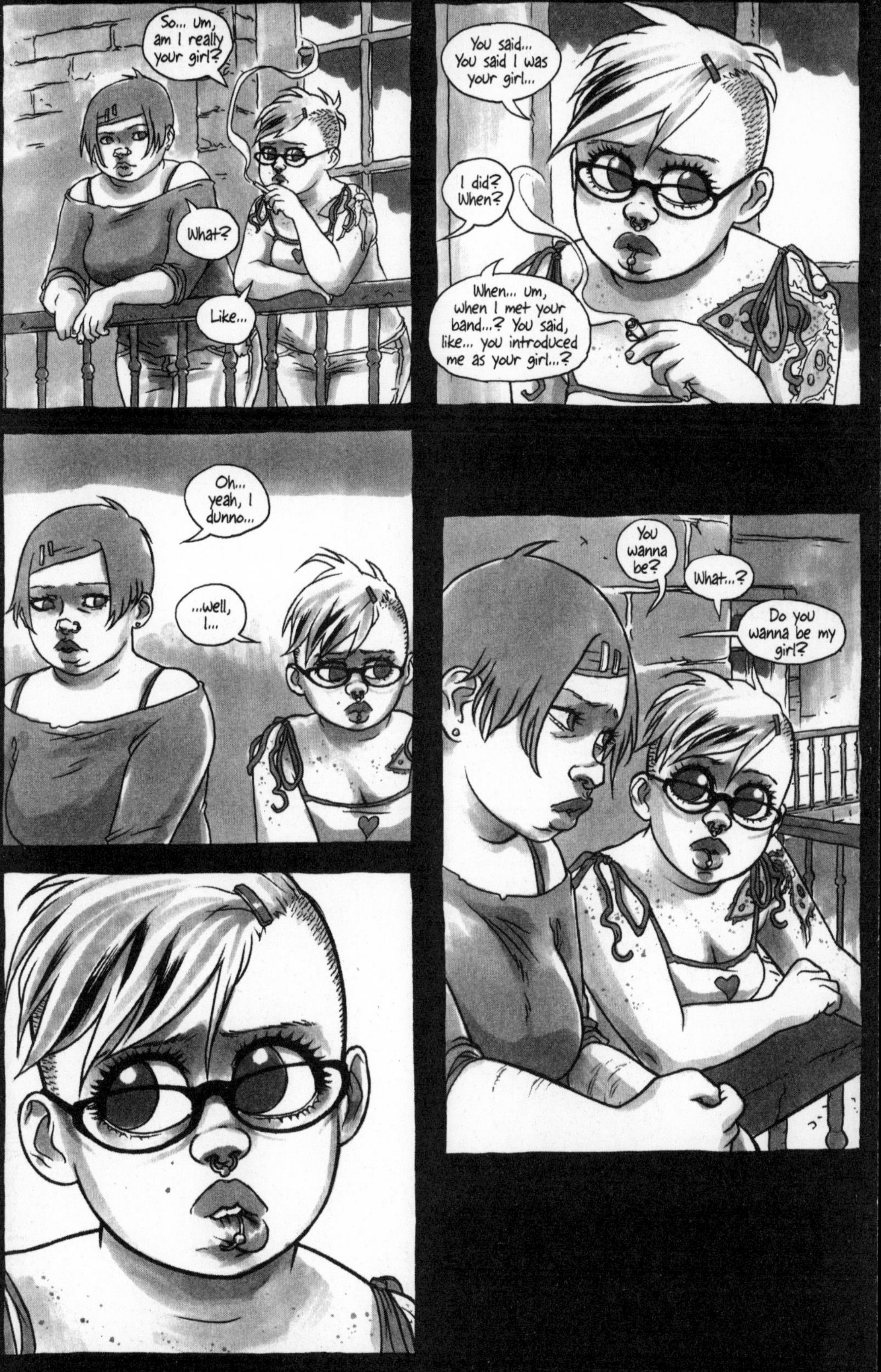
So... Um, am I really your girl?
What?
Like...
You said... You said I was your girl...
I did? When?
When... Um, when I met your band...? You said, like... you introduced me as your girl...?
Oh... yeah, I dunno...
...well, I...
You wanna be?
What...?
Do you wanna be my girl?

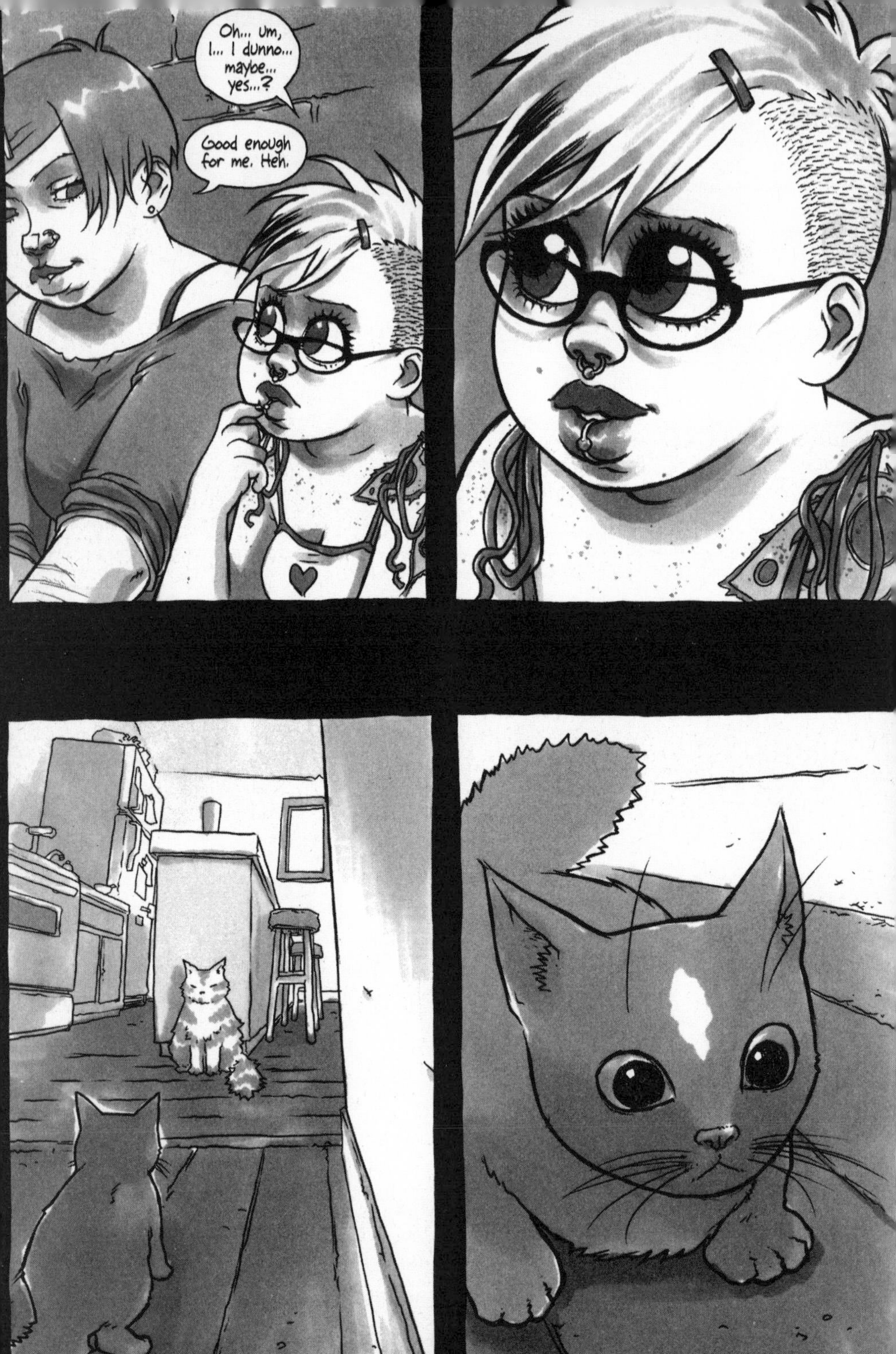
Oh... um, I... I dunno... maybe... yes...?
Good enough for me. Heh.

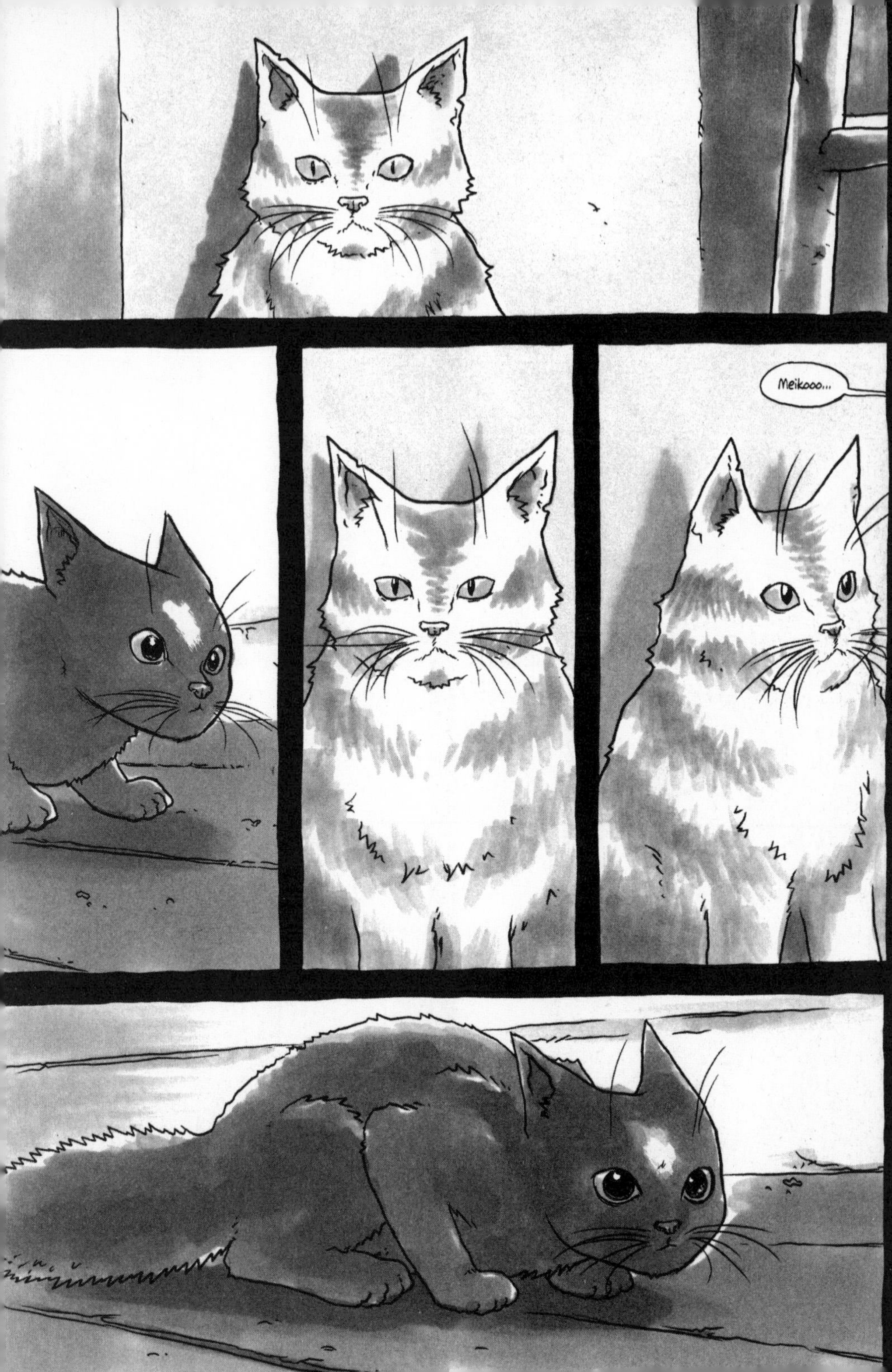
Meikooo...

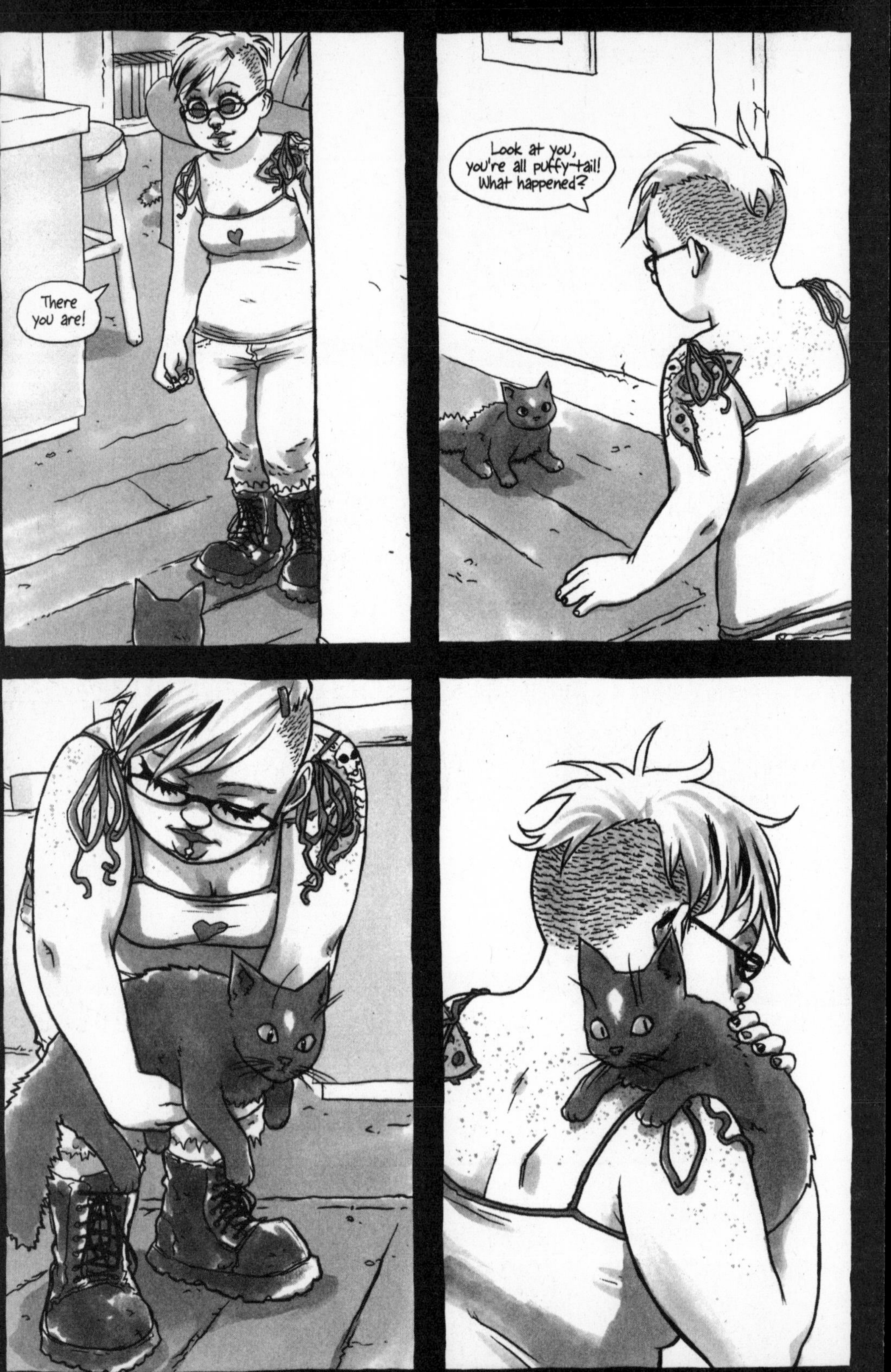
There you are!
Look at you, you're all puffy-tail! What happened?

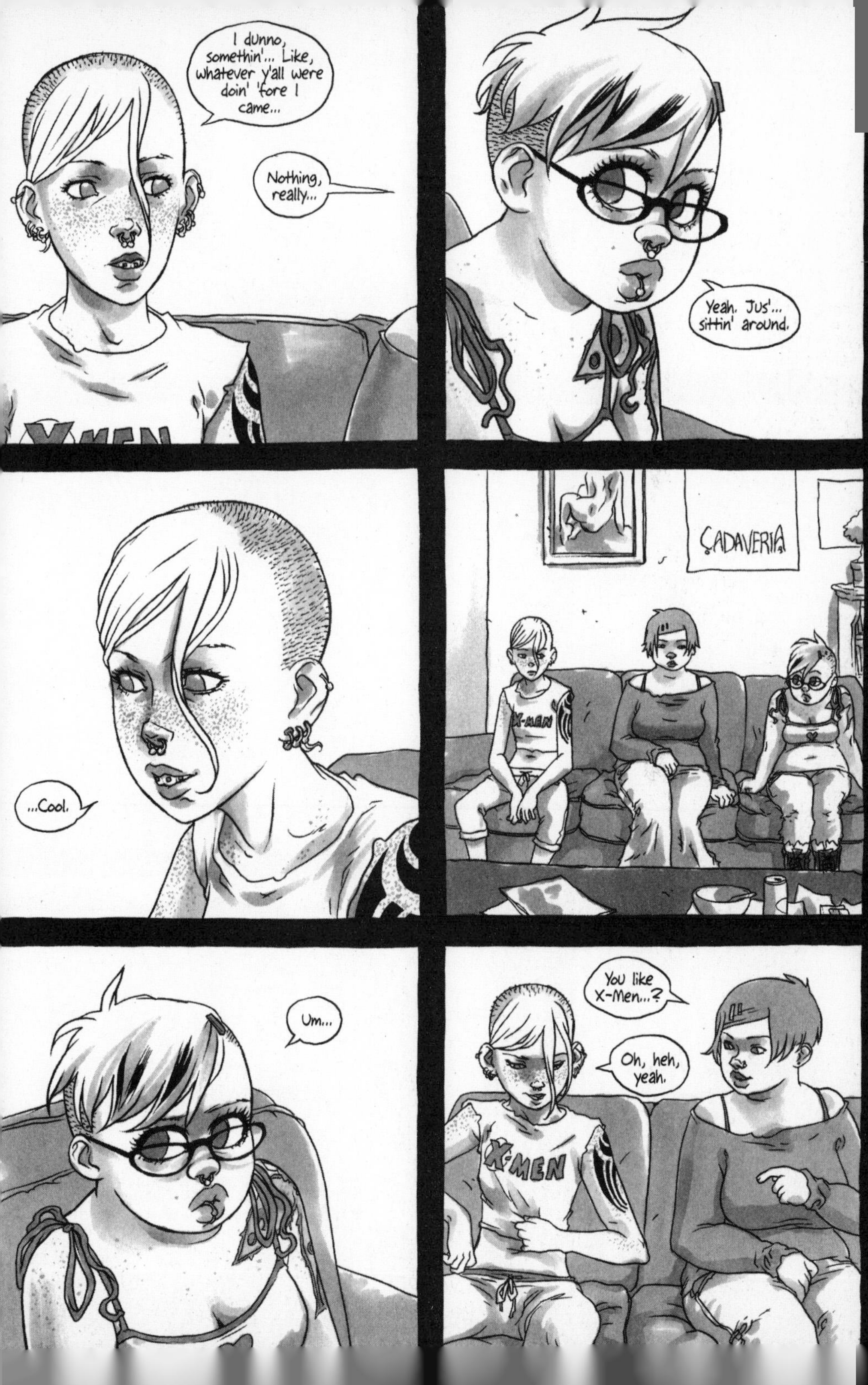
I dunno, somethin'... Like, whatever y'all were doin' 'fore I came...
Nothing, really...
Yeah. Jus'... sittin' around.
...Cool.
ÇADAVERIA
Um...
You like X-Men...?
Oh, heh, yeah.

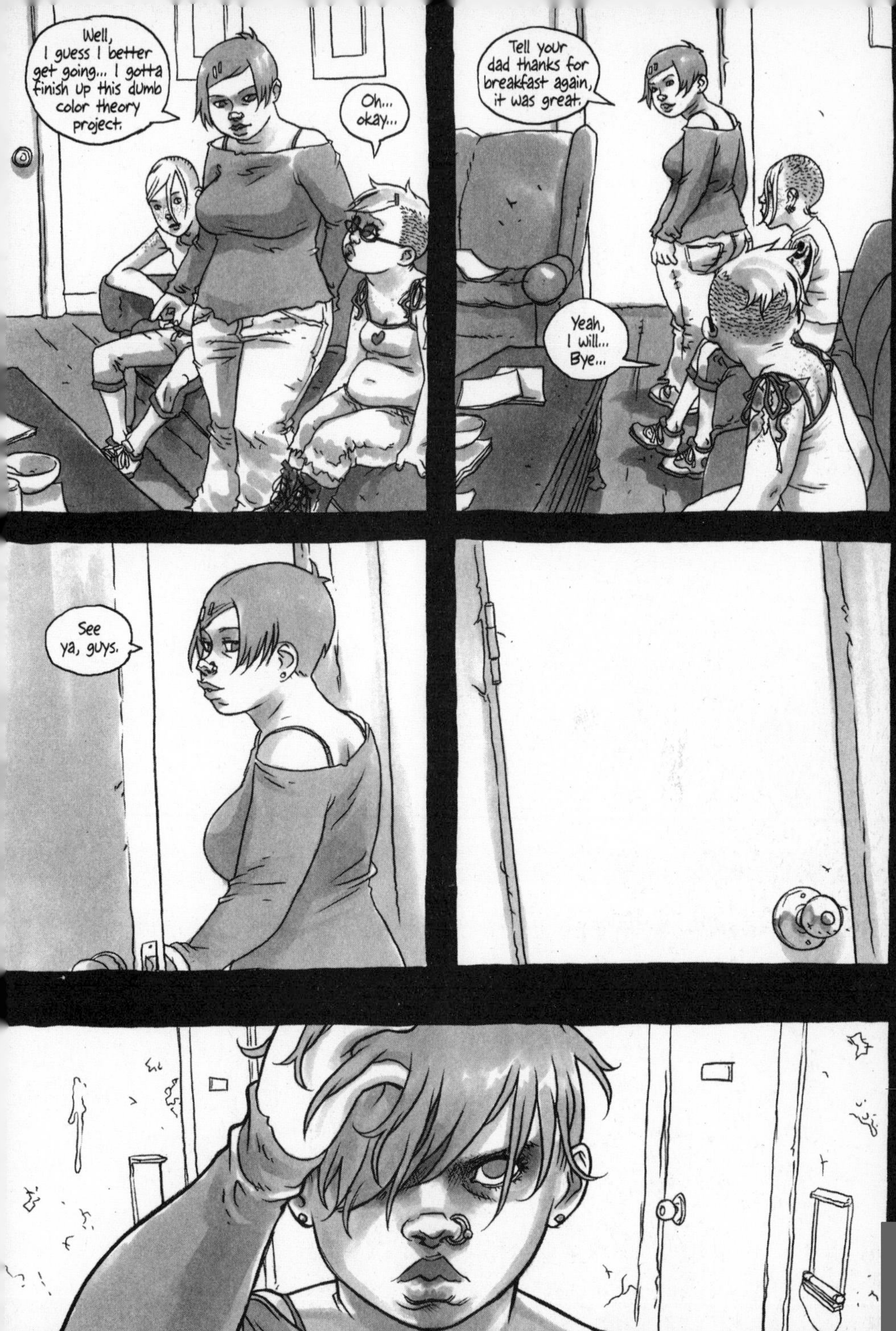
Well, I guess I better get going... I gotta finish up this dumb color theory project.
Oh... okay...
Tell your dad thanks for breakfast again, it was great.
Yeah, I will... Bye...
See ya, guys.

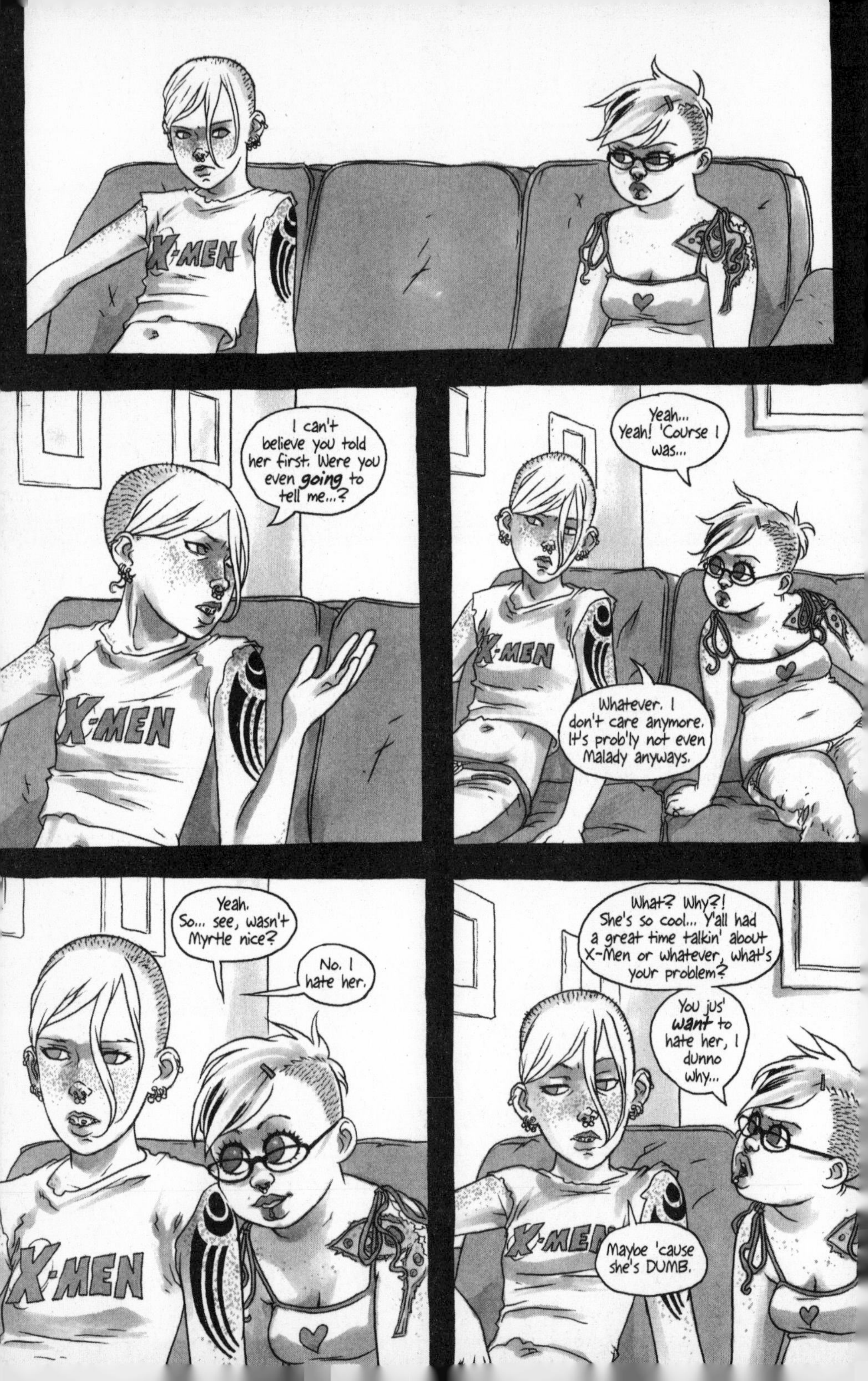
I can't believe you told her first. Were you even going to tell me...?
Yeah... Yeah! 'Course I was...
Whatever. I don't care anymore. It's prob'ly not even Malady anyways.
Yeah. So... see, wasn't Myrtle nice?
No. I hate her.
What? Why?! She's so cool... Y'all had a great time talkin' about X-Men or whatever, what's your problem?
You jus' want to hate her, I dunno why...
Maybe 'cause she's DUMB.

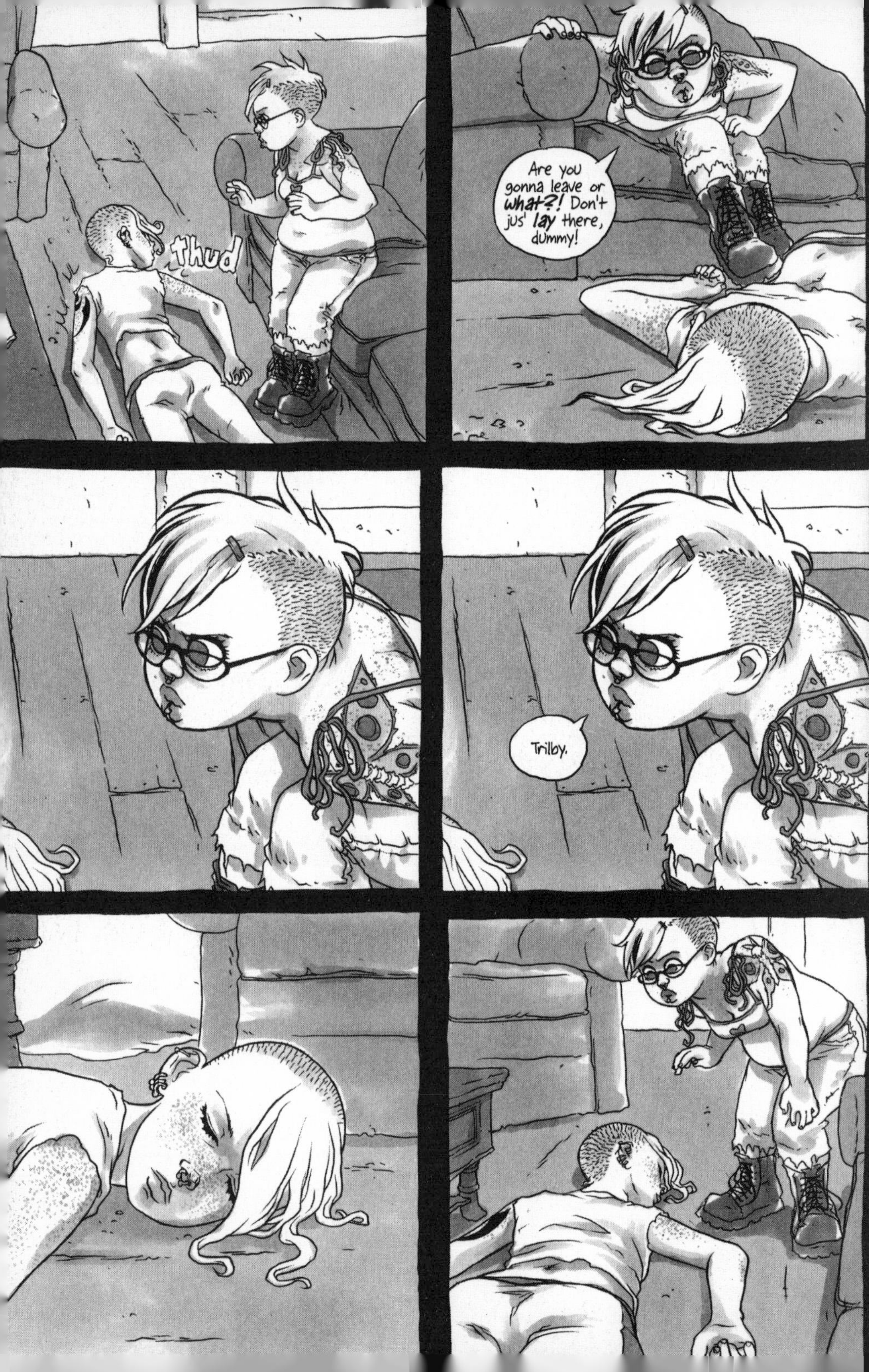
thud
Are you gonna leave or what?! Don't jus' lay there, dummy!
Trilby.

Tril...?

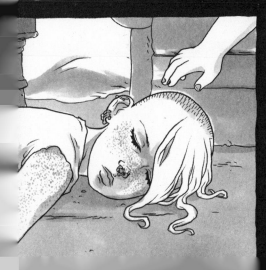

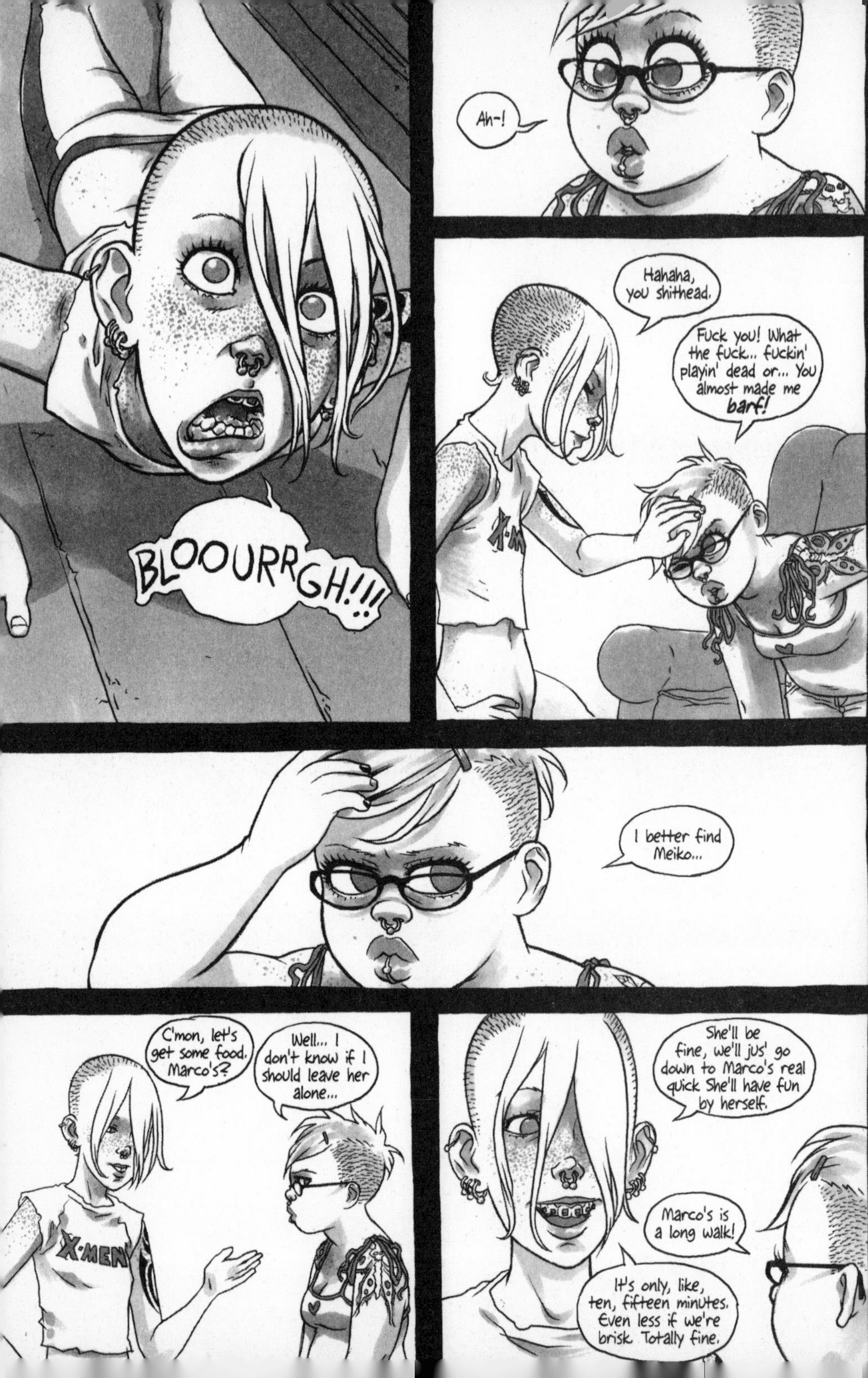
BLOOURRGH!!!
Ah-!
Hahaha, you shithead.
Fuck you! What the fuck... fuckin' playin' dead or... You almost made me **barf!**
I better find Meiko...
C'mon, let's get some food. Marco's?
Well... I don't know if I should leave her alone...
She'll be fine, we'll jus' go down to Marco's real quick She'll have fun by herself.
Marco's is a long walk!
It's only, like, ten, fifteen minutes. Even less if we're brisk. Totally fine.

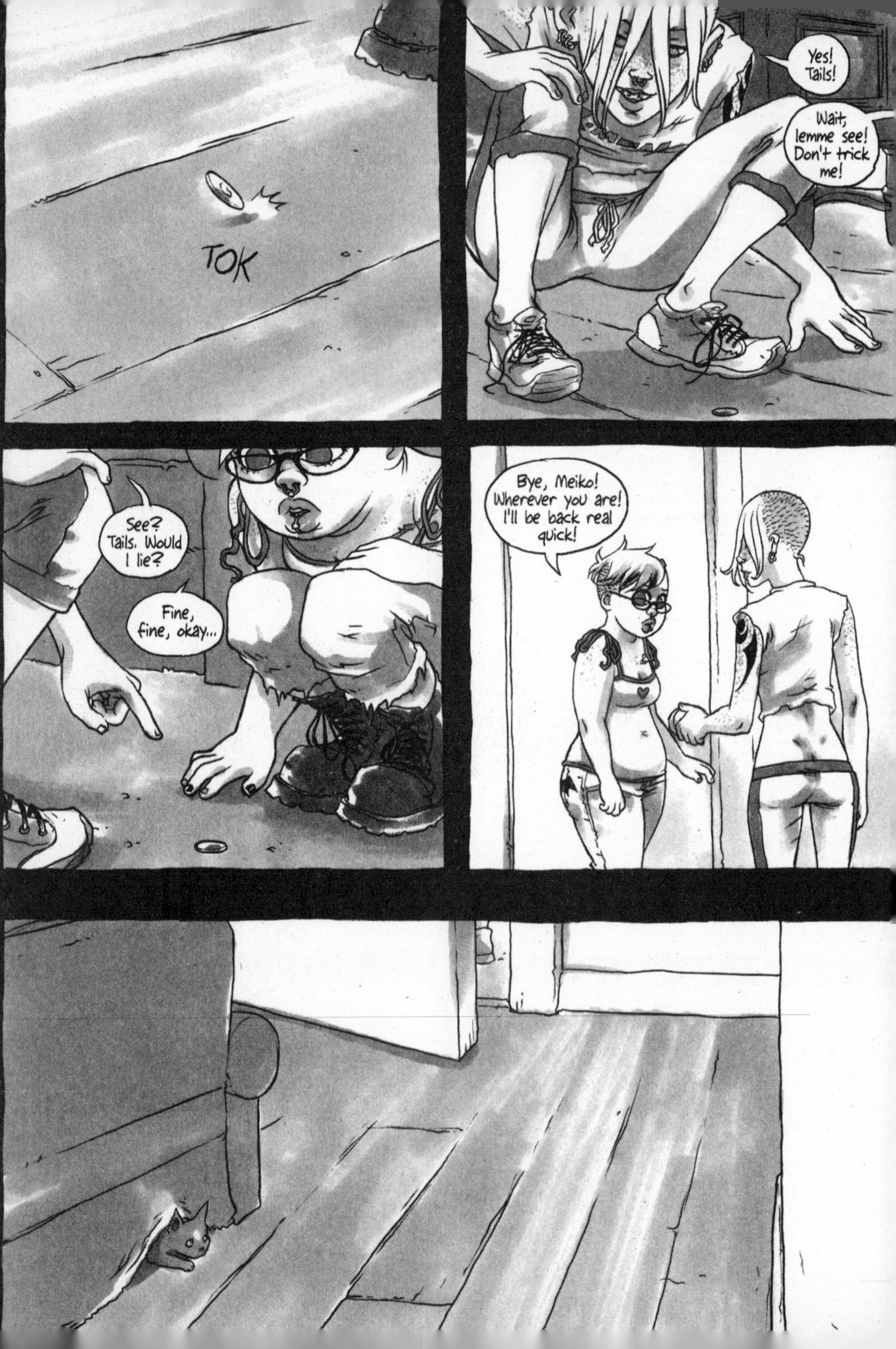
TOK
Yes! Tails!
Wait, lemme see! Don't trick me!
See? Tails. Would I lie?
Fine, fine, okay...
Bye, Meiko! Wherever you are! I'll be back real quick!

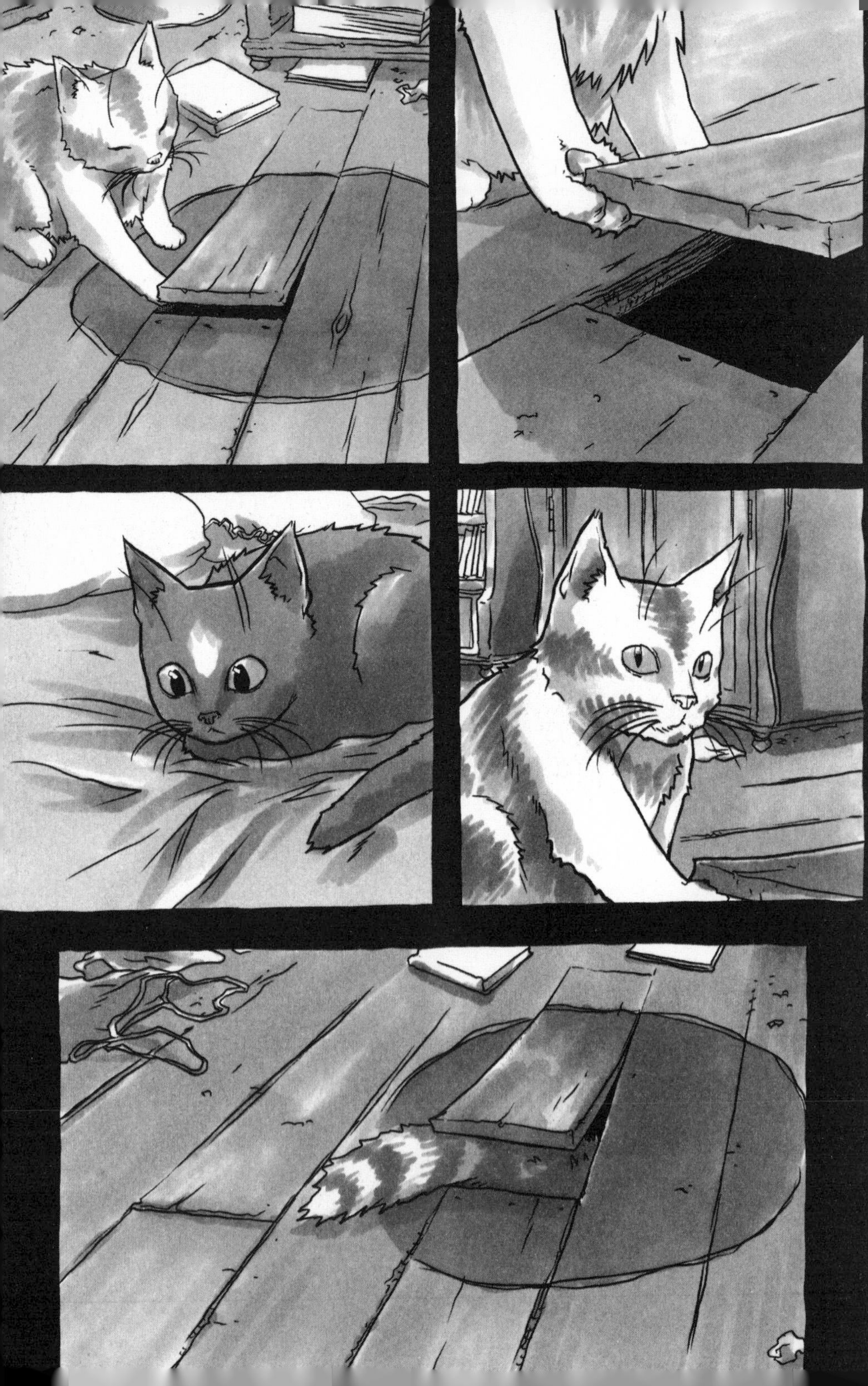

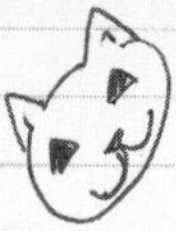

October Something
Meiko ran away. Penny might be pregnant. Everything is going crazy. Meiko has to come back, I don't know what I'd do. I don't know where the fuck she went. I don't think any of the doors or windows were open, but I've checked the whole place and she's absolutely not here. Oh god, I don't know. Where is she??!!

Meiko came back! And then Penny! Oh my god! She's probably pregnant, but I just know she is! I really hope she keeps the baby, I want to be an aunt, and it would be cool to have a baby grand. Everything sucks. I don't feel like writing anymore.

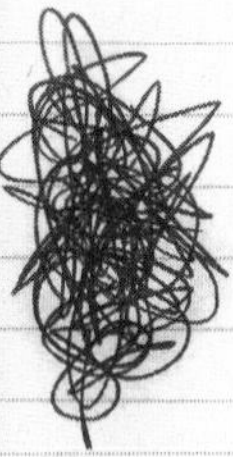

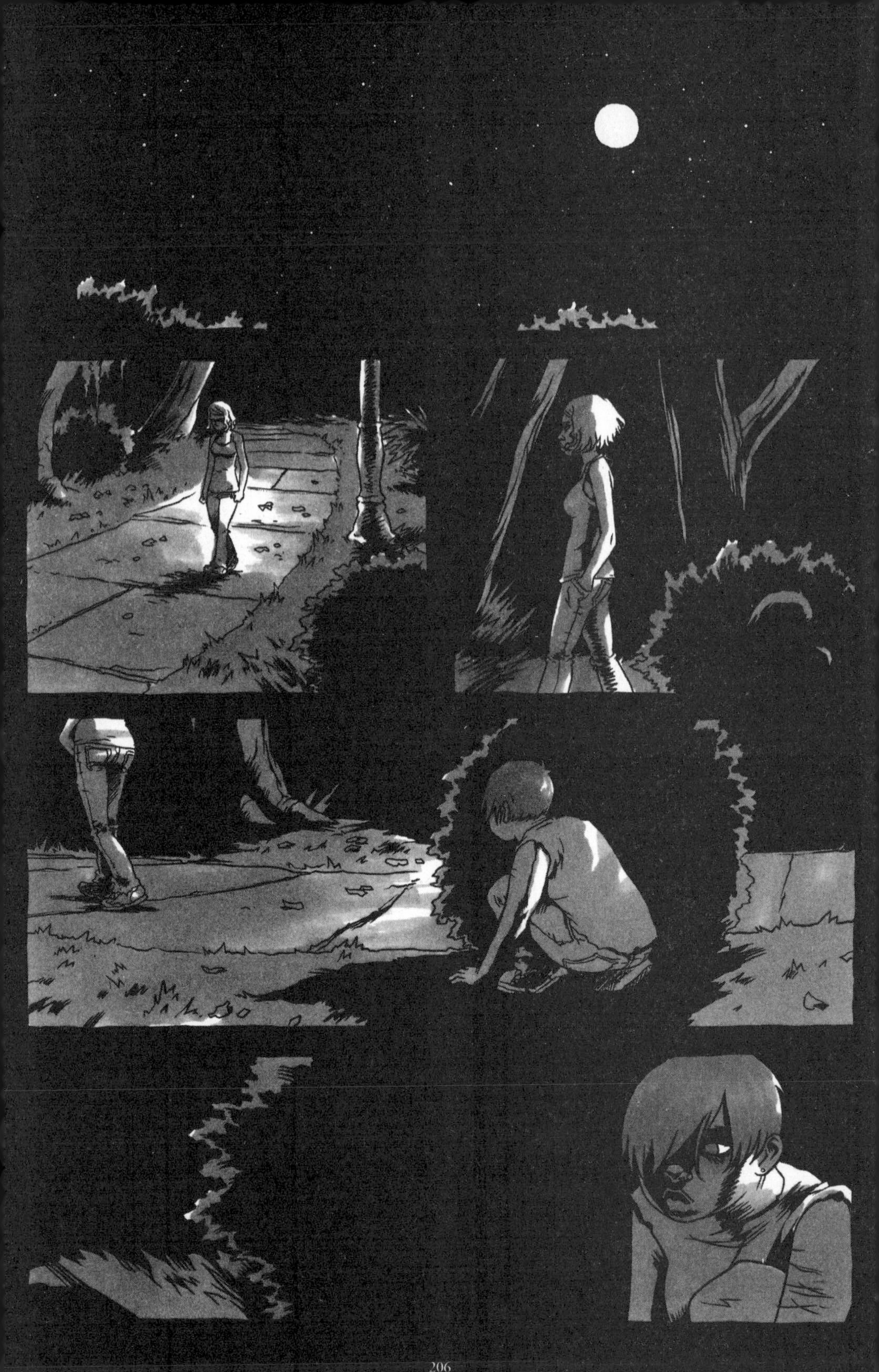

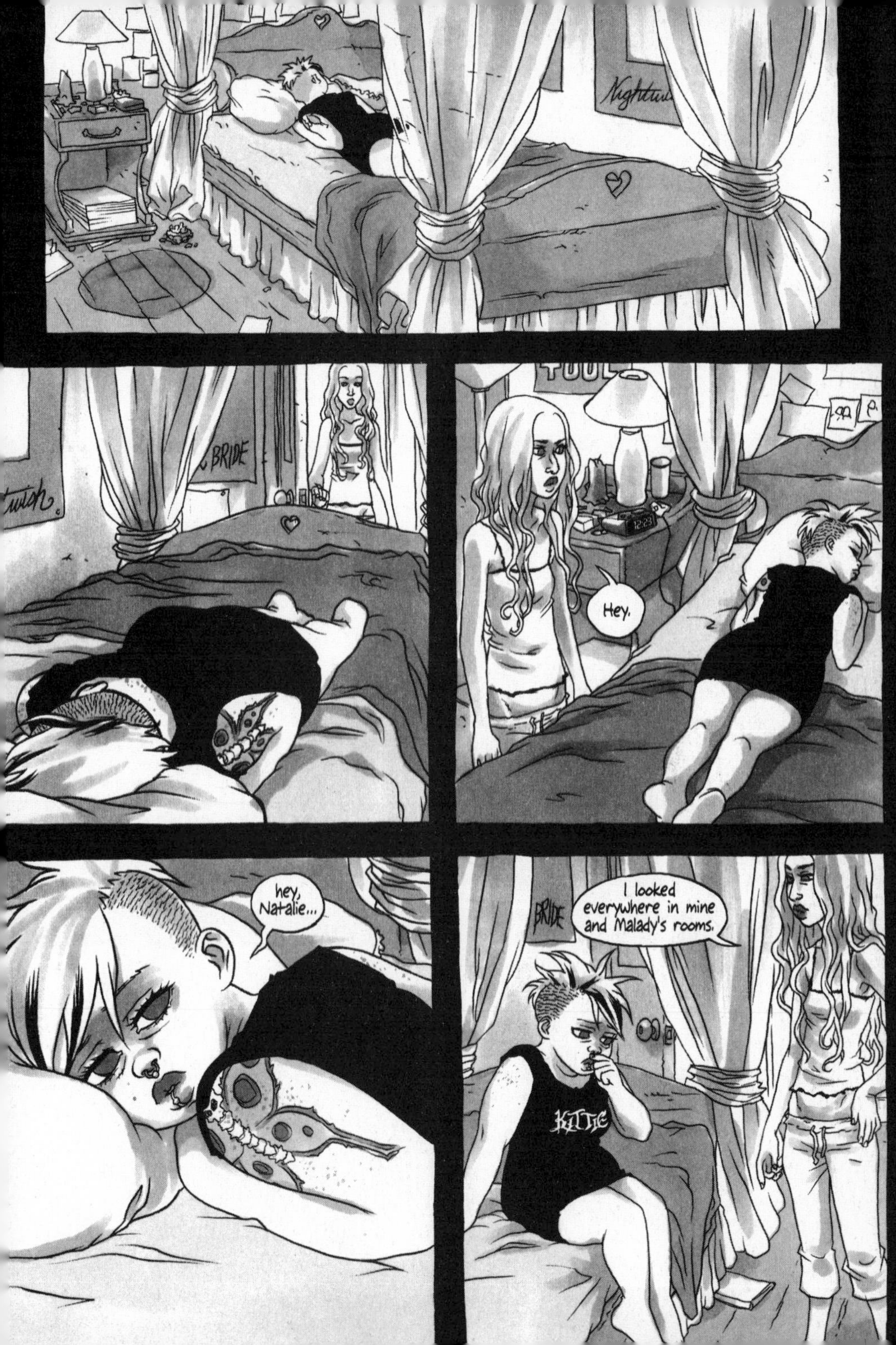
Hey.
hey, Natalie...
I looked everywhere in mine and Malady's rooms.

209

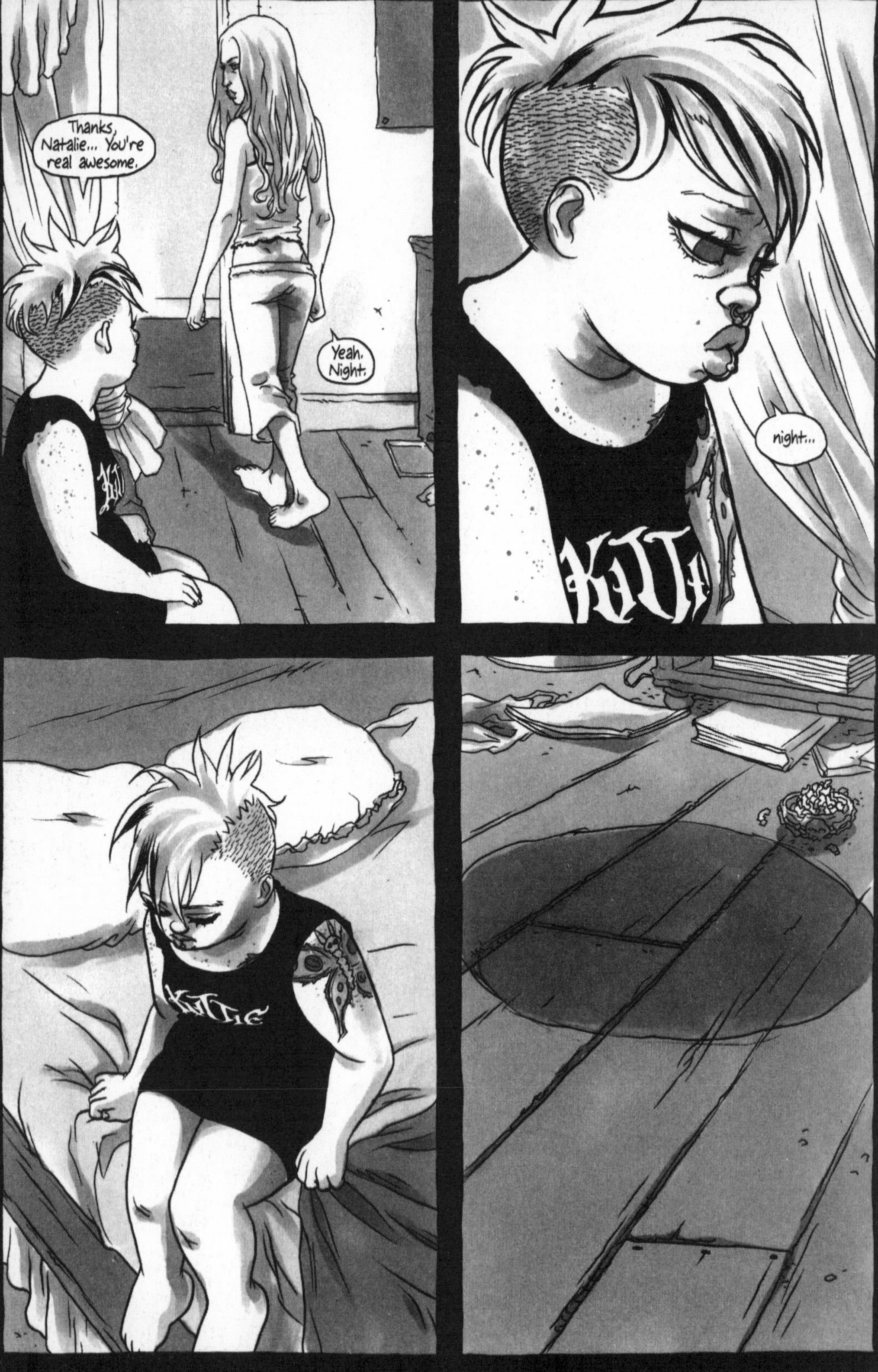
Thanks, Natalie... You're real awesome.
Yeah. Night.
night...

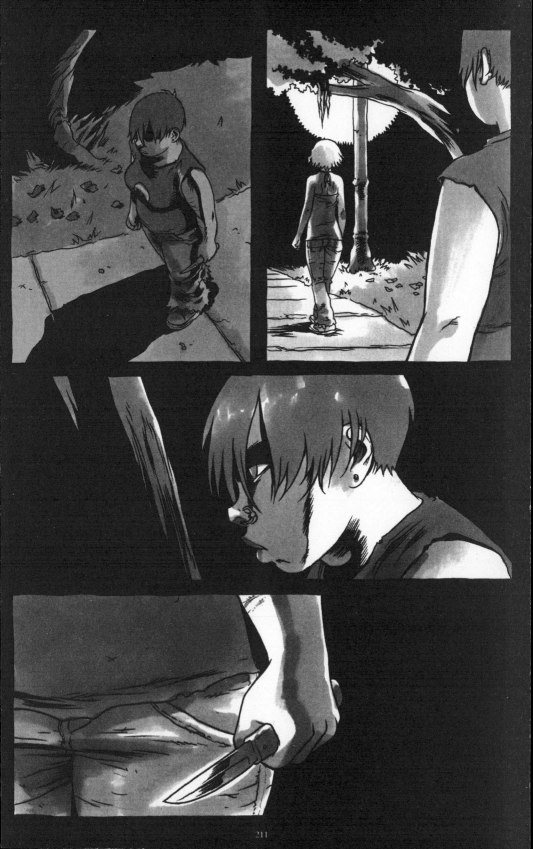

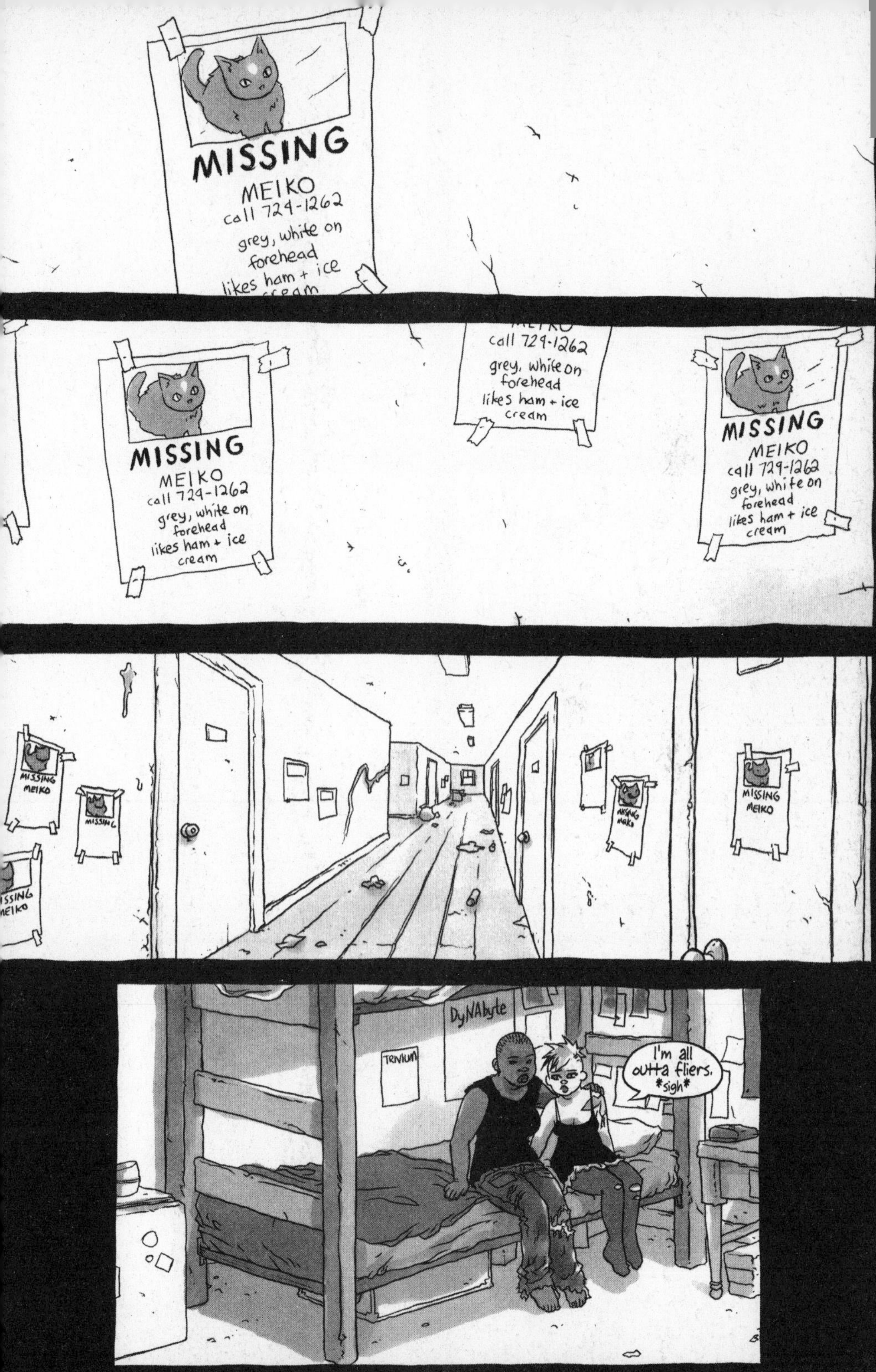
MISSING
MEIKO
call 729-1262
grey, white on forehead
likes ham + ice cream
call 729-1262
grey, white on forehead
likes ham + ice cream
MISSING
MEIKO
call 729-1262
grey, white on forehead
likes ham + ice cream
MISSING
MEIKO
call 729-1262
grey, white on forehead
likes ham + ice cream
MISSING MEIKO
MISSING
MISSING MEIKO
MISSING MEIKO
DyNAbyte
TRIVIUM
I'm all outta fliers.
sigh

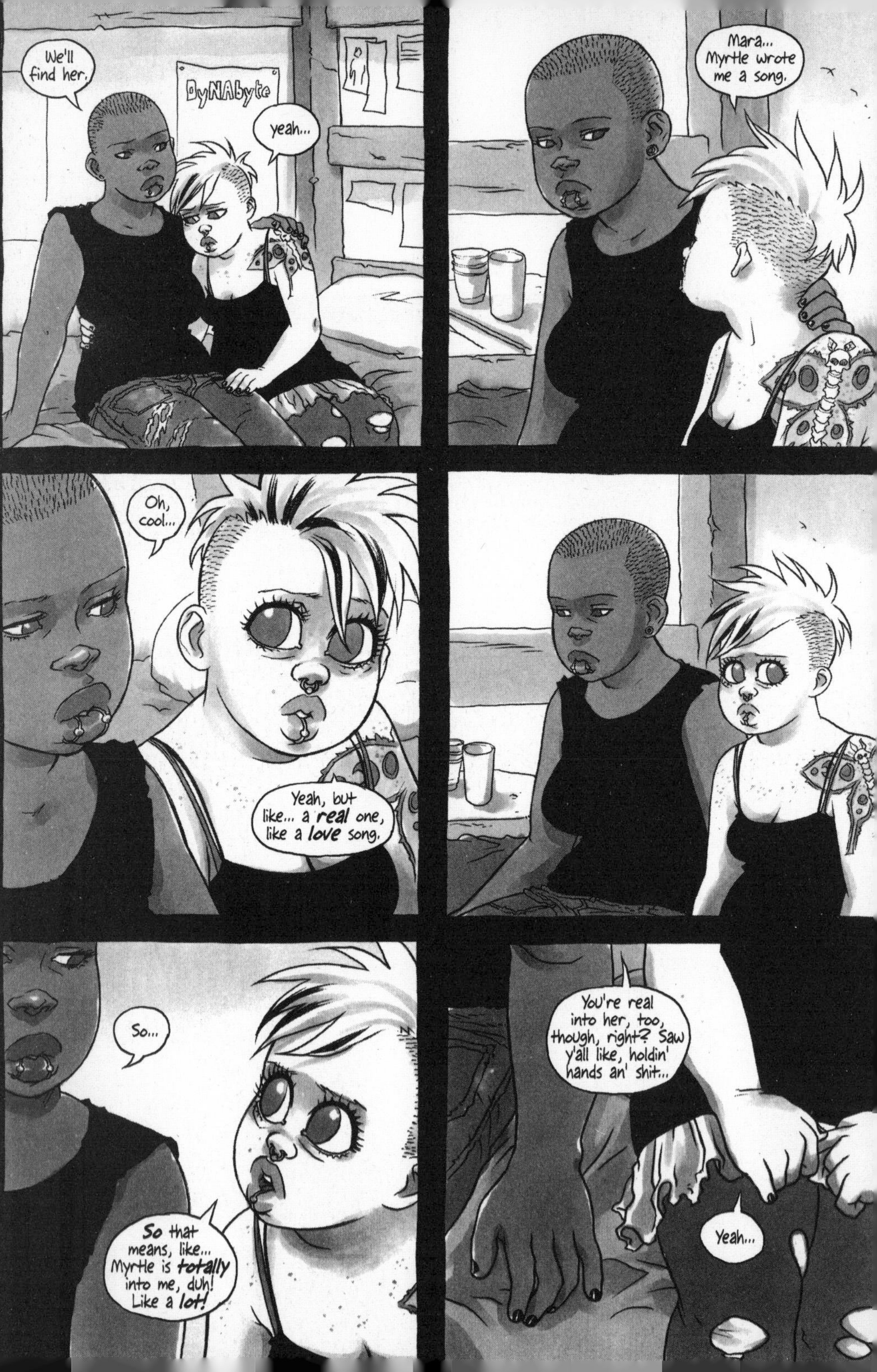
We'll find her.
DyNAbyte
yeah...
Mara... Myrtle wrote me a song.
Oh, cool...
Yeah, but like... a **real** one, like a **love** song.
So...
So that means, like... Myrtle is **totally** into me, duh! Like a **lot**!
You're real into her, too, though, right? Saw y'all like, holdin' hands an' shit...
Yeah...

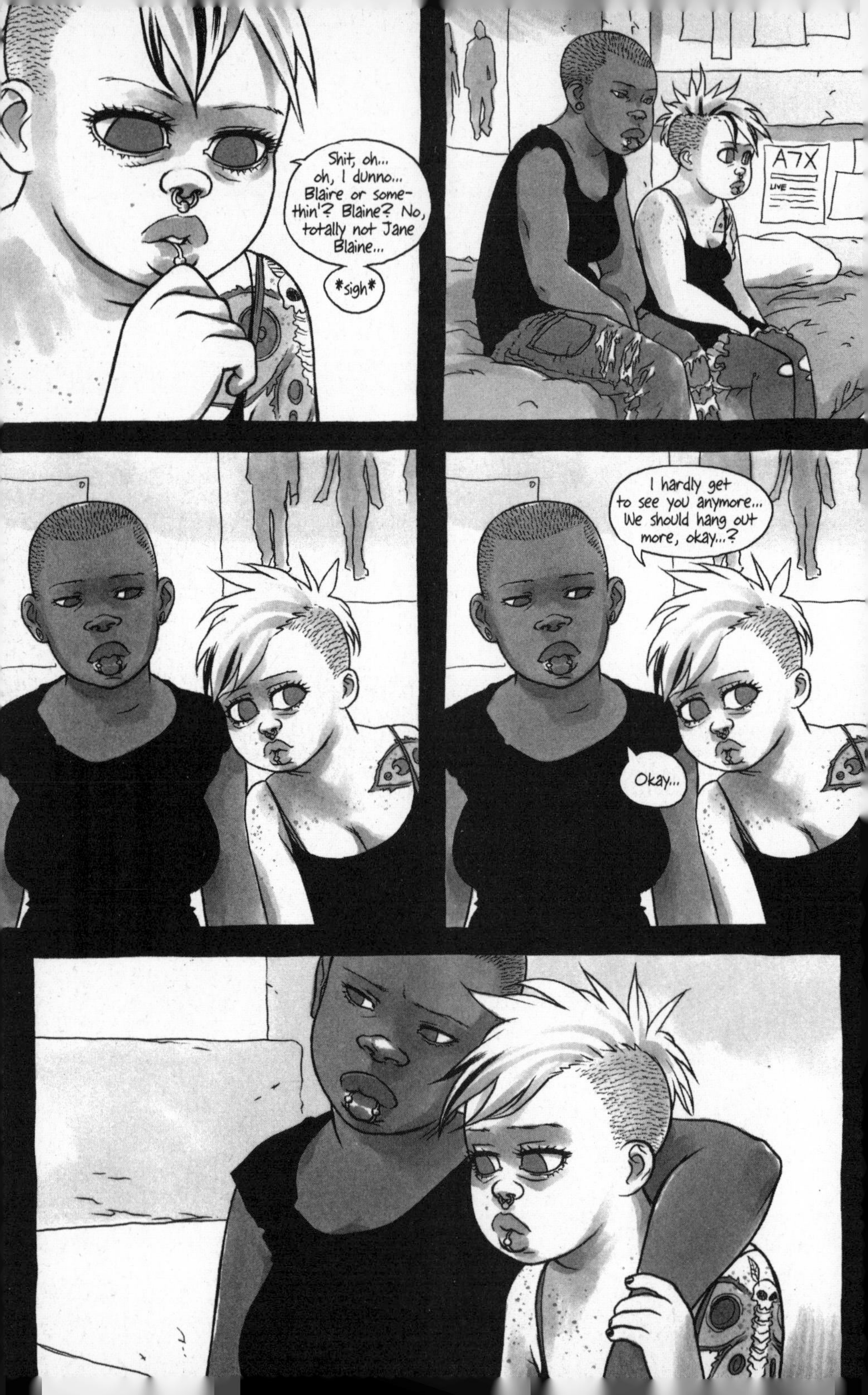
Shit, oh... oh, I dunno... Blaire or somethin'? Blaine? No, totally not Jane Blaine...
sigh
A7X
LIVE
I hardly get to see you anymore... We should hang out more, okay...?
Okay...

something breaks inside of me
something wicked
rise
screams lift into the air louder still
purge the demons from my mind

[Bella Morte]

16

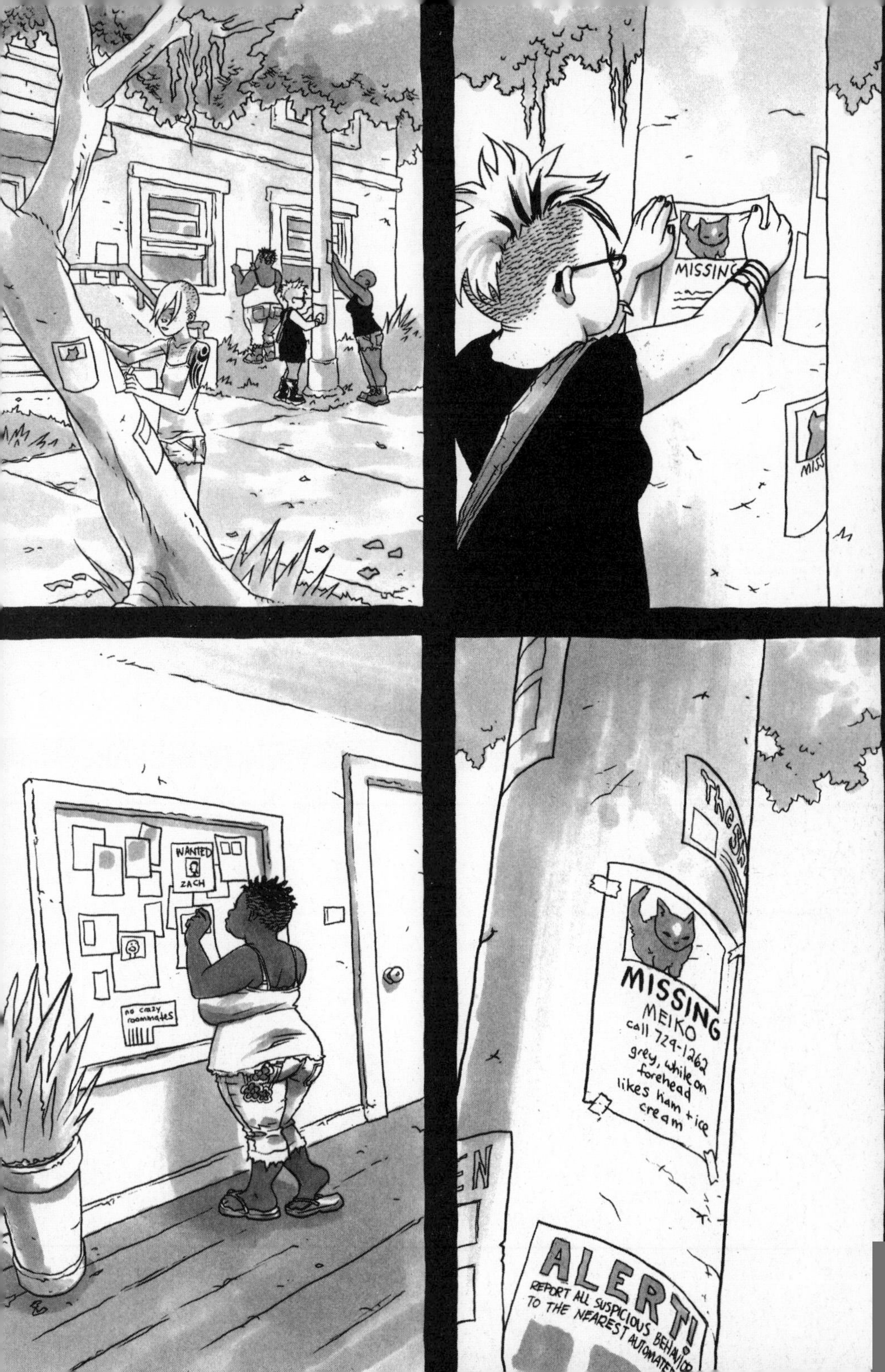
MISSING
WANTED
ZACH
no crazy roommates
MISSING
MEIKO
call 729-1262
grey, white on forehead
likes ham + ice cream
ALERT!
REPORT ALL SUSPICIOUS BEHAVIOR
TO THE NEAREST

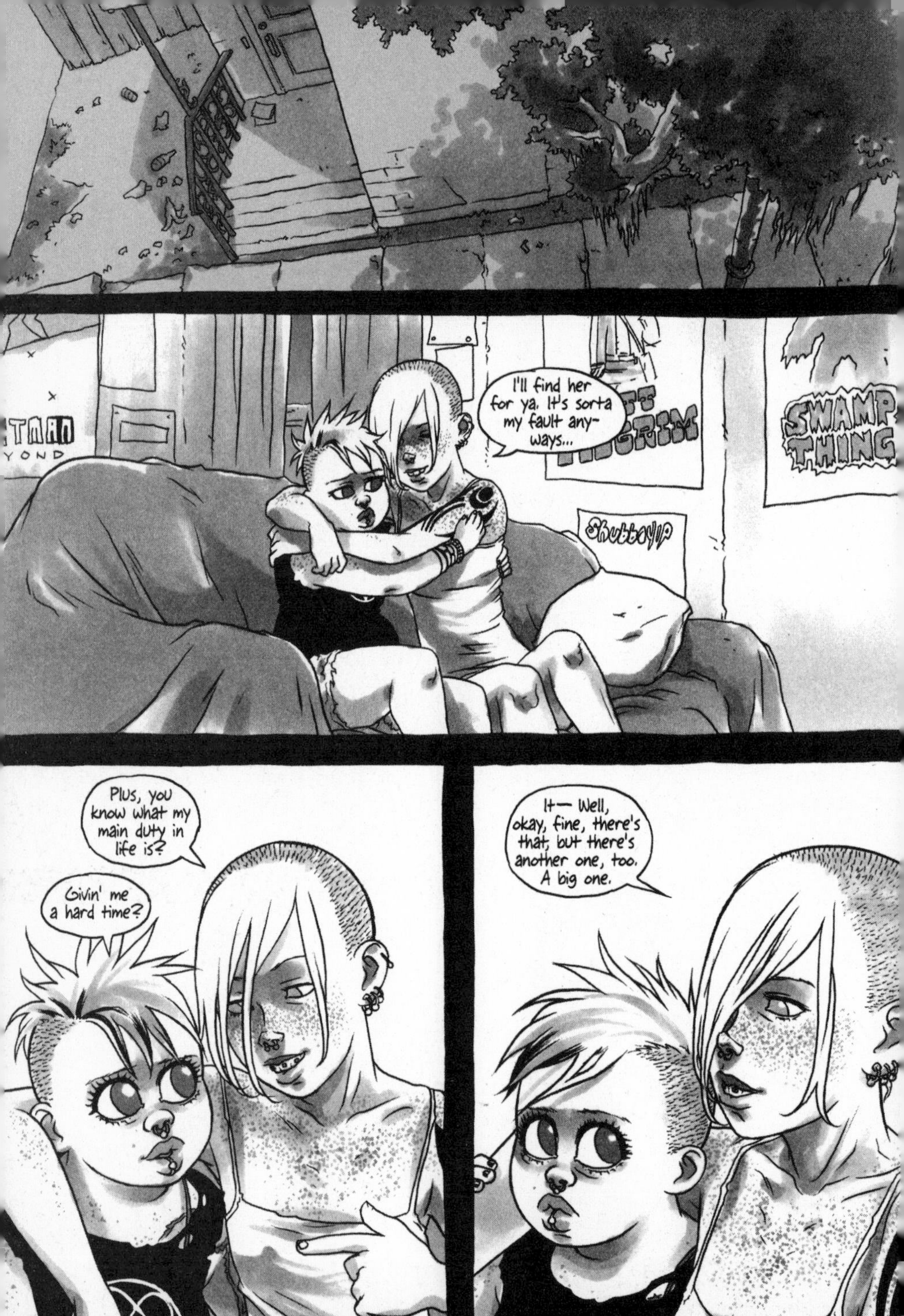
TMAN
YOND
I'll find her for ya. It's sorta my fault any- ways...
SWAMP THING
Shuttayip
Plus, you know what my main duty in life is?
Givin' me a hard time?
It— Well, okay, fine, there's that, but there's another one, too. A big one.

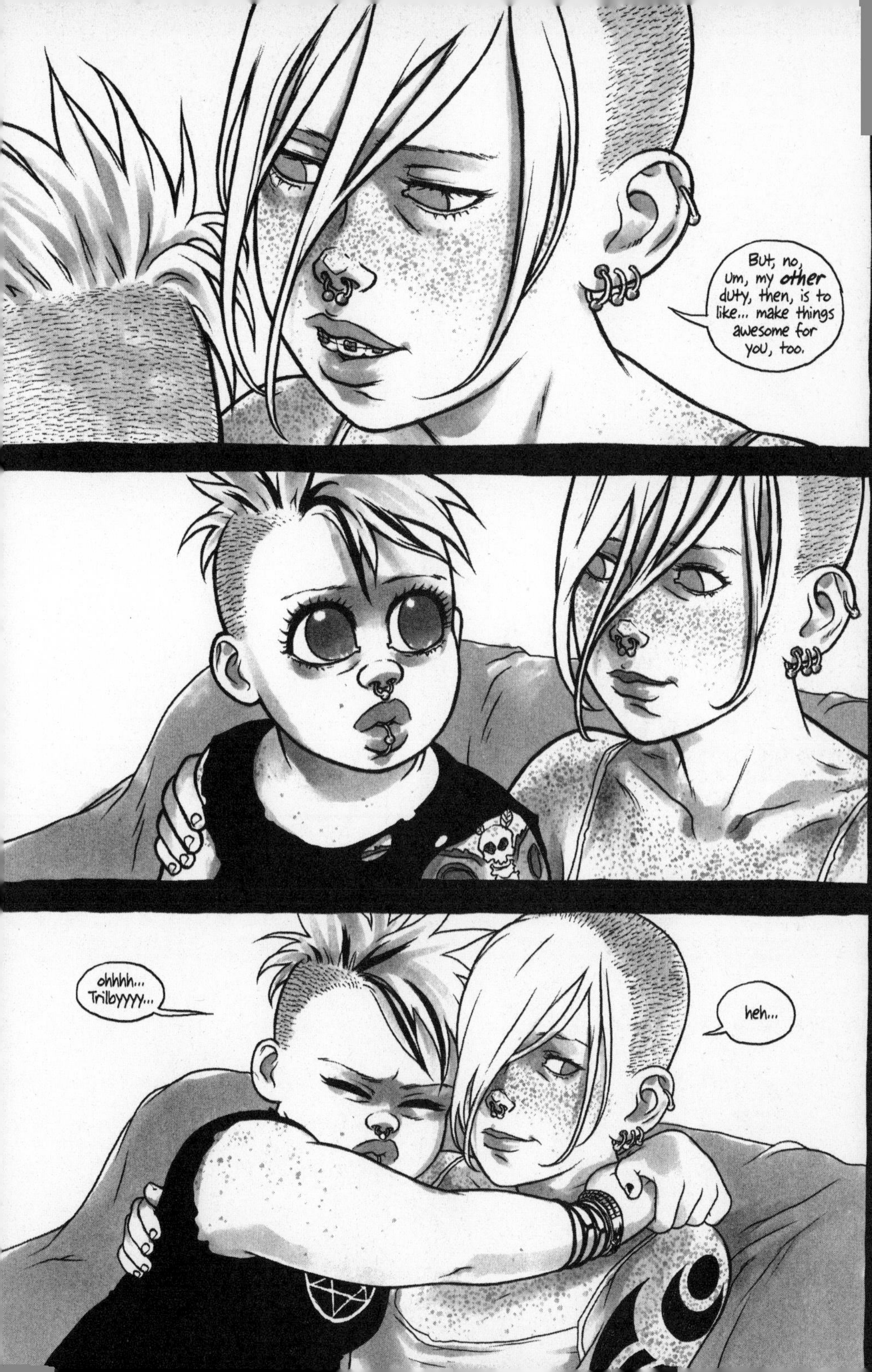
But, no, um, my other duty, then, is to like... make things awesome for you, too.
ohhhh... Trilbyyyy...
heh...

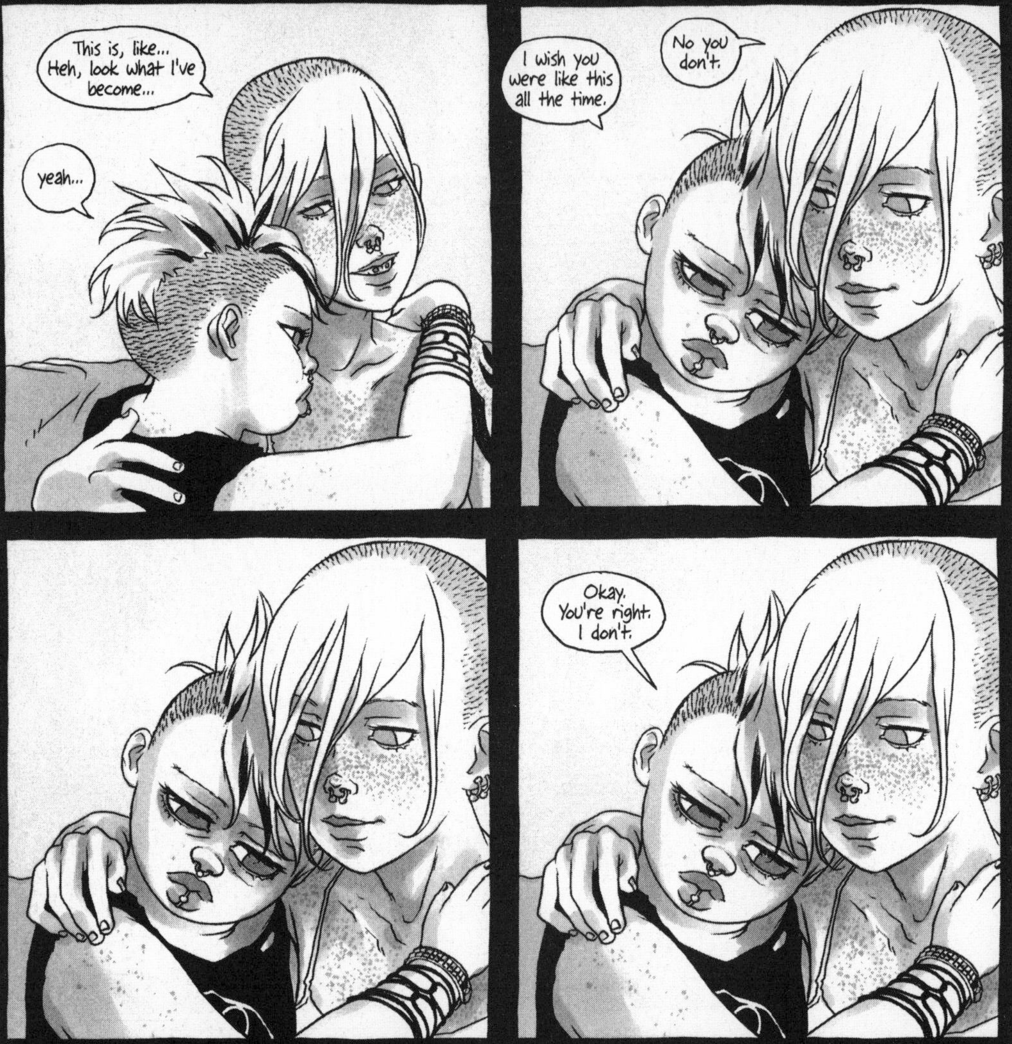
This is, like... Heh, look what I've become...
yeah...
I wish you were like this all the time.
No you don't.
Okay. You're right. I don't.

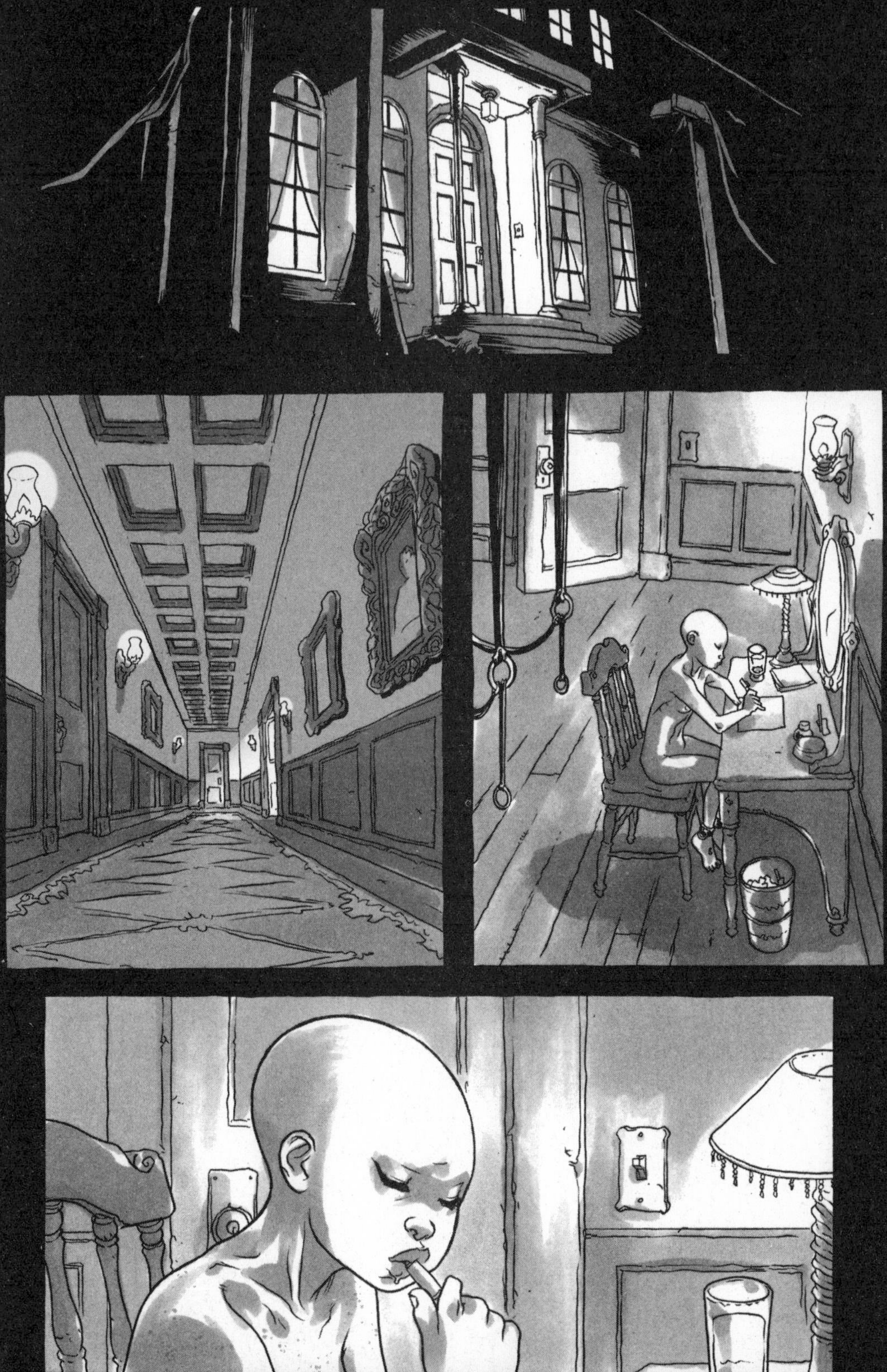

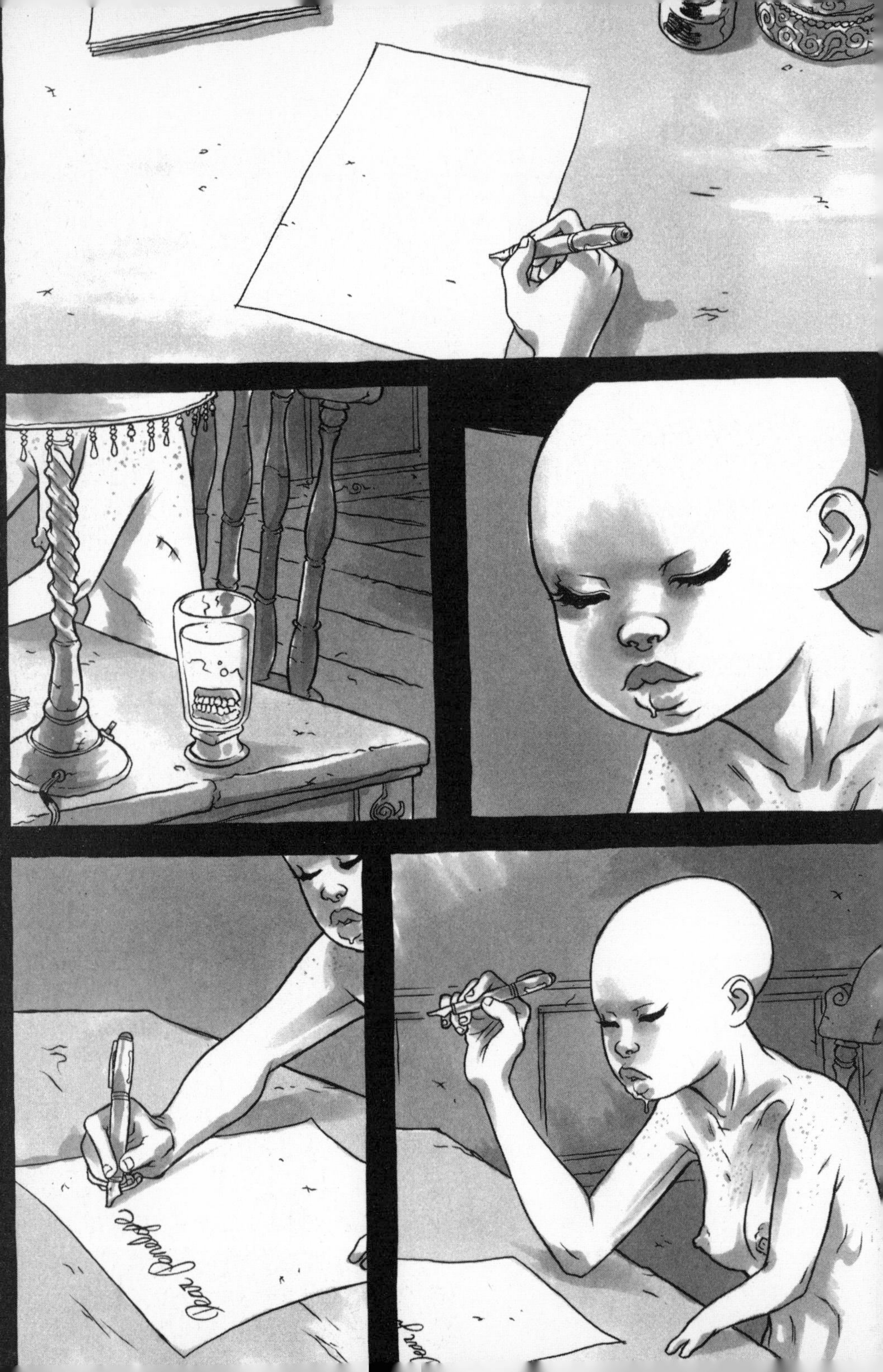
Dear Penelope

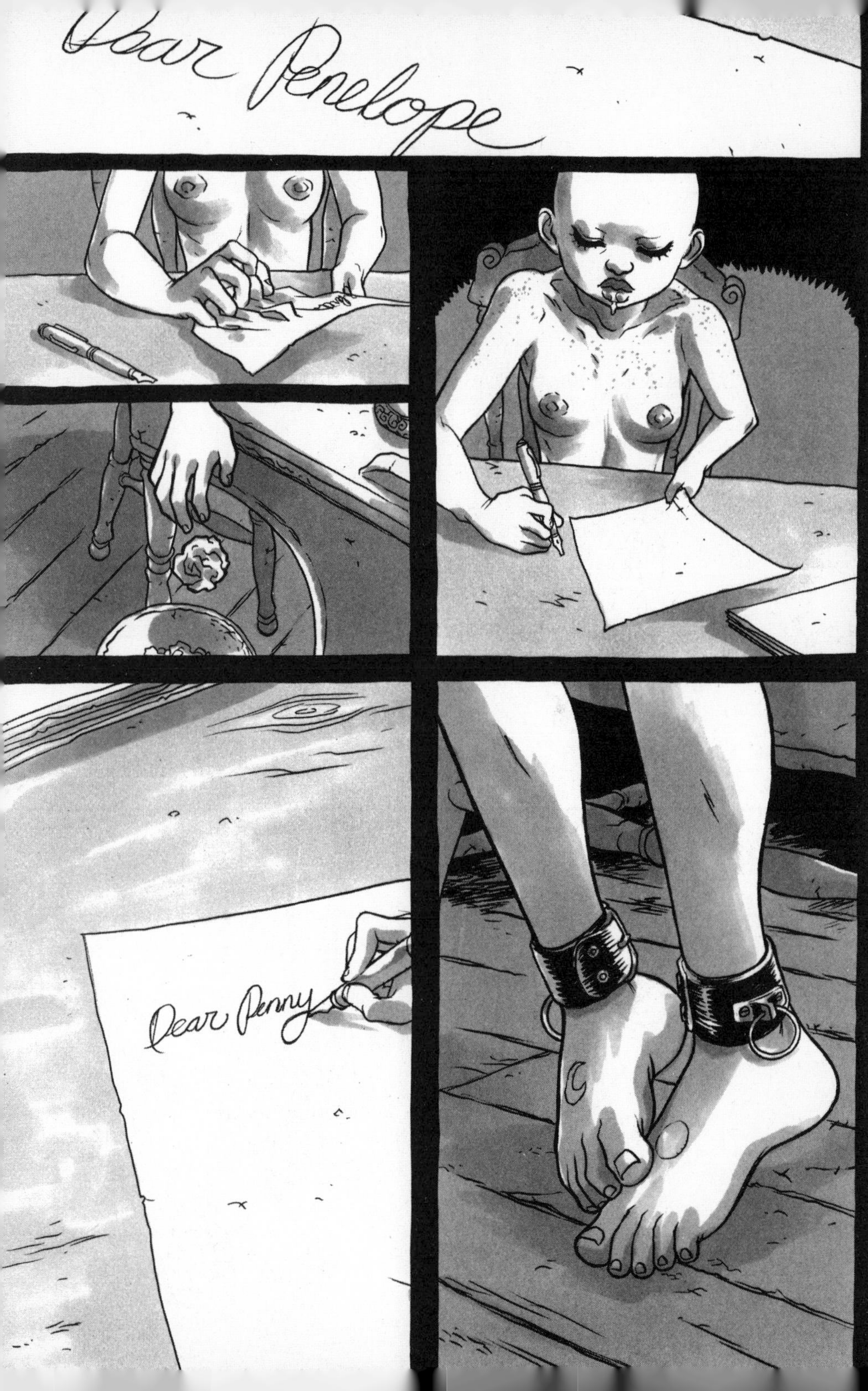
Dear Penelope
Dear Penny

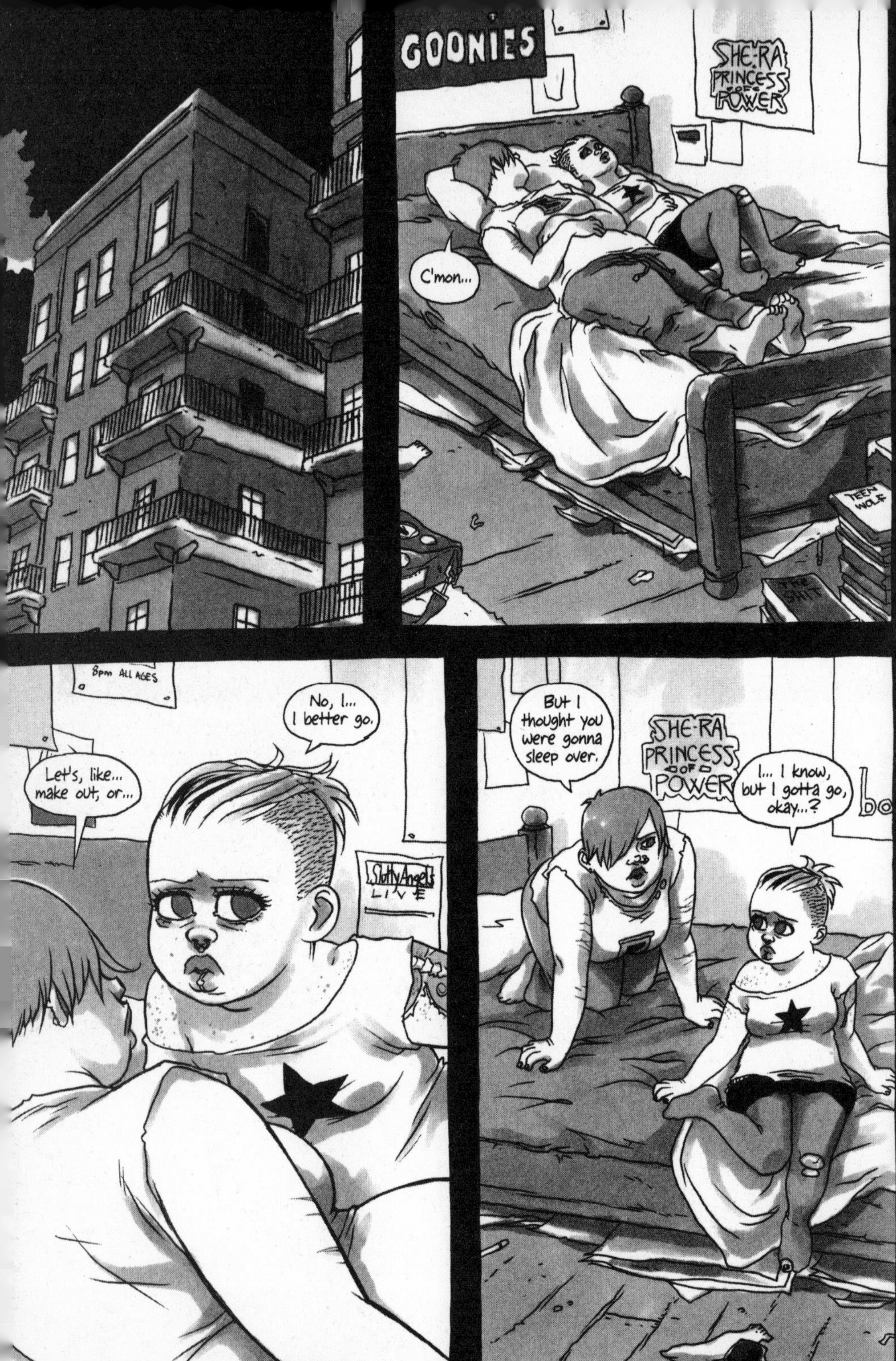
GOONIES
SHE-RA PRINCESS OF POWER
C'mon...
TEEN WOLF
8pm ALL AGES
Let's, like... make out, or...
No, I... I better go.
Slutty Angels LIVE
But I thought you were gonna sleep over.
SHE-RA PRINCESS OF POWER
I... I know, but I gotta go, okay...?

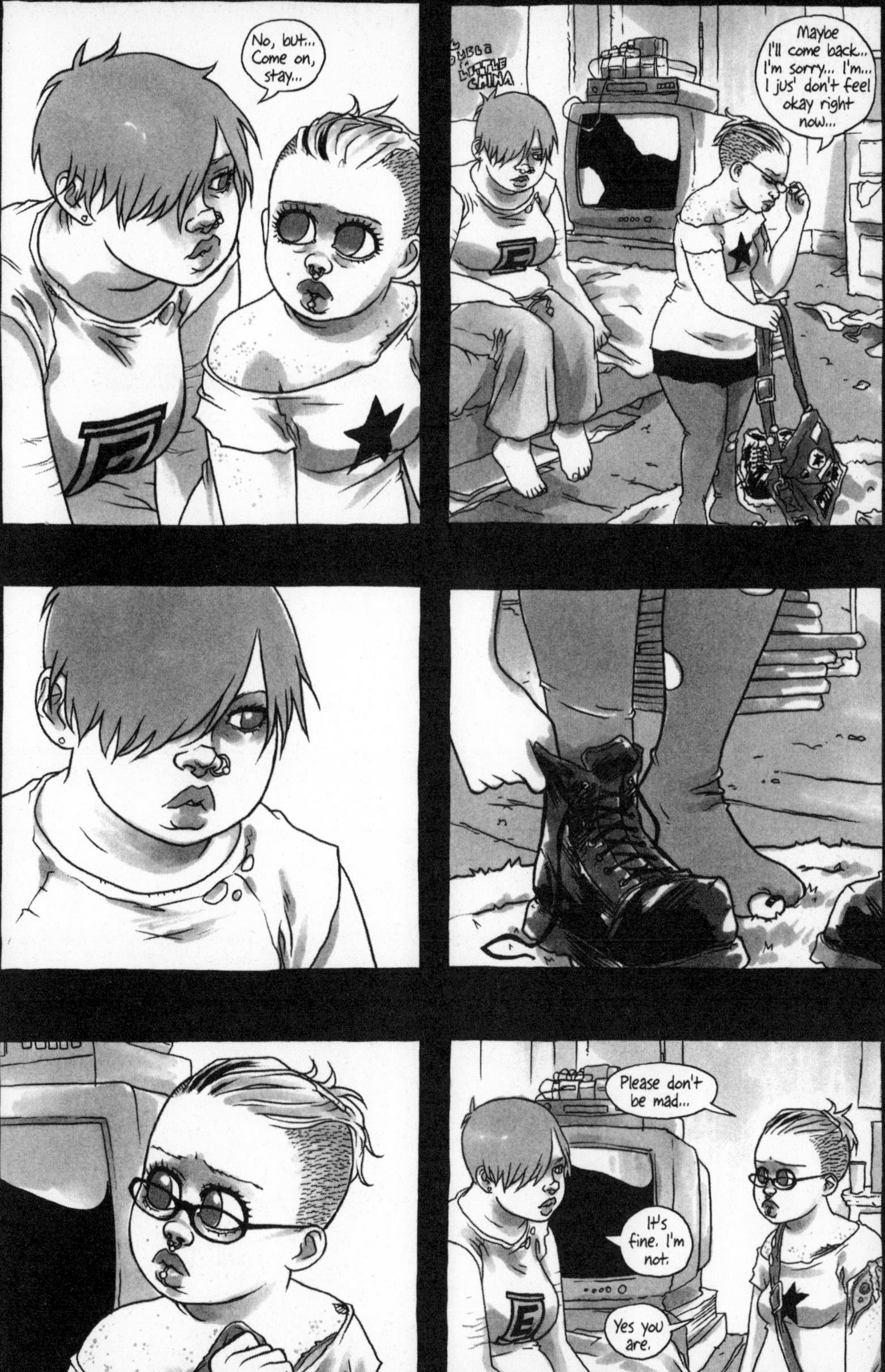
No, but... Come on, stay...
LITTLE CHINA
Maybe I'll come back... I'm sorry... I'm... I jus' don't feel okay right now...
Please don't be mad...
It's fine. I'm not.
Yes you are.

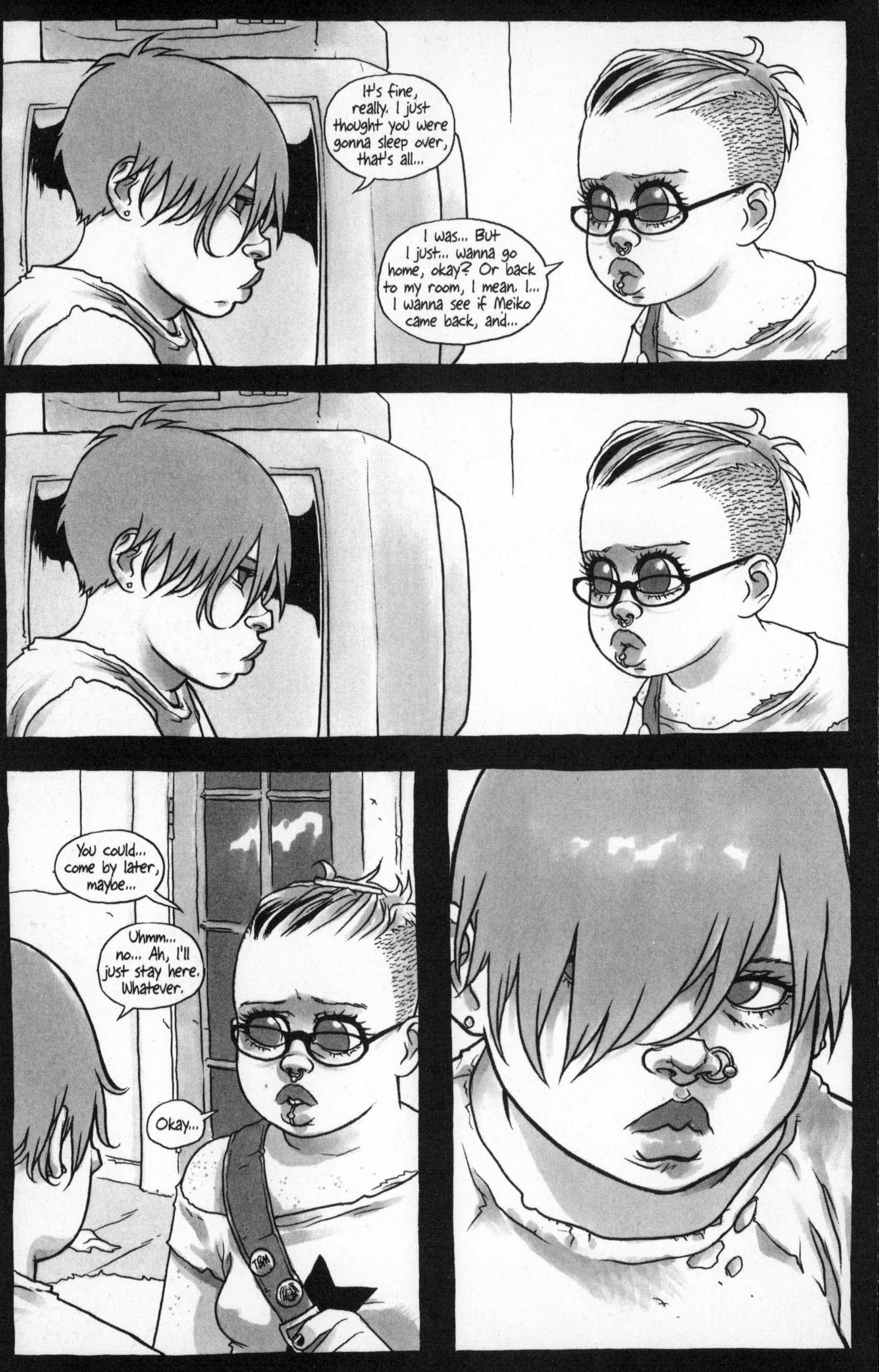
It's fine, really. I just thought you were gonna sleep over, that's all...
I was... But I just... wanna go home, okay? Or back to my room, I mean. I... I wanna see if Meiko came back, and...
You could... come by later, maybe...
Uhmm... no... Ah, I'll just stay here. Whatever.
Okay...

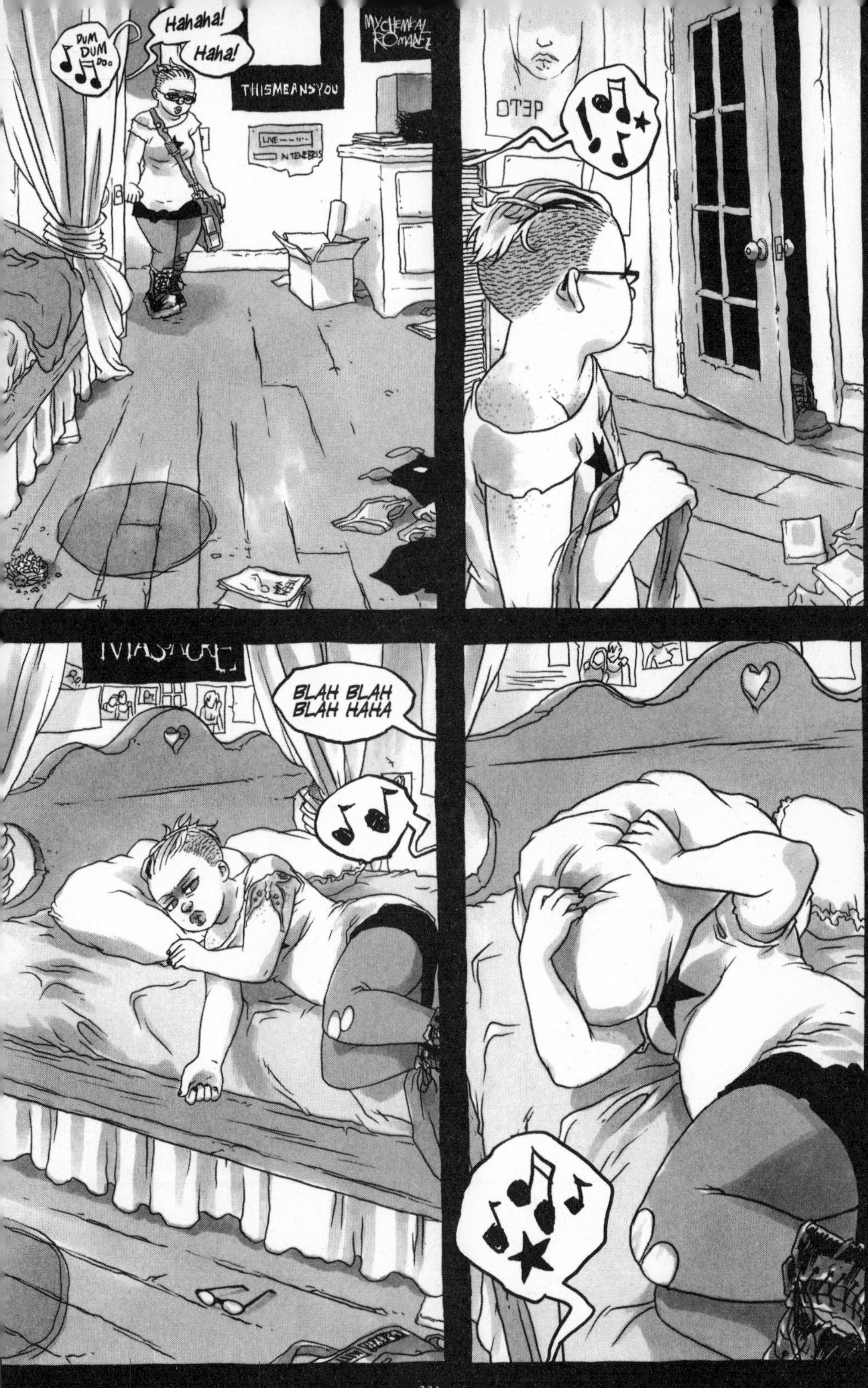
DUM DUM DOO
Hahaha!
Haha!
MY CHEMICAL ROMANCE
THISMEANSYOU
LIVE
IN TENEBRIS
OTEP
BLAH BLAH BLAH HAHA

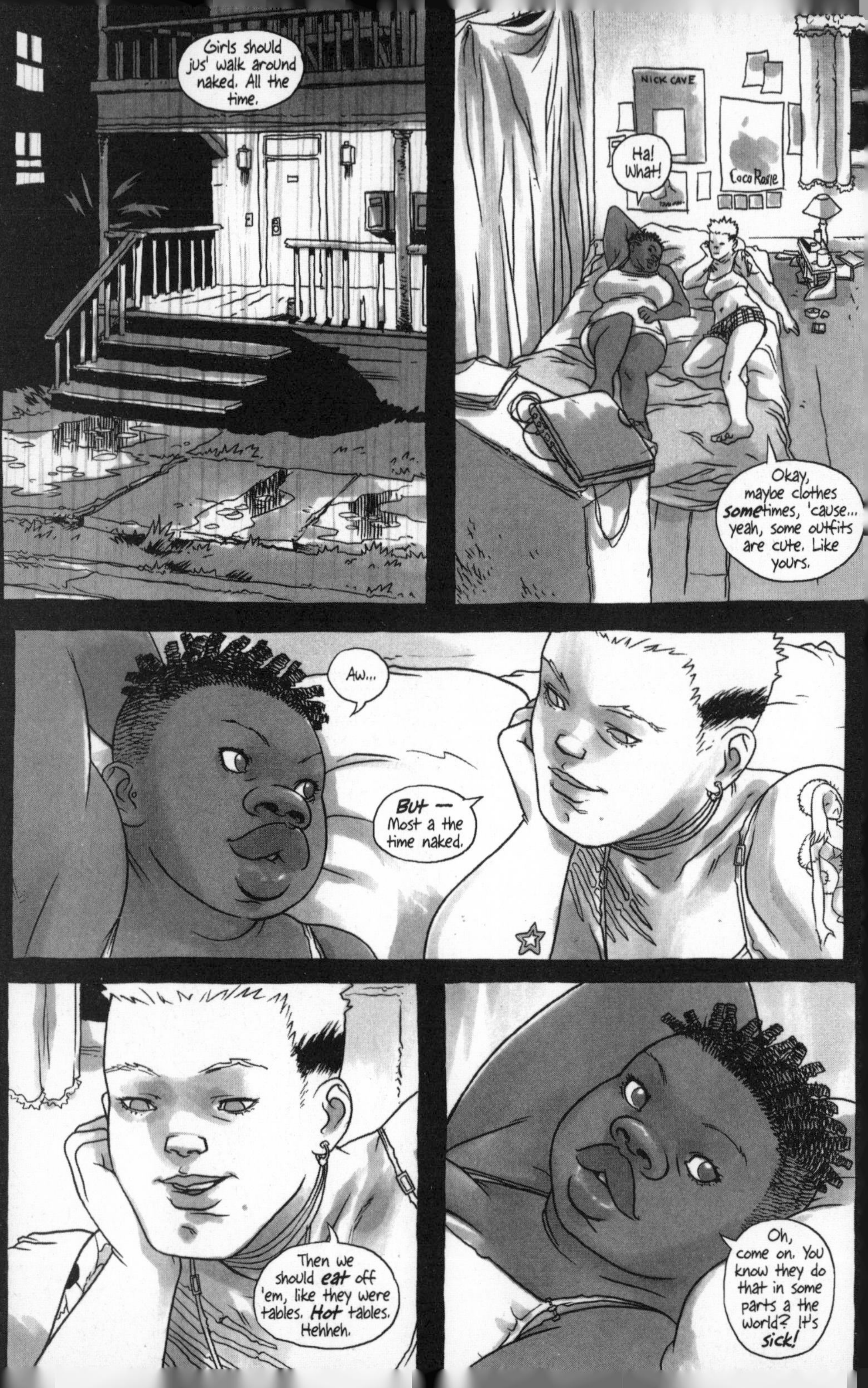
Girls should jus' walk around naked. All the time.
NICK CAVE
CocoRosie
Ha! What!
Okay, maybe clothes sometimes, 'cause... yeah, some outfits are cute. Like yours.
Aw...
But — Most a the time naked.
Then we should eat off 'em, like they were tables. Hot tables. Hehheh.
Oh, come on. You know they do that in some parts a the world? It's sick!

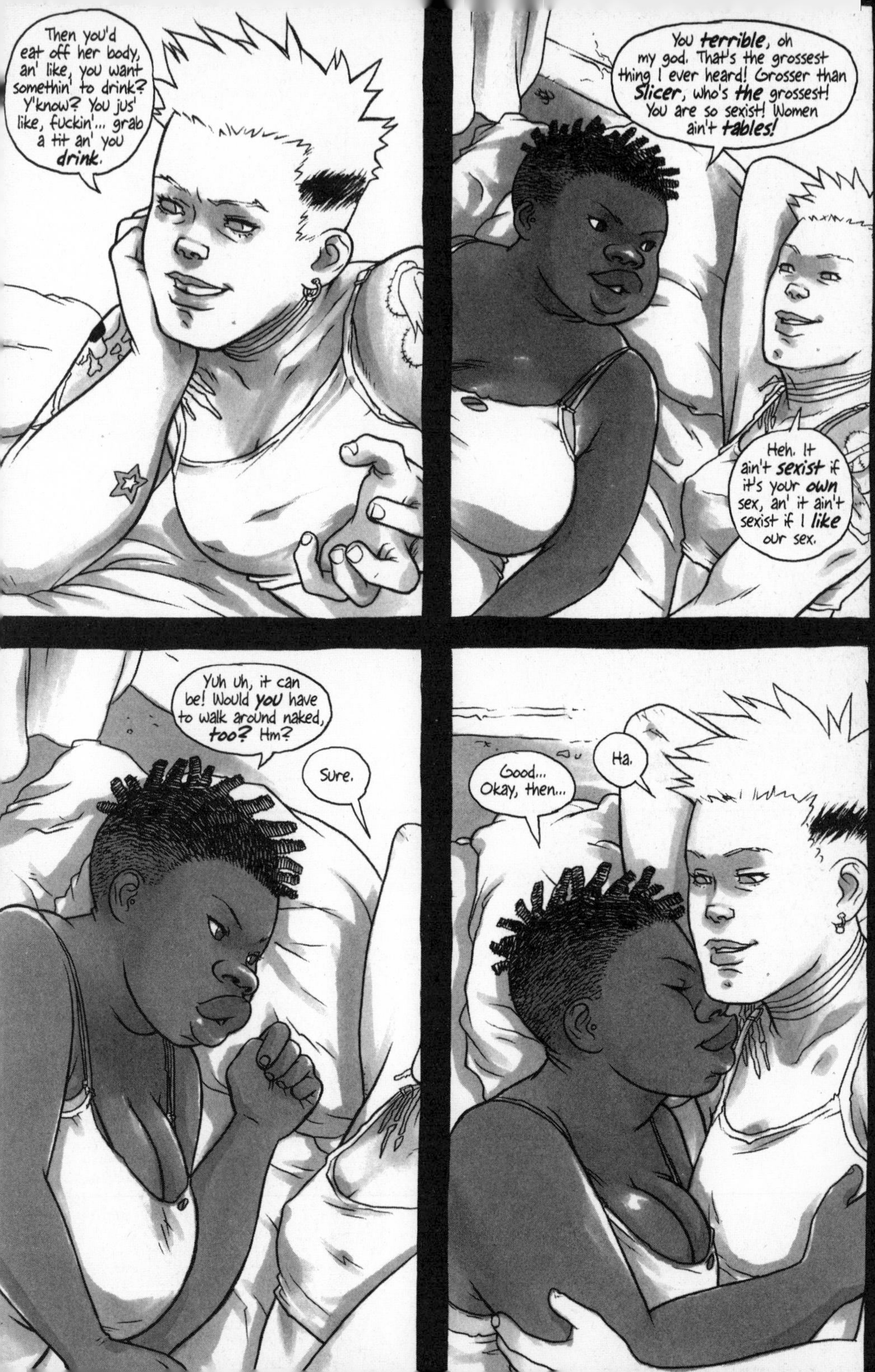
Then you'd eat off her body, an' like, you want somethin' to drink? Y'know? You jus' like, fuckin'... grab a tit an' you **drink**.
You **terrible**, oh my god. That's the grossest thing I ever heard! Grosser than **Slicer**, who's **the** grossest! You are so sexist! Women ain't **tables!**
Heh. It ain't **sexist** if it's your **own** sex, an' it ain't sexist if I **like** our sex.
Yuh uh, it can be! Would **you** have to walk around naked, **too?** Hm?
Sure.
Good... Okay, then...
Ha.

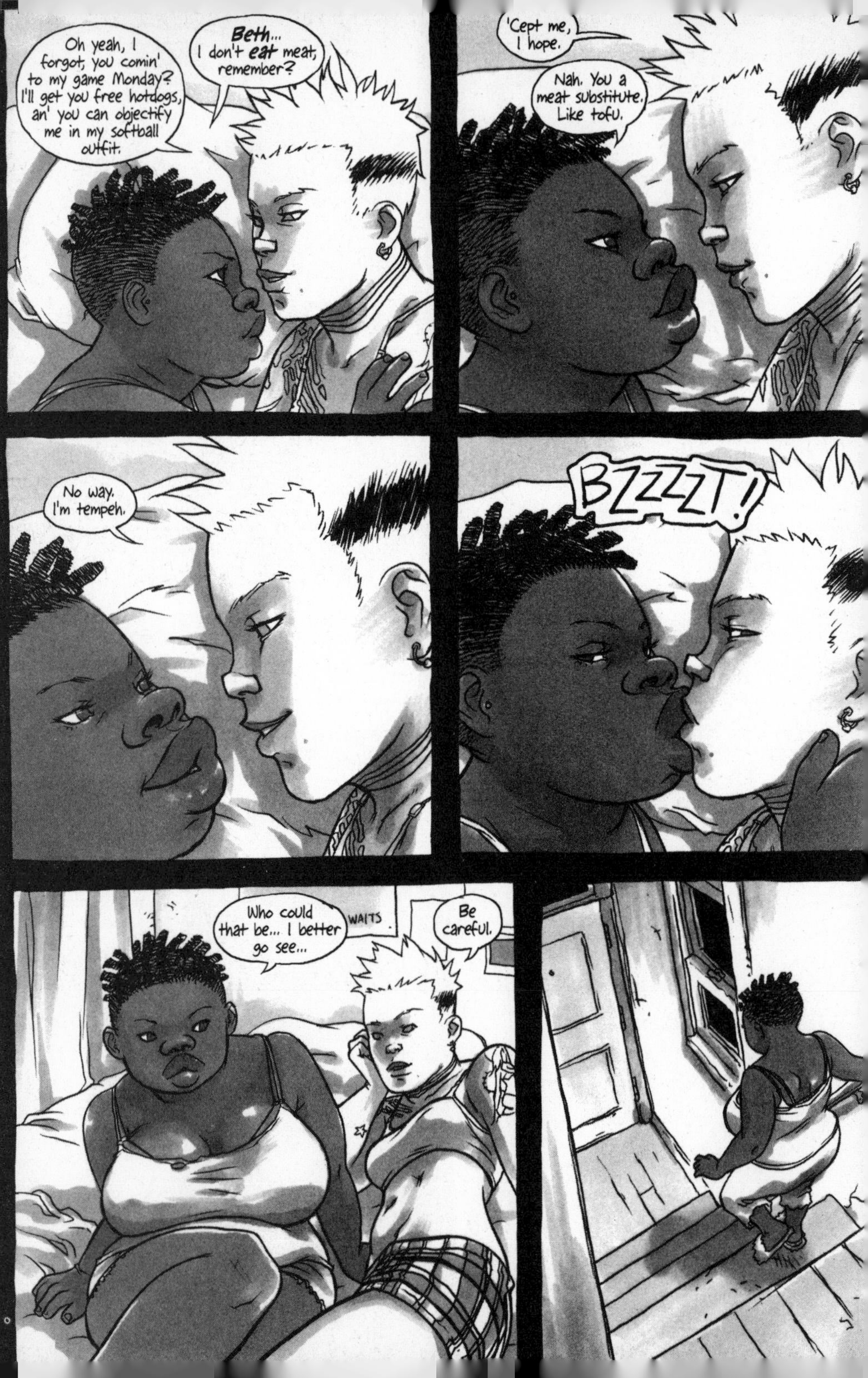
Oh yeah, I forgot, you comin' to my game Monday? I'll get you free hotdogs, an' you can objectify me in my softball outfit.
Beth... I don't eat meat, remember?
'Cept me, I hope.
Nah. You a meat substitute. Like tofu.
No way. I'm tempeh.
BZZZZT!
Who could that be... I better go see...
WAITS
Be careful.

235

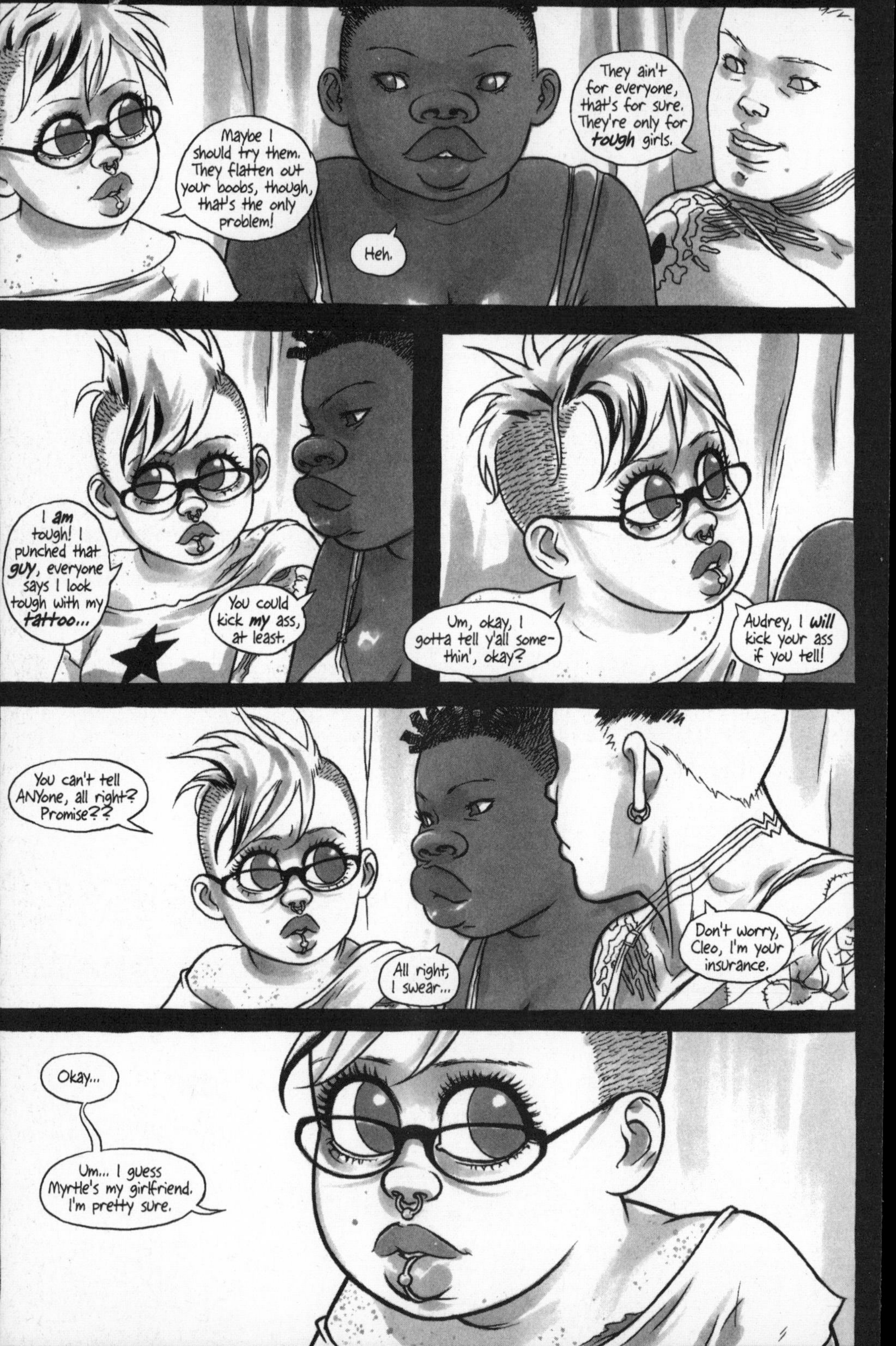
Maybe I should try them. They flatten out your boobs, though, that's the only problem!
Heh.
They ain't for everyone, that's for sure. They're only for **tough** girls.
I **am** tough! I punched that **guy**, everyone says I look tough with my **tattoo...**
You could kick **my** ass, at least.
Um, okay, I gotta tell y'all some-thin', okay?
Audrey, I **will** kick your ass if you tell!
You can't tell ANYone, all right? Promise??
All right, I swear...
Don't worry, Cleo, I'm your insurance.
Okay...
Um... I guess Myrtle's my girlfriend. I'm pretty sure.

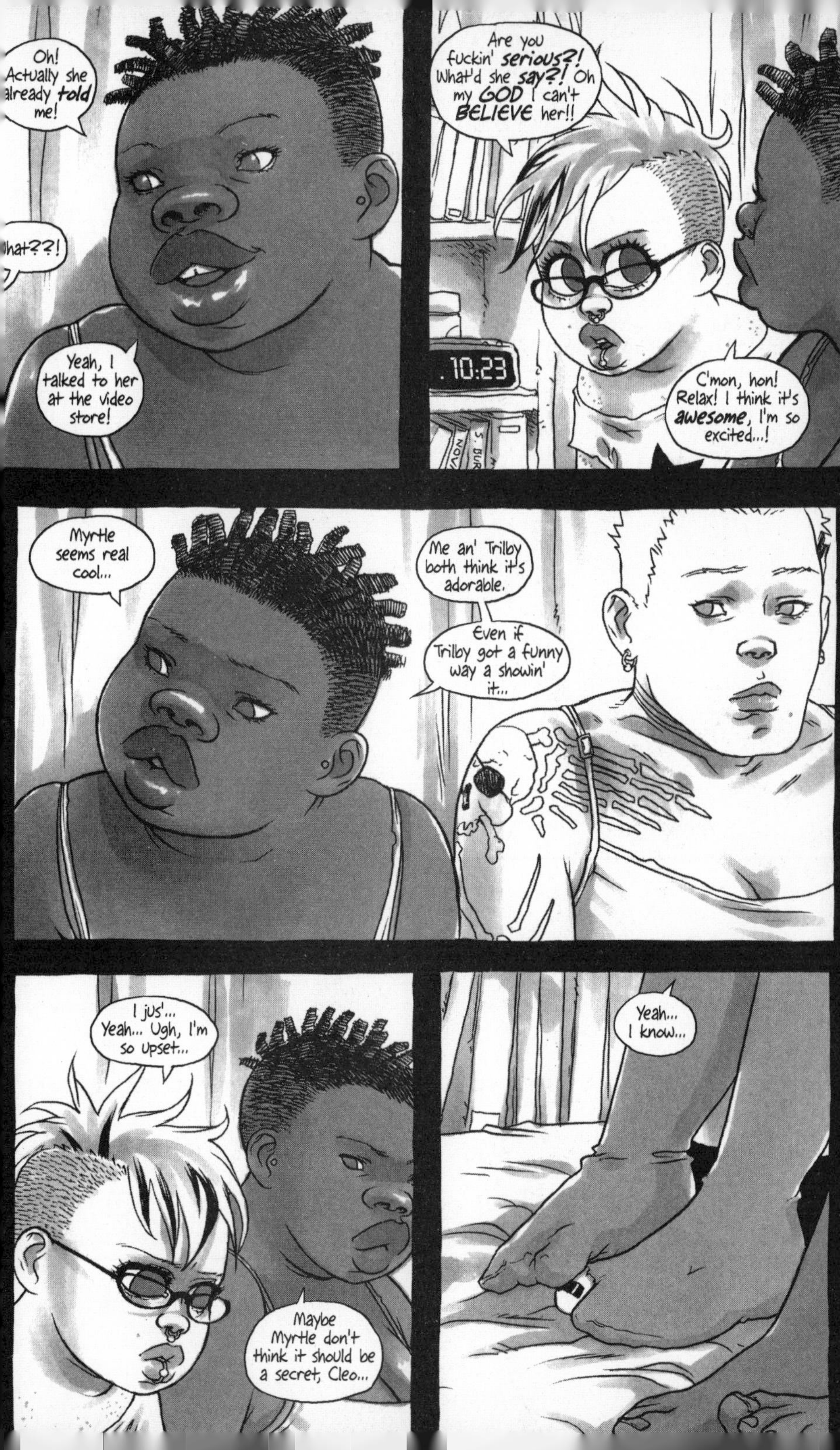
Oh! Actually she already told me!
What??!
Yeah, I talked to her at the video store!
Are you fuckin' serious?! What'd she say?! Oh my GOD I can't BELIEVE her!!
.10:23
C'mon, hon! Relax! I think it's awesome, I'm so excited...!
Myrtle seems real cool...
Me an' Trilby both think it's adorable.
Even if Trilby got a funny way a showin' it...
I jus'... Yeah... Ugh, I'm so upset...
Maybe Myrtle don't think it should be a secret, Cleo...
Yeah... I know...

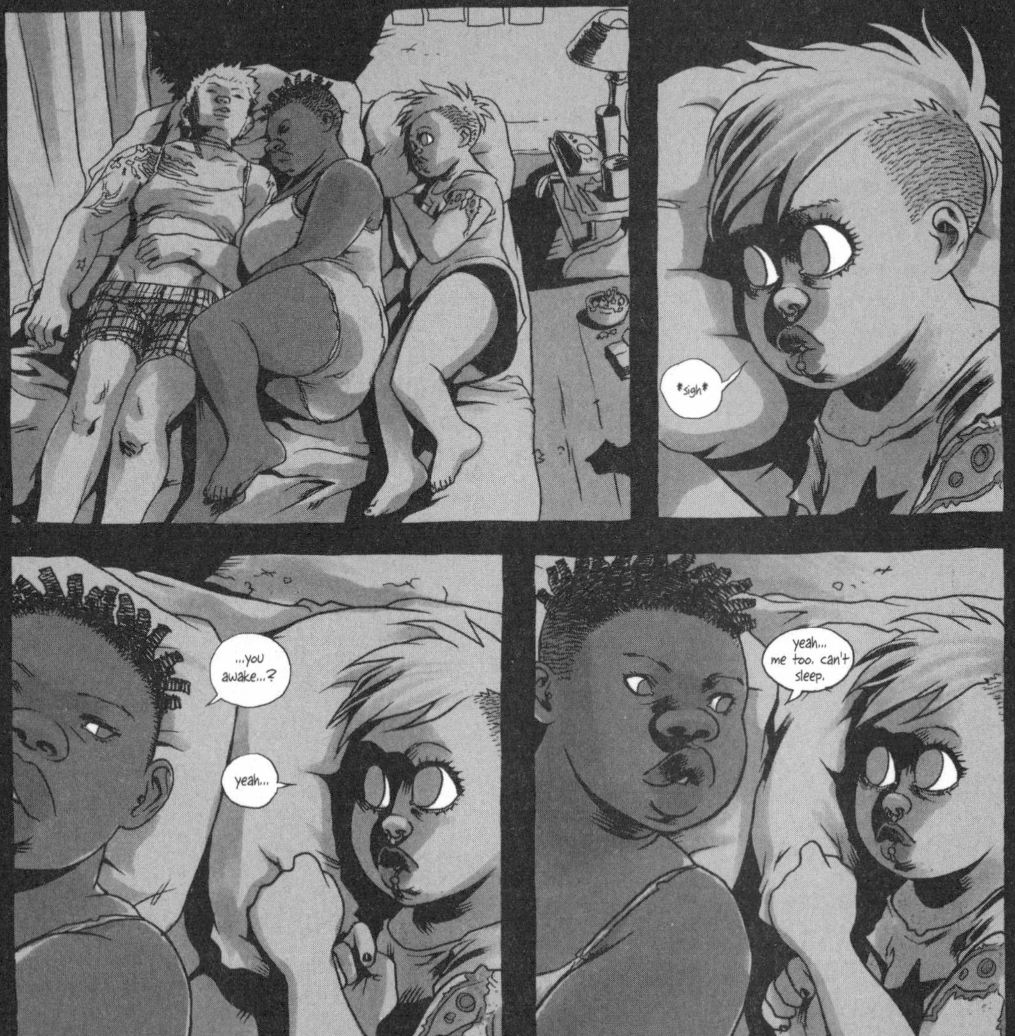
sigh
...you awake...?
yeah...
yeah... me too, can't sleep.

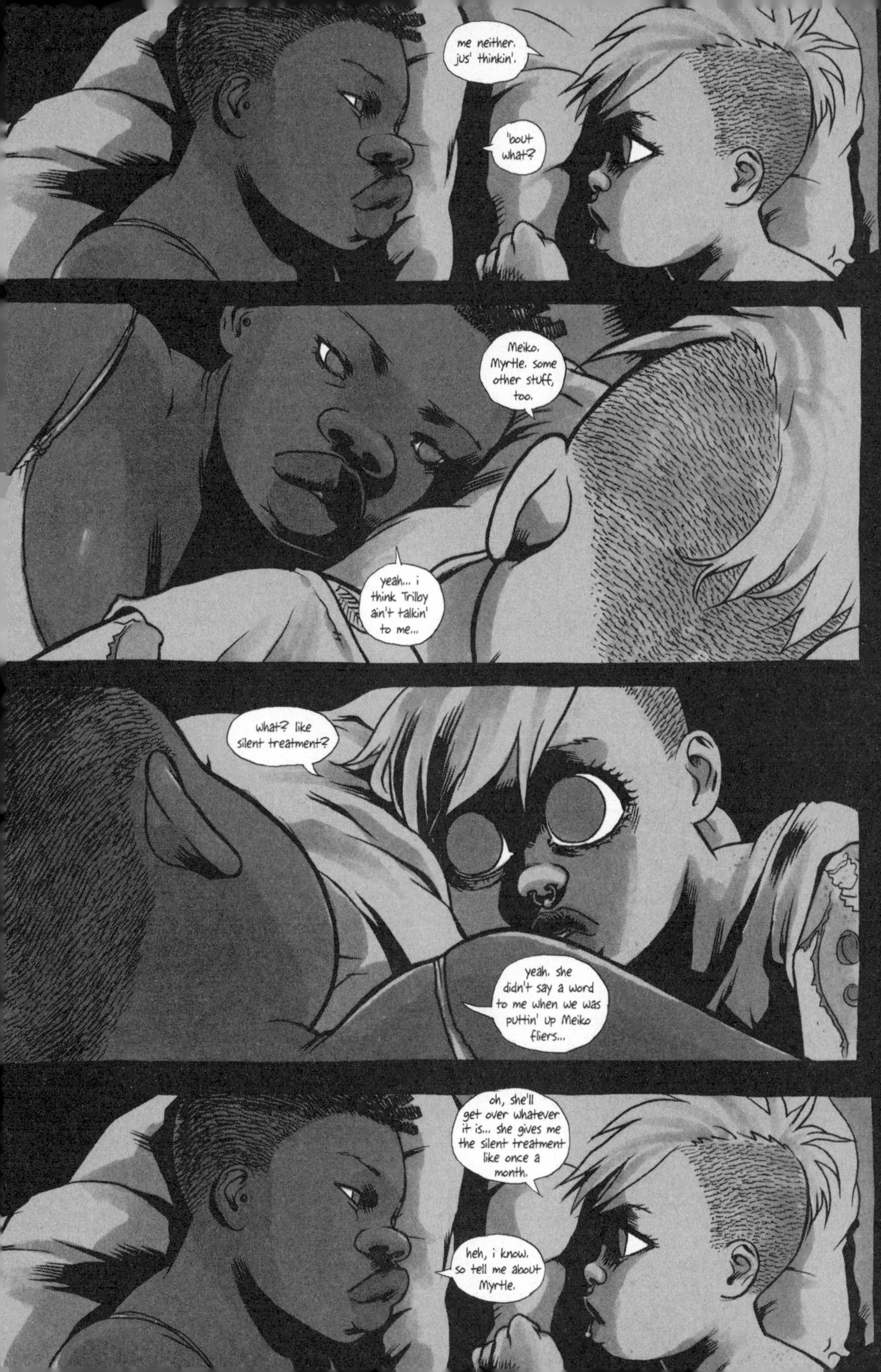
me neither. jus' thinkin'.
'bout what?
Meiko. Myrtle. some other stuff, too.
yeah... i think Trilby ain't talkin' to me...
what? like silent treatment?
yeah. she didn't say a word to me when we was puttin' up Meiko fliers...
oh, she'll get over whatever it is... she gives me the silent treatment like once a month.
heh, i know. so tell me about Myrtle.

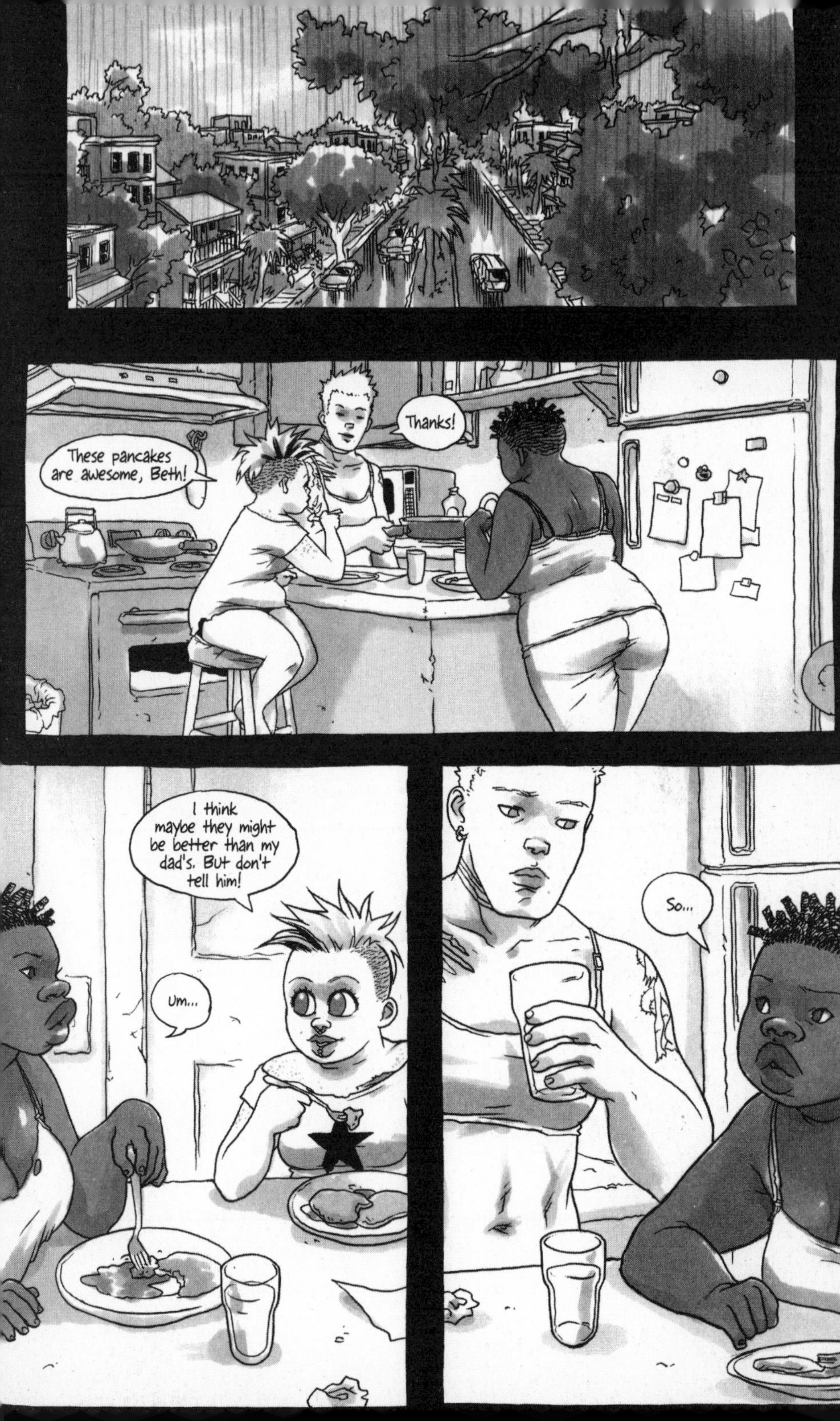
Thanks!
These pancakes are awesome, Beth!
I think maybe they might be better than my dad's. But don't tell him!
Um...
So...

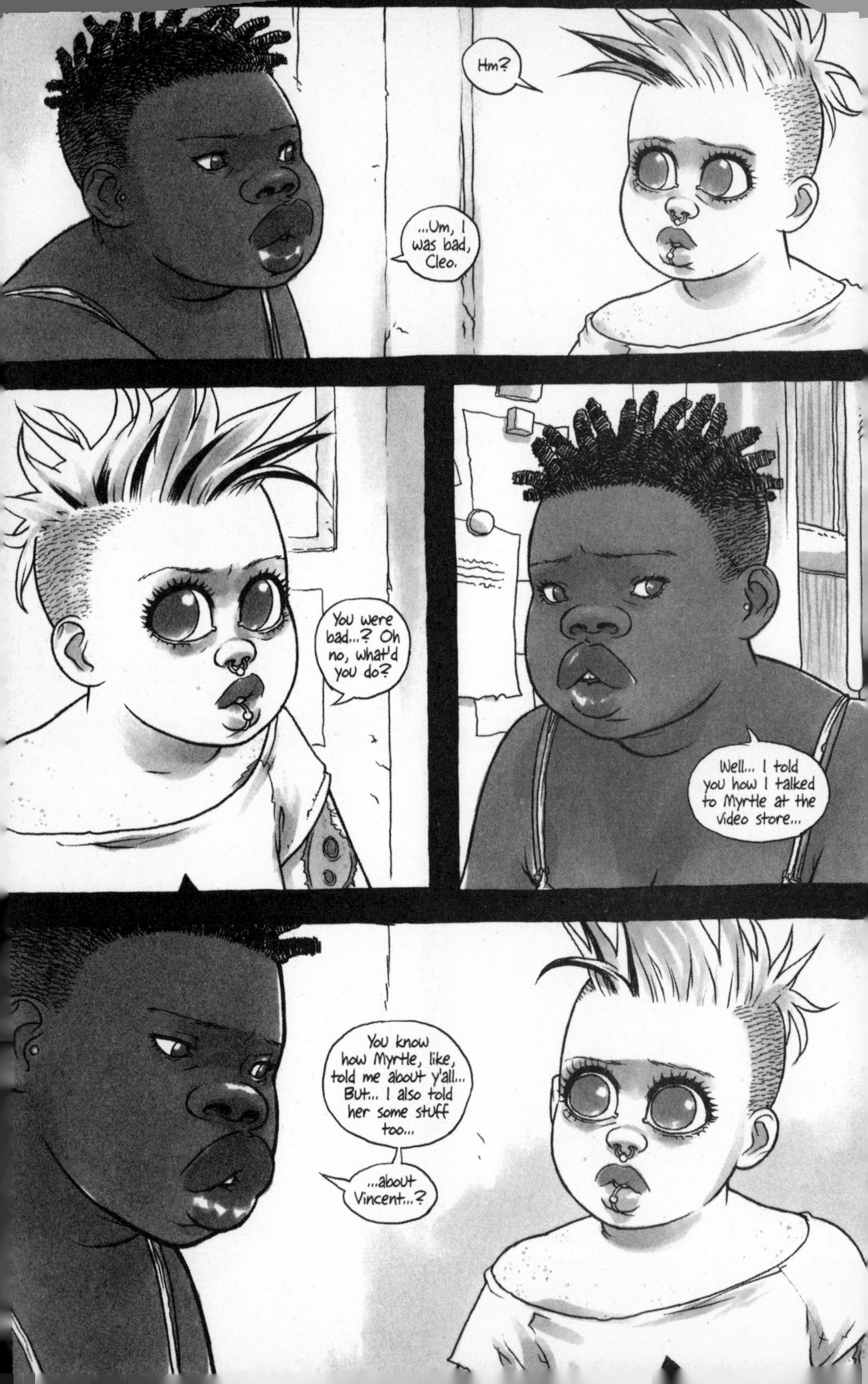
Hm?
...Um, I was bad, Cleo.
You were bad...? Oh no, what'd you do?
Well... I told you how I talked to Myrtle at the video store...
You know how Myrtle, like, told me about y'all... But... I also told her some stuff too...
...about Vincent...?

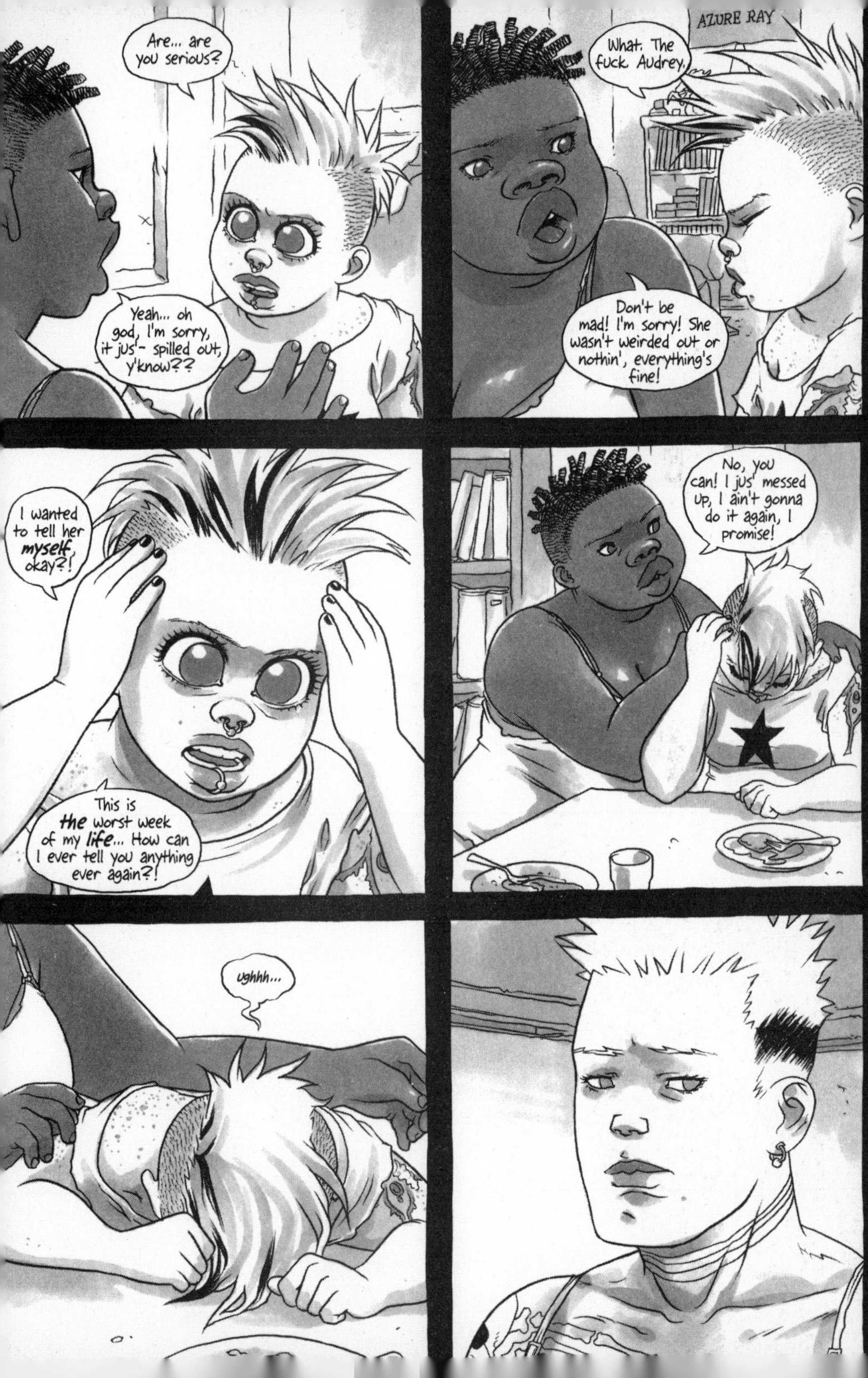
Are... are you serious??
AZURE RAY
What. The fuck. Audrey.
Yeah... oh god, I'm sorry, it jus'- spilled out, y'know??
Don't be mad! I'm sorry! She wasn't weirded out or nothin', everything's fine!
I wanted to tell her *myself*, okay?!
This is **the** worst week of my *life*... How can I ever tell you anything ever again?!
No, you can! I jus' messed up, I ain't gonna do it again, I promise!
ughhh...

The Wonders At Your Feet

[friendtoroaches@gmail.com]

Recent Entries Archive Friends User Info

mara's journal

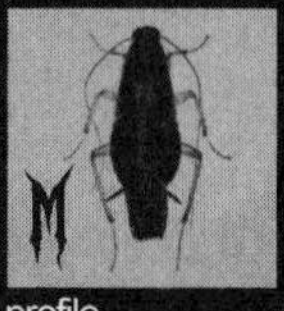

profile

October 19th, 1:22am

TREAD THE WORLD WITH STEEL AND BURNING BLADES

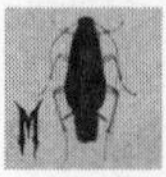

i got up even earlier today. and i went running. i haven't gone for a run in such a long time it felt like, at least since 10th grade i think. it was great except that i really felt the shit in my lungs, it's weird how i hardly ever noticed until now. i really have to quit, i'll never hack it in softball if i don't. i'd hit a homerun and collapse before i'd made it to third base. Cleo's been smoking longer than me, i don't know how she can take it. i think she usually smokes like over a pack a day but i smoke only about half a pack on good days. it's really gross. anyway the run was great, i'm doing it again tomorrow and i hope i can keep it up and start a routine to get in shape again. and then i'll figure out how to stop smoking. then i will rock. i'm sick of my friends and i know i was all talking about how i like being alone so much in my last post but i think i might look for some new friends. at least ones for casual hanging out, i don't know. it's hard to set up new close friendships with people you haven't already known for years from when you were a kid. i think i'm going to take another jog and then stop over at Bowden House and see if Natalie's there. i can't leave things with her hanging on my last two weird, awkward, shitty run-ins. it's going to be good this time.

mood: excited
current music: dynabyte - i'll rise

[0 comments | leave a comment]

October 16th, 3:47pm

THIS RIVER BANK HOLDS SECRETS

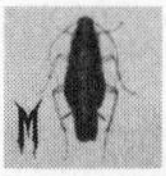

today i got up around 2pm, that's a good start. Cleo is seeing this girl Myrtle, i've mentioned her before. i didn't really think about it at first but i'm pretty much positive now that it's a romantic thing between them. Myrtle actually came up to the window in our European Romanticism class to bug Cleo. who does that? then after that i saw them holding hands. i guess it's cool. i think i'm going to start playing softball again. i walked past the field today and i got all nostalgic and remembering when i used to play. me and Trilby both played and i know Trilby still does so that might be weird with her on the team too. but i know i should really do this, i'm going to tryouts next week. i used to hit some killer home runs. it'll be great to be playing for the Wet Moon Worm Lizards again. maybe this means i'll have to stop smoking.

Trilby being with Martin, Cleo with Myrtle and Audrey with Beth sort of half makes me want to be with someone too, like this subconscious, passive peer pressure. nobody's actively trying to get me to do anything, but it's this presence that's still there. i like being the one single girl though, there's something appealing about it. when all my friends are off with their significant others i'm pretty much left alone, and while i sort of know my roomate Claire i don't really have anyone else to hang out with but i kind of like that, being forced to be by myself and entertain myself. it gives me a lot of time to do things i'd never normally do or read things i wouldn't normally think of to read. there's something also really cool about going out to eat by yourself. either in a restaurant or the dining hall. or even getting takeout alone is cool. i can't imagine myself dating anyone right now anyway, i can't imagine how anyone could really pull me out of this. everyone always rubs me the wrong way or i piss them off and everything goes down the shitter so i might as well keep to myself for now.

mood: nostalgic
current music: thismeansyou - river

[2 comments | leave a comment]

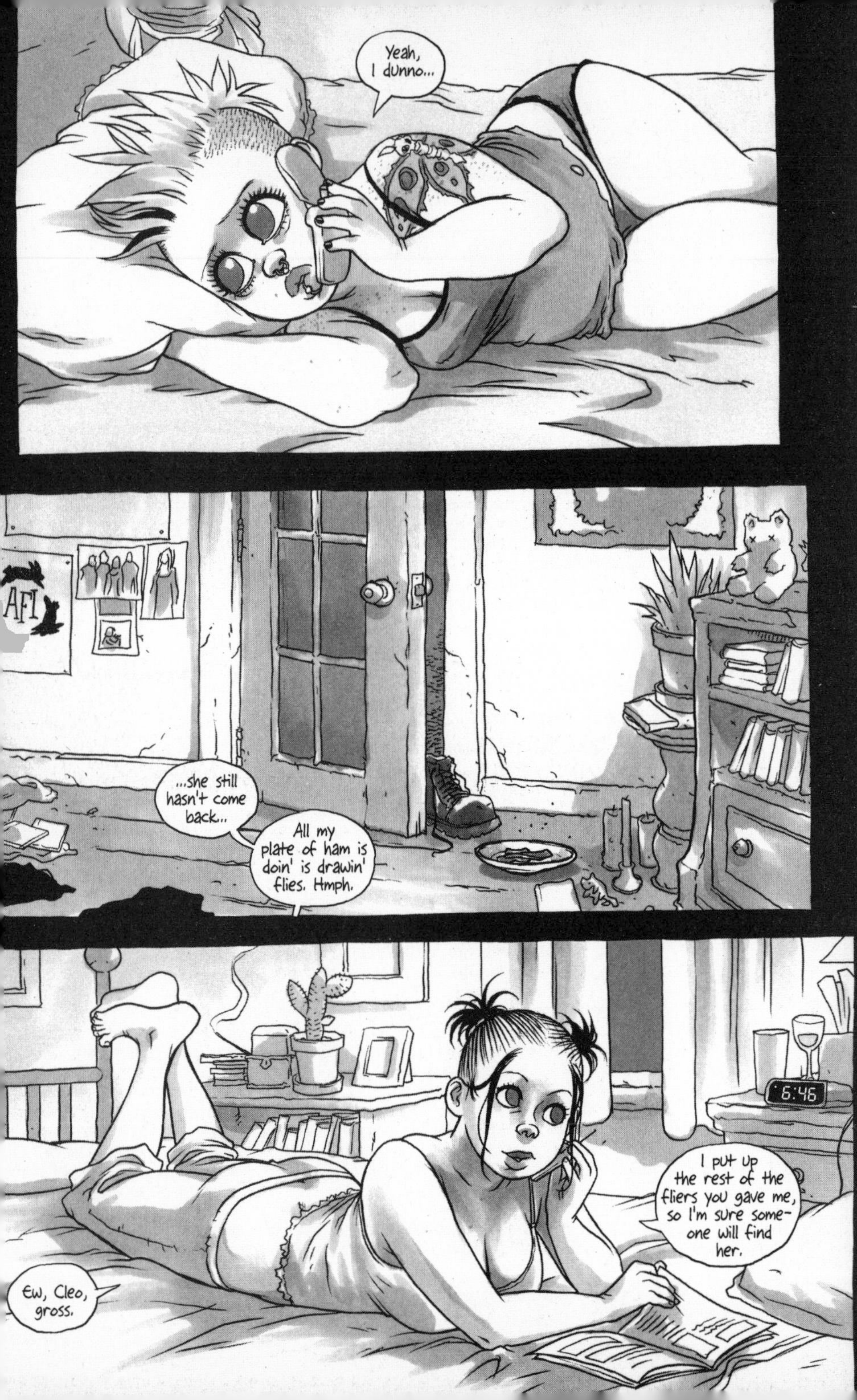
Yeah, I dunno...
...she still hasn't come back...
All my plate of ham is doin' is drawin' flies. Hmph.
6:46
I put up the rest of the fliers you gave me, so I'm sure some-one will find her.
Ew, Cleo, gross.

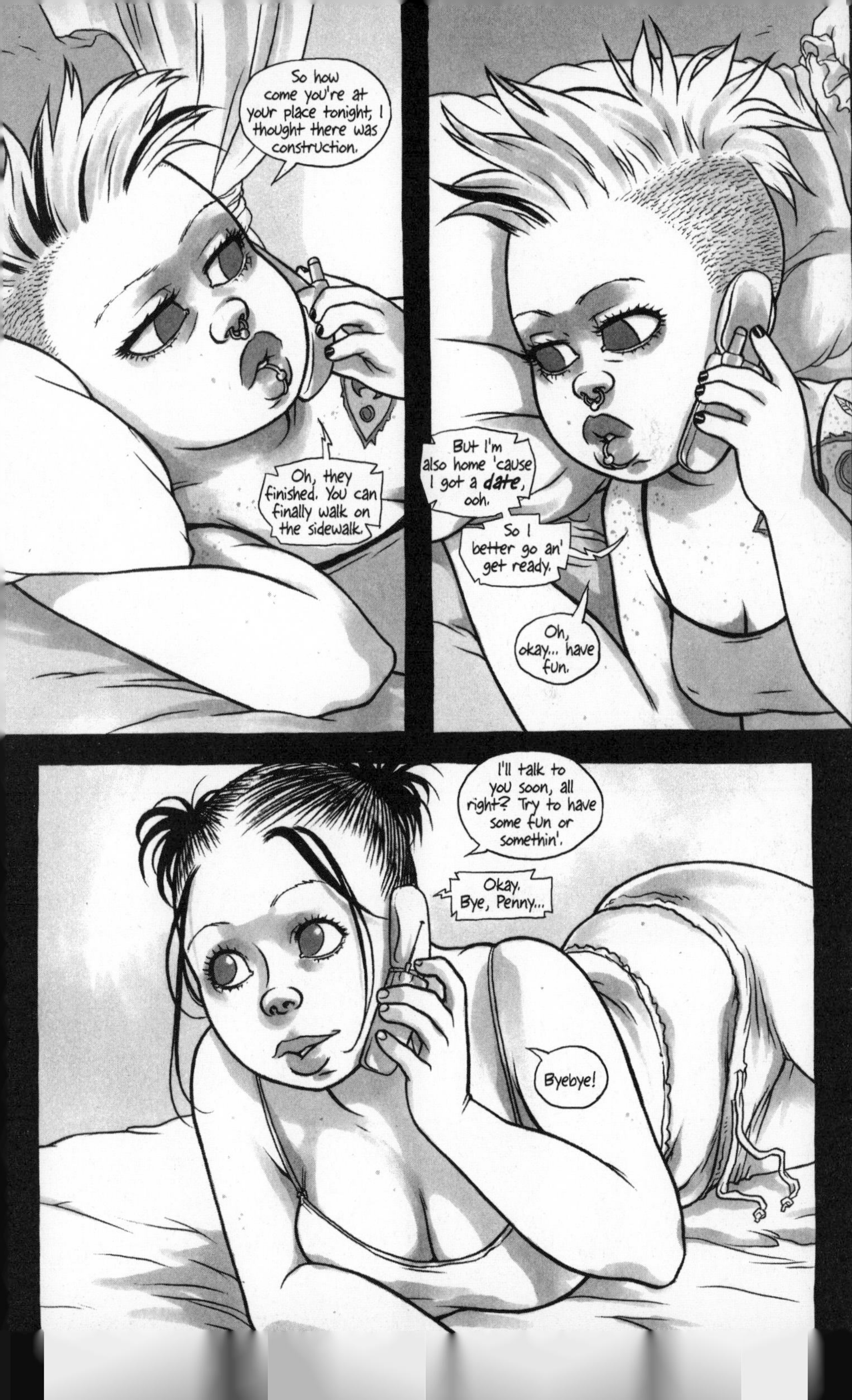
So how come you're at your place tonight, I thought there was construction.
Oh, they finished. You can finally walk on the sidewalk.
But I'm also home 'cause I got a **date**, ooh.
So I better go an' get ready.
Oh, okay... have fun.
I'll talk to you soon, all right? Try to have some fun or somethin'.
Okay. Bye, Penny...
Byebye!

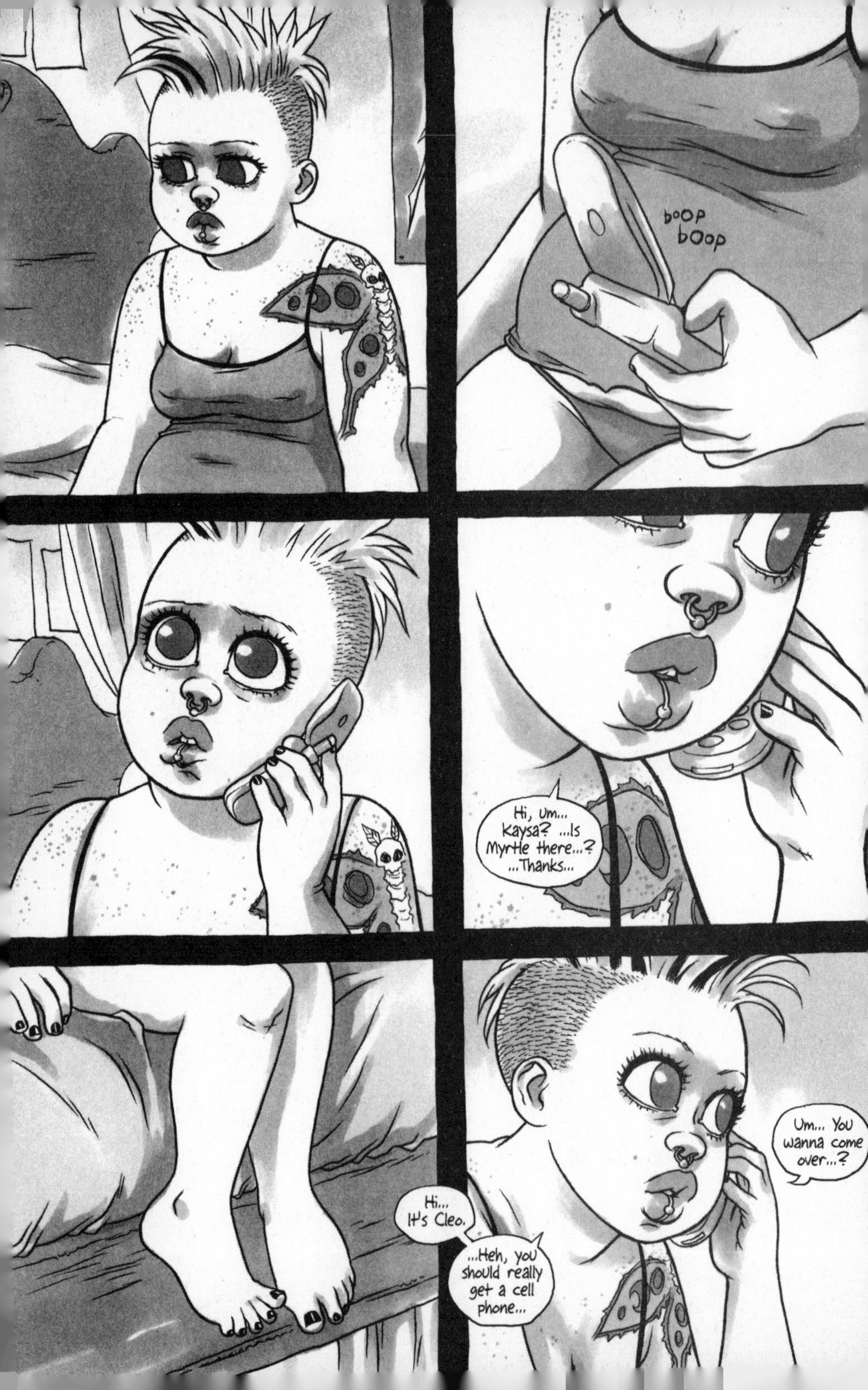
boop
boop
Hi, um... Kaysa? ...Is Myrtle there...? ...Thanks...
Hi... It's Cleo.
...Heh, you should really get a cell phone...
Um... You wanna come over...?

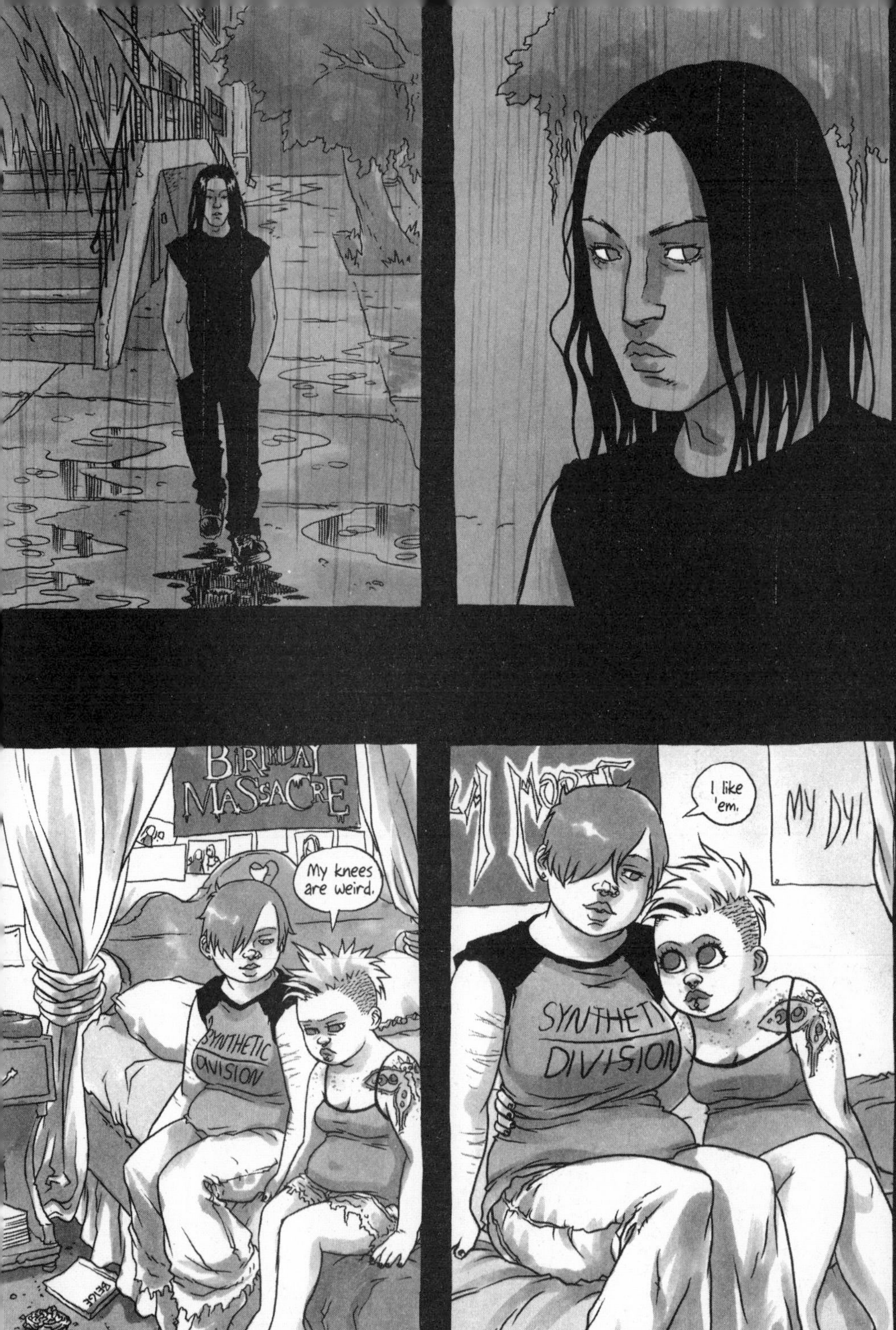
BIRTHDAY MASSACRE
My knees are weird.
SYNTHETIC DIVISION
I like 'em.
SYNTHETIC DIVISION

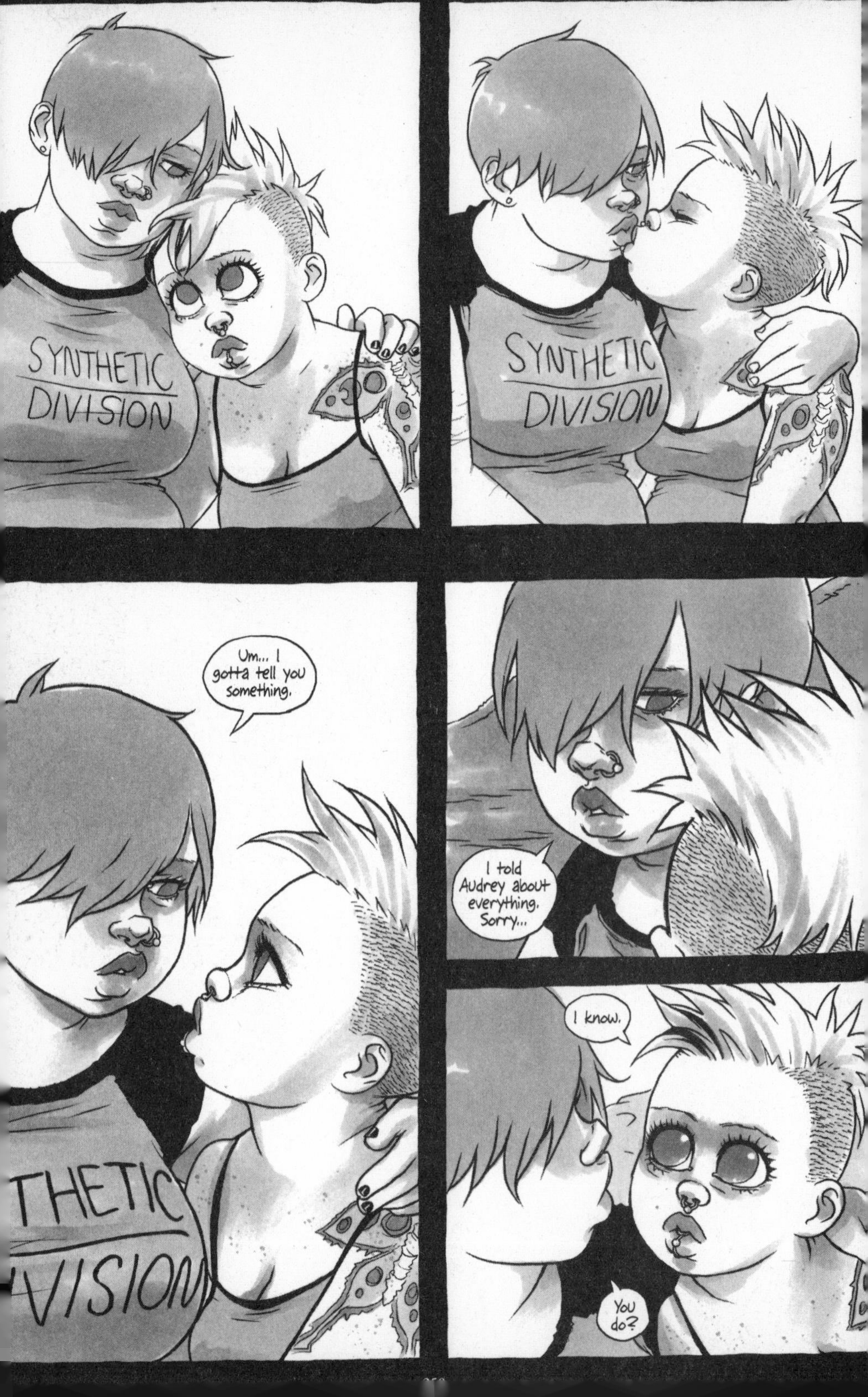
SYNTHETIC DIVISION
SYNTHETIC DIVISION
Um... I gotta tell you something.
THETIC VISION
I told Audrey about everything. Sorry...
I know.
You do?

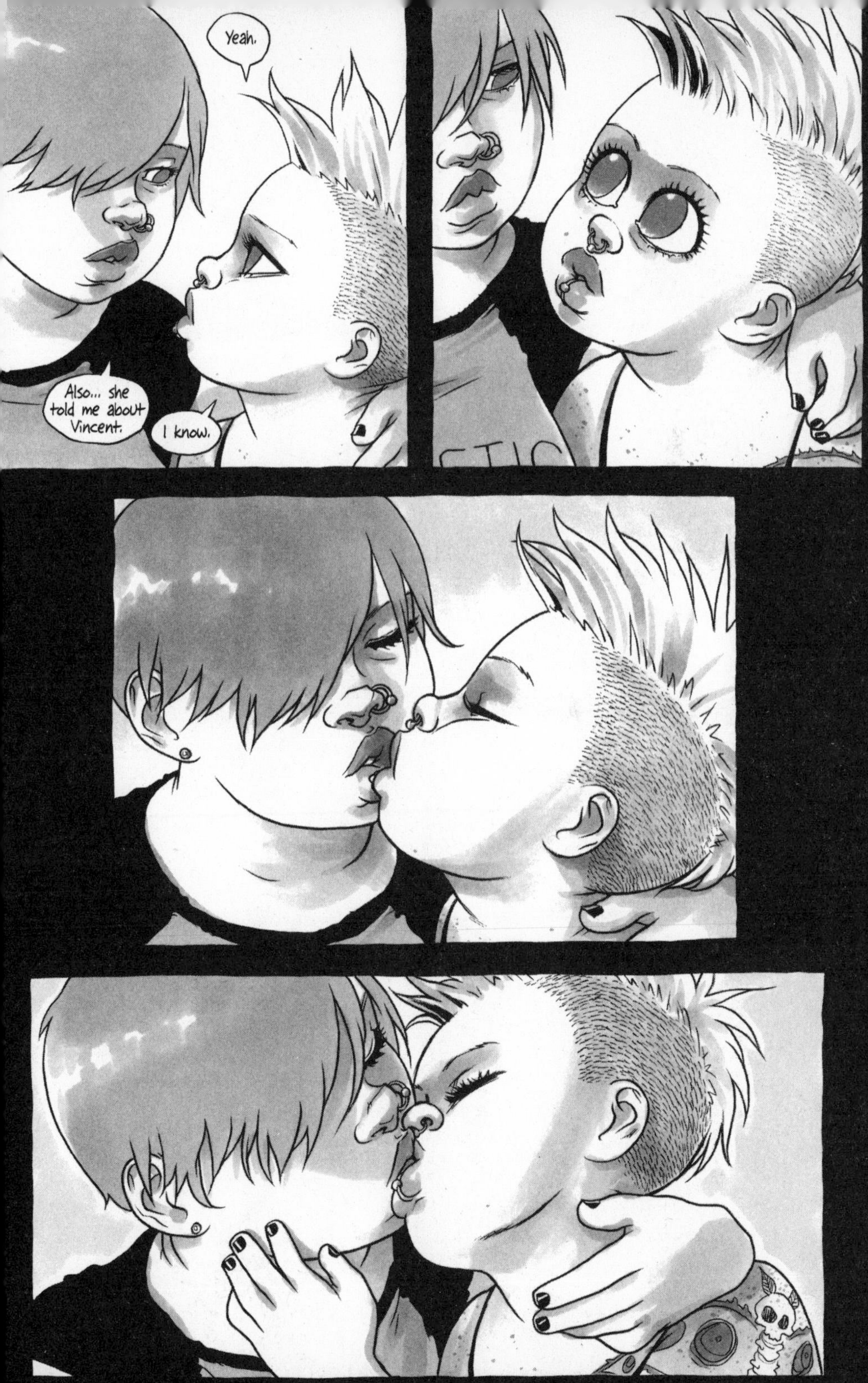
Yeah.
Also... she told me about Vincent.
I know.

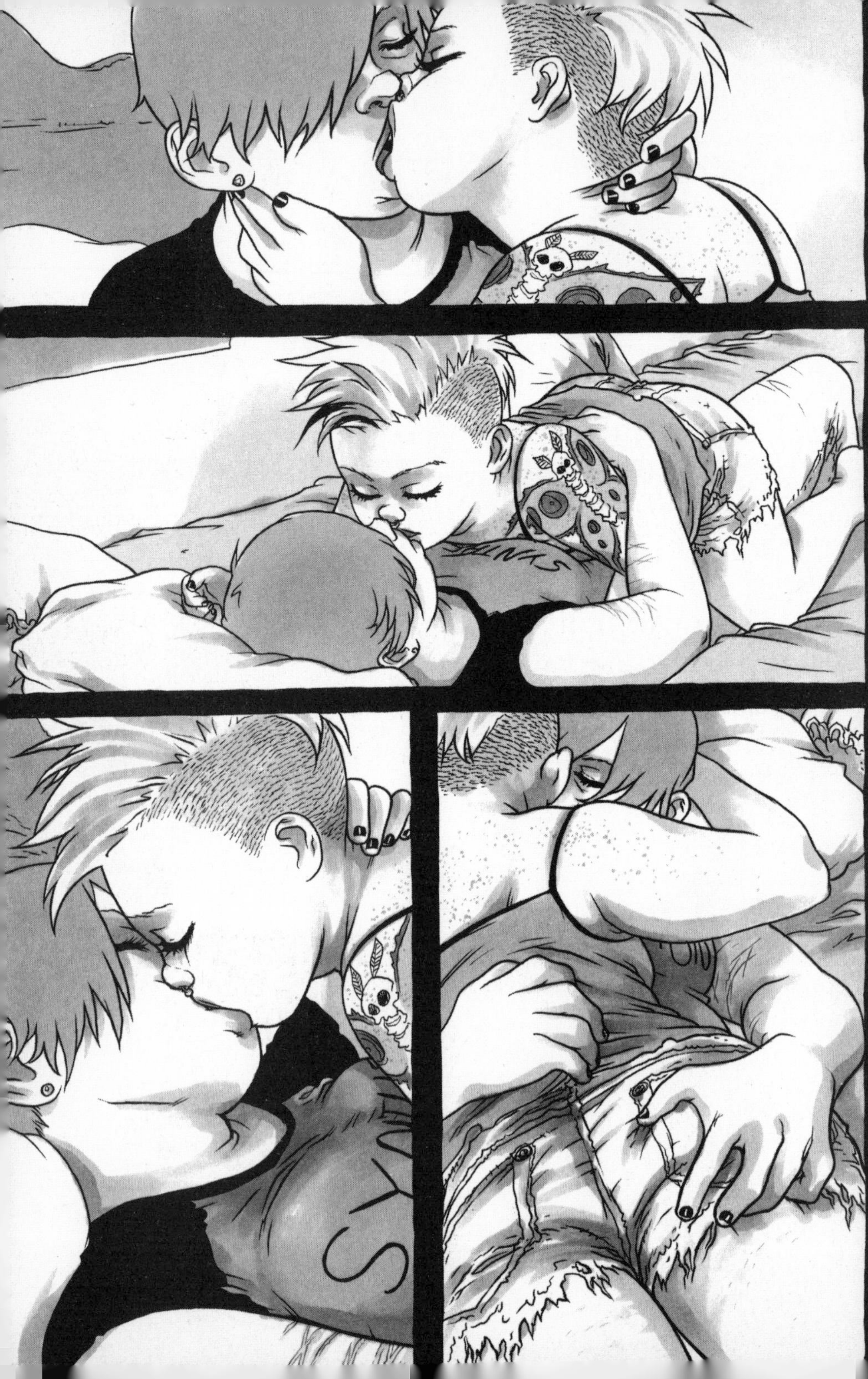

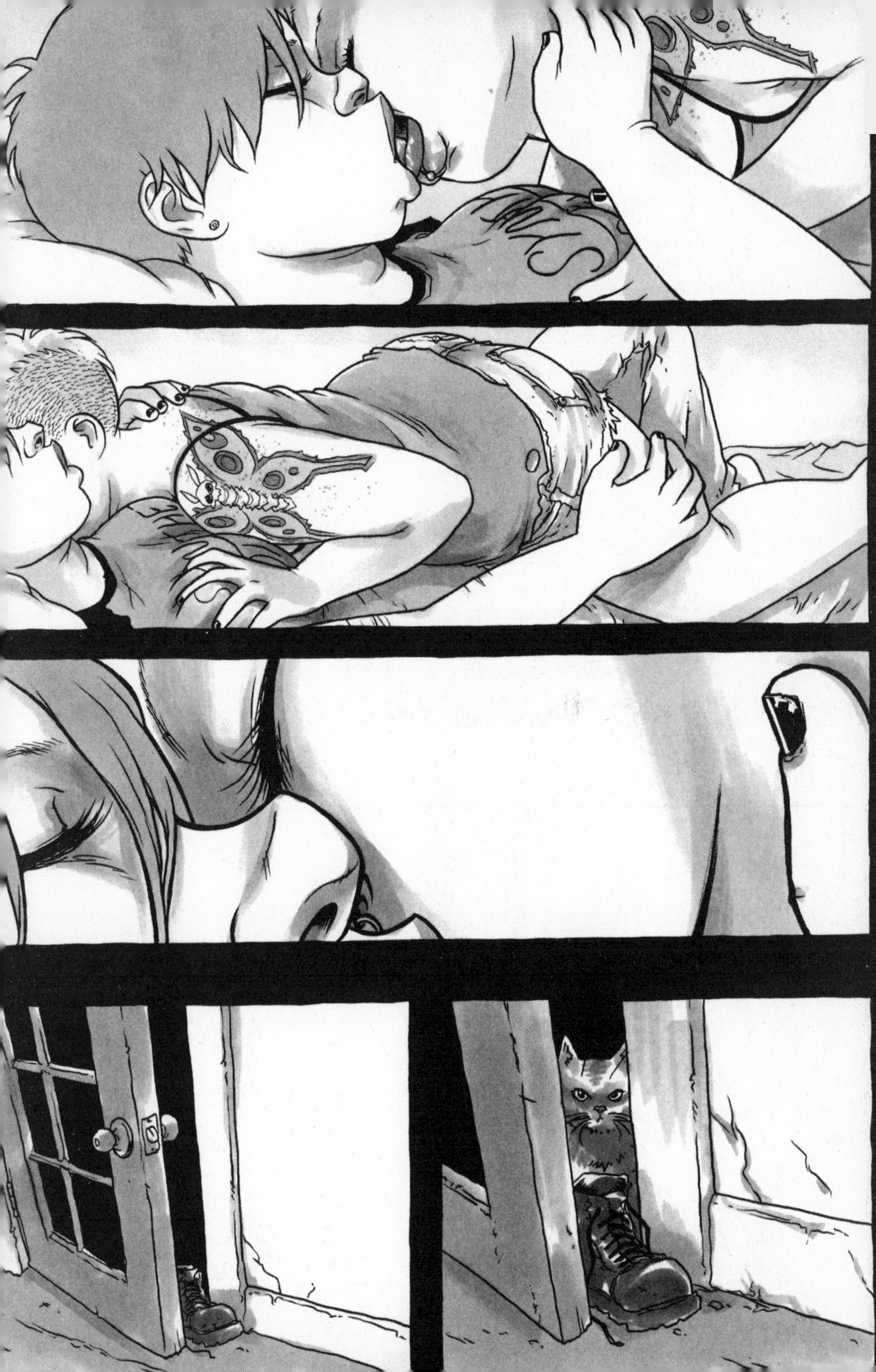

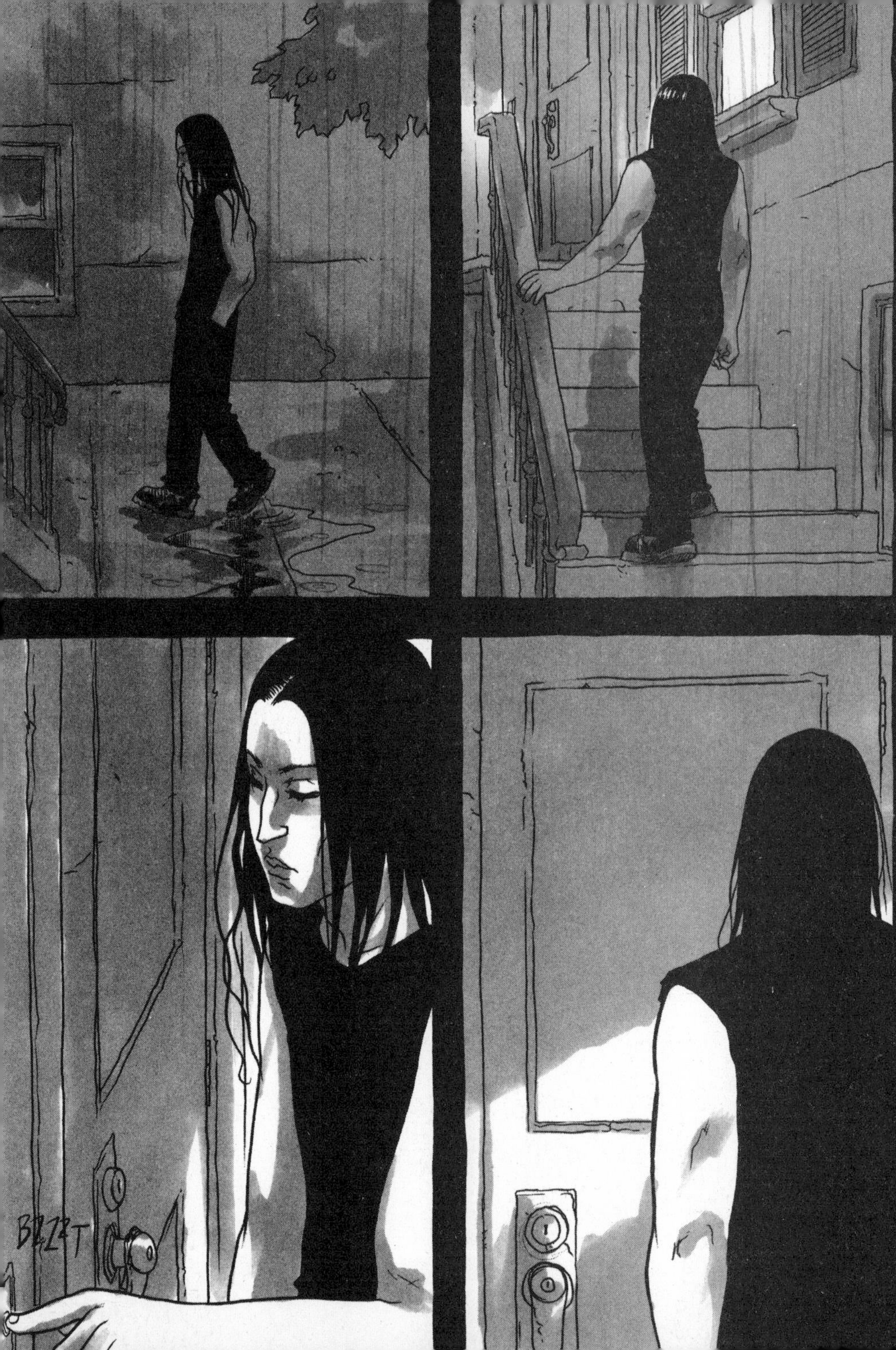
BZZZT

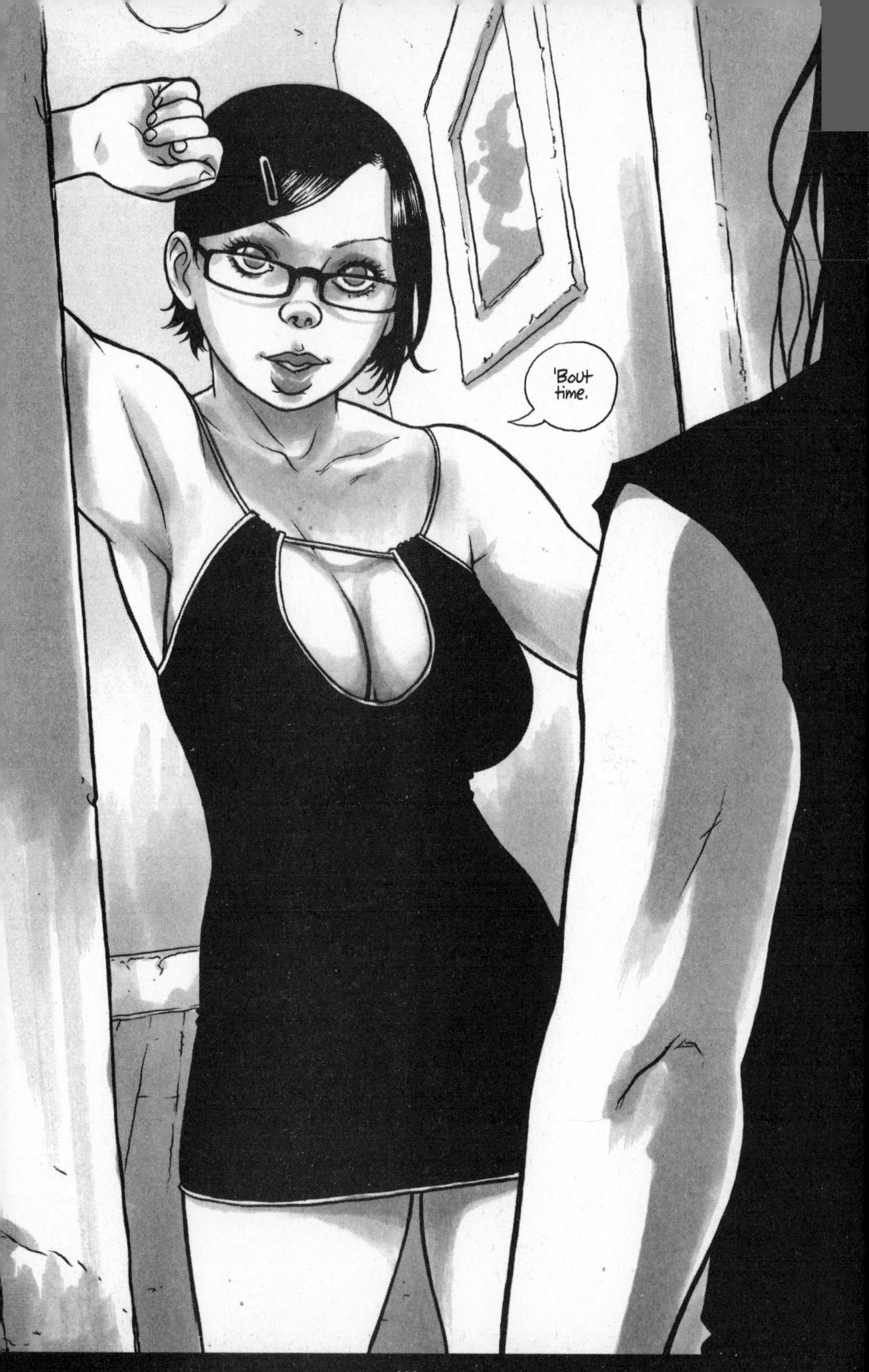
'Bout time.

NEXT:

Cleo gets a job!
Mara kicks some ass!
Beth beats up somebody else!
Audrey vs. stupid little kids!
Trilby's secret origin!
The UltraCon!

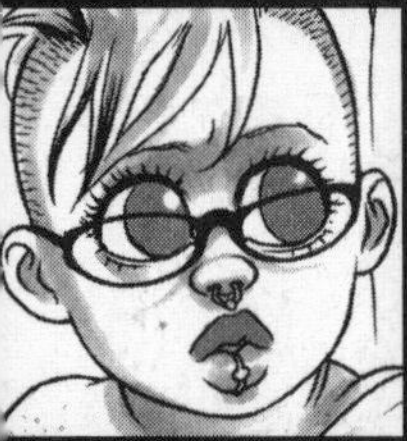
cleo lovedrop
(18)

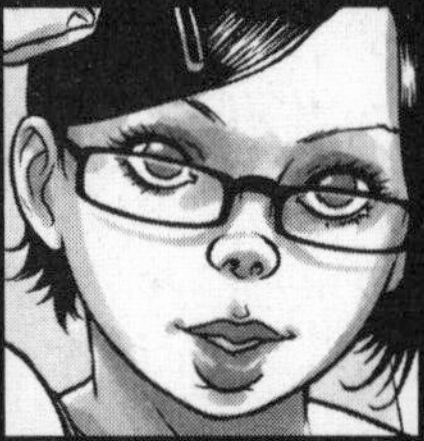
penny lovedrop
(23)

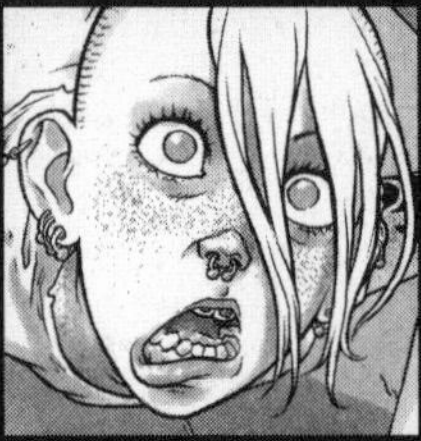
trilby bernarde
(18)

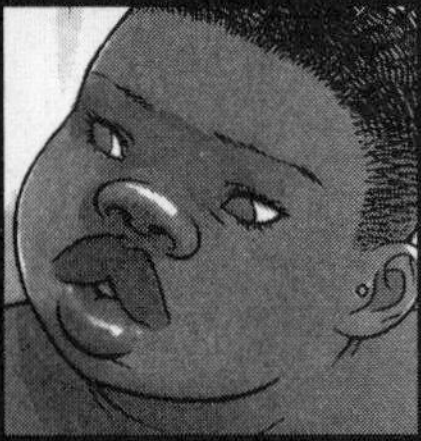
audrey richter
(19)

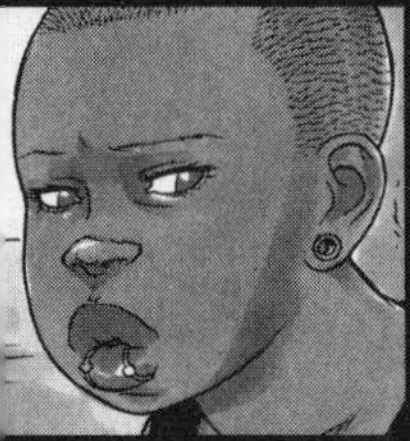
mara zuzanny
(18)

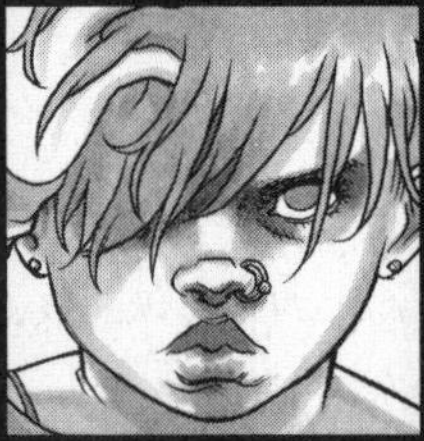
myrtle turenne
(19)

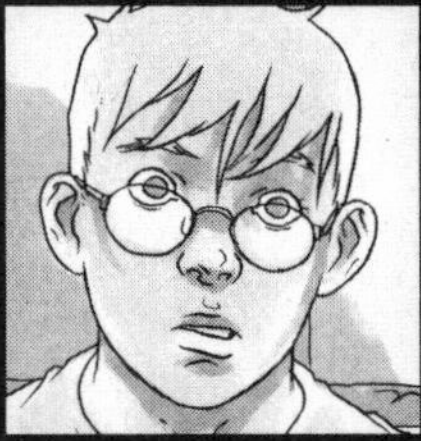
martin samson
(21)

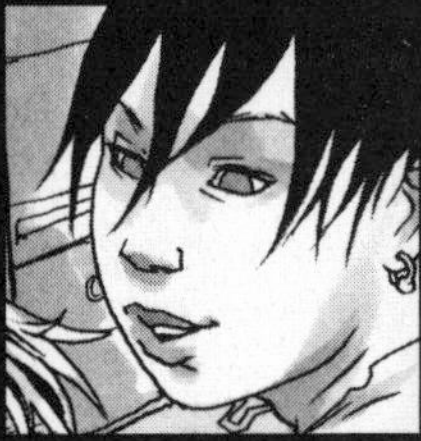
glen neuhoff
(20)

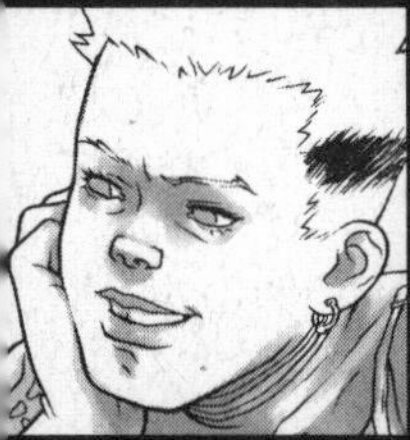
beth mckenzie
(17)

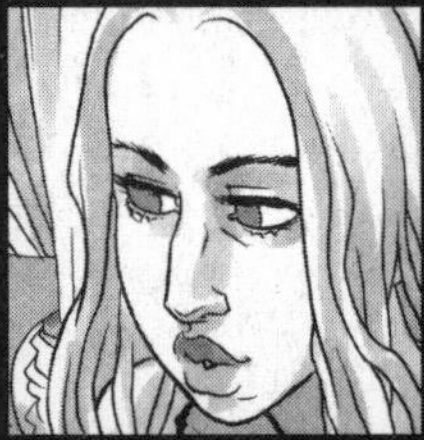
natalie ringtree
(21)

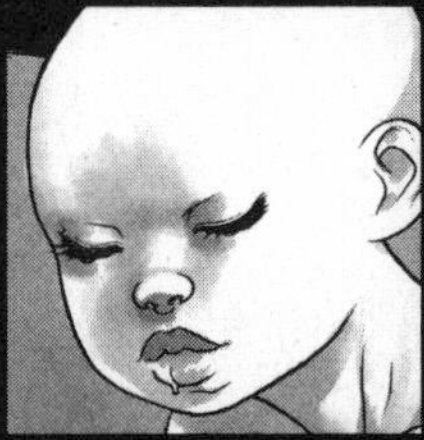
fern
(age unknown)

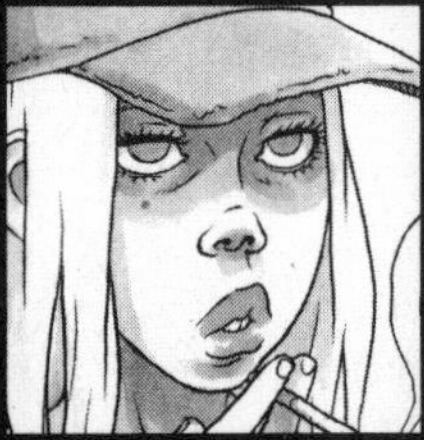
fall swanhilde
(15)

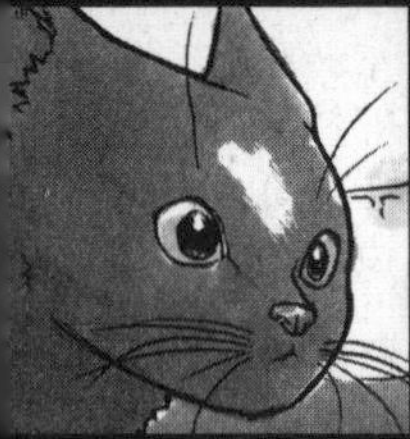
meiko
(5)

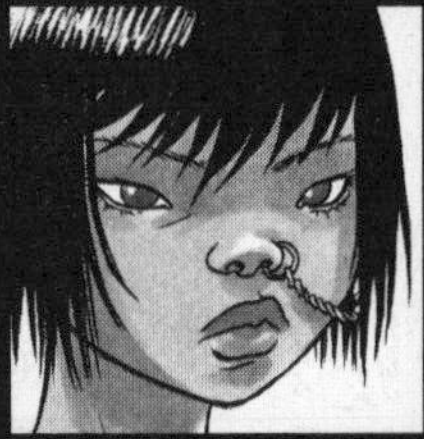
kinzoku
(19)

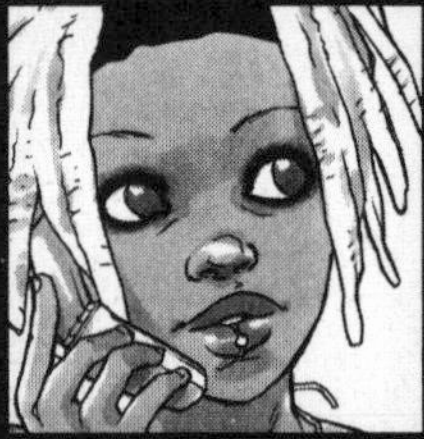
malady mayapple
(20)

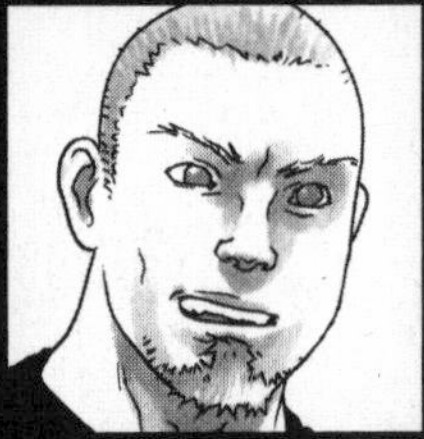
connor eakle
(23)

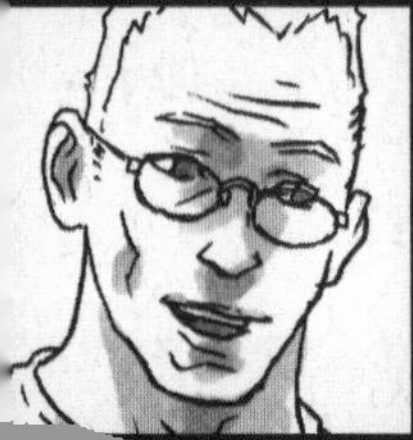

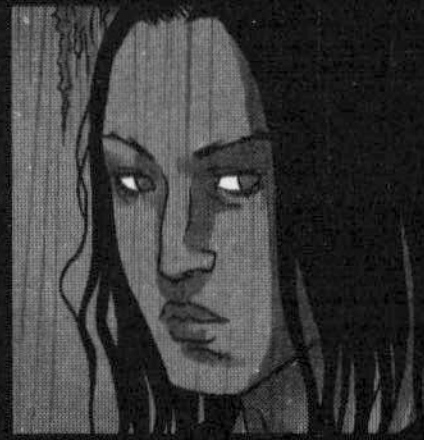

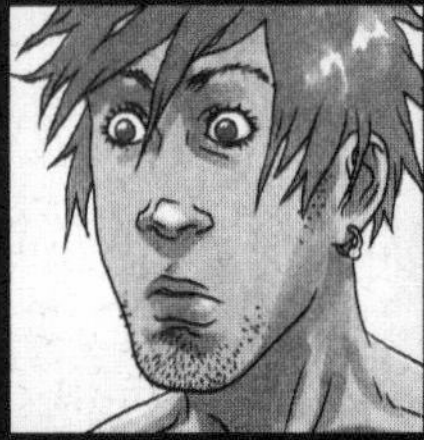

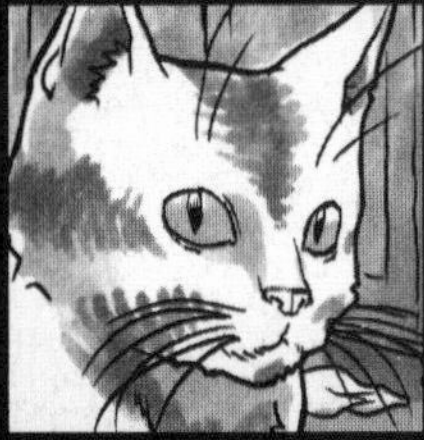

Special thanks to: mom, dad, james, joe, jess c., becky, zach, shelly, carlie, dan, nate, julie, brandon g., the Bella Morte guys (andy, tony, tony 2, micah & jordan, and formerly gopal), rea, jessica p., vasilis, kirk, robert haines, everyone at deviantart and everyone who reads my books.

No thanks to: bill goodin, the supersquirrel(s), my digestive tract, fleas, the wall-bat, the window-bird.

Plugs: bellamorte.com, thismeansyou.com, theprotomen.com, cadaveria.com, synthetic-division.com, roaringshark.com

About the author: Ross Campbell is an art monk who currently lives in Rochester, New York. His first published work was for White Wolf Publishing's *Exalted* RPG books, which he continues to do illustrations for today. He made his comics debut doing the flashbacks in Jen Van Meter's *Too Much Hopeless Savages*, published by Oni Press. Ross spends his time working and not much else, but he gets some time off to watch a movie or two every Friday. His personal website is www.greenoblivion.com, and his deviantArt gallery is at mooncalfe.deviantart.com (and keep an eye out for www.wet-moon.com, your one stop for all things *Wet Moon*). He likes monsters, zombies, Tifa Lockhart, Fefe Dobson, unsolved mysteries, great white sharks, alien artifacts, tea, outer space, and cats. He hates neighbors, ketchup, frogs, traveling, sunny weather, and pretty much everything else.

Other books by Ross: Spooked (drawn by, written by Antony Johnston/Oni), *Wet Moon* volumes 1 & 2 (Oni), *The Abandoned* (Tokyopop), *Mountain Girl* #1-2 (self-published), Water Baby (DC/Minx. early 2008)

OTHER BOOKS FROM ROSS CAMPBELL & ONI PRESS...

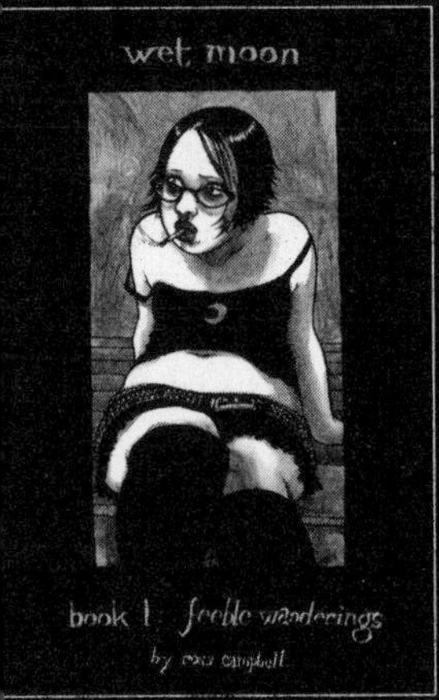

wet moon
book 1: feeble wanderings
by ross campbell

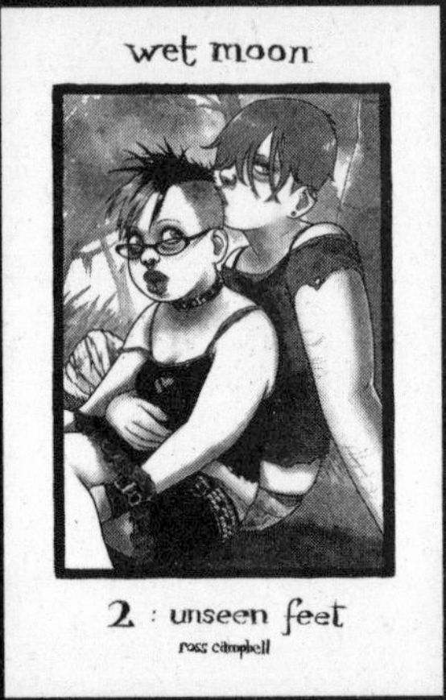

wet moon
2 : unseen feet
ross campbell

WET MOON, VOL. 1:
FEEBLE WANDERINGS
By Ross Campbell
176 pages, 6"x9" trade paperback
black and white interiors
ISBN 978-1-932664-07-2

WET MOON, VOL. 2:
UNSEEN FEET
By Ross Campbell
184 pages, 6"x9" trade paperback
black and white interiors
ISBN 978-1-932664-47-8

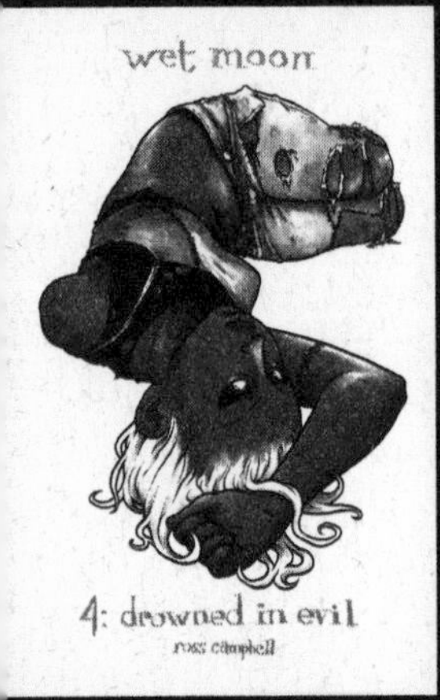

wet moon
4: drowned in evil
ross campbell

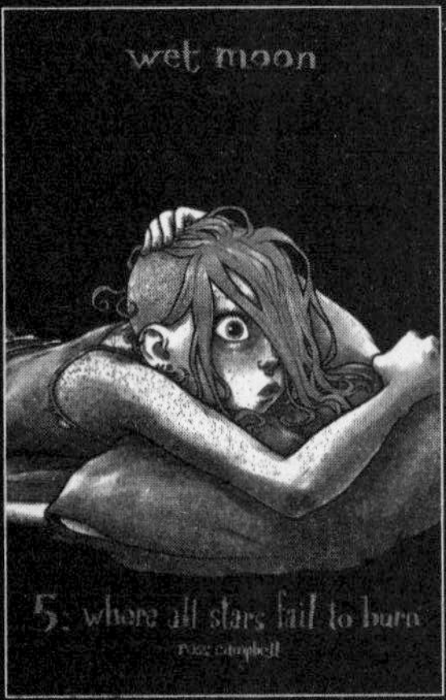

wet moon
5: where all stars fail to burn
ross campbell

WET MOON, VOL. 4:
DROWNED IN EVIL
By Ross Campbell
184 pages, 6"x9" trade paperback
black and white interiors
ISBN 978-1-934964-09-5

WET MOON, VOL. 5:
WHERE ALL STARS FAIL TO BURN
By Ross Campbell
168 pages, 6"x9" trade paperback
black and white interiors
ISBN 978-1-934964-25-5

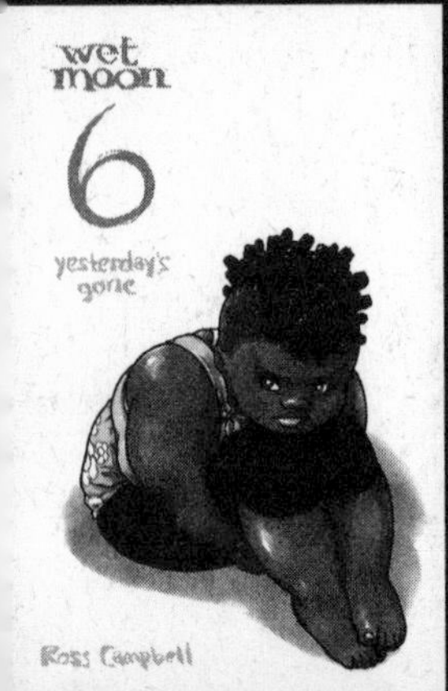

wet moon
6
yesterday's gone
Ross Campbell

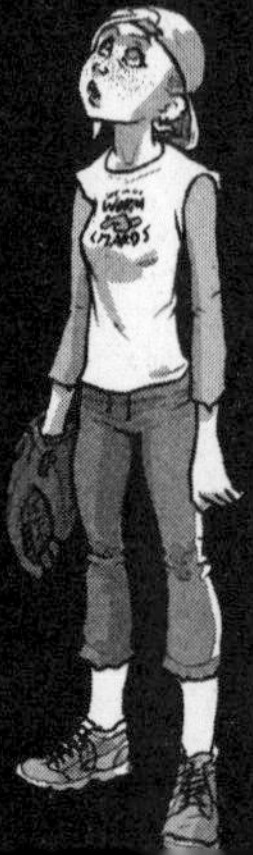

WET MOON, VOL. 6:
YESTERDAY'S GONE
By Ross Campbell
168 pages, 6"x9" trade paperback
black and white interiors
ISBN 978-1-934964-83-5